SHAKESPEAREAN TRAGEDY
AND GENDER

SHAKESPEAREAN TRAGEDY AND GENDER

EDITED BY

SHIRLEY NELSON GARNER
AND
MADELON SPRENGNETHER

INDIANA UNIVERSITY PRESS
BLOOMINGTON AND INDIANAPOLIS

The paper used in this publication meets the minimum
requirements of American National Standard for Information
Sciences—Permanence of Paper for Printed Library Materials,
ANSI Z39.48-1984.

∞™

Manufactured in the United States of America

Library of Congress Cataloging-in-Publication Data

Shakespearean tragedy and gender / edited by Shirley Nelson Garner and
Madelon Sprengnether.
p.   cm.
Includes bibliographical references and index.
ISBN 0-253-32964-7 (cl : alk. paper). — ISBN 0-253-21027-5 (pa :
alk. paper)
1. Shakespeare, William, 1564-1616—Tragedies.   2. Shakespeare,
William, 1564-1616—Characters—Women.   3. Women and literature—
England—History—16th century.   4. Women and literature—England—
History—17th century.   5. Gender identity in literature.   6. Sex
role in literature.   7. Tragedy.   I. Garner, Shirley Nelson, date.
II. Sprengnether, Madelon.
PR2983.S4498   1996
822.3'3—dc20   95-21677

1   2   3   4   5   01   00   99   98   97   96

❖ FOR MY FAMILY, FRANK, HART, AND·CELIA ❖
FOR MY DAUGHTER, JESSICA LEE GOHLKE
—SHIRLEY GARNER AND MADELON SPRENGNETHER

CONTENTS

Acknowledgments *ix*

Introduction: The Gendered Subject of Shakespearean Tragedy *1*
Madelon Sprengnether

Part One: Tragic Subjects

1. History into Tragedy: The Case of *Richard III* *31*
Phyllis Rackin

2. A Woman of Letters: Lavinia in *Titus Andronicus* *54*
Sara Eaton

3. "Documents in Madness": Reading Madness and Gender in Shakespeare's Tragedies and Early Modern Culture *75*
Carol Thomas Neely

4. "Born of Woman": Fantasies of Maternal Power in *Macbeth* *105*
Janet Adelman

5. "Magic of bounty": *Timon of Athens,* Jacobean Patronage, and Maternal Power *135*
Coppélia Kahn

Part Two: Implicating *Othello*

6. Desdemona's Disposition *171*
Lena Cowen Orlin

7. "The Moor of Venice," or the Italian on the
Renaissance English Stage *193*
Margo Hendricks

8. The Heroics of Marriage in *Othello* and *The Duchess of Malfi* *210*
Mary Beth Rose

Part Three: Shakespeare Our Contemporary?

9. The Fatal Cleopatra *241*
Carol Cook

10. What's Love Got to Do with It? Reading the Liberal Humanist
Romance in *Antony and Cleopatra* *268*
Linda Charnes

11. Shakespeare in My Time and Place *287*
Shirley Nelson Garner

12. Leaving Shakespeare *307*
Gayle Greene

Notes on Contributors *317*

Index *321*

❖
_____

ACKNOWLEDGMENTS

WE wish to thank the Graduate School at the University of Minnesota for grants-in-aid of research, which allowed us to employ two research assistants in our work on this book. In the early stages, Stephanie Athey, a graduate student in English and now an assistant professor at Stetson University in Deland, Florida, compiled a bibliography of relevant research. Shannon Olson, a graduate student in Creative Writing, assisted us near the end, handling many of the tasks that are necessary to complete a manuscript. We are particularly grateful for her energy, good humor, sense of organization, and eye for detail.

Many scholars have helped to shape our thinking on this subject. They include participants in a double seminar on Shakespearean Tragedy and Gender at the annual meeting of the Shakespeare Association of America held in Seattle in 1987; graduate students at the University of Minnesota in Shirley Garner's seminars on the subject; and those in Madelon Sprengnether's "The Revolution in Shakespeare Studies: 1980–1990." During the time in which this book has been in preparation, we have benefited from the support and advice of a number of Shakespeare scholars and are especially grateful for the contributions of the following: Peter Erickson, Kirby Farrell, Dianne Hunter, David Sundelson, and Valerie Traub.

❖

INTRODUCTION
The Gendered Subject of Shakespearean Tragedy

MADELON SPRENGNETHER

The Subject of Tragedy

I HAVE LONG been intrigued by Goneril's parting line in *King Lear:* "Ask me not what I know" (5.3.160).[1] Having poisoned her sister, her dalliance with Edmund discovered, Goneril exits refusing us insight into her presumably desperate state of mind. She will die by her own hand, unloved and unmourned, her fate the antithesis of that of a tragic hero, the opacity of her consciousness an emblem of the lot of women generally in Shakespeare's tragedies. For the ingeniousness lavished on the development of the tragic hero, from his first fatal error to his final agonized awareness of his ignorance or transgression, does not extend to the women he resists, idolizes, or reviles. We will never know what they know.[2] The subject position not only of Shakespeare's tragedy but of tragedy defined as a genre in the Aristotelian tradition seems to preclude this very possibility. What is feminist criticism, after nearly two decades of development, to make of this? The essays gathered here will explore this question from many angles, attesting to the diversity of perspectives that characterize contemporary feminist analysis, while putting pressure throughout on the gendered subject of Shakespearean tragedy.

In order to frame this project, I would like to look first at a contemporary retelling of the Lear story, this time by a woman novelist. In *A Thousand Acres,* Jane Smiley deliberately disrupts the gender economy of Shakespeare's plot, choosing not Lear but Goneril (named Ginny) as narrator, displacing not only the locus of masculine subjectivity but also its implicit claim to universal significance. Changing the traditional "subject" of tragedy, moreover, has generic repercussions which transcend Smiley's choice of fiction over drama to include a transformation of the idea of tragic action. While events are set in motion by a father's division of his property among his daughters, the focus of Smiley's narration is not on errors committed (or repented) in the present, but on the gradual revelation of a corrupted past, including the fateful role of father-daughter incest in the evolution of family dynamics.

As if to correct for Goneril's parting words, Smiley centers her story around Ginny's slow coming to awareness, not only of her own repressed history but of the meanings contained in her relations to each member of her family: her father, her two sisters, her husband, and her nieces. From a state of not knowing, in which she innocently thinks of her life as secure and good, she enters one of hyperlucidity, where nothing painful can remain hidden. Reflecting on this transformation, she says,

> The strongest feeling was that now I knew them all. That whereas for thirty-six years they had swum around me in complicated patterns that I had at best dimly perceived through murky water, now all was clear. I saw each of them from all sides at once. I didn't have to label them as Rose had labeled herself and Pete: "selfish," "mean," "jealous." Labeling them, in fact, prevented knowing them. All I had to do was imagine them, and how I "knew" them would shimmer around them and through them, a light, an odor, a sound, a taste, a palpability that was all there was to understand about each and every one of them. (305)

This knowledge is like "being drenched with insight, swollen with it like a wet sponge," and as excruciating as it is to arrive at such a state, it nonetheless gives the satisfaction of being real. "Rather than feeling not myself," Ginny concludes, "I felt intensely, newly, more myself than ever before" (305).

Although the cost of Ginny's knowledge is high (including the deaths of her father, her sister Rose, and her brother-in-law Pete), she is not, like Goneril, a malevolent agent in her family's catastrophic fall. Neither is she an innocent bystander. Her behavior is not only adulterous (she has a brief affair with the son of a neighboring farmer) but also potentially criminal (she attempts to poison her sister for doing the same). Still, the reader is not asked to condemn her, but rather to absorb what she knows, to participate finally in her capacity to embrace the unimaginable, including what she refers to as the "gleaming obsidian shard" of her father's violent and self-willed nature (371).

In rewriting the plot of *King Lear*, Smiley performs a piece of literary analysis in addition to offering a metacritical commentary on the issue of tragic form. Her choice to portray both Ginny and her sister Rose as victims of father-daughter incest, for instance, is surely based on the desire for exclusivity that pervades Lear's language of relationship to Cordelia. By displacing this implicit motif from Cordelia to her two sisters, Smiley provides motivation for their reactions of anger, indifference, or revenge. In a single stroke, moreover, she reverses both the gender hierarchy and the trajectory of desire embedded in the classic Aristotelian example of tragedy, *Oedipus Rex*. As if thumbing her nose at an entire humanist tradition, from its origins in Sophocles and Aristotle through its transformations in Shakespeare and Freud, Smiley deliberately dislocates the subject of tragedy—on the level of narrative as well as gender.

By beginning with a discussion of Smiley's revisionary novel, I do not mean to sweep aside considerations of history or culture but rather to indicate the very situatedness of the notion of tragedy, including the specificity of the critical traditions that have shaped our expectations and analyses of Shakespeare's drama. From the beginning of this century until fairly recently, these expectations (in Anglo-American criticism) have remained remarkably consistent, despite inevitable differences of emphasis due to the temperaments of individual critics or their choice of interpretive models. A brief overview of the positions of two representative figures in this tradition will indicate the radical nature of the departure occasioned by contemporary critical approaches, while underscoring the specific contributions of feminism.

The World We Have Lost

In his classic pre–World War I introduction to his lectures on *Hamlet, Othello, King Lear,* and *Macbeth,* A. C. Bradley set the parameters of discussion for decades to come (*Shakespearean Tragedy* 15–41). For Bradley, character is the basis of action, while inner conflict reveals the essence of character. "The dictum that, with Shakespeare, 'character is destiny' is no doubt an exaggeration," he allows, yet "it is the exaggeration of a vital truth" (21). The hero, he continues, "though he pursues his fated way, is at least at some point, and sometimes at many, torn by an inward struggle; and it is frequently at such points that Shakespeare shows his most extraordinary power" (25). In order to appreciate the full tragedy of Lear, for instance, we must remember not only the "part played by the hero in bringing it on" (231) but also the conflicting elements in his nature that predispose him to his error.

Bradley's conception of character is sufficiently broad, however, for him to describe it in rather generic terms. Thus Lear is "unsuspicious, of an open and free nature," though also "choleric by temperament" (232). Bradley's tendency to generalize the issue of character reappears in his next requirement—that the hero be an "exceptional being," in order to elicit the appropriate tragic response of sympathy and terror. "What a piece of work is man," he exclaims, "so much more beautiful and so much more terrible than we knew! Why should he be so if this beauty and greatness only tortures itself and throws itself away?" (28).

Finally, Bradley understands fate in terms of the hero's implication in the convulsion of a moral system that destroys him in the process of reasserting its imperative. Hence the horrors unleashed by Lear's rash actions cause us to "feel that this world is so far at least a rational and a moral order, that there holds in it the law, not of proportionate requital, but of strict connection between act and consequence" (234). "The ultimate power in the tragic world," he assures us, is precisely such a "moral order" (37).

Bradley's emphasis on character (particularly in regard to the intrinsic worth of the tragic hero) combined with his insistence on the reassertion of a moral order have had an enduring impact, surviving the transformations of the New Criticism to reemerge, most recently, in the work of neo-Aristotelian Richard Levin. Before moving to a consideration of Levin's attack on feminist criticism of Shakespeare, however, I want to look at an intermediary figure in the New Critical tradition who establishes a line of continuity between his work and that of Bradley.

While dissociating itself from the type of character analysis typified by Bradley, the New Criticism treats character as exemplary, thus reinforcing Bradley's conception of the tragic hero as an "exceptional being." Though widely individual in their approaches, New Critics share Bradley's assumptions about the centrality of the hero's experience and its generalizability to that of "mankind," about the wholeness of Shakespeare's vision as represented by the canon, about the centeredness of themselves and their subject. Needless to say, there is no category of gender analysis to challenge any of these presuppositions. In order to measure the full distance between this Shakespearean world view and the one we inhabit today, I would like to look at one of its most eloquent (yet not too far removed) expressions: Maynard Mack's *King Lear in Our Time.*

First published in 1965, two years after Betty Friedan's *The Feminine Mystique, King Lear in Our Time* was reprinted in paperback in 1972, two years after the appearance of Kate Millet's *Sexual Politics,* and a scant four years before the first MLA session on Feminist Criticism of Shakespeare in 1976. Read in this light, the book has an eerie premonitory quality, as if its author already suspected how quickly his ideas would come to seem outdated—as if he wrote against the tide of that very awareness.

Although Mack's strategies for interpreting *Lear*—displacing the question of character onto an emblem of humanity at large, then affirming the essential human values of the play—are by now familiar, there is a particular urgency to them, as evidenced by the emphasis in the title on "our time," coupled with scattered textual allusions to Hiroshima and the Holocaust. It is as though Mack's aim is not only to render Lear's drama newly relevant to a late twentieth-century audience, but also, and even more pointedly, to preserve something under threat.

The nature of this threat emerges in Mack's discussion of the performance history of the play, where he lays stress on the improbabilities of character and action that make the play seem incoherent, if not impossible to stage with any credibility. "If *King Lear*," he concludes,

> as a work of literature, is either Shakespeare's greatest achievement, freely compared by its devotees to the sublimest inventions of the artistic imagination, or else a work of childish absurdity inspiring "aversion and weariness" in others besides Tolstoi; if as a play it is either unsuited to actual stage performing, or on the contrary is only understood when performance has tied together the "series of intellectual strands" which compose it and drawn our attention "away from what otherwise might seem puzzling, distasteful, or foolish," clearly we have a problem. (7)

The "problem" Mack identifies has to do with the extreme heterogeneity of the play, which threatens to diminish or undermine its claim to tragic sublimity. As a first step in addressing this issue, he argues against psychological realism as a means of interpreting character. "The siren's rock on which efforts to bring *King Lear* to the stage . . . oftenest split," Mack tells us, "is the desire to motivate the bizarre actions that Shakespeare's play calls for in some 'reasonable' way" (29). In place of such motivation, he focuses on Shakespeare's appeal to parable and archetype. "Do we see in the play's grand opening a rash choice merely or something more like an archetype of all choosing, a pattern of the mind's act of will as that act begins to grow and branch in the material world, locking subject to object on a wheel of fire?" (48) This approach has the immediate advantage of nullifying any objections to Lear's behavior in the beginning of the play, whether in denouncing Cordelia and dividing his kingdom, or simply in allowing his knights to carouse. It not incidentally also frees us from any obligation to consider the plight of Goneril and Regan, who are referred to as "paradigms of evil" (31), prey to an "anarchy of appetite" (53), which reduces them to "unmitigated badness" (76).

Mack displaces the question of Lear's character upward—onto a consideration of Everyman (57). On this level, "hints of childishness, imperiousness, decaying powers, and incipient fury" that an actor may wish to project in any given interpretation of Lear must yield to his awareness that there is also "an *esse* in his role which, like that of the Morality hero, *must* present itself surrounded by forces of evil and good to which it is blinded by vanity and passion, *must* make a wrong choice and live to rue it, because that is the lot of man" (68). Otherwise, "we wind up in Mr. Empson's position, appalled by an old man's 'ridiculous and sordid' obsession," a position evidently to be avoided at all cost (69).

Having first eliminated any necessity of understanding Lear in terms of psychological motivation and then elevated him to the status of representative of mankind, Mack is now free to redeem his common humanity, which serves to reaffirm the moral foundation of human social order while enabling us to identify with him as a fully individualized and expressive human being. At this stage in Mack's argument, a loving, suffering, and enduring Lear emerges to elicit our sympathy and awe.

What Mack wants to say, I think, in his last chapter is that he himself identifies with Lear. But such a statement, in the context of the rigorous exclusion of the personal mandated by the New Criticism, would be unthinkable. His solution to this problem is to maintain that Lear represents all of "us." Mack's embrace of this passionate plural indicates not only his uneasiness in expressing his personal point of entry into the play, but also his intensity of response. "For the abysses of the play," he lyricizes, are "wrapped in the enigma of our own ignorance of the meaning of existence, its peaks echo with cries of triumph and despair so equivocal that we are never sure they are not ours" (84).

Increasingly, Mack invokes this simultaneously personalized and universal "we" as his argument rises to its crescendo. "Existence is tragic in *King Lear*," he states, "because existence is inseparable from relation; we are born from and to it; it envelops us in our loves and lives as parents, children, sisters, brothers, husbands, wives, servants, masters, rulers, subjects—the web is seamless and unending" (110). Expanding eloquently on this theme, Mack writes as if he no longer makes any distinction between the specific conditions of Lear's life and his own. "Old, we begin our play with the need to impose relation—to divide our kingdom, set our rest on someone's kind nursery, and crawl toward our death" (111). Ultimately, Mack focuses on the phrase "we came crying hither" as expressive of Lear's, his, and our tragedy. Lear's suffering, he concludes, "is the suffering that is rooted in the very fact of being human, and its best symbol is the birth cry of every infant, as if it knew already that to enter humanity is to be born in pain, to suffer pain, and to cause pain" (111).

Mack's emphasis on the "birth cry of every infant" leads him to affirm this basic human vulnerability as the source of tragic dignity and meaning. The book comes to a close on this powerful (and unconventional) note: "When we come crying hither, we bring with us the badge of all our misery; but it is also the badge of the vulnerabilities that give us access to whatever grandeur we have" (117). The Lear Mack finds compelling is not the imperious or infirm old man of the beginning of the play (whose possible motivations he dismisses as irrelevant to our concern) but rather the defeated monarch rendered childlike and defenseless through his ordeal. In order to endorse such a position of vulnerability, however, Mack must first nullify the question of Lear's complicity in the events that cause his suffering, then universalize his plight so as to render it accessible to identification. As a result, he puts forth a notion of tragedy based on human relatedness from which all traces of specific human relations (in terms of character or motivation) have disappeared.

If *King Lear in Our Time* reads anachronistically to us, it is because it attempts to shore up a set of assumptions already in danger of collapse at the moment of its writing. Curiously, it raises, only to dismiss, the very issues and areas of interest that would preoccupy succeeding generations of not only feminist but also psychoanalytic, deconstructive, new historicist, and cultural materialist critics. Along with psychological speculation, for instance, Mack sweeps aside the objection that the play cannot be unified; he brings in an instance of historical anecdote (the story of Cordell and her sister Lady Wildgoose) only to drop it as tangential to his argument; and to the extent that he discusses issues of class conflict (in the relations between Edmund and Edgar, for instance), he subordinates them to an assertion of the necessity for traditional order and hierarchy. Such elements might almost be considered the repressed content of his text, struggling for articulation yet relentlessly marginalized. It is as though Mack understood how these differing emphases would disrupt the profoundly humanist view of tragedy which he espoused. In his own highly individualistic way, he strove to rearticulate this view in what he considered contemporary terms, precisely in order to defend it against the depredations of "our time."

Difference and Dispersal

Mack had reason to be concerned. By 1980, it was no longer possible to invoke the royal "we" to authorize such a particular viewpoint. A watershed year, 1980 witnessed the publication of three books which would effectively decenter the humanist tradition of Shakespeare studies: *The Woman's Part:*

Feminist Criticism of Shakespeare, edited by Carolyn Ruth Swift Lenz, Gayle Greene, and Carol Thomas Neely; Stephen Greenblatt's *Renaissance Self-Fashioning;* and *Representing Shakespeare: New Psychoanalytic Essays,* edited by Murray Schwartz and Coppélia Kahn. In a series of complementary moves, *The Woman's Part* would question basic assumptions about the irrelevance of gender to the process of interpretation, *Representing Shakespeare* would subvert humanist assumptions about rationality by focusing on the duplicitous and fantasmatic aspects of dramatic form, and *Renaissance Self-Fashioning* would introduce a practice of reading which denies the special status of literary over other kinds of texts. Under pressure from these challenges and others from the direction of cultural materialist and poststructural theory, the critical world view of Maynard Mack would finally crumble and dissolve into a rich diversity of overlapping and competing perspectives.[3]

The Woman's Part had the effect of decentering the significance of the tragic hero to the point of challenging traditional assumptions about tragedy as a genre. In their introduction, the editors articulate the premises underlying the collection which lead to this result. Female readers, they observe, bring their own subjectivity into the reading process and trust their own responses. In this way they compensate for the bias in Shakespeare criticism in favor of male characters, themes, and fantasies. They adapt reading strategies from various critical traditions: historical, psychological, New Critical—and create their own. They owe a special debt to the New Criticism for its techniques of close textual analysis, but also violate New Critical strictures concerning the significance of social and historical contexts, the subjective experience of the individual reader, and the political implications of literary works.

The focus on gender as an analytic category gives rise to a profound skepticism about the meanings male critics from A. C. Bradley to Maynard Mack have attributed to Shakespeare's tragedies. "While in comedy," the editors note, "the heroines achieve their ends gracefully by playing a part, in tragedy they are condemned for acting, accused of being deceitful even when they are not, or relegated to the position of audience to male acting. Good women are often powerless, and powerful women are always threatening and often, in fact, destructive. And, as has been noted, the women in the tragedies almost invariably are destroyed, or are absent from the new order consolidated at the conclusions" (6). Carol Neely, who reads *Othello* from the decentered position of Emilia, brings out some of the more radical implications of this statement ("Women and Men in *Othello*").

Neely deliberately chooses a marginalized position from which to interpret the play. She looks through the eyes of not only a woman, but one who is neither upper-class nor pivotal to the main action—as is Desdemona, for instance. From this down-to-earth perspective, the men (in their envy, idealism, and obsession) come across poorly. "In *Othello*," she states, "the men's murderous fancies are untouched by the women's affection, wit, and shrewishness. The play ends as it began, in a world of men—political, loveless, undomesticated" (215).[4] Embedded in this observation is an implicit statement of value, but one which Neely does not find confirmed by the play. Hence, she is unmoved by its conclusion. For her, the play ends "on the note of arrested growth, devastated fertility. 'The object poisons sight'; it signifies destruction without catharsis, release without resolution. The pain and division of the ending are unmitigated, and the clarification it offers is intolerable" (234-35). When we attempt to look, not through Shakespeare's eyes, Neely implies, nor through those of the tragic hero, a dislocation occurs so profound as to alter our very understanding of tragedy. While feminist critics themselves have not always emphasized this point, at least one neotraditionalist critic has attempted to reckon with its impact.

In a highly polemical article published in PMLA in 1988, Richard Levin launched an attack on feminist criticism of Shakespeare by condemning it as "thematic" (rather than character-based) in approach ("Feminist Thematics and Shakespearean Tragedy").[5] While it is clear that what he means is "ideological" rather than "thematic," his actual target is the view of tragedy that emerges from this by now large and wide-ranging body of criticism. His objections are threefold: that the tragic hero no longer appears admirable, that there is no recognition of restoration or renewal, and, perhaps worst of all, that there is no possibility of "catharsis." As a result, there is an inevitable loss of "tragic effect" (131).

In an argument as tendentious as this, it is difficult to isolate a single strand of concern, yet one might be adduced from Levin's overly protective stance vis-à-vis the tragic hero. In feminist criticism, he laments, "most of the heroes emerge as a sorry lot indeed, having lost virtually all their admirable qualities and even their individuality" (131). Instead of regaining their "earlier noble stature" in the end, they are homogenized "down to the lowest moral level" (131), with the result that "the protagonist, who is usually the most individualized and most admirable character, will suffer the greatest diminution on both counts" (131). Such a relentless "denigration of the tragic hero," of course, destroys the tragic effect, which depends on an implicit emotional identification missing from this type of criticism. Catharsis, Levin states, includes not only "some kind of restoration of order," but also "a renewal or enhancement of our positive feelings for the hero," leading to "tragic sympathy" for his plight, "none of which can be recognized by this group of critics" (132). Believing as he does in the intrinsic worth of the tragic hero, Levin simply cannot understand why feminists don't seem to like him.

For Levin, the idea of tragedy refers to a fixed set of conventions and responses, which the individual interpreter is not at liberty to question. "Most of these critics," he complains, "do not see Shakespeare deliberately setting out to write a tragedy where the nature of the genre (its conventions, expectations, and appropriate pleasures) might determine the nature of the gender relations portrayed in the play, rather than the other way around" (133). Levin rightly detects a threat to his own view of tragedy in the decentering moves of feminist criticism, but he cannot imagine admitting more than one perspective on this subject. Effacing his own indebtedness to Aristotle via Bradley, Levin writes as though his conception of tragedy were not a matter of historical and critical engagement, but rather one of timeless universals. If, from this position, genre is responsible for producing a specific configuration of gender relations, then there is no point in analyzing their effects. Feminist criticism, in contrast, not only historicizes the notion of tragedy but also reverses Levin's trajectory of value. By interrogating the dynamics of gender in Shakespeare's tragedies, feminist critics implicitly, if not openly, question the meanings traditionally invested in tragedy as a genre.[6]

Levin's conception of tragedy situates itself comfortably in a line of twentieth-century British and American criticism stretching back to Bradley. This view depends on a faith in a unified subjectivity (in author, critic, and text) which underwrites the possibility of articulating a universal truth, applicable not only to both genders but also to all classes, races, and sexualities. Writing in 1988, Levin was confronted by a radical erosion of this faith. Although he chose to address a specific form of gender analysis, he might have targeted a number of other critical approaches as equally hostile to his assumptions.[7] While the first wave of feminist criticism had the effect of dislodging the tragic hero from his privileged status as the generator of tragic meaning, other interpretive strategies have continued this process of decentralization to the point of radical dispersal. The tragic subject has, on all levels, come into question.

Lacanian psychoanalysis and poststructuralism, while incongruent in many respects, share certain assumptions about the nature of subjectivity which have contributed to the deconstruction of a character-based mode of interpretation, along with the kind of communal critical response represented in the use of "we." For Lacan, the subject constituted as such through the mirror stage can never wholly comprehend itself. Rather, it must depend for its coherence on a "mirror image" which supplies only an illusion of wholeness or integrity, masking a condition of internal dispersal and dis-integration ("The Mirror Stage"). Such a subject can no more assume a coherence of self hood or awareness in the tragic hero than it can pretend to know itself. Derridean poststructuralism further diffuses the notion of a stable subjectivity by locating it along a continuum of signifiers, themselves divorced from the possibility of material reference or fixed construction of meaning. Immersed in such a fluid medium, the self can never be apprehended for more than a moment, nor can it be pinned to any of its diverse manifestations.[8] A criticism that relies on either Lacanian or Derridean assumptions regarding self hood can hardly subscribe to the notion of the hero's exemplary character, much less to the idea of an unproblematized restoration of moral order—both at the heart of humanist interpretation.

From a different angle, the practices of both new historicism and cultural materialism (including the new gay and lesbian and colonial discourse studies) have assisted in the displacement of the tragic hero from the center of tragic construction and significance.[9] Each of these schools focuses on the functioning of social codes in the production of power relations which inform textual practices and meanings, hence subordinating issues of formal aesthetics to ones of ideology and culture.[10] In this light, the hero's fate does not so much devolve from defects of individual character or judgment as it reflects the mapping of his social world in both its conservative and disruptive forms. Rather than stressing his role as a self-willed, autonomous subject, these approaches emphasize the tragic hero's implication in a highly complex, as well as internally conflicted, field of social discourses. From this perspective, he suffers a reduction of the stature automatically accorded him in the humanist tradition of interpretation.

Until sometime roughly in the mid-seventies, Shakespeare criticism could assume a high degree of consensus on issues regarding the centrality of the tragic hero, his representative nature, and the special status of tragedy as a genre. Contemporary critics, in contrast, stress matters of difference: in the processes of language, representation, and the construction of self hood, in addition to the gender, racial, sexual, and class locations of the interpreter.[11] On the whole, they are more preoccupied with these concerns than they are with questions of genre. While the New Criticism enjoyed hegemony, for a time, over other critical practices, today there is no such hierarchy or cohesion. Rather, a diversity of critical perspectives simultaneously flourish, freely borrowing from each other even as they challenge one another's political and philosophical assumptions.

This anthology does not aim to mediate local disputes among these approaches, but rather to indicate how richly they interact in their varied contributions to the subject of gender in Shakespeare's tragedy. Hence Shirley Garner and I as editors have chosen essays that represent not only differing strategies of interpretation but also differing conclusions. Taken as a group, however, what these essays demonstrate is how significantly gender figures in the construction and devolution of tragic subjectivity and action. For Shakespeare, they collectively imply, gender and genre (both derived from the Latin *genus*) are as interinvolved in the interpretation of tragedy as they are in their linguistic origins.

The first five essays in this collection deal with Shakespeare's construction of tragic subjectivity—out of the materials and conventions of the history play, in relation to the deployment of literacy and contemporary discourses of madness, and in terms of fantasies regarding maternal power. These essays document the displacement of dangerous female energy from the center of the action, as the tragic hero gains in richness of dramatic representation. In this perilous gender dynamic, women characters dwindle while their male counterparts expand. As these essays demonstrate, the scold, the witch, and the madwoman, along with the merely literate aristocratic female, are effectively silenced, tamed, or otherwise banished from the tragic scene.

In "History into Tragedy: The Case of *Richard III*," Phyllis Rackin shows how Shakespeare's shift from the loose chronicle form of his early history plays to the tightly focused structure of tragedy restricted the range of possible roles for women. What Shakespeare's tragic women gain in terms of sympathetic portrayal, they lose in terms of transgressive, even demonic, power. The male hero, in the meantime, moves center stage, occupying the *platea*, the site of soliloquy, and hence privileged subjectivity. Rackin relates these changes in dramatic form to the emergence of a capitalist economy and a nation-state "that increasingly employed the mystified image of a patriarchal family to authorize masculine privilege and rationalize monarchical power."

Sara Eaton explores the question of women's positioning in tragedy by exploring Shakespeare's deployment of early modern discourses concerning learned women. Eaton reads the fate of Lavinia in *Titus Andronicus* as expressive of the anxieties she generates as an educated, and hence potentially unruly, woman. Lavinia's rape and mutilation, she argues, not only deprives her of the power to speak and write, but also makes brutally evident the nature of her social function as an object of exchange among men. Whereas "Titus' recourse to writing ennobles his actions and allows his family to transcend his opponents socially," thus contributing to his tragic stature, Lavinia's body, as Eaton succinctly states, becomes "her alphabet," the means by which we may interpret her position as an educated aristocratic woman.

Carol Thomas Neely approaches the portrayal of madness in Shakespeare's tragedies from the standpoint of shifting attitudes in the culture at large. She argues that Shakespeare contributed to a general process by which madness came to be secularized, medicalized, and psychologized as well as gendered. The specific gender marking of madness is evident in the contrast between the way in which male and female characters behave in states of psychic extremity. Whereas Hamlet, as a victim of melancholy, merely feigns madness, Ophelia, a hysteric, succumbs to her ailment and dies a helpless suicide. While Macbeth projects his fears into hallucinations yet remains fully functional as a warrior, Lady Macbeth breaks down and kills herself. Even Lear, who descends into paranoid psychosis, recovers full tragic dignity, along with his sanity, by the end of the play. When men go mad in Shakespeare, they either remain in control or manage to recover agency; women, in contrast, lose command over themselves and their fates.

The next two essays consider more closely the tensions in the masculine psyche that structure the treatment of women in tragedy. Janet Adelman reads *Macbeth* in terms of a dual fantasy structure, which posits a "virtually absolute and destructive female power" along with the simultaneous and absolute escape from it. Lady Macbeth joins with the witches, in this logic, to subject her husband to fantasies of unmanning and hence vulnerability to maternal rage, at the same time that the play permits the circulation of a counterfantasy of autonomous male generation and hence immortality. While Macbeth himself succumbs in the end, this latter fantasy survives through the ambiguous prophecy concerning Macduff as one "not of woman born." Order is restored, moreover, at the expense of the women in the play, not one of whom is left alive, thus solving "the problem of masculinity by eliminating the female."

Coppélia Kahn explores the way in which the fantasy of an all-bountiful yet ultimately rejecting mother underlies the system of male patronage that structures the action of *Timon of Athens*. She sees Timon's excessive display of generosity to his friends as an analogue of the dynamic of social exchange favored by James I, whose own compulsive giving turned the crown surplus that he inherited at his accession into a staggering burden of debt. In a play striking for its absence of significant women's roles, Timon first usurps the role of a benevolent (and maternal) Fortune, then reacts, angrily, like her betrayed offspring. In this way, Shakespeare "portrays a radical mistrust of women in a male subject, which the male projects onto woman as her aggression toward him."

While the first five essays focus on Shakespeare's construction of male tragic subjectivity and its corresponding constriction of women's roles, the next three essays explore the early modern discourses of marriage and race that determine Desdemona's fate. Taken together, these essays reveal further how both actors in Othello's tragic wife-murder live out the contradictions regarding race and gender embedded in their culture.

Lena Cowen Orlin points to the moral import of physical disposition in early modern texts dealing with wifely conduct. In them, a woman who leaves her home eludes male control and hence may be suspected of infidelity. The uncertainty of Desdemona's "disposition" in first escaping her father's house, then lodging at the Sagittary, and finally taking up residence in a military camp, suggests for the men in the play that she is loose by temperament. Rather than displaying any inner consistency of character by which we may construct a plausible interpretation of her contradictory actions and utterances, Desdemona behaves in ways that enable the unfolding of Othello's tragedy. As such, she is "an artfully created embodiment of female behavior and feminine responses" which serves to expose the patriarchal assumptions underlying the play's dramatic action.

Margo Hendricks, refusing a simplistic racialized reading of the conclusion of Othello as the murder of a "white" woman by her enraged "black" husband, looks instead at the radically unstable meanings attributed to Venice as a source for the gender and racial politics of the play. Early modern discourses concerning Venice carried within them the binary divisions so painfully enacted in Othello's perceptions of himself and of Desdemona. Venice, Hendricks argues, was understood alternatively as an ideal image of the well-governed state and as a site of political and sexual corruption. To the extent that both Othello and Desdemona are "Venetian" (one by birth, the other by assimilation), both are subject to the violent oscillations contained in this discourse. Thus the white/black and virgin/whore dichotomies which drive the action of the play are less the result of individual consciousness or error than of an entire social field of awareness.

Mary Beth Rose further contextualizes the action of Othello by locating it within the field of Protestant discourse concerning marriage. She sees Desdemona's character as expressive of the conflict embedded in this discourse between women as spiritually and socially equal to their husbands yet subordinate. While Shakespeare's tragedy works to expose this inherent contradiction, it provides no satisfactory resolution. Instead, it victimizes the women who attempt to fulfill such warring expectations. Contrasting the death of Desdemona with that of the Duchess of Malfi, Rose comments on the greater latitude for female heroism that Webster allows. Yet Jacobean tragedy as a whole, by representing irreconcilable ambiguities, also acts to contain them, thus serving conservative aims.

Rose emphasizes the resistance to change inherent in the elegiac function of tragedy, which articulates "the need for a future by destroying the past and then mourning its disappearance." Each of the next four essays strives to locate a position from which to disrupt this conservative logic. For Carol Cook, Cleopatra represents a principle of linguistic challenge to phallocentric assumptions. For Linda Charnes, Shirley Nelson Garner, and Gayle Greene, it is the feminist interpreter herself who may most effectively perform this role by measuring the critical distance between herself and Shakespeare.

Carol Cook moves from patriarchy as a system of social relations to the issue of phallocentrism in representation. Drawing on the work of French feminist Luce Irigaray, she argues that the radical ambiguity encoded in Cleopatra's punning language offers a means of disrupting or subverting the binary logic of hierarchy and opposition that structures all other relations in the play. Cleopatra functions less as a character with a recognizable psychology than as "a figure for a certain kind of textual operation," which points to that which escapes representation altogether. Only in this way can the reader or spectator imagine her as eluding Roman Caesar's attempts to objectify and contain her. By calling attention to the limits of representation itself, Cleopatra gestures toward another space, one which calls into question the gender and power politics of the play.

While Cook emphasizes Cleopatra's freedom from sexual stereotyping in her playful references to cross-dressing and to the conventions of stage transvestism, Linda Charnes stresses the frequency with which critics exalt the love-death conclusion of the play in ways that reinscribe traditional gender roles. To counter this tendency, she suggests that we read the love plot of *Antony and Cleopatra* in terms of Harlequin romance. These popular love stories for women typically obscure the actual difficulties of women's lives, in much the same way that the "transcendent love" interpretation of *Antony and Cleopatra* obliterates matters of sociopolitical concern. According to Charnes, the rhetoric of epic love in the play serves not only to camouflage Antony's obvious weaknesses, but also to restore gender decorum by emphasizing Cleopatra's self-sacrifice as romantically motivated. Identifying this mode of interpretation as typical of liberal humanism, Charnes calls instead for a recognition of the complex web of sociopolitical meanings masked by such rhetoric.

The remaining two essays in this volume introduce a series of personal reflections on Shakespearean tragedy, through autobiographical accounts of what it has meant to be a gender-sensitive critic of Shakespeare in the latter half of the twentieth century. Like Linda Charnes, Shirley Nelson Garner and Gayle Greene balance respect for the enduring impact of Shakespeare's plays with a clear-eyed assessment of their own needs as contemporary women.

Shirley Garner explores her educational experience of Shakespeare (as student, then teacher) as a means of probing her current engagement with the question of gender and tragedy. By coming to her reading of Shakespeare as a woman and an "outsider," she was able to penetrate the aura of reverence which (still) surrounds his work and, by defamiliarizing the experience of the tragic hero, to register the impact of his misogyny. The tragedies engage her imagination more than the comedies or romances, "but should they?" she asks. Is this a "perverse taste" that inevitably turns her against herself? Her efforts to comprehend her responses as well as those of her students have persuaded her of the need not only to locate Shakespeare firmly within his time and place, but also to recognize the claims of her own.

Gayle Greene takes us on a journey through her years with Shakespeare, from her first adolescent "crush" on Richard II and her fascination with such ambivalent figures of male power, through her dawning awareness of the importance of language in mediating crises of signification, to her final disillusionment with the narratives of canonized male authors. Comparing her involvement with Shakespeare to the process of falling in and out of love, she describes how she made the transition to her current work on contemporary women writers—out of her mature conviction that their concerns more nearly match her own. Refusing to sever her ties with her past, however, she pays tribute to her early love for Shakespeare while acknowledging that it no longer seems to satisfy. In middle age, she implies, it no longer pays to valorize this kind of romantic attachment.

Rewriting Tragedy, Rewriting Ourselves?

In our early conversations about this anthology project, Shirley Garner and I talked about the ways in which the insertion of gender into the discussion of

Shakespeare's tragedies altered our understanding of tragedy as a genre—an understanding which was very much a product of our own educations as influenced by A. C. Bradley and his intellectual heirs. This view of tragedy, we came to see, rests on the assumption of a unified, universal, male subjectivity which no longer compels our allegiance. For critics such as Richard Levin, such apostasy signals a crisis in literary studies, if not in society at large; for us it suggests both a liberation and an opportunity. The very elements that elicit his anxiety and indignation also release our hope and imagination.

A novel such as Jane Smiley's *A Thousand Acres*, although it makes no allusion to feminist criticism of Shakespeare, could hardly have been written without the emergence of second-wave feminism and the tide of critical reevaluation it launched. Most notably a work of fiction, *A Thousand Acres* also functions as literary interpretation, critiquing and revising the very assumptions on which Levin's notion of tragedy depends.[12] Deliberately choosing an undutiful daughter through which to tell her story of family disorder and decay, Smiley summarily disposes of such issues as the (male) hero's exemplary character and tragic dignity in favor of a humbler set of aims and values. Not only is Ginny's knowledge more inclusive than that of Lear, but it also spares her as knower. Smiley opts against the traditional tragic denouement in which the hero pays for his awareness with his life and affirms instead Ginny's capacity to endure. Tragedy so understood need not victimize women; so revised, it may even offer forms and strategies for our survival.

If compelled to choose, Shirley Garner affirms that she would respond to Maynard Mack's question "Who would be Horatio if he could be Hamlet?" by taking Horatio's part.[13] After all, she reminds us, Horatio loves, survives, and Shakespeare leaves him to tell Hamlet's story. Several years ago, when my daughter was in high school and reading Shakespeare seriously for the first time, she expressed a similar view. Musing out loud about the plays she had read, she paused to comment extensively on *Hamlet*. The only character she really liked, she said, was Horatio. She couldn't see why Hamlet willed his kingdom to Fortinbras, whose only distinguishing characteristic was his willingness to risk hundreds of lives for a worthless piece of ground, when Horatio was really qualified to be king. Laertes she dismissed as a fool. She thought Hamlet's telling Ophelia to go to a nunnery was ridiculous and remarked on the difficulty and pain of Ophelia's position. She was especially perturbed by Hamlet's jumping into Ophelia's grave and acting sentimental when he had effectively driven her to suicide. Hamlet, she concluded, was responsible for much carnage—a somewhat sorry excuse for a hero.

There is much that I could have said to counterbalance this view, but I didn't have the heart. My daughter's assessment struck me as shrewd and more likely to be of use to her in the world than any rehabilitation of Hamlet that I might offer. I was reluctant to undermine her faith in her own judgment and reality.

If the price of sustaining the humanist evaluation of tragedy (as represented by Bradley, Mack, and Levin) is the displacement or denigration of one's own experience, intelligence, and most fully informed understanding, then it is too high. In the words of Catherine Belsey, "Shakespeare's plays reveal with great subtlety the shifts that language is put to in defence of a Renaissance masculinity which so engrosses meaning to itself that it constantly risks the exclusion of its defining [female] other" ("Afterword" 260). *Macbeth*, in particular, "demonstrates the instabilities of a patriarchy which confines woman to motherhood and promises to man everything else that it means to be human" (261). The failure to critique such exclusionary moves, she implies, helps to reconstitute the very structures that organize difference in hierarchical and oppositional terms.

Gary Taylor's encyclopedic survey of critical and dramatic interpretations of Shakespeare from the Restoration to the present demonstrates just how culturally mediated our images of Shakespeare are (*Reinventing Shakespeare*). This might also be said of tragedy, which reflects not a universal essence but rather a historically specific encoding of practices and values. If feminist criticism has contributed to the dissolution of a certain humanist consensus about the proper subject of tragedy, it has also released a diversity of plots and possibilities. If some feel dismay at such an open prospect, others (like the editors and contributors to this volume) will welcome the opportunity for creative play.

NOTES

1. This line is attributed to Goneril in the 1608 Quarto, to Edmund ("Bast.") in the 1623 Folio. Until recently, most editors of *King Lear* have constructed a composite text based on these two sources under the assumption that both derive from a more definitive, "lost" version. This assumption has been challenged by a group of scholars who argue rather that the Folio version of the play represents Shakespeare's revision of the Quarto and hence that the two texts must be considered independently of each other. For fuller accounts of this controversy, see Steven Urkowitz, *Shakespeare's Revision of "King Lear"*; Gary Taylor and Michael Warren, eds., *The Division of the Kingdoms: Shakespeare's Two Versions of "King Lear"* (especially the essays by Stanley Wells and Steven Urkowitz); Michael Warren, "Quarto and Folio *King Lear* and the Interpre-

tation of Albany and Edgar"; and Gary Taylor, *Reinventing Shakespeare* (356–62). Randall McLeod analyzes the major differences between the Quarto and Folio in terms of their characterizations of Goneril ("No more, the text is foolish"). The Folio, he argues, portrays her somewhat more sympathetically than the Quarto. He distinguishes between Goneril's departure from the stage in the two versions as follows:

> In F, it is true, Gonerill leaves the stage challenged, but she is in a position of strength, and asserts that she is above the law—even as her dismissive "An enterlude" asserted that she was real while her husband was role-playing in a farce. Exactly what Gonerill will do after her exit eventually proves pitiful, of course; but at the moment the unknown is part of her strength. . . . In Q, however, Gonerill leaves the stage already defeated and shamefaced. Having claimed at first to stand above the law, she ultimately implies her guilt; not denying her husband's charge, she attempts merely to suppress it and run away from it. Her exit in defeat and her suicide, when it is revealed, do not contradict each other, as they do in the *Tragedie*. (188)

Clearly it makes a difference to interpretation whether or not Goneril says "Ask me not what I know," yet my choice of attribution here is not critical to my general point about the opacity of Shakespeare's tragic women, nor it is necessary to my interpretation of Smiley's novel, although it is certainly consistent with my reading of her transformation of Goneril into Ginny.

2. In " 'This is and is not Cressid': The Characterization of Cressida," Janet Adelman argues that the character of Cressida diminishes in the second half of the play in such a way as to make her motivations inscrutable. Marianne Novy detects a similar structure in several of Shakespeare's tragedies, where the women who begin in an active mode are gradually marginalized and subordinated in development to the more expansive consciousness of the male hero ("Shakespeare's Female Characters as Actors and Audience").

3. For an overview of the broad structural changes that took place in the 1980s, see Gary Taylor's highly readable chapter "Present Tense" in *Reinventing Shakespeare*. Taylor's view of the current stage of critical fragmentation is happily relativistic. "Everything is related to everything else," he genially concludes. "So everything is relevant to Shakespeare, and Shakespeare is relevant to everything. Shakespeare, the apex of the inverted pyramid of interpretation, is also the tip of a funnel through which the whole world can be poured. And that tip belongs to criticism" (352).

4. In "Loss and Recovery: Homes Away from Home," Neely describes this essay as "paradigmatic of seventies American feminist literary criticism" in its blindness to issues of race and class in *Othello*. While she sees the danger of essentializing "men" and "women" in the text, she continues to affirm the value of a decentered reading, one now complicated by an understanding of the plural points of identification involved in subject formation. In a recent essay, presented at the 1992 meeting of the Shakespeare Association of America, she argues for a reading of Othello's tragedy as devolving from his multiple and conflicting, hence *mestizo*, identities.

5. Levin's article prompted a collective response, appearing in a subsequent issue

of *PMLA*, in the form of a letter cosigned by twenty-four scholars, most of whose work had been assailed by Levin ("Forum"). This letter has generated new defenses (and critiques) of his position. The controversy continues to rage, as witnessed by a special session at the 1989 meeting of the Modern Language Association dealing with the pros and cons of Levin's attacks on ideological forms of criticism. This session, in turn, provided the basis for an anthology on the topic, titled *Shakespeare Left and Right*.

6. The body of criticism I refer to here, much of it in article form, which appeared in the seventies and early to mid-eighties, is simply too large to credit in full. Several landmark books from this period, however, deserve individual mention: Linda Bamber, *Comic Women, Tragic Men: A Study of Gender and Genre in Shakespeare;* Diane Dreher, *Domination and Defiance: Fathers and Daughters in Shakespeare;* Peter Erickson, *Patriarchal Structures in Shakespeare's Drama;* Coppélia Kahn, *Man's Estate: Masculine Identity in Shakespeare;* Carol Thomas Neely, *Broken Nuptials in Shakespeare's Plays;* Marianne Novy, *Love's Argument: Gender Relations in Shakespeare;* and Richard Wheeler, *Shakespeare's Development and the Problem Comedies: Turn and Counter-Turn.* Recent books which deal (in part) with the issue of gender and Shakespearean tragedy include Janet Adelman, *Suffocating Mothers: Fantasies of Maternal Origin in Shakespeare's Plays, "Hamlet" to "The Tempest";* Dympna Callaghan, *Women and Gender in Renaissance Tragedy;* Peter Erickson, *Rewriting Shakespeare, Rewriting Ourselves;* Ania Loomba, *Gender, Race, Renaissance Drama;* Karen Newman, *Fashioning Femininity and English Renaissance Drama;* Phyllis Rackin, *Stages of History: Shakespeare's English Chronicles;* Mary Beth Rose, *The Expense of Spirit: Love and Sexuality in English Renaissance Drama;* and Valerie Traub, *Desire and Anxiety: Circulations of Sexuality in Shakespearean Drama.*

7. In "The Poetics and Politics of Bardicide," published in a later issue of *PMLA*, Levin takes issue with Marxist cultural materialist and "neo-Freudian" readings of Shakespeare. While he condemns these approaches for being politically motivated, he assumes that his own interpretive stance is free of cultural or personal bias.

8. The collection *Shakespeare and the Question of Theory*, ed. Patricia Parker and Geoffrey Hartman, offers several examples of such deconstructive readings. See, in particular, Howard Felperin, " 'Tongue-tied our queen?': The Deconstruction of Presence in *The Winter's Tale*"; Elizabeth Freund, " 'Ariachne's Broken Woof': The Rhetoric of Citation in *Troilus and Cressida*"; Geoffrey Hartman, "Shakespeare's Poetical Character in *Twelfth Night*"; and Patricia Parker, "Shakespeare and Rhetoric: 'Dilation' and 'Delation' in *Othello*." Joel Fineman's essay in that volume, "The Turn of the Shrew," relies on a specifically Lacanian psychoanalytic framework. For other Lacanian approaches, see Barbara Freedman, "Misrecognizing Shakespeare," and David Willbern, "What Is Shakespeare," in *Shakespeare's Personality*, ed. Norman Holland, Bernard Paris, and Sidney Homan. Jacqueline Rose, in "Sexuality in the Reading of Shakespeare: *Hamlet* and *Measure for Measure*," interprets the roles of Gertrude and Isabella through a feminist Lacanian lens in order to emphasize the disruptive possibilities of the feminine within representation. From a Derridean standpoint, Terry Eagleton, in "Lan-

guage: *Macbeth, Richard II, Henry IV,*" argues that the witches in *Macbeth* (by virtue of their radically ambiguous speech) are the real heroines of the play. Others whose readings of Shakespeare seek to undermine the notion of a stable subjectivity include Marguerite Waller, in "Usurpation, Seduction, and the Problematics of the Proper: A 'Deconstructive,' 'Feminist,' Rereading of the Seductions of Richard and Anne in Shakespeare's *Richard III*," and Christopher Norris, in "Post-structuralist Shakespeare: Text and Ideology."

9. Feminism and new historicism regarded each other at first with some suspicion. From the perspective of feminism, new historicism (in its early stages of development) seemed insufficiently concerned with gender. For new historicists, first-wave feminist critics of Shakespeare seemed too narrowly focused on character and not enough on sociopolitical context. As younger critics have entered this field of debate, the terms have softened somewhat, primarily because of the plurality of critical approaches to which they have been exposed in their graduate training. While new historicists do not invariably concern themselves with gender, there is nothing in their methodology that prevents them from doing so. Hence a generation of feminist new historicists has emerged, whose work interweaves gender analysis with issues of cultural critique. *The Matter of Difference,* Valerie Wayne's collection of feminist materialist essays on Shakespeare, bears witness to the degree to which feminist criticism has appropriated the perspectives and interpretive techniques of new historicism (and cultural materialism) without losing its own clear-eyed focus on gender.

10. In "Professing the Renaissance: The Poetics and Politics of Culture," Louis A. Montrose articulates the assumptions regarding the construction of subjectivity which underlie the new historicist and cultural materialist approaches to literary analysis. "The writing of texts," he explains, "as well as the processes by which they are circulated and categorized, analyzed and taught, are being reconstrued as historically determined and determining modes of cultural work; apparently autonomous aesthetic and academic issues are being reunderstood as inextricably though complexly linked to other discourses and practices—such linkages constituting the social networks within which individual subjectivities and collective structures are mutually and continuously shaped" (15). As a result, "the freely self-creating and world-creating Individual of so-called liberal humanism is—at least, in theory—now defunct" (21). Catherine Belsey in *The Subject of Tragedy: Identity and Difference in Renaissance Drama* and Jonathan Dollimore in *Radical Tragedy: Religion, Ideology and Power in the Drama of Shakespeare and His Contemporaries* both make the case for a deconstruction of the notion of the tragic hero as an autonomous individual with easily recognized and comprehensible motivations. For Terry Eagleton, the character of Hamlet is constructed around a void. "Hamlet has no 'essence' of being whatsoever, no inner sanctum to be safeguarded: he is pure deferral and diffusion, a hollow void which offers nothing determinate to be known. . . . In this sense, Hamlet is even more proleptic than Coriolanus, looking forward to a time (our own?) when that individualistic conception of the self will itself enter into crisis" ("Nothing" 72–75). Proceeding from such a nonnaturalistic conception

of the individual, new historicist and cultural materialist readings of Shakespeare's tragedies tend to focus not on the hero per se but on the political/ideological force fields of the plays. See, for instance, Stephen Greenblatt's interpretation of *King Lear*, "Shakespeare and the Exorcists," which stresses the role of theater in negotiating social change, and Peter Stallybrass's reading of *Othello*, "Patriarchal Territories: The Body Enclosed," which analyzes the class dynamics of the play in terms of cultural fantasies about women's bodies. Terence Hawkes's essay on *Hamlet*, "Telmah" (Hamlet backward), announces by its very title its refusal to approach the play through the personality of its eponymous hero.

11. Analysis of colonialist discourse and gay and lesbian approaches to Shakespeare's work are yielding productive new readings of his plays. Yet, with the exception of *Othello* criticism, most of this work does not focus on the tragedies. While *The Tempest* has become a locus classicus for studies in colonialist discourse, Shakespeare's comedies have proved to be a rich ground for interpreting the gender-bending effects of cross-dressing on the Renaissance stage. See, for instance, Francis Barker and Peter Hulme, "Nymphs and Reapers Heavily Vanish: The Discursive Contexts of *The Tempest*"; Paul Brown, " 'This thing of darkness I acknowledge mine': *The Tempest* and the Discourse of Colonialism"; Thomas Cartelli, "Prospero in Africa: *The Tempest* as Colonialist Text and Pretext"; Stephen Greenblatt, "Learning to Curse: Aspects of Linguistic Colonialism in the Sixteenth Century"; Jean Howard, "Renaissance Antitheatricality and the Politics of Gender and Rank in *Much Ado about Nothing*"; Lisa Jardine, *Still Harping on Daughters*; and Valerie Traub, "Desire and the Differences It Makes." Laura Levine's "Men in Women's Clothing: Antitheatricality and Effeminization from 1579 to 1642" and Stephen Orgel's "Nobody's Perfect: Or Why Did the English Stage Take Boys for Women," while not directly concerned with Shakespeare's comedy, have helped to open the subject of gender indeterminacy in Shakespeare's handling of this genre. For recent analyses of the racial discourses that inform *Othello*, see Jack D'Amico, *The Moor in English Renaissance Drama;* Emily Bartels, "Making More of the Moor: Aaron, Othello, and Renaissance Refashionings of Race"; Phyllis Natalie Braxton, "Othello: The Moor and the Metaphor"; Paul Cantor, "*Othello:* The Erring Barbarian among the Supersubtle Venetians"; Karen Newman, " 'And Wash the Ethiop White': Femininity and the Monstrous in *Othello*"; and Patricia Parker, "Fantasies of 'Race' and 'Gender': Africa, *Othello*, and Bringing to Light."

12. *Women's Re-Visions of Shakespeare*, edited by Marianne Novy, offers a spectrum of critical responses to the ways that women writers from 1664 to the present have transformed Shakespearean plots and motifs by weaving them into their own work. Peter Erickson's book *Rewriting Shakespeare, Rewriting Ourselves* focuses first on Shakespeare, then on the efforts of writers such as Gloria Naylor and Adrienne Rich to alter Shakespeare's legacy by revealing the limitations of his perspective in the light of their own concerns. Novelist Valerie Miner tells me that she had Shakespeare's *Hamlet* in mind when she wrote *Blood Sisters*. Her most recently published novel, *A Walking Fire*, revises the plot of *King Lear* by recounting its story of paternal wrath through the perspective of Lear's banished, and virtually silenced, daughter Cordelia (named Cora). In

this retelling, Cora's banishment (to Canada) results from her radical political protest against the Vietnam War. Her return, motivated by her father's failing health, sparks a series of reminiscences, which interweave the intimate politics of gender and family with those of national policy. The appropriation of Shakespeare by a woman writer, as each of these instances reveals, acts as a form of critical analysis.

13. The paper by this title was presented at a seminar on Shakespeare and Gender at the World Shakespeare Congress in Stratford-upon-Avon in 1981. For a fuller description of the content of this essay, see Shirley Nelson Garner's essay in this volume.

WORKS CITED

Adelman, Janet. *Suffocating Mothers: Fantasies of Maternal Origin in Shakespeare's Plays, "Hamlet" to "The Tempest."* New York: Routledge, 1992.

———. " 'This is and is not Cressid': The Characterization of Cressida." *The (M)other Tongue: Essays in Feminist Psychoanalytic Interpretation.* Ed. Shirley Nelson Garner, Claire Kahane, and Madelon Sprengnether. Ithaca: Cornell UP, 1985. 119–41.

Bamber, Linda. *Comic Women, Tragic Men: A Study in Gender and Genre in Shakespeare.* Stanford: Stanford UP, 1982.

Barker, Francis, and Peter Hulme. "Nymphs and Reapers Heavily Vanish: The Discursive Contexts of *The Tempest.*" *Alternative Shakespeares.* Ed. John Drakakis. London: Methuen, 1985. 191–205.

Bartels, Emily. "Making More of the Moor: Aaron, Othello, and Renaissance Refashionings of Race." *Shakespeare Quarterly* 41 (1990): 433–54.

Belsey, Catherine. "Afterword: A Future for Materialist Feminist Criticism?" *The Matter of Difference: Materialist Feminist Criticism of Shakespeare.* Ed. Valerie Wayne. Ithaca: Cornell UP, 1991. 257–70.

———. *The Subject of Tragedy: Identity and Difference in Renaissance Drama.* London: Methuen, 1985.

Bradley, A. C. *Shakespearean Tragedy.* New York: Ballantine/Random House, rpt. 1986.

Braxton, Phyllis Natalie. "Othello: The Moor and the Metaphor." *South Atlantic Review* 55 (1990): 1–17.

Brown, Paul. " 'This thing of darkness I acknowledge mine': *The Tempest* and the Discourse of Colonialism." *Political Shakespeare: New Essays in Cultural Materialism.* Ed. Jonathan Dollimore and Alan Sinfield. Ithaca: Cornell UP, 1985. 48–71.

Callaghan, Dympna. *Women and Gender in Renaissance Tragedy.* New York: Harvester, 1989.

Cantor, Paul. "Othello: The Erring Barbarian among the Supersubtle Venetians." *Southwest Review* 75 (1990): 296–319.

Cartelli, Thomas. "Prospero in Africa: *The Tempest* as Colonialist Text and Pretext." *Shakespeare Reproduced: The Text in History and Ideology.* Ed. Jean Howard and Marion O'Connor. New York: Methuen, 1987. 99–115.

D'Amico, Jack. *The Moor in English Renaissance Drama.* Tampa: South Florida UP, 1993.

Dollimore, Jonathan. *Radical Tragedy: Religion, Ideology and Power in the Drama of Shakespeare and His Contemporaries.* Brighton: Harvester, 1984.

Dreher, Diane. *Domination and Defiance: Fathers and Daughters in Shakespeare.* Lexington: U of Kentucky P, 1986.

Eagleton, Terry. "Language: *Macbeth, Richard II, Henry IV.*" *William Shakespeare.* Oxford: Basil Blackwell, 1986. 1–17.

———. "Nothing: Othello, Hamlet, Coriolanus." *William Shakespeare.* Oxford: Basil Blackwell, 1986. 64–75.

Erickson, Peter. *Patriarchal Structures in Shakespeare's Drama.* Berkeley: U of California P, 1985.

———. *Rewriting Shakespeare, Rewriting Ourselves.* Berkeley: U of California P, 1991.

Felperin, Howard. " 'Tongue-tied our queen?': the Deconstruction of Presence in *The Winter's Tale.*" *Shakespeare and the Question of Theory.* Ed. Patricia Parker and Geoffrey Hartman. New York: Methuen, 1985. 3–18.

Fineman, Joel. "The Turn of the Shrew." *Shakespeare and the Question of Theory.* Ed. Patricia Parker and Geoffrey Hartman. New York: Methuen, 1985. 138–59.

Forum. *PMLA* 104 (1989): 78–79.

Freedman, Barbara. "Misrecognizing Shakespeare." *Shakespeare's Personality.* Ed. Norman Holland, Bernard Paris, and Sidney Homan. Berkeley: U of California P, 1990. 244–60.

Freund, Elizabeth. " 'Ariachne's Broken Woof': The Rhetoric of Citation in *Troilus and Cressida.*" *Shakespeare and the Question of Theory.* Ed. Patricia Parker and Geoffrey Hartman. New York: Methuen, 1985. 19–36.

Friedan, Betty. *The Feminine Mystique.* New York: Norton, 1963.

Garner, Shirley Nelson. "Who Would Be Horatio If He Could Be Hamlet?" Paper presented at seminar on Shakespeare and Gender, World Shakespeare Congress, Stratford-upon-Avon, 1981.

Greenblatt, Stephen. "Learning to Curse: Aspects of Linguistic Colonialism in the Sixteenth Century." *Learning to Curse: Essays in Early Modern Culture.* New York: Routledge, 1990. 16–39.

———. *Renaissance Self-Fashioning.* Chicago: U of Chicago P, 1980.

———. "Shakespeare and the Exorcists." *Shakespeare and the Question of Theory.* Ed. Patricia Parker and Geoffrey Hartman. New York: Methuen, 1985. 163–87.

Hartman, Geoffrey. "Shakespeare's Poetical Character in *Twelfth Night.*" *Shakespeare and the Question of Theory.* Ed. Patricia Parker and Geoffrey Hartman. New York: Methuen, 1985. 37–53.

Hawkes, Terence. "Telmah." *That Shakespeherian Rag.* New York: Methuen, 1986. 92–119.

Howard, Jean. "Renaissance Antitheatricality and the Politics of Gender and Rank in *Much Ado about Nothing.*" *Shakespeare Reproduced.* Ed. Jean Howard and Marion O'Connor. New York: Methuen, 1987. 163–87.

Jardine, Lisa. *Still Harping on Daughters: Women and Drama in the Age of Shakespeare.* Totowa, N.J.: Barnes and Noble, 1983.

Kahn, Coppélia. *Man's Estate: Masculine Identity in Shakespeare.* Berkeley: U of California P, 1981.

Kamps, Ivo. *Shakespeare Left and Right.* New York: Routledge, 1991.

Lacan, Jacques. "The Mirror Stage." *Écrits: A Selection.* Trans. Alan Sheridan. London: Tavistock, 1977. 1–7.

Lenz, Carolyn Ruth Swift; Gayle Greene; and Carol Thomas Neely, eds. *The Woman's Part: Feminist Criticism of Shakespeare.* Urbana: U of Illinois P, 1980.

Levin, Richard. "Feminist Thematics and Shakespearean Tragedy." *PMLA* 103 (1988): 125–38.

———. "The Poetics and Politics of Bardicide." *PMLA* 105 (May 1990): 491–504.

Levine, Laura. "Men in Women's Clothing: Antitheatricality and Effeminization from 1579 to 1642." *Criticism* 28 (Spring 1986): 121–43.

Loomba, Ania. *Gender, Race, Renaissance Drama.* Oxford: Oxford UP, 1992.

Mack, Maynard. *King Lear in Our Time.* Berkeley: U of California P, 1965, rpt. 1972.

McLeod, Randall. "No More, the Text Is Foolish." *The Division of the Kingdoms: Shakespeare's Two Versions of King Lear.* Ed. Gary Taylor and Michael Warren. Oxford: Oxford UP, 1986. 153–93.

Millet, Kate. *Sexual Politics.* New York: Doubleday, 1970.

Miner, Valerie. *Blood Sisters.* New York: St. Martin, 1982.

———. *A Walking Fire.* Albany: SUNY P, 1994.

Montrose, Louis A. "Professing the Renaissance: The Poetics and Politics of Culture." *The New Historicism.* Ed. H. Aram Veeser. New York: Routledge, 1989. 15–36.

Neely, Carol Thomas. *Broken Nuptials in Shakespeare's Plays.* New Haven: Yale UP, 1985.

———. "Circumscriptions and Unhousedness: Othello at the Crossroads." Paper presented at the annual meeting of the Shakespeare Association of America, Kansas City, 1992.

———. "Loss and Recovery: Homes Away from Home." *Changing Subjects: The Making of Feminist Literary Criticism.* Ed. Gayle Greene and Coppélia Kahn. New York: Routledge, 1993. 180–94.

———. "Women and Men in *Othello*: 'What should such a fool / Do with so good a woman?' " *The Woman's Part.* Ed. Carolyn Ruth Swift Lenz, Gayle Greene, and Carol Thomas Neely. Urbana: U of Illinois P, 1980. 211–39.

Newman, Karen. " 'And Wash the Ethiop White': Femininity and the Monstrous in *Othello.*" In *Shakespeare Reproduced: The Text in History and Ideology.* Ed. Jean E. Howard and Marion F. O'Connor. New York and London: Methuen, 1987. 143–62.

———. *Fashioning Femininity and English Renaissance Drama.* Chicago: U of Chicago P, 1991.

Norris, Christopher. "Post-structuralist Shakespeare: Text and Ideology." *Alternative Shakespeares.* Ed. John Drakakis. London: Methuen, 1985. 47–66.

Novy, Marianne. *Love's Argument: Gender Relations in Shakespeare.* Chapel Hill: U of North Carolina P, 1984.

———. "Shakespeare's Female Characters as Actors and Audience." *The Woman's Part.* Ed. Carolyn Ruth Swift Lenz, Gayle Greene, and Carol Thomas Neely. Urbana: U of Illinois P, 1980. 256–70.

Novy, Marianne, ed. *Women's Re-Visions of Shakespeare.* Urbana: U of Illinois P, 1990.

Orgel, Stephen. "Nobody's Perfect: Or Why Did the English Stage Take Boys for Women." *South Atlantic Quarterly* 88 (Winter 1989): 7–29.

Parker, Patricia. "Fantasies of 'Race' and 'Gender': Africa, Othello, and Bringing to Light." *Women, Race, and Writing in the Early Modern Period.* Ed. Margo Hendricks and Patricia Parker. New York: Routledge, 1994. 84–100.

———. "Shakespeare and Rhetoric: 'Dilation' and 'Delation' in *Othello.*" *Shakespeare and the Question of Theory.* Ed. Patricia Parker and Geoffrey Hartman. New York: Methuen, 1985. 54–74.

Rackin, Phyllis. *Stages of History: Shakespeare's English Chronicles.* Ithaca: Cornell UP, 1990.

Rose, Jacqueline. "Sexuality in the Reading of Shakespeare: *Hamlet* and *Measure for Measure.*" *Alternative Shakespeares.* Ed. John Drakakis. London: Methuen, 1985. 95–118.

Rose, Mary Beth. *The Expense of Spirit: Love and Sexuality in English Renaissance Drama.* Ithaca: Cornell UP, 1988.

Schwartz, Murray, and Coppélia Kahn, eds. *Representing Shakespeare: New Psychoanalytic Essays.* Baltimore: Johns Hopkins UP, 1980.

Shakespeare, William. *King Lear.* The Arden Shakespeare. Ed. Kenneth Muir. London: Methuen, 1972, rpt. 1986.

Smiley, Jane. *A Thousand Acres.* New York: Knopf, 1991.

Stallybrass, Peter. "Patriarchal Territories: The Body Enclosed." *Rewriting the Renaissance: The Discourses of Sexual Difference in Early Modern Europe.* Ed. Margaret

Ferguson, Maureen Quilligan, and Nancy Vickers. Chicago: U of Chicago P, 1986. 123–42.

Taylor, Gary. *Reinventing Shakespeare: A Cultural History from the Restoration to the Present.* New York: Weidenfeld and Nicolson, 1989.

Taylor, Gary, and Michael Warren, eds. *The Division of the Kingdoms: Shakespeare's Two Versions of King Lear.* Oxford: Oxford UP, 1983.

Traub, Valerie. *Desire and Anxiety: Circulations of Sexuality in Shakespearean Drama.* New York: Routledge, 1992.

———. "Desire and the Differences It Makes." *The Matter of Difference.* Ed. Valerie Wayne. Ithaca: Cornell UP, 1991. 81–114.

Urkowitz, Steven. " 'The Base Shall to the Legitimate': The Growth of an Editorial Tradition." *The Division of the Kingdoms.* Ed. Gary Taylor and Michael Warren. Oxford: Oxford UP, 1983. 23–43.

———. *Shakespeare's Revision of "King Lear."* Princeton: Princeton UP, 1980.

Waller, Marguerite. "Ursurpation, Seduction, and the Problematics of the Proper: A 'Deconstructive,' 'Feminist' Rereading of the Seductions of Richard and Anne in Shakespeare's *Richard III.*" *Rewriting the Renaissance.* Ed. Margaret Ferguson, Maureen Quilligan, and Nancy Vickers. Chicago: U of Chicago P, 1986. 159–74.

Warren, Michael. "Quarto and Folio *King Lear* and the Interpretation of Albany and Edgar." *Shakespeare, Pattern of Excelling Nature.* Ed. David Bevington and Jay L. Halio. Newark: U of Delaware P, 1978. 95–107.

Wayne, Valerie. "Introduction." *The Matter of Difference.* Ed. Valerie Wayne. Ithaca: Cornell UP, 1991. 1–26.

Wells, Stanley. "The Once and Future King Lear." *The Division of the Kingdoms.* Ed. Gary Taylor and Michael Warren. Oxford: Oxford UP, 1986. 1–22.

Wheeler, Richard. *Shakespeare's Development and the Problem Comedies: Turn and Counter-Turn.* Berkeley: U of California P, 1981.

Willbern, David. "What Is Shakespeare." *Shakespeare's Personality.* Ed. Norman Holland, Bernard Paris, and Sidney Homan. Berkeley: U of California P, 1990. 226–43.

PART ONE

TRAGIC SUBJECTS

1

HISTORY INTO TRAGEDY

The Case of *Richard III*

PHYLLIS RACKIN

AN AUDIENCE COMING to *Richard III* from the Henry VI plays and *King John* witnesses a remarkable transformation in the roles and representations of female characters. On the one hand, women are much more sympathetically portrayed. They take on their tragic roles as suffering victims and assume their tragic status as central objects of male concern. On the other hand, they lose the vividly individualized voices and the subversive theatrical power that made the female characters in Shakespeare's earlier history plays formidable antagonists to the masculine project of English history-making (Rackin 151–60).

Robert Weimann's distinction between *locus* and *platea* can be used to chart both the elevation of the female characters and their containment. Weimann associates the *locus* with the upstage site of mimetic illusion, "aloofness from the audience, and representational closure" which privileges the authority of the objects represented, the *platea* with the forestage where actors addressed their audiences, a liminal space where the authority of the represented narrative could be challenged by calling attention to the immediate theatrical occasion with all its subversive potential.[1] Although not always or necessarily literalized in specific locations on the physical stage, the different acting styles and different relationships between actor and audience that Weimann associates with *locus* and *platea* provide a useful basis for understanding the transformation of women's roles in *Richard III*. Ennobled, the female characters move into the privileged *locus* of hegemonic representation, but this move also subsumes them in the patriarchal project of that representation and distances them from the present theater audience.[2] Still the dominant figure in the *locus*, the male protagonist now dominates the *platea* as well. When Richard speaks to the audience, the *platea* begins to assume the function it would have in plays such as *Hamlet* and *Macbeth* as the site of the soliloquies where the masculine subject of tragedy was to be constructed.[3]

I

Although the First Folio classifies *Richard III* with Shakespeare's other English histories, the title pages of the Quartos suggest generic difference. In the case of *2 Henry VI*, the title page indicates both the episodic chronicle structure of the play and its historical subject: "The First part of the Contention betwixt the two famous Houses of Yorke and Lancaster, with the death of the good Duke Humphrey: and the banishment and death of the Duke of *Suffolke*, and the Tragicall end of the proud Cardinall of *Winchester*, with the notable Rebellion of *Iacke Cade: And the Duke of Yorkes first claime unto the Crowne.*" The Quarto of *Richard III*, by contrast, designates at once its self-consciously dramatic form as a tragedy, its origins as a script for theatrical performance, and its strongly centered focus on the male protagonist: "The Tragedy of Richard the third, Containing, His treacherous Plots against his brother Clarence: the pittiefull murther of his iunocent nephewes: his tyrannicall usurpation: with the whole course of his detested life, and most deserved death. As it hath beene lately Acted by the Right honourable the Lord Chamberlaine his servants."

In Shakespeare's time, the story of Richard III was repeatedly identified as tragic. Edward Hall had entitled his account of Richard's reign "The Tragical Doynges of Kynge Richard The Thirde" (374). Richard's story (along with those of Clarence, Hastings, Buckingham, and Jane Shore) was identified as a tragedy in *A Mirror for Magistrates.* Thomas Legge's Latin play *Richardus Tertius*, performed at Cambridge in 1579, is identified in contemporary texts as an exemplary tragedy, singled out by Sir John Harington (210) and Thomas Heywood (sig. F4ᵛ) to illustrate the beneficial effects of tragic drama and by Francis Meres in his list of "famous tragedies" (319–20). Yet another play about Richard, anonymously published in 1594 and entitled "The True Tragedy of Richard III," begins with a dialogue between Truth and Poetrie that identifies "Tragedia" as a player in the coming action and the subject of the play as a "Tragedie" (sig. A3ʳ).

This essay is an attempt to delineate the ways the movement from history to tragedy transvalued the representations of women and the construction of femininity on Shakespeare's stage. I should begin, however, by acknowledging that the distinction between history and tragedy was by no means clear. The protagonists of tragedy, like those of history, were understood to be characters of high rank. Moreover, in the Renaissance as in antiquity, plays identified as tragedies frequently took their subjects from history (Shakespeare himself is a good case in point: of the eleven plays designated as tragedies in the First Folio, all but *Romeo and Juliet* and *Othello* have historical subjects).[4]

Despite the many similarities between the subjects of the two genres, contemporary descriptions of the ways they affected their audiences are strikingly different in regard to issues of gender. Antitheatrical invective typically attacked all theatrical performance as effeminating, but the English history play offered a significant exception.[5] Thomas Nashe, in fact, used the example of the English history play to defend theatrical performance against its detractors: "our forefathers valiant acts . . . are revived," he declared, "than which, what can be a sharper reproofe to these degenerate effeminate dayes of ours?" Commemorating the valiant deeds of heroic forefathers and celebrating the masculine virtues of courage, honor, and patriotism, the theatrical representation of English historical subjects could redeem theatrical performance as a means of reclaiming the endangered masculinity of the men in the theater audience.

Tragedy, on the other hand, was likely to inspire womanly emotions in its spectators. According to Stephen Gosson, "The beholding of troubles and miserable slaughters that are in Tragedies, drive us to immoderate sorrow, heavines, womanish weeping and mourning, whereby we become lovers of dumpes, and lamentation, both enemies to fortitude" (215).[6] The claim that tragedy produced womanly softness in its spectators was not confined to antitheatrical discourse. Sir Philip Sidney recounts a story from Plutarch in which the performance of a tragedy "drewe aboundance of teares" from the eyes of a tyrant "who, without all pitty, had murthered infinite nombers, and some of his owne blood" (177–78). Arguing for the salutary effects of tragedy, Sidney does not identify them as effeminating. The terms of his argument, however, suggest just that. He claims, for instance, that tragedy "openeth the greatest wounds, and sheweth forth the Ulcers that are covered with Tissue." As Gail Paster has demonstrated, men's bodies opened and wounded were gendered feminine; and the ulcer image directly parallels the terms in which Hamlet will address his guilty mother: "Lay not that flattering unction to your soul, / That not your trespass but my madness speaks; / It will but skin and film the ulcerous place, / Whiles rank corruption, mining all within, / Infects unseen" (3.4.145–49).

Women, in fact, were especially prominent in descriptions of the effects of tragedies on early modern audiences. In a 1620 recollection of a performance of *The Spanish Tragedy*, for instance, "Ladyes in the boxes" are said to have

"Kept time with sighes and teares to [the player's] sad accents." As Richard
Levin points out, the numerous contemporary accounts that describe "women
weeping in the theatre" suggest a perception "that women had a special sensi-
tivity to, and perhaps a special preference for, pathetic plots and situations."[7]

In *An Apology for Actors*, Thomas Heywood recounts three anecdotes to
illustrate the beneficial effects of tragedies on their auditors. Two of them center on women who had murdered their husbands. In the first, "a townes-
woman (till then of good estimation and report)" watching a play about a
woman who had committed a similar crime "suddenly skritched and cryd out
Oh my husband, my husband! I see the ghost of my husband fiercely threatning
and menacing me" and subsequently confessed her crime to the people about
her in the audience. In the second, the particulars of the tragic plot are somewhat different, but they have exactly the same effect on the wicked woman:
during the performance of a play in which a laborer, envied by his fellow work-
ers for his diligence, is murdered by having a nail driven into his temples, "a
woman of great gravity" becomes "strangely amazed" and "with a distracted
& troubled braine oft sighed out these words: Oh my husband, my husband!":

> The play, without further interruption, proceeded; the woman was to her
> owne house conducted, without any apparant suspition, every one coniectur-
> ing as their fancies led them. In this agony she some few dayes languished, and
> on a time, as certaine of her well disposed neighbours came to comfort her,
> one amongst the rest being Church-warden, to him the Sexton posts, to tell
> him of a strange thing happening him in the ripping up of a grave: see here
> (quoth he) what I have found, and shewes them a faire skull, with a great nayle
> pierst quite through the braine-pan, but we cannot coniecture to whom it
> should belong, nor how long it hath laine in the earth, the grave being con-
> fused, and the flesh consumed. At the report of this accident, the woman, out
> of the trouble of her afflicted conscience, discovered a former murder. For 12
> yeares ago, by driving that nayle into that skull, being the head of her husband,
> she had trecherously slaine him. This being publickly confest, she was ar-
> raigned, condemned, adiudged, and burned. (Sigs. G1^v, G2^v)

Heywood's lurid examples represent an extreme case. In the first place, the
plays he describes belong to the subgenre of domestic tragedy, an innovative
dramatic form that moved down the social scale and into the home to find its
subjects in a domestic space where female characters could and did play central
roles (Dolan). Not all of the female spectators of tragedy were imagined as
"guilty creatures sitting at a play," and not all of the spectators of tragedy were
imagined as women. Nonetheless, the spectators were repeatedly and consis-

tently described in contemporary accounts as moved to emotions and responses (compassion, remorse, pity, tears) that were understood as feminine. This conception of the effects of tragedy as feminizing, although not always explicitly stated, is remarkably consistent: it appears in arguments for and against the theater, in the prologues and epilogues to plays, in accounts of actual experience as well as in prescriptive directions.

The Induction to *A Warning for Fair Women* (1599) begins with the stage direction *"Enter at one doore, Hystorie with Drum and Ensigne: Tragedie at another, in her one hand a whip, in the other a knife."* During the ensuing dispute with Comedie and Hystorie, Tragedie's feminine gender receives repeated emphasis. She is addressed by the others as "mistris buskins" and "my Ladie *Tragedie*," and she describes the kind of performance she requires as one that will evoke feminine responses from the audience:

I must have passions that must move the soule,
Make the heart heave, and throb within the bosome,
Extorting teares out of the strictest eyes,
. . . Untill I rap the sences from their course . . .
(Sigs. A2^v, A3^r)

Over half a century later, Margaret Cavendish, the Duchess of Newcastle, described the effects of Shakespeare's tragedies in similar terms:

in his Tragick Vein, he Presents Passions so Naturally, and Misfortunes so Probably, as he Peirces the Souls of his Readers with such a True Sense and Feeling thereof, that it Forces Tears through their Eyes. . . . [8]

In direct contrast to Nashe's celebration of the history play, which imagines an audience of men inspired by the representation of a heroic masculine world to emulate the manly virtues of the forefathers, tragedy is repeatedly described as appealing to women as well as men; and its appeal to men is repeatedly described as directed toward their feminine sympathies, softening hard hearts, piercing guilty souls with remorse, ravishing the entire audience with the feminine passions of pity and fear, and forcing them to weep.

A similar gendered difference characterized the subjects of the two genres. On the stage as in the audience, the exemplary subjects of tragedy—"Gods and Goddesses, Kynges and Queenes"—were understood to include women as well as men (Webbe 249).[9] Because history sought to commemorate the past, reconstituted as a nostalgically idealized world of the fathers, women and sexuality occupied only marginal roles. Both tragedy and comedy, however, assigned important roles to women and marriage. In comedy, conflicts between older and newer social dispensations are characteristically resolved in marriage; in tragedy they often constitute the hero's predicament, which is typically defined at least partly in terms of his relationship to women. This is true not only in plays such as *Romeo and Juliet*, *Othello*, and *Antony and Cleopatra*, which center on romantic relationships, but also in most of Shakespeare's other tragedies as well.

Shakespeare's history plays opposed the troubling realities of cultural change by projecting a better world in the past; his tragedies played out those cultural contradictions in the struggles of an individual heroic figure destroyed by the irreconcilable conflicts they produced.[10] Deeply implicated in those contradictions, the ambivalent place of women in Shakespeare's world and the instability of the gender ideology that attempted to contain them were central issues in tragic drama (Rose; Callaghan). With the possible exceptions of Juliet and Cleopatra, Shakespeare reserves the role of tragic hero for a man; but, as Mary Beth Rose has argued, the increasing importance assigned to marriage "as the basis of an ordered society" allowed female characters to play central roles in non-Shakespearean Jacobean tragedies such as *The Duchess of Malfi*, which "bear witness to a particular historical moment when private life was beginning . . . to be related analogously, rather than hierarchically, to public affairs" (96–98).

II

The reconstruction of history as tragedy and the transformation of women's roles in *Richard III* can be associated with an earlier stage of this process. Paradoxically, however, even as the female characters in *Richard III* are ennobled, they are also disempowered. Because the traditional subjects of English history were the heroic deeds and dynastic struggles of kings and noblemen, most of the female characters in Shakespeare's other English history plays are defined in gendered antithesis by low social status and foreign nationality. Some are literally alien—such as the French women in *1 Henry VI* and *Henry V* and the Welsh women in *1 Henry IV*. Others, such as the women in the Boar's Head Tavern, are excluded from the scene of historical representation by their confinement to the anachronistically modern settings of the fictional, plebeian, comic subplots. The foreign tongues spoken by the Welsh woman in *1 Henry IV* and the French women in *Henry V* and the malapropisms that disfigure the speech of Mistress Quickly signal their inability to enter the official discourse of English history. In direct antithesis, all of the female characters in *Richard III* are highborn English women who speak in the undifferentiated, formal blank verse that constitutes the standard language of the playscript. Recruited in the service of the hegemonic project of the plot, the accession of Henry VII to the English throne, the women are also subsumed in its hegemonic discourse. As Nicholas Brooke has observed, "the flexibility of private speech" in this play is almost entirely "confined to Richard" (108). Even Margaret, the most powerful of Richard's female antagonists, speaks in the generalized rhetorical terms that constitute the normative language of the play.

Assuming their tragic roles as pitiable victims, female characters are no longer represented as dangerous, demonic Others. The subversive theatrical energy of the peasant Joan is replaced by the pathos of suffering English queens.[11] Margaret, the adulterous wife and bloodthirsty warrior of the Henry VI plays, is transformed into a bereaved and suffering prophet of divine vengeance for the crimes of the past. In the Henry VI plays, the female characters are defined as opponents to the masculine project of English history-making. In *Richard III*, all of the women support the desired conclusion of the historical plot, the foundation of the Tudor dynasty.

Although the overarching goal of the dramatic action in *Richard III* (as in all of Shakespeare's English histories and a number of his tragedies as well) is the maintenance of a legitimate royal succession, in this play, unlike the earlier histories, it is the male protagonist who opposes the patriarchal project. The threats to patrilineal succession represented in the Henry VI plays by Joan's sexual promiscuity and Margaret's adultery are replaced by Richard's murders of his brother's innocent children, the rightful heirs to the throne he usurps, and his deceitful efforts to deny their legitimacy and that of their royal father. In *Richard III*, the subversive power associated with female characters in the earlier plays is demystified, and all the power of agency and transgression is appropriated by the male protagonist. The threat of adultery is no longer real, and the character who threatens to displace legitimate heirs is not any adulterous woman but the slanderous man who brings the charge. Witchcraft, the quintessential representation of the dangerous power of women, is similarly reduced from a genuine threat to a transparent slander. Both Joan in *1 Henry VI* and Eleanor Cobham in *2 Henry VI* summon demons to the stage. In *Richard III*, however, there are only Richard's unsupported and obviously false charges against Queen Elizabeth and Jane Shore.

Joan in *1 Henry VI* is the prototype for the marginal and criminal status of the women in the Henry VI plays and also for their subversive, theatrical energy. Her inexplicable military power, first explained as deriving from the Blessed Virgin, is finally revealed as witchcraft and punished with burning. Her very subversiveness, however, paradoxically authorizes her dramatic power. As both Catherine Belsey and Karen Newman have observed, the custom of requiring witches to confess from the scaffold "paradoxically also offered women a place from which to speak in public with a hitherto unimagined authority which was not diminished by the fact that it was demonic." These public occasions were also theatrical. As both critics note, "the crowds at trials and executions" were frequently described as "beholders" or "the audience," and "Pamphleteers often describe[d] the scene of execution explicitly as a play" (Newman 67; Belsey, *The Subject of Tragedy* 190–91).

Two episodes, one near the beginning of the play and one near its end, illustrate the way the powerful role of demonic other, occupied by women in the Henry VI plays, is now transferred to Richard. The longer of these is the second, the encounter near the end of Act IV between Richard and Queen Elizabeth, where Shakespeare altered his historical source in order to ennoble the character of the widowed queen. As Barbara Hodgdon observes, Shakespeare "displaces those attributes the chronicler ascribes to the Queen onto Richard" (109–10).[12] In Hall's version, Queen Elizabeth exemplifies female "inconstancie," first promising her daughter Elizabeth (or, in the event of Elizabeth's death, her next daughter, the Lady Cecile) to Richmond (391), then, persuaded by promises of "promocions innumerable and benefites," agreeing to Richard's demands:

> . . . putting in oblivion the murther of her innocente children, the infamy and dishonoure spoken by the kynge her husbande, the lyvynge in avoutrie leyed to her charge, the bastardyng of her daughters, forgettyng also ye feithfull promes & open othe made to the countesse of Richmond mother to ye erle Henry, blynded by avaricious affeccion and seduced by flatterynge wordes, first delivered into kyng Richards handes her. v. daughters as Lambes once agayne committed to the custody of the ravenous wolfe. (406)

Shakespeare's widowed queen, unlike Hall's, keeps faith with Richmond and adamantly refuses Richard's urgings to forget past wrongs. Insistently recalling the fate of her murdered children, she charges, "No doubt the murd'rous knife was dull and blunt / Till it was whetted on thy stone-hard heart / To revel in the entrails of my lambs" (4.4.227–29). Shakespeare thus appropriates for Elizabeth's use against Richard the very arguments, and even the terms, by which the authoritative narrative voice in Hall's chronicle condemns her action.

In Shakespeare's representation, it is Richard and not Elizabeth—or any of the women—who becomes the sole object of condemnation; but at the same time that the female characters are ennobled, they are also deprived of theatrical power and agency, both of which are appropriated by Richard, along with their demonic roles. The audience is never allowed to see Elizabeth deciding to bestow her daughter on Richmond. All we get is Stanley's laconic report that "the Queen hath heartily consented / He [Richmond] should espouse Elizabeth her daughter" (4.5.7-8); and a number of critics have accepted Richard's judgment at the end of their encounter that the queen is a "relenting fool, and shallow, changing woman."[13] Like the other women in *Richard III*, Elizabeth serves as a kind of ventriloquist's dummy. She gives forceful and eloquent voice to Richard's crimes, but her own motives can remain ambiguous because they are finally irrelevant to the outcome of the plot. What is important is that Richmond marries her daughter; whether or when the queen gives her consent is of so little consequence that it is never clearly specified in Shakespeare's script.

The earlier incident is much more brief, a telling moment in Act I when Richard literally appropriates the demonic power of a woman's voice. Margaret of Anjou, sent at the end of *3 Henry VI* back to France (where her historical prototype died in 1482), returns unhistorically in *Richard III* like a voice from the dead to recall the crimes of the past and pour out curses on her old enemies. In Act I, Scene III, she comes on stage as an eavesdropper who punctuates the dialogue with bitter comments delivered to the audience, unheard by the other characters. Finally, she moves forward to dominate the stage with a great outpouring of curses and denunciations, directed at each of the other characters in turn. When she comes to Richard, however, he interrupts the stream of malediction to turn Margaret's curses back upon herself. "O, let me make the period to my curse!" she complains. " 'Tis done by me," he replies, "and ends in 'Margaret' " (1.3.216-38).

This exchange dramatizes what will be a major source of Richard's theatrical power—his appropriation of the woman's part.[14] Characterized throughout in terms of warlike masculinity and aggressive misogyny, Richard also commands the female power of erotic seduction. His monopoly of both male and female sexual energy is vividly portrayed in his seduction of Anne. The turning point comes when Richard lends her his sword and lays his breast "naked" for her penetration (1.2.177). Overwhelmed by Richard's aggressive passivity, Anne's resistance quickly collapses, whereupon Richard seals his sexual conquest by enclosing her finger with his ring. "Look how my ring encompasseth thy finger," he says. "Even so thy breast encloseth my poor heart" (1.2.203–204). Owner of both the sword and the naked breast, both penetrated ring and penetrating heart, Richard has become, as Rebecca Bushnell points out, "both the man who possesses and the woman who submits" (124).

The power that Richard takes from women is not only the power to curse and seduce; it is also the power to transcend the frame of historical representation, the ability to address the audience directly without the knowledge of the other characters, and the theatrical energy that serves to monopolize the audience's attention. The structure of Richard's exchange with Margaret is also the structure of the early scenes in the play: it is always Richard who has the last word—along with the first. Each scene is punctuated by soliloquies in which Richard addresses the audience, predicting the action to come, responding to the action just past, flaunting his witty wickedness, gloating at the other characters' weakness and ignorance, and seducing the fascinated playgoers into complicity with his diabolical schemes.

The association between the transgressive, the demonic, and the theatrical is consistently used to characterize Richard. It is, in fact, associated with his story from its beginning in More's *History of King Richard the thirde* (ca. 1513–1518), written about thirty years after Richard's death, the source for the versions Shakespeare found in Hall and Holinshed.[15] In Shakespeare's representation, as in his sources, Richard's wickedness is repeatedly and explicitly associated with his characterization as an actor. These associations are established even in *3 Henry VI*. Just before his murder by Richard, Henry asks, "What scene of death hath Roscius now to act?" (5.6.10). Earlier in the play, Richard has a long soliloquy in which he identifies himself as a villain in exactly the same terms that Renaissance writers typically used to describe actors:

Why, I can smile, and murther whiles I smile,
And cry "Content" to that which grieves my heart,
And wet my cheeks with artificial tears,
And frame my face to all occasions.
. . . . . .
I can add colors to the chameleon,
Change shapes with Proteus for advantages,
And set the murtherous Machevil to school
(3.2.182–93)[16]

In *Richard III* Richard's identity as a master performer not only is reiterated, as, for instance, when he instructs Buckingham on the performance techniques that will enable him to "counterfeit the deep tragedian" (3.5.1–9); it also becomes the structural principle of the dramatic action. As Alexander Leggatt has observed, this "is the only play of Shakespeare's to begin with a soliloquy by one of its characters." Not only the central character in the *locus* of historical representation, Richard also monopolizes the *platea* of direct address to the audience; he "is not just hero but chorus and presenter as well" (32).[17] The early scenes of the play are punctuated by asides and soliloquies in which Richard announces his chosen dramatic role ("to prove a villain"), shares his wicked plots with the audience before stepping back into the frame of representation to execute them upon the other characters, and then returns to the *platea* to gloat about the efficacy of his performance.

By defining his villainy as theatrical *tour de force*, Richard invites the audience to suspend their moral judgment and evaluate his actions simply as theatrical performance. Significantly, the most striking instance of this maneuver occurs in the soliloquy at the end of the scene when he seduces Anne. "Was ever woman in this humor woo'd?" he asks the audience. "Was ever woman in this humor won?"

> What? I that kill'd her husband and his father,
> To take her in her heart's extremest hate,
> With curses in her mouth, tears in her eyes,
> The bleeding witness of my hatred by,
> Having God, her conscience, and these bars against me,
> . . . .
> Hath she forgot already that brave prince,
> Edward, her lord, whom I, some three months since,
> Stabb'd in my angry mood at Tewksbury?
> A sweeter and a lovelier gentleman,
> Fram'd in the prodigality of nature—
> Young, valiant, wise and (no doubt) right royal—
> The spacious world cannot again afford.
> And will she yet abase her eyes on me,
> That cropp'd the golden prime of this sweet prince
> And made her widow to a woeful bed?
> On me, whose all not equals Edward's moi'ty?
> (1.2.227–49)

This soliloquy, which ends the scene, goes on for thirty-six lines, reminding the audience of the historical wrongs that should have made Anne reject his suit, flaunting the theatrical power that made her forget the past. Here, and throughout the first act of the play, Richard performs a similar seduction upon the audience.[18] Once the power of theatrical agency is appropriated by the male protagonist, the audience in the playhouse is reduced, along with the other characters on stage, to a state of feminine passivity. For the audience as for

Anne, the seduction requires the suspension of moral judgment and the era-
sure of historical memory, since Shakespeare's contemporaries would have
entered his theater well aware of the demonic role that Richard had been assigned in Tudor historiography; but the sheer theatrical energy of Richard's
performance supersedes the moral weight of the hegemonic narrative.

The conflation of the historical seduction represented on stage with the theatrical seduction of the present audience, of the character Richard with the
actor who played his part, and of the feminine character he seduces on stage
with an audience interpellated as feminine is implicit in two well-known
anecdotes associated with the play from the beginning of the seventeenth century. In March 1602, John Manningham recorded in his diary an account of a
"citizen" in the audience "upon a tyme when Burbidge played Rich. 3." who
"greue soe farr in liking with him, that before shee went from the play shee
appointed him to come that night unto hir by the name of Ri: the 3."[19] Another
anecdote, not explicitly sexual, also attests the identification of Richard with
the actor who played his part. Bishop Richard Corbet, a friend of Ben Jonson,
described a visit to the site of the Battle of Bosworth Field in which his host,
"when he would have said, King Richard dyed, / And call'd—A horse! a
horse!—he, Burbidge cry'de."

Both of these anecdotes point to a subtle but significant difference between
conceptions of tragedy and history, a difference which helps to explain both
the ennobling and the disempowering of the female characters in *Richard III.*
Contemporary descriptions of the history play genre focus on the historical
objects of representation. Celebrating "our domesticke histories," Thomas
Heywood asks,

> what English blood seeing the person of any bold English man presented and
> doth not hugge his fame, and hunnye at his valor, pursuing him in his enter-
> prise with his best wishes, and as beeing wrapt in contemplation, offers to him
> in his hart all prosperous performance, as if the Personater were the man Per-
> sonated. . . . What English Prince should hee behold the true portrature ofthat
> amous King *Edward* the third, foraging France, taking so great a King captive
> in his owne country, quartering the English Lyons with the French Flower-
> delyce, and would not bee suddenly Inflam'd with so royall a spectacle, being
> made apt and fit for the like atchievement. So of *Henry* the fift. (Book I, sig. B4ʳ)

Thomas Nashe makes essentially the same claims for the theatrical performance of English history. For Nashe as for Heywood, the value of the history
play is identified with the value of the objects of historical representation.
"What a glorious thing it is," he insists, "to have *Henrie* the fifth represented

on the Stage, leading the French King prisoner." He imagines "How would it have joyed brave *Talbot* (the terror of the French) to thinke that after he had lyne two hundred yeares in his Tombe, hee should triumphe againe on the Stage and have his bones newe embalmed with the teares of ten thousand spectators at least (at severall times) who, in the Tragedian that represents his person, imagine they behold him fresh bleeding?" (4:238–39). The thought of the weeping spectators, however, leads inexorably to the thought of the "Tragedian": the present actor who elicits the spectators' feminine tears replaces the historical character who constitutes the object of masculine emulation.

Conceived as historical drama, the play features the objects of representation. Conceived as tragedy, it features the theatrical power of the actor. In either case, the role of the protagonist is reserved for a male character, but so long as that protagonist is identified, like Heywood's Edward III or Nashe's (and Shakespeare's) Talbot, with the *locus* of historical representation, the transgressive power of theatrical performance can be mobilized by a woman such as Joan (or a disorderly, effeminate man such as Falstaff) to subvert the hegemonic narrative. Once the protagonist assumes the role of tragic hero, however, he can also dominate the *platea*. Not only the character privileged in the represented action, the tragic hero is also the actor privileged in theatrical performance.

III

The movement in *Richard III* from historical chronicle to tragical history is also a movement into modernity. Tragedy, as Catherine Belsey has shown, was deeply involved with the emergent conception of an autonomous masculine identity defined in performance. The history play was doubly associated with the past, not only with the traditional heroes of the historical chronicles it represented but also with an older conception of masculine identity rooted in patrilineal inheritance. As a dramatic genre, moreover, tragedy represented the wave of the future, while the vogue of the history play was remarkably short-lived, beginning in the 1580s and ending soon after the accession of James I (Levy 233; Rackin 30–32).

Both transitory and transitional, the Shakespearean history play was shaped by the same process of rapid cultural transformation that quickly produced its obsolescence as a dramatic genre. The plays combine two potentially contradictory versions of national and personal identity, rationalizing new conceptions of royal authority and masculine identity by reference to old models of patrilineal inheritance, amalgamating medieval cultural structures of dynastic succession with emergent concepts of personal achievement and private property. In so doing, they anticipate the new concept of feudalism that Richard Halpern describes as James I's "major innovation on the absolutist claims of the Tudors," the conception of the crown as a piece of property inherited by the king. As Halpern explains,

> [The older] theory relies on a divine conception of *political* authority, which is mystically passed from the body of the ruling king to his successor; it regards the monarch as the political representative of God and therefore invests the office of kingship with certain unique qualities. The [emergent] "feudal" theory, by contrast, envisions not a mysterious transmission of power but a legal transmission of property, with the king as little more than a particularly privileged landlord. Political authority derives not from divine sanction but from the prerogatives of property ownership, and is conterminous with it. To vary James's own aphorism, "No Land, No King." (220–23)

One way to state the problem in *Richard III* is in terms of the contradiction between these two models of royal authority. Representing the end of the old Plantagenet dynasty and its replacement by the House of Tudor, the project of the play is to ratify the property rights that Richmond acquired by his victory at Bosworth Field with the warrant of God's grace expressed throughout the play by prophecies, dreams, and curses and the patriarchal legitimacy that he appropriates by his marriage to Elizabeth.

The new conception of royal authority was implicated in new understandings of masculine identity. In the older, feudal model, not only a man's property but also his title, status, and personal identity were all determined by patrilineal succession. Increasingly, however, a man's status and identity were determined simply by his wealth. Instead of an inheritance, ratified by time and patriarchal succession, a man's place in the social hierarchy became increasingly dependent upon his own performance. Ultimately, even the ideal of the landed hereditary aristocrat would give way to that of the self-made man. For the time being, the status and land purchased by new money were validated by genealogical fictions of aristocratic lineage.

This transition involved a transformation of the functions of marriage. In a society where social and economic status were based on patrilineal succession, the most important function of marriage was to produce legitimate heirs. In an economy where wealth could be rapidly acquired or lost and a culture where social status was increasingly subject to renegotiation, marriage served less as an instrument of reproducing patriarchy over time, more as a basis for producing new wealth and status within its own time. As many critics have remarked, the earlier conception of marriage as a necessary alternative to whoredom—i.e., the lesser of two evils—was increasingly displaced by celebrations of ordered family life as the model and foundation for the good order of the state (Rose; Newman 25). This transition is generally associated with the movement from Roman Catholic asceticism to Protestant celebration of marriage. However, it also involves the replacement of the notion that marriage is valuable only as a means of procreation of legitimate heirs by the belief that it is valuable in itself; and as such it can be seen as a concomitant of the transition from feudalism to an early form of capitalism in which the family was the basic unit of economic production among the emergent middle classes.

Authority was still gendered masculine and rationalized historically, but there were significant differences in the ways a man's place in the status hierarchy (and therefore his identity) was established. In the older, feudal model, status was grounded in land, inherited from an authorizing father and transmitted through the body of an effaced mother. In the newer model—the product of an emergent capitalism and an emergent nation-state—the material basis for power and authority was monetary wealth. That wealth did not need to be inherited; it could just as well be obtained by a man's own efforts, and it could be derived either from land or from some other source of monetary income, including the acquisition of a wealthy wife.

Transforming the structure and functions of the family, the cultural transformation that led in the long run from the masculine ideal of the hereditary feudal aristocrat to that of the self-made capitalist man also produced a new conception of women (Belsey, "Disrupting Sexual Difference"). Women become a form of property: acquiring a woman, like acquiring any other property, became a means of validating masculine authority and manhood. Within the feudal, dynastic model of cultural organization, a man was defined as his father's son, and the ideal woman was a chaste mother who transmitted the father's legacy. Once a man's status came to be defined by his own performance, however, the ideal woman became the marriageable heiress, the prize to be attained by a man's own efforts, the material basis for the establishment of his own wealthy household.

This is not to say, of course, that wealthy and aristocratic wives were not valued by feudal noblemen, or that chaste mothers had no place in the logic of bourgeois gender ideology. The simple schematic opposition I propose cannot begin to account for the richly textured variety of social practice and socially conditioned desire, for differences over time and across class, or for the ways variations in the material conditions of individual lives qualified the force of prescriptive ideals. Even within the relatively closed discursive field of Shakespeare's English history plays, both models of the family and of gendered identity can be seen, although, since history was a conservative genre, the patriarchal, feudal model predominates. The alternative performative model, although it becomes increasingly prominent in the second tetralogy, is much more fully elaborated in the comedies and tragedies.[20]

In the Henry VI plays, marriage is represented as dangerous and destructive to men. Both Henry VI and Edward IV reject prudent dynastic marriages in order to marry on the basis of personal passion; both marriages are represented as disastrous mistakes that weaken the men's authority as kings and destabilize the political order of their realms. *Richard III*, on the other hand, reaches its happy resolution in the marriage between Richmond and Elizabeth, the foundation of the Tudor dynasty. In so doing, it looks forward to Shakespeare's representation of Henry V, where the successful courtship of Katherine is presented as the culminating event of Henry's triumphant reign. The resolutions of those plots in marriage literalize the scripture from Proverbs, widely quoted in contemporary marriage handbooks and sermons, "A good wife is the crown of her husband" (Newman 15). Like a newly prosperous commoner who acquired a coat of arms in order to authorize his new wealth in genealogical fictions of hereditary entitlement, both kings authorize their possession of the lands they have won in military conquest by marrying women who can secure that land by genealogical authority to their heirs.

Although both marriages are historical facts, their deployment in Shakespeare's plays is a product of dramatic selection. Their location as the satisfying theatrical culminations of the represented stories also satisfies the ideological imperatives of an emergent capitalist economy and an emergent nation-state that increasingly employed the mystified image of a patriarchal family to authorize masculine privilege and rationalize monarchical power.[21] The hero the Chorus calls the "mirror of all Christian kings" (2.Cho.6), Shakespeare's Henry V is also a prototype for the emergent ideal of modern masculinity, a gender identity that can be established only in the performance of heterosexual conquest. The act of sexual domination constitutes Henry's greatest triumph. The association of royal authority with the authority of a married man looks ahead, in fact, to Jacobean ideology, to Filmer's *Patriarcha*, to the emergent construction of the masculine paradigm as *paterfamilias*.

In keeping with this ideal, all the female characters in *Richard III* are related by blood or marriage to English kings and defined by their familial relation-

ships—as wife, as prospective wife, as mother, as widow. Unlike the Henry VI
plays, where both Joan and Margaret appeared on stage in masculine battle
dress and led armies on fields of battle, the female characters in *Richard III* are
confined to domestic roles and domestic settings. The domestication and sexualization of women represents a movement into modernity; it adumbrates the
rising barriers that were to confine respectable women within the household,
defined as a separate, private sphere. *Richard III,* like the plays of the second
tetralogy, is noticeably more modern in its representations of women, of gender roles, of the English state, and of the family.

The movement into modernity reaches its culmination in the concluding
speech, when Richmond seals his victory at Bosworth Field by announcing his
intention to marry Elizabeth of York. It is only by appropriating Elizabeth's
genealogical authority as the last survivor of the House of York that Richmond
can authorize himself as king and authorize the legitimacy of the Tudor
dynasty, only by becoming a *paterfamilias* that he can secure his new identity
as king. Elizabeth, moreover, literalizes the legal status of a married woman as
a *feme covert,* reduced to a disembodied name, a place marker for the genealogical authority that Richmond's son will inherit.

The female characters who do appear in the play are also recruited in Richmond's project; and like Elizabeth, they are also sacrificed to it. Richmond's
victory, in fact, reenacts in benevolent form Richard's earlier appropriation of
the feminine. Just as the play begins with Richard's appropriation of Margaret's
power of subversive speech, it ends with Richmond's appropriation of the
moral authority of bereaved and suffering women to authorize his victory.
To serve that purpose, the female characters must lose their individuality
and become an undifferentiated chorus of ritual lamentation, curse, and
prophecy. Like the ghosts who appear on the night before the Battle of Bosworth Field, these "poor mortal-living ghost[s]" (4.4.26) record the oblitera-
tion of patrilineal genealogy and invoke the higher authority of divine provi-
dence to validate Richmond's accession (Hodgdon 114). The new man is
authorized by God's blessing, the possession of a good wife, and the disempowerment of women, who need him to protect them and act on their behalf.

In praying for Richmond's victory, the ghosts of Richard's victims speak for
the entire nation, which is now identified as a helpless, suffering woman. This
identification is reiterated in Richmond's final speech: "Abate the edge of trai-
tors, gracious Lord," he prays, "that would reduce these bloody days again /
And make poor England weep in streams of blood!" The suffering victim of
Richard's bloody tyranny, England is also the cherished object of Richmond's

compassionate concern. Both here and in his oration before the battle, Richmond characterizes himself as a loving, protective *paterfamilias,* and he also promises his soldiers the rewards that go with that role:

> If you do fight in safeguard of your wives,
> Your wives shall welcome home the conquerors;
> If you do free your children from the sword,
> Your children's children quits it in your age
>
> (5.3.259–62)

Richard, by contrast, resorts to jingoistic appeals to masculine honor and misogynist charges that Richmond is a "milksop" and his soldiers "bastard Britains [i.e., Bretons], whom our fathers / Have in their own land beaten, bobb'd, and thump'd." "If we be conquered," he says, "let men conquer us" (5.3.325–34).

Interpellated as feminine by the preceding action, the audience is prepared to reject Richard's aggressively masculine rhetoric and respond instead as Richmond's "loving countrymen" who desire to "sleep in peace." They are not, however, prepared to accept a female image of royal or theatrical authority. When Richmond invites the audience to join him in a prayer that the descendants of his union with Elizabeth will "Enrich the time to come with smooth-fac'd peace, / With smiling plenty, and fair prosperous days," he appeals to their feminine desires for peace and prosperity and invokes the authority of their own female monarch to sanction his accession to the throne. But just as the Elizabeth Richmond marries can never appear on stage, the Elizabeth he foretells is never mentioned by name or identified as a woman.

Assuming the role of benevolent *paterfamilias,* Richmond constructs himself in direct antithesis to the solitary individualism of the tragic hero he supplants, the murderer of the young princes, the character who defined himself from the beginning by his contempt for women and his separation from the loving bonds of kinship. Nonetheless, the play ends as it begins, with a male character speaking from the *platea* empowered by his appropriation of the woman's part and his performative self-construction as the object of a feminized audience's desire.

NOTES

A previous version of this essay, entitled "Engendering the Tragic Audience: the Case of *Richard III*," was published in *Studies in the Literary Imagination* 26, No. 1 (Spring 1993): 47–65.

I am indebted to Rebecca Bushnell, Jean Howard, Donald Rackin, and Carroll Smith-Rosenberg for careful readings and helpful criticisms of earlier versions of this essay.

1. *Shakespeare and the Popular Tradition* 73–85 and "Bifold Authority" 409–10. For an excellent analysis of *Richard III* in terms of Weimann's theory, see Mooney.

2. On the exclusion of female characters from the *platea*, see Helms 554–65. Helms associates the male monopoly of the *platea* in public theater plays with the fact that men's roles were played by adult shareholders in the companies, while women's roles were played by boy apprentices. However, see Forse 71–99 for an argument that female parts were also played by adult shareholders, including William Shakespeare.

3. For arguments that emphasize the differences between Richard and later tragic heroes, see Belsey, *Subject of Tragedy* 37–39, and Adelman 9. In Belsey's view, Richard's isolation and self-assertion declare his alignment with the Vice "rather than defining an emerging interiority." To Adelman "the effect" in Richard's final soliloquy "is less of a psyche than of diverse roles confronting themselves across the void where a self should be." She sees Richard as possessing a "powerful subjectivity" in *3 Henry VI*, which is emptied out in *Richard III*, as Richard remakes himself "in the shape of the perfect actor who has no being except in the roles he plays" (8–9). For a discussion that emphasizes Richard's status as prototype for the modern tragic hero, see Weimann, *Shakespeare and the Popular Tradition* 159–60. In Weimann's view, Richard "marks the point of departure for modern tragedy . . . the *Charakterdrama* of an individual passion and a self-willed personality" who combines the self-expressive theatrical energy of the traditional Vice with the "mimetic requirements of a *locus*-oriented royal personage." Weimann concedes that "*Richard III*, of course, only points the way," but he also insists that "the pattern seems clear."

4. On the convergence of history and tragedy, see Lindenberger 72–78. For Aristotle, the ideal tragic protagonist was "highly renowned and prosperous—a personage like Oedipus, Thyestes, or other illustrious men of such families"—and also historical: Unlike comic poets, "tragedians still keep to real names" (*Poetics* XIII, IX). Cf. Lope de Vega 543: "For a subject tragedy has history and comedy has feigning."

5. Although early modern beliefs about the effeminating effects of theatrical performance and attributions of feminine characteristics to actors have received considerable attention in recent criticism, see especially Howard, *Stage and Social Struggle*, Levine, and Singh.

6. Gosson's charge that tragedy would incite womanly passions in its spectators had an ancient and respectable precedent in Book X of Plato's *Republic*, where Socrates condemned the sympathetic raptures stirred up by the tragedian as "the part of a woman" (39). For a perceptive discussion of the effeminacy of the tyrant figure, see Bushnell.

7. "Women in the Renaissance Theatre Audience" 170–71. Levin quotes the description of the ladies in the *Spanish Tragedy* audience from the beginning of Thomas May's *The Heir*.

8. CCXI. *Sociable Letters* (1664), reprinted in *The Riverside Shakespeare* 1847, and

also quoted in Levin, "Relation of External Evidence" 12. For an impressive array of similar descriptions, see Levin's entire article.

9. This is a familiar list. On the marginal roles of women in Shakespeare's English history plays, see Rackin, *Stages of History,* chapter 4.

10. In the words of Herbert Lindenberger, "Tragedy . . . gives history a way of making 'sense' out of what might otherwise be a chaos of events; or the catastrophe whose inevitability it demonstrates works to confirm our worst fears about the nature of events and, by one of those apparent paradoxes that we often find when we examine the effects of art, it ends up helping us to cope with an otherwise unbearable reality" (73).

11. On the widespread use in English Renaissance drama of female characters, and especially of bereaved mothers, as "a symbolic focus of pity" rather than individual figures "involved in an action through [their] own motive and volition," see McLuskie 136 and chapter 6 passim.

12. Hodgdon explains Shakespeare's transformation of Elizabeth's character as an effort to protect the name of Elizabeth's descendant and living, reigning namesake.

13. See, e.g., the editorial comment in the Arden edition (296): "Commentators have laboured to settle the impossible, whether Elizabeth's acceptance was real or feigned."

14. See Bushnell 118–26 for a brilliant exposition of this aspect of Richard's characterization. Cf. 3.7.51, when Buckingham will advise Richard to "play the maid's part, still answer nay and take it"—a misogynist joke that defines the female part as an eroticized and deceptive form of theatrical performance.

15. See Hammond 77–78 for two striking examples, especially notable because, as Hammond points out, they occur in a passage that Shakespeare did not use in his play.

16. In addition to the repeated use of similar descriptions in antitheatrical invective, it is noteworthy that Burbage himself, the actor who first played Richard's role, was compared in admiring contemporary descriptions to Proteus, the shape-shifter. For a good summary of Elizabethan descriptions of actors, including Burbage, see Montrose 56–57. On the image of Proteus as applied to actors, see Barish 99–107.

17. Compare Weimann's suggestive analysis in *Shakespeare and the Popular Tradition* 159–60.

18. This (along with the contrasting effects of Richard's later wooing of Elizabeth) seems to be the scene's *raison d'être.* As Judith Anderson points out, except for the fact that Richard married Anne Neville, the wooing scene has no historical basis (112); it is also completely unnecessary to the dramatic narrative of Richard's ascent to the throne.

19. Reprinted in *The Riverside Shakespeare* 1836. A similar account, quoted by Schoenbaum 205–206, appeared in Thomas Wilkes's *A General View of the Stage* (1759) 220–21.

20. For the distinction between patriarchal and performative masculinities, see Jeffords. Many critics have remarked on the patriarchal structures of Shakespeare's

English chronicle plays, but see especially Kahn, chapter 3. On the differing structures of masculine identity in the comedies, see Williamson.

21. Many writers have made this point, but see especially Williamson, chapter 3, and Schochet.

WORKS CITED

Adams, Hazard, ed. *Critical Theory since Plato*. New York: Harcourt, 1971.

Adelman, Janet. *Suffocating Mothers: Fantasies of Maternal Origin in Shakespeare's Plays, "Hamlet" to "The Tempest."* London: Routledge, 1992.

Anderson, Judith. *Biographical Truth: The Representation of Historical Persons in Tudor-Stuart Writing*. New Haven: Yale UP, 1984.

Anon. *The True Tragedy of Richard III*. London: Thomas Creede, 1594. Rpt. Oxford: Malone Society, 1929.

———. *A Warning for Fair Women: A Critical Edition*. Ed. Charles Dale Cannon. The Hague: Mouton, 1975.

Barish, Jonas. *The Antitheatrical Prejudice*. Berkeley: U of California P, 1981.

Belsey, Catherine. "Disrupting Sexual Difference: Meaning and Gender in the Comedies." *Alternative Shakespeares*. Ed. John Drakakis. London: Methuen, 1985. 166–90.

———. *The Subject of Tragedy: Identity and Difference in Renaissance Drama*. London: Methuen, 1985.

Brooke, Nicholas. "Reflecting Gems and Dead Bones: Tragedy versus History in *Richard III.*" *Shakespeare's Wide and Universal Stage*. Ed. C. B. Cox and D. J. Palmer. Manchester: Manchester UP, 1984. 104–16.

Bushnell, Rebecca W. *Tragedies of Tyrants: Political Thought and Theater in the English Renaissance*. Ithaca: Cornell UP, 1990.

Callaghan, Dympna. *Woman and Gender in Renaissance Tragedy*. Atlantic Highlands, N.J.: Humanities P International, 1989.

Chambers, E. K. *The Elizabethan Stage*. 4 vols. Oxford: Clarendon P, 1951.

Corbet, Richard. *Iter Boreale*. Furness 591.

Dolan, Frances E. "Gender, Moral Agency, and Dramatic Form in *A Warning for Fair Women*." *SEL* 29 (1989): 201–18.

———. "Home-Rebels and House-Traitors: Murderous Wives in Early Modern England." *Yale Journal of Law and the Humanities* 4 (Winter 1992): 1–31.

Evans, G. Blakemore, et al., eds. *The Riverside Shakespeare*. Boston: Houghton Mifflin, 1974.

Forse, James H. *Art Imitates Business: Commercial and Political Influences in Elizabethan Theatre.* Bowling Green, Ohio: Bowling Green State U Popular P, 1993.

Furness, Horace Howard Jr., ed. *The Variorum Edition of Shakespeare's Richard III.* Philadelphia: Lippincott, 1908.

Gilbert, Allen, ed. *Literary Criticism: Plato to Dryden.* Detroit: Wayne State UP, 1962.

Gosson, Stephen. *Playes Confuted in five Actions.* Chambers 4: 213–19.

Hall, Edward. *The Union of the Two Noble and Illustre Famelies of Lancastre & Yorke.* 1548; rpt. London: J. Johnson et al., 1809.

Halpern, Richard. *The Poetics of Primitive Accumulation: English Renaissance Culture and the Genealogy of Capital.* Ithaca: Cornell UP, 1991.

Hammond, Anthony, ed. The Arden Edition of Shakespeare's *King Richard III.* London: Methuen, 1981.

Harington, Sir John. *A Preface, or rather a Briefe Apologie of Poetrie.* 1591. Smith 2: 194–222.

Helms, Lorraine. " 'The High Roman Fashion': Sacrifice, Suicide, and the Shakespearean Stage." *PMLA* 97 (1992): 554–65.

Heywood, Thomas. *An Apology for Actors.* London, 1612.

Hodgdon, Barbara. *The End Crowns All: Closure and Contradiction in Shakespeare's History.* Princeton: Princeton UP, 1991.

Howard, Jean E. *The Stage and Social Struggle in Early Modern England.* London: Routledge, 1994.

Howard, Jean E., and Marion F. O'Connor, eds. *Shakespeare Reproduced: The Text in History and Ideology.* London: Methuen, 1987.

Jeffords, Susan. "Performative Masculinities, or, 'After a Few Times You Won't Be Afraid of Rape at All.' " *Discourse* 13 (1991): 102–18.

Kahn, Coppélia. *Man's Estate: Masculine Identity in Shakespeare.* Berkeley: U of California P, 1981.

Leggatt, Alexander. *Shakespeare's Political Drama: The History Plays and the Roman Plays.* London: Routledge, 1988.

Levin, Richard. "The Relation of External Evidence to the Allegorical and Thematic Interpretation of Shakespeare." *Shakespeare Studies* 13 (1980): 1–29.

———. "Women in the Renaissance Theatre Audience." *Shakespeare Quarterly* 40 (1989): 165–74.

Levine, Laura. *Men in Women's Clothing: Anti-theatricality and Effeminization 1579–1642.* Cambridge: Cambridge UP, 1994.

Levy, F. J. *Tudor Historical Thought.* San Marino, Calif.: The Huntington Library, 1967.

Lindenberger, Herbert. *Historical Drama: The Relation of Literature and Reality.* Chicago: U of Chicago P, 1975.

McLuskie, Kathleen. *Renaissance Dramatists.* Atlantic Highlands, N.J.: Humanities P International, 1989.

Meres, Francis. *Palladis Tamia, Wits Treasury.* 1598. Smith 2: 309–24.

Montrose, Louis Adrian. "The Purpose of Playing: Reflections on a Shakespearean Anthropology." *Helios* n.s. 7 (1980): 51–74.

Mooney, Michael E. "Language, Staging, and 'Affect': *Figurenposition* in *Richard III.*" *Shakespeare's Dramatic Transactions.* Durham, N.C.: Duke UP, 1990. 23–50.

Nashe, Thomas. *Pierce Penilesse his Supplication to the Divell.* 1592. Chambers 4: 238–40.

Newman, Karen. *Fashioning Femininity and English Renaissance Drama.* Chicago: U of Chicago P, 1991.

Paster, Gail Kern. " 'In the spirit of men there is no blood': Blood as Trope of Gender in *Julius Caesar.*" *Shakespeare Quarterly* 40 (1989): 284–98.

Plato. *Republic.* Trans. Benjamin Jowett. Rpt. Adams 19–41.

Rackin, Phyllis. *Stages of History: Shakespeare's English Chronicles.* Ithaca: Cornell UP, 1990.

Rose, Mary Beth. *The Expense of Spirit: Love and Sexuality in English Renaissance Drama.* Ithaca: Cornell UP, 1988.

Schochet, Gordon. *Patriarchalism in Political Thought: The Authoritarian Family and Political Speculation and Attitudes Especially in Seventeenth-Century England.* Oxford: Blackwell, 1975.

Schoenbaum, Samuel. *William Shakespeare: A Compact Documentary Life.* New York: Oxford UP, 1978.

Shakespeare, William. *The Riverside Shakespeare.* Ed. G. Blakemore Evans et al. Boston: Houghton Mifflin, 1974.

Sidney, Sir Philip. *An Apologie for Poetrie.* 1595. Smith 1: 148–207.

Singh, Jyotsna. "Renaissance Antitheatricality, Antifeminism, and Shakespeare's *Antony and Cleopatra.*" *Renaissance Drama* n.s. 20 (1989): 99–122.

Smith, G. Gregory, ed. *Elizabethan Critical Essays.* 2 vols. Oxford: Oxford UP, 1904.

de Vega, Lope. *The New Art of Making Comedies.* 1609. Trans. Olga Marx Perlzweig. Gilbert 541–48.

Webbe, William. *A Discourse of English Poetrie.* 1586. Smith 1: 226–302.

Weimann, Robert. "Bifold Authority in Shakespeare's Theatre." *Shakespeare Quarterly* 39 (1988): 401–17.

———. *Shakespeare and the Popular Tradition in the Theater: Studies in the Social Dimension of Dramatic Form and Function.* Ed. Robert Schwartz. Baltimore: The Johns Hopkins UP, 1987.

Williamson, Marilyn. *The Patriarchy of Shakespeare's Comedies.* Detroit: Wayne State UP, 1986.

2

A WOMAN OF LETTERS

Lavinia in *Titus Andronicus*

SARA EATON

> I will learn thy thought;
> In thy dumb action will I be as perfect
> As begging hermits in their holy prayers.
> Thou shalt not sigh, nor hold thy stumps to heaven,
> Nor wink, nor nod, nor kneel, nor make a sign,
> But I, of these, will wrest an alphabet,
> And by still practice learn to know thy meaning.
>
> —(3.2.39–45)

TITUS SPEAKS TO Lavinia in my epigraph, and he terms her a "map of woe" whose body must "talk in signs" (3.2.11), since, as Marcus puts it, "that delightful engine of her thoughts, / That babbl'd them with such pleasing eloquence, / Is torn from forth that pretty hollow cage" (3.1.81–84). Their metaphors heighten the theatrical effects of Lavinia's grisly appearance after her rape and mutilation, but they also anticipate scenes for the "wresting" of meaning, for the "practice" of reading and writing in the play, which follow the loss of Lavinia's eloquent (theatric) voice and gestures and the sacrifice of Titus's hand. Because of this arrangement in the plot, reading and writing in *Titus* are perceived by the characters and audience as supplementary to the body's "usual" means of communication; in a sense, reading and writing are the spectacular products of extremity, depicted in the play as a "private" activity transformed by political violence into a "public" utterance.[1]

Acts of literacy become violent, visualized ones. But Shakespeare replicates in this play contemporary understandings about reading and writing. Recent critical studies of humanism, an ideology promoting the kind of literacy the Andronici exhibit, and its effects on early modern England have emphasized the social and psychological violence encoded within it. Mary Thomas Crane, for example, describes in detail how, in their educational practices, "humanists . . . reach toward transformation of the self but can only depict it as a painful violation, closely related to corporal punishment" and "depict their students as fragmented subjects, both alienated from and controlled by language" (76). These depictions of the self, manifested in literate behavior, infiltrated schools for both the upwardly mobile and the elite by the later sixteenth century and, Crane argues, were intentionally positioned against traditional aristocratic-values: "Instead of the display of innate superiority at such courtly pastimes as hunting, singing, dancing, and romantic interchange, English humanists sought to establish a serious demeanor, aphoristic style, and constructive use of time as the signs of a powerful subject" (78). These humanist attributes Titus will come to display, in seeming contrast to Tamora and her brood, who murder as part of a hunt, and whose "romantic interchanges" are depicted as infidelity and rape.

But there is more at stake in the confrontation between Tamora and Titus than contested value systems. By the late sixteenth century, humanists and their heirs were the educators of monarchs and their most powerful advisers, making up the bulk of Elizabeth's bureaucracy, but not without serious resistance from unreconstructed aristocrats and the humanist-trained elite who vied for access to the queen and the patronage system.[2] In effect, the system which had educated Shakespeare and his contemporaries also signified, literally, a fragmented subject's desires for public exercise of power. Moreover, for the English, the potential violence encoded in the educational training of humanist subjects and the implementing and display of their social power, as well as the frustration of it, acquired additional resonance in the context of the religious wars. The print revolution and subsequent increases in literacy facilitated the Reformation and maintained its momentum; as Elizabeth Eisenstein puts it, "The theme of printing as proof of spiritual and cultural superiority, first sounded in Rome in its crusade against 'illiterate' Turks, was taken over by German humanists trying to counter Italian claims" (147). As John Foxe explained it in *Acts and Monuments*, "The Lord began his work for His Church not with sword and target to subdue His exalted adversary, but with printing, writing, and reading" (as qtd. in Eisenstein 148). *Titus*, I will argue, reproduces variants on all these social attitudes and tensions by displaying literacy as a weapon, by adopting pedagogical metaphors, by pitting the literate Andronici, who initially wish only to advise the king, against Tamora's politics of "kind" or blood, and by depicting Titus as an explicitly humanist revenger, valued for his depictions of subjectivity as he cleanses the state of corruption.

In addition, Shakespeare also depicts the literally bloody action of the play as one inflected by gender. The play reflects contemporary sexualized attitudes toward aristocratic women as they are viewed, again, from a humanist perspective characterized by substitution and displacement of affect. Stephanie Jed has argued that humanism has its origins in the figure of Lucrece, another famous rape victim, and the fascinated responses of fifteenth-century humanists to her suicide, significant because the Roman republic thus has its beginnings in her defilement and death. The many treatments of Lucrece, Jed argues, are "inscribed in a language that invites sexual violence" (7) and infect humanist habits of reading and writing, re-reading and re-writing with "an eagerness to hear this tale over and over again, an eagerness which is, however, covered over by a certain solemnity and detachment from the rape" (7–8). The pattern of re-reading/writing Jed describes also can be applied to Shakespeare's treatment of Lavinia and Tamora, the revisions of his source and the classical myths in the play, Titus's own revisions, and much of the critical response to the play, as well as to Shakespeare's own return to the scene of rape, his *Lucrece,* printed in 1594. While Lavinia's body, like Lucrece's, becomes the site for reproductive warfare and a successful repulsion of "barbaric" invaders, the play transforms the conflict into a matter of class and kind of rhetorical education, a social war juxtaposing the persuasive powers of speech to the equally compelling powers of writing.[3] As a result, Lavinia's dismemberment is a sign of the omnipresent violence which marks the play, a violence which encodes and politicizes contemporary attitudes toward humanist education and its products, reading and writing, especially in relation to learned women, the staple of reproductive exchange in early modern England's aristocracy.

The physical instruments, or signs, for what become a humanist production of meaning—a letter, more letters attached to bundles of weapons and arrows, other texts, a stick, and, most important, the hand—become the stimulus for action in *Titus* after the initial attacks on the Andronici. The signs supplementing the tongue, the "delightful engine of thought," transform dramatic action and produce it. The characters' recourse to literacy reflects their sense that reading that writing and each other are similar interpretive and imitative behaviors, persuasive acts performed by humanist "teachers" and imitated by "students" which can supplement and finally transcend speech.[4]

Significantly, writing and the effects of reading permeate the play after Lavinia's rape and the loss of her tongue. Chiron's mockery immediately following Lavinia's rape—"Write down thy mind, bewray thy meaning so, / And if thy stumps will let thee play the scribe" (2.4.3-4)—anticipates when Titus will write his "heart's deep languor, and my soul's sad tears" (3.1.13) in the dust when his sons are judged murderers, and when his dismembered "good hand" (3.1.235) is carried in an "employ'd" Lavinia's mouth (3.1.282) to signify his revengeful intentions. From his study, a room designed for private "ruminations" (5.1.6) and writing, and a fairly recent architectural innovation in the uses of domestic space, Titus writes coded (i.e., Latin) messages of his intentions attached to weapons, messages which "decipher" (4.2.8)[5] his enemies, "blazoning [their] unjustice everywhere" (4.4.18).

Failing to read well (or interpret correctly) has social and political consequences. When Chiron, the play's representation of the naive or impolitic reader, responds to the message on Titus's "gift" as a schoolboy would ("O, 'tis a verse in Horace, I know it well, / I read it in the grammar long ago"), Aaron remarks, "Ay, just—a verse in Horace, right, you have it. / [Aside] Now what a thing it is to be an ass!" (4.2.22-25). A wiser reader, Saturninus, the Emperor, reads Titus's missives and responds by plotting with Tamora what becomes under Titus's revisions the banquet scene in the last act. Titus cooks by the book: his text is drawn explicitly from Ovid's description of Progne's revenge of her sister in the *Metamorphosis*. First a reader, Titus then becomes the dramatist creating a spectacle when he declares, "for what I mean to do / See here in bloody lines I have set down: / And what is written shall be executed" (5.2.13-15), and then an actor in it, becoming "the cook" who dismembers Chiron and Demetrius for his "play" (5.2.205). Mixing also his texts, Titus justifies his killing of Lavinia by finding a "pattern" (5.3.44) for his action in the story of Virginius: "I am as woeful as Virginius was, / And have a thousand times more cause" (5.3.50-51). But the violent textual connections between humanist thoughts, words, and deeds are perhaps most poignantly made theatric ones in the scene in Act 4 when Lavinia gives Titus, Lucius, and Marcus a "lesson" (4.1.106), ironically reproducing both Chiron's and her father's directives, first by drawing their attention to Ovid's text and the story of Philomela, and then writing the names of her attackers in the sand by holding a stick in her mouth and guiding it with her stumps.[6]

Lavinia's "lesson" in this scene is one of numerous allusions in the play to the humanist pedagogy of reading and writing. Teaching someone a lesson, of course, is the motivation behind revenge, but these scenes are frequently placed as an alternative to the social organization of a dramatic world based on kinship, or "kind," a world characterized as "headless" (1.1.186), dismembered, and governed by persuasive speech.[7] Lavinia suggests such divisions when she appeals to Tamora to stop her rape on the basis of their shared femininity and then appeals to her sons on the basis of their difference: "O, do not learn her wrath—she taught it thee" (2.3.142). She tries again with Tamora: "O, be to me, though thy hard heart say no, / Nothing so kind, but something pitiful!" When Tamora retorts, "I know not what it means," Lavinia pleads, "O, let me teach thee" (2.3.155–58). Even if her voice fails her, Lavinia assumes here that education can change minds.

Lavinia has some practice in teaching social reform; she has read the classics to Lucius's son like "Cornelia" (4.1.12).[8] But Aaron, the only one of his kind in the play until the birth of his son, whose birth becomes, ironically, the cause of his death, repeats the assumption that learning transcends "kind" when he declares that he has been Chiron and Demetrius's "tutor," asserting "that codding spirit had they from their mother": "That bloody mind I think they learn'd of me" (5.1.98–99, 101).[9] Likewise a tutor, Titus tells his grandson, who he hopes will "bear his pretty tales in mind / And talk of them when he is dead and gone" (5.3.165–66), that he will "teach [him] another course" (4.1.119) for revenge after they read Lavinia's words in the sand. Keeping his father's words in mind, Lucius, his son, after the revenge is completed, pleads to the Roman populace,

> O, let me teach you how to knit again
> This scattered corn into one mutual sheaf,
> These broken limbs again into one body.
> (5.3.70–73)

All of these scenes of teaching, reading, and writing, realized as political acts occurring when a humanist ideology collides with one based on lineage or "kind," symbolized by and enacted through physical dismemberment, describe the scene for the humanist production of writing in early modern England, according to Jonathan Goldberg, in an essay in *Shakespeare Quarterly* exploring similar images in *Hamlet*. Goldberg cites two contemporary sources, among many:

Gregory of Nyssa, for instance, who writes that "it was above all for language that nature added hands to our bodies." "Hands are the characteristic of rational nature," he continues, since "it is, in effect, one of the marks of the presence of reason to express itself through letters." Or I might have cited the Spanish writing master Andres Brun, writing in 1583: "Plato says that the difference which divides us humans from the animals is that we have the power of speech and they do not. I, however, say that the difference is that we know how to *write* but they do not. . . . " (307)

Goldberg argues that the hand that writes is a symbol of man as a rational creature to many in this period; in Goldberg's analysis, the hand produces characters and character, identifying the writer and reproducing him inside a social structure determined by "written marks" serving as "class markers" (317).[10] The popular and numerous copybooks in the period which demonstrate how to hold the pen and hand and how to form the letters correctly are like the similarly popular conduct books: they show how to simulate character. Goldberg argues, and I would emphasize, that writing thus creates a persona, a theatric character (316). The writing/written self in humanist ideology is a supplementary—or self-conscious—one.

As if to reveal to readers that the written characters may be detached from the writer's character, all of the books Goldberg saw illustrated the text by picturing hands "detached from bodies, severed arms ruled by the pictorial frame" (317). These pictures, Goldberg writes, "illustrate the material circuit from a hand writing to handwriting, a production of value—good or naught—and an implicit idealization and dematerialization of the hand inserted within the practice of writing. . . . [T]he body has been detached from the hand, and the material production of letters has been moralized, spiritualized, placed, in short, within a regime of value that appears to take its source from some transcendent realm" (317). In a sense, as Goldberg says, "the mind arises from the hand" (319).

Goldberg's interests are the applications of his research to *Hamlet*'s character(s), but his arguments can be applied more literally to *Titus*, a play abounding with severed hands and lopped limbs.[11] Clearly, reading and writing in the play supplement the lost active hand, creating humanist scripts for social correction and change and a way of "knitting" the political body back together. While writing can teach and create social change, the words, the supplement, become the public expression of the body: they display the private hand which produced the writing, the hand which cannot be seen. If the results of writing by the right kinds of hands are reified in the play—"moralized, spiritualized," to repeat Goldberg—so are the writers. Titus's recourse to writing ennobles his actions and allows his family to "transcend" his opponents socially, to vanquish them, because he has the textual justifications. At the same time, he is social-ized. The more Titus writes, the more he sheds the look of the savage patriarch of act 1 who kills his son, his own kind, for disobeying him and acquires an interiority signified by humanist pedagogy and writing, the look of the "mad" Senecan avenger.[12] And the more psychologically complex Titus appears, the more Tamora and her sons are characterized as "beasts and birds of prey" (5.3.198), unlettered, devoid of humanity, needing to be taught a lesson.

Goldberg suggests that "the hand moves in language, and its movement retraces the 'being' of the individual inscribed with social practice" (317). The social practice of writing produces the signs of a displaced subjectivity, of a distinctly humanist subjectivity, in Titus's world, transcending the "kind" that Tamora inhabits. Hers is also constructed of words, but for her the spoken word informs the attached hand. She declares to Chiron and Demetrius that "your mother's hand shall right your mother's wrong" (2.3.121), and to herself, how "high-witted Tamora to gloze with all" (4.4.35) will accomplish her revenge. But her unmarked body signifies her words, and these are rendered "hollow," unpersuasive, in this sense, unremarkable except as examples of monstrosity, by others' (re)actions in the play.

Her quarrel with Titus begins when he ignores her words and kills her son. And Aaron and his "teachings," his letter writing and scripting of the murders and rape at the pit, inform the revenge she does accomplish. Tamora presumes she will "enchant the old Andronicus" to his doom "with words more sweet, and yet more dangerous / Than baits to fish" (4.4.89–91):

> For I can smooth and fill his aged ears
> With golden promises, that, were his heart
> Almost impregnable, his old years deaf,
> Yet should both ear and heart obey my tongue.
> (4.4.96–99)

Significantly, when she announces that she wants to talk at his study door, Titus notes their difference: "No, not a word, how can I grace my talk, / Wanting a hand to give['t] that accord?" (5.2.16–18). Tamora's assumption that her "mon-strous" powers translate as linguistic powers, that her attached hands and tongue render her remarkable in her world, is heard as evidence of the politics of "kind."[13] Titus does not "obey" her "words more sweet, and yet more dangerous." Instead, she falls into Titus's hands and script. As he says as he plans his revenge, he "o'erreaches them in their own devices" (5.2.143).

Titus refers to the rules of rhetoric here; "overreaching" is Puttenham's term for the hyperbolic or the "loud lyer," one of the ornaments or figures used in persuasion. Titus knows his revenge is a "great diffimulation," to quote Puttenham, one that "if we fhall meafure it by the rule of exact veritie, is but an vntruth, yet a more cleanly commendation then was maifter Speakers" (192). The "overreaching" that Puttenham discusses in this passage concerns the praising of a prince, and illustrates how humanist rhetoric and politics were intrinsically intertwined in early modern England. In this sense, Titus perceives himself as a "better" and more politic liar than Tamora, one whose actions are "more cleanly" commended.

If Titus's revenge is successful as a humanist demonstration of rhetorical art with social and political effects, his actions and the action of the play also link what Patricia Parker, in her study of Renaissance rhetorics and literary texts, has termed "something described as divinely sanctioned or 'naturall' to something that can not only be learned and manipulated but disrupted, and hence is in need of being hedged about by careful distinctions, social enforcements, and laws" (118).[14] If Shakespeare's play assumes that the written and spoken word are both "divinely sanctioned" and potentially disruptive of the social order, what the play also demonstrates is how the dismembered hand, and by implication the alienated rhetorical subject, invested with "Roman" or humanist social practice and "being" triumphs, how the written word supersedes the spoken, because writing reifies and thus transforms social and political action. And, since Tamora speaks while Titus writes, the practice of writing is also, inevitably, gendered.

The act of writing differentiates Titus and his family from Tamora's kind. Not surprisingly, opposing Titus, the revered "grandsire" (5.3.172), the "head" of the family, Tamora is perceived as "beastly" in her actions by the other characters and critics alike, analogous to the pit which has entrapped the Andronici, a great "swallowing womb" (2.3.239), a devouring mother, juxtaposed to the edifice built to honor the patriarchal family, the Andronici tomb.[15] Between Titus and Tamora and what they signify, Lavinia writes—and is written on.

Lavinia, like Helena, Olivia, Portia, and Rosalind in the comedies, is a humanist-trained and educated woman—a rarity in her day.[16] She is well read in the classics, "sweet poetry and Tully Orator" (4.1.14), obviously Ovid, and she has overseen the education of her nephew. According to Marcus, in the much-commented-on apostrophe following her rape and mutilation, her voice was a "heavenly harmony" (2.4.48) of modulation, her "pretty fingers . . . sewed better than Philomel" (2.4.42–43), her "lily hands" could "tremble like aspen leaves upon a lute / And make the silken strings delight to kiss them" (2.4.44–46).[17] She is chaste and obedient, ready to marry Saturninus at her father's bidding, then loyal to Bassianus and Saturninus when she chastises Tamora for her infidelity.

Lavinia is Shakespeare's picture of the "Roman" matron, the educated and humanist aristocratic woman, the courtier's lady. Castiglione describes this woman in the third book of *The Book of the Courtier*:

> I will that this woman have a sight in letters, in musicke, in drawing, or painting, and skilfull in dauncing, and in devising sports and pastimes, accompanying with that discrete sober moode, and with the giving a good opinion of her selfe, the other principles also that have beene taught the Courtier. And thus in conversation, in laughing, in sporting, in jesting, finally in everie thing she shal be had in great price. . . .
> And albeit stayednesse, noblenesse of courage, temperance, strength of the minde, wisdom, and the other vertues, a man would thinke belonged not to entertaine, yet will I have her endowed with them all, not so much to entertaine (although notwithstanding they may serve thereto also) as to be vertuous: and these vertues to make her such a one, that she may deserve to bee esteemed, and all her doings framed by them. (Castiglione [tr. Hoby] 195; qtd. in Jardine 6–7)

Castiglione ends this passage with conjectures that these learned "vertues" result in potential political and social role reversals: "I wonder then quoth the Lorde Gasper smyling, since you give women both letters, and stayednesse, and nobleness of courage, and temperance, ye will no have them also to beare rule in cities, and to make lawes, and to leade armies, and men to stand spinning in the kitchin" (195; Jardine 7). The educated woman is potentially unruly, "a threat in the social and sexual sphere," as Lisa Jardine puts it (7), and is consistently ambiguously portrayed in humanist texts, popular pamphlets, and plays.

In early modern England, a humanist education for women was viewed as training, as a supplement to essential femininity, rather than a cultivation of what was inherited—i.e., the mind. "On the one hand," Jardine suggests, "the [humanist texts on the education of women] encourage female aspiration towards real learning; on the other, faced with female intellectual achievement, male writers consistently *mythologize* it into iconic chastity, or into a glorious emblem of the cultivatedness of the courts of Europe" (5). If education was perceived as an overlay, a potential making manly of the feminine body, humanist practice also rendered that body iconic, thus re-feminizing it as an object to be praised, an object to be observed, and an object to be read. Thus, Lavinia is "framed" by her doings as the image of the educated woman, but ravished, she becomes Titus's "greatest spurn" (3.1.101); he says, "Had I but seen thy picture in this plight / It would have madded me; what shall I do / Now I behold thy lively body so?" (3.1.103–105).

Even though both Titus and Lavinia have lost their hands, the psychological "growth" as a tragic hero that Titus shows because he writes is not given to Lavinia, the tragic heroine. She does not acquire subjectivity because she, too, writes. Instead, the play emphasizes her "lively body" and her reinscription as a woman in a patriarchal humanist script.[18] She carries Titus's hand in her mouth, her "lively body" articulating her father's words, fulfilling in macabre fashion Goldberg's analysis of "the path of the hand towards its human destination, the hand filled like a mouth, given interiority (and mind) by the external imposition of a disciplinary regime" (*Matter* 97).[19] For that reason, Titus, when informing Chiron and Demetrius of how and why he will kill them, paints a picture of social and political miscegenation rather than detailing the violation done to Lavinia's "mind" as evidenced in hand and tongue:

> Here stands the spring whom you have stain'd with mud,
> This goodly summer with your winter mix'd. . . .
> Both her sweet hands, her tongue, and that more dear
> Than hands or tongue, her spotless chastity,
> Inhuman traitors, you constrain'd and forc'd.
> (5.2.170–71, 175–77)

I want to stress that Titus's attitudes toward Lavinia do not change during the play as he becomes more complex psychologically and thus a humanist hero in the Senecan fashion; in fact, his attitudes toward Lavinia's worth are reflected in others' attitudes toward women generally. From the beginning, the play emphasizes the value of being female in a fragmented dramatic world. Lavinia is an object of exchange in Titus's political dealings with Saturninus, her proposed marriage to him an "advance" of name and family (1.1.238–39) in exchange for Titus's vote of allegiance to Saturninus. While Titus translates his sons' behavior in Lavinia's abduction and subsequent marriage to Bassianus as traitorous and dishonorable, a view shared to advantage by Saturninus, who prefers Tamora's "hue" (1.1.261) and some distance from the Andronici,

Titus simultaneously calculates that Tamora will be "beholden to the man [himself] / That brought her for this high good turn so far[.] / Yes, and will nobly him remunerate" (1.1.396–98). The exchange of women in this dramatic world creates an arena of political and social remuneration in "public" and "private" spheres which are nearly indistinguishable. The politics of kind are conducted through marriages, as one would expect, but sexual preferments, sexual politics, create the "real" social and political world of the play, a world perceived by all of its inhabitants as fragmented and chaotic, "headless," in its social structures.

In this world, Lavinia is a "changing piece" (1.1.309), her humanist education but an ornament, her only "real" value the possession of her chaste femininity. A "pretty hollow cage," she is simultaneously perceived as potentially unruly and uniquely chaste, a paradoxical sign of constant change and stasis. Like Titus, her rapists also read her in that context; Demetrius argues:

> She is a woman, therefore may be woo'd,
> She is a woman, therefore may be won,
> She is Lavinia, therefore must be lov'd.
> What, man, more water glideth by the mill
> Than wots the miller of, and easy it is
> Of a cut loaf to steal a shive.
>
> (2.1.82–87)

Passages similar to this one, Peter Stallybrass has argued, represent the articulations of the class aspirant in this period. He notes three possible class positions: the first, "the one attempting to maintain social closure and exclusion"; the second, "subverting class but reinforcing gender hierarchy"; the third, desiring a closed social structure worthy of his aspiration but flexible enough to admit him (134). Stallybrass suggests that the class aspirant's "conceptualization of woman will . . . be radically unstable; she will be perceived as oscillating between the enclosed body (the purity of the elite to which he aspires) and the open body (or else how could he attain her?), between being 'too coy' and 'too common' " (134).

It is tempting to label Lavinia "too coy" and Tamora "too common" and suggest an easy and static dichotomy in how the play represents its women, but the social and political structure of *Titus* is much as Stallybrass describes, from the opening scenes, when Bassianus and Saturninus with Titus compete to be emperor, to its close, when Lucius does the same. Creating among themselves the conditions for "headless" social chaos, the men are in ceaseless competition for honors, from marriage to proper burials, and their exchanged women are in this sense a sign of their agonistic struggle. Their rivalry is gendered and imagined as a war of regeneration between matriarchal and patriarchal would-be rulers, between Tamora's and Titus's families, the play thus replicating the political tensions of England in the 1590s.

From this perspective, Lavinia and Tamora are similar "changing pieces," as are their actions; their images "oscillate." Both are motivated by the need for revenge, Tamora's by the death of her son, Lavinia's by the deaths of her brothers and husband. Tamora's bloodthirsty words are countered by the image of Lavinia holding the bowl in her mouth under Chiron's and Demetrius's slit necks. If Tamora marries Saturninus too easily given her preference for Aaron, similarly Lavinia will marry either brother as her father or brothers dictate.

While productions of the play usually indicate through gesture an affection between Lavinia and Bassianus and there are textual references to a prior betrothal her father may not be aware of, nothing she says reveals more than loyal obedience to her father and husband, much like Tamora's vigilant protection of Saturninus's rule even though she seems unimpressed by her new role. Tamora's affair with Aaron, her absence of chastity, is balanced by Lavinia's rape, defined as "lust," even a version of Petrarchan love (cf. 2.1.), by her attackers. Both women suffer devaluation, what Aaron terms a "trimming" (5.1.94), as a result of the play's action from this point of view, and Titus kills them both, enclosing them as participants, as actors, in the humanist revenge script he reads, writes, and enacts, because they inspire "a pattern, president, and lively warrant / For [Titus], most wretched, to perform the like" (5.3. 44–45).

But the women are not perceived as "like." Tamora is perceived as the "beast," the monster mother, because of her adultery with Aaron and her attacks on the Andronici. Tamora speaks, incorporating into herself all of the stereotypes concerning unruly women as a result. Much has been written by Shakespeare's contemporaries and twentieth-century critics concerning these stereotypes.[20] Perhaps, in this case, the most pertinent texts for the woman who would speak or write come from humanist writers, from the conduct book writer Richard Brathwait, who said, "Silence in a Woman is a mouing Rhetorike, winning most, when in words it wooeth least" (90), and the educator and humanist Juan Luis Vives, who said, in *The Instruction of a Christian Woman*, "But I give no license to a woman to be a teacher, nor to have authority of the man but to be in silence" (1585 ed. 30; qtd. in Kaufman 893). Discussing this commonly held view that "rhetoric is one thing that women should not be taught," Parker locates writing and speech specifically in attitudes toward the gender of the public and private bodies which spoke and wrote:

> It was the public nature of rhetoric—taking women outside their proper "province" or place—which disqualified them, in a long tradition dating from as ancient an authority as Aristotle's strictures that women were to be not only silent but identified with the property of the home and with the private sphere, with a private rather than a common place. (At least one Renaissance poet also linked this private place, in the *Politics*, with the Aristotelian distinction, in the *Rhetoric*, between *koinoi topoi* or "common places" and *idio topoi* or "private places," and their sexual counterparts.) (104)

A woman who spoke displayed her voice, Parker argues, and was by definition a "public woman" and a "whore" (104)—a woman, I would add, like Tamora, who not only would rule her sons and husband, but literally travels to Rome and then freely moves about the "public" areas of the play and whose body is finally cast out.

Lavinia, who begins the play potentially unruly in her speech and her humanist education, her writing, her teaching, is rendered a macabre and reified image of the chaste, silent, and obedient wife and daughter after her mutilation—or because of it—and is from her rape enclosed in her father's house. From the play's beginning, and iconically, from the moment of her mutilation, Lavinia's written words are not the signs of the text to be read. Her mutilated body is her "alphabet," the sign of her meanings, her consciousness. Her missing hands and tongue signify the loss of her chastity, where the attack on her father has occurred, her dismembered body resembling Rome's politicized images of itself. Lavinia's mutilated body duplicates and genders, in this sense, the fragmented political system at work in the play and its attitudes toward writing, its attitudes toward humanism, demonstrating what Francis Barker describes as "a materiality that is fully and unashamedly involved in the processes of domination and resistance which are the inner substance of social life" (25). But these "inner" workings are mapped on the exterior of Lavinia's body, in a literal paradox, on her "trimmed" and missing limbs. From Stallybrass's and Barker's perspectives, Lavinia is turned inside out. The invisible "inner" sign of social value, her chastity, is written on her missing extremities, and, as the ideal aristocratic woman, her "private" place is "publicly" revealed to all who view her.[21]

She is revenged. Titus enacts the consequences of a "public" and alienated patriarchal subjectivity by reading Lavinia and killing her, Tamora, and Tamora's children. But humanist discourse makes for differences. Tamora, in spite of her staged reproductive capabilities, is rendered "hollow," monstrous, one of her kind in a world which "swallows her own increase" (5.2.191) like her spoken words, the excess in a political world inscribed finally as a dismembered and dismembering female. Conversely, Lavinia, by definition of Tamora's kind but self-inscribed and inscribing, becomes a visible woman of letters and a product of that extremity, capable of reproducing a humanist world in and on her body. Her missing tongue and limbs confirm her as an object of value and desire, signifying how her world violently possesses and exchanges women through a dislocation of words and hands. As the frontispiece to Martin Billingley's *The Pens Excellencie or The Secretaries Delight* (1618) declares:

Lingua, Penna: Mentis Muta
1. The pen is the mute tongue of the mind.
2. The tongue is the mute pen of the mind.
3. The mute pen is the tongue of the mind.
4. The mute tongue is the pen of the mind.
5. The tongue of the mind is a mute pen.
6. The pen of the mind is a mute tongue. (As qtd. in Goldberg, *Matter* 276)

Lavinia is the visible sign of a humanist ideology which would displace the location of the subject and inscribe invisible—but "public"—social and political distinctions on women's bodies: she is the image of the educated aristocratic woman.

NOTES

My title for this essay was inspired by Carolyn Kizer's poem "Pro Femina, Three," which begins "I will speak about women of letters . . . " (1973).

1. What is designated "private" and "public" has been the focus of much critical attention, especially in relation to the iconic condition of primarily aristocratic women's bodies on the stage. See especially Stallybrass and Barker. Other critics have focused on the iconic value of such displays and politicized them, in effect politicizing what we would term "private" or personal; see Bergeron, Goldberg's work on James, Montrose, and Tennenhouse. This intersection of the "private" with the political is one both Elizabeth and James were cognizant of; both referred to themselves as "set on stages" (as qtd. in Heisch; also *Basilikon Doron* 163, as quoted in Bergeron 43). Stage metaphors are pervasive in this period, but these critiques concerning the display of

the "private" female aristocratic body have influenced my reading of Lavinia. She is transformed into a "private" icon or text, read by her family as the motivation for revenge.

Other critics have particularized how royal icons were read in regard to shifting historical moments as the monarchs changed; see Berry, King, Levin, and Patterson. *Titus*, most likely written by 1594, reformulates an aristocratic Elizabethan political iconography for the stage. See Tennenhouse especially, who argues that Lavinia's body functions as "synecdoche and the emblem of the disorder of things" (107). If the rivalry between Rome's warring factions is mapped on her dismembered body, that rivalry is also gendered and imagined as a war of regeneration between matriarchal and patriarchal would-be rulers, between Tamora's and Titus's families. The play thus replicates what Lena Cowen Orlin has described as the social instability of patriarchal attitudes in the 1590s. Arguing that "domestic patriarchalism . . . preceded political patriarchalism," which, because of Elizabeth's position on the throne, would achieve fuller expressions during the Stuarts' reigns, Orlin demonstrates how "as a domestic philosophy, patriarchalism was subverted in one key aspect. The patriarchal locus of power was necessarily defined with reference to those who were obliged to relinquish power, as it was the presence in the patriarchal schema of the woman—in her dual role as wife and mother—that was a radically destabilizing factor" (29). While Orlin's comments would seem to apply most aptly to Tamora's actions in the play, it is Lavinia's mutilated body which literally externalizes and visualizes this debate.

2. Crane discusses at length these tensions in relation to Cecil, Lord Burghley's control of the Court of Wards, noting that "young aristocrats like Essex and Oxford resisted his attempts to educate them into submission, while members of the upwardly mobile gentry and middle class (Sir Philip Sidney, Edmund Spenser) were frustrated by Burghley's attempts to arrogate to aristocrats the traditional humanist credentials for upward mobility. How, under Burghley, was fitness for preferment to be displayed?" (128). See also Carole Levin's discussion of Essex's wooing of Elizabeth during the 1590s and his subsequent rebellion as a sustained bid for economic preferment (149ff.).

3. Thomas Docherty suggests that this juxtaposition, "broadly, the authority of writing and that of the voice, typographical literacy versus vocal orality, as it were," "is central to an age in which, after Gutenberg, writing itself has become more of a social issue, related to questions of power" (7). Docherty's work traces the historical emergence of the self-conscious author, what I will argue Titus himself becomes. Many critics of the play subsume speech and writing under a general category of oratory, rhetoric, or words, in juxtaposition to the body: S. Clark Hulse, for example, emphasizes that "as Titus learns to 'wrest the alphabet' of his mangled daughter, he learns a new action that supplants the old Roman oratory, because it alone can simultaneously probe the inner wounds of the spirit and inflict outer wounds on his enemies" (108). R. Stamm argues that the play is a study in logocentrism and translates what is seen into what is said, a point repeated by D. J. Palmer and Jane S. Carducci in their studies of the relationship between language and gesture in the play. Mary Laughlin Fawcett also emphasizes how the play works to "literalize [words] by writing them out on the stage" (263), with the

result that the Andronici "become words" and "reduce their enemies to bodies" (272). Jane Hicks argues that the play depicts a rhetorical war between Titus and Tamora, and that once Titus substitutes "written discourse for oral, it is a small step to a metonymy of action that discloses all" (71). The metonymy of action Hicks describes is the violent disintegration of metaphors, of language itself, "as words disengage from casual usage and become literalized" (299) for Gillian Murray Kendall.

4. Crane documents the humanist belief that its training reproduces itself in the values held by its practitioners and their students, becoming the means for a humanist self-fashioning; Jed sexualizes that account.

5. According to the *OED*, "decipher" meant "to convert into ordinary *writing*" (emphasis mine).

6. Much has been written concerning the overt textual allusions to Ovid's *Metamorphosis* in the play, most notably by Eugene M. Waith and Barbara Mowat. Douglas E. Green discusses both the critics and these allusions in depth, but argues that "it is largely through and on the female characters that Titus is constructed and his tragedy inscribed" (319). In his discussion of the impact of writing in early modern Europe and the construction of the authorial self, Docherty suggests that "what is written can be considered as some kind of 'pre-text' of its performance" (12), an idea with obvious application to what I have been discussing. Docherty himself argues that Lavinia in this scene is "entirely dependent on anterior authority in the form of Ovid, through which she manages to reveal the tale of her rape" (126).

7. The events in act 1, especially the election of Saturninus by voice vote or acclamation, emphasize this state of affairs. Historians of early modern England have long debated the importance of "kin" or kinship in its social organization. David Cressy discusses this debate and concludes that "the English kinship system was egocentric and bilateral, contextual and informal. Although a patrilineal lineage bias affected the transmission of property, in other regards the system was fluid and flexible" ("Kinship" 67).

8. Cornelia was "the mother of the Gracchi, Roman political reformers, whose education she had carefully supervised," according to a textual note in the Riverside edition (n.12;1038).

9. Green argues that "the live burial of the still-railing Aaron and the casting forth of Tamora's body signify what this patriarchy cannot digest. The unassailable elements—racial as well as sexual otherness, and all that issues from such difference—crystallize in the sign of other life: at the end, whether dead or alive, whether an absence or a silent presence, the child of Aaron and Tamora, the infant for whom the Moor gave himelf up, cannot be contained by Lucius' new order or by Shakespeare's play" (326). In contrast, Palmer thinks that "swallowing" as epitomized by the murderous pit, Lavinia's mouth, and Aaron's burial is "a nauseous and abhorrent act" (332). In terms of my argument to follow concerning the reification of writing, perhaps Aaron's head is left above ground in this last scene to signify that he is both a writer and the unassimilated other, a Moor or Turk.

10. David Cressy's work on literacy in the period informs Goldberg's argument and my own. Cressy has studied the numbers of English who could sign their names on public documents, assuming that the ability to sign corresponds with the ability to read. While people could read without writing, Cressy argues in some convincing ways that writing one's name assumes an ability to both read and write.

11. Goldberg extends his discussion of writing in *Hamlet* to argue the political dimensions of writing and pedagogy in *Writing Matter*, in which he makes explicit how the act of writing conveys not only subjectivity but social class. "Letters," he argues, "are inscribed within nature, *and they inscribe nature, the human, and the social/ideological within their domain*" (*Matter* 225).

12. Gordon Braden describes the seemingly paradoxical collapse of revenge with humanism in the depiction of the Senecan revenger.

13. Crane suggests that the humanist "educational program in turn gave rise to a version of authorship that was collective instead of individualistic, published instead of private, *inscriptive instead of voice-centered*, and aphoristic or epigrammatic instead of lyric or narrative" (4; emphasis mine). Her argument does not conflict with Goldberg's as much as this quote would imply; both emphasize a fractured or "dismembered" humanist subjectivity.

14. Parker adds here that "it may be for this reason that rhetoric and language were so much the locus of anxieties about the problem of control, including the link between the ordered 'chain' of discourse and the disposition of a potentially wayward or unruly female *materia*" (118–19).

15. See, in particular, Marion Wynne-Davies's discussion of the rape theme and Tamora's dramatic treatment: "The pit in *Titus* functions as both a womb and a consuming mouth. As the play attempts to repress female sexuality through rape, so it denies female speech when Lavinia has her tongue cut out. Tamora's unheeded plea for her sons is likewise a reminder of women's muted state. Yet it is through the 'consumption' of a pen that Lavinia regains the power of communication, and at the end of the play, Tamora will literally eat her sons" (136).

16. David Cressy estimates that the illiteracy rate for women in England in the 1590s was well over 90 percent (145). While his methodology has been criticized, Cressy's figures still demonstrate how rapidly this situation changes in the seventeenth century. For examples of later women writers, see Margaret George.

17. Kendall comments that Lavinia's "literal lack of hands becomes equated with an ability to write, sew, or in any way create her story" (303).

18. Mary Laughlin Fawcett suggests that "contained in this scrowl-emblem of the father's hand as tongue in the daughter's mouth are ideas about the patriarchal nature of language (her tongue *is* her father), about the equivalence between speaking (tongue) and doing (hand), and about writing (what the hand does) as a substitute for speaking (what the tongue does). . . . The mother-tongue for this speaker is a father-

hand inserted incestuously between the teeth of a ruined mouth, a vagina dentata" (261–62). Her arguments concerning Lavinia's role anticipate my own in many ways.

19. It is coincidence that Goldberg here seems to imagine *Titus*. He is discussing how the acts of writing and speaking are naturalized through pedagogy in the chapter in *Matter* titled "The Violence of the Letter."

20. Recent studies on the unruly woman have been done by Jean E. Howard, Karen Newman, Mary Beth Rose, and David Underdown. Their studies focus on the disruptive potential of the unruly woman and how "such behavior is a form of simulation, a confusion that elides the conventional poles of sexual difference by denaturalizing gender-coded behaviors; such simulations pervert authorized systems of gender and power" (Newman 33).

21. To some extent repeating Laqueur's hypothesis in *Making Sex*, Emily Martin notes that during this period, "what could be seen on men's bodies was assumed as the pattern for what could not be seen of women's" (30); more to my point, she compares historical attitudes of women and the medical authorities toward women's reproductive lives, ending in the present, where, she says, "but [the metaphor of] dismemberment is with us still, and the 'hold on the body' has not so much slackened as it has moved from law to science" (21). Elaine Scarry's work on the psychodynamics of torture is illuminating on this point. She argues that the infliction of pain is an attempt by the torturer to project, or inscribe, self-perceptions on the other, seemingly inert, body of the tortured. In the process of torturing, the body is "substantiated," becomes as the torturer would perceive it, because it expresses pain. Pain validates perceptions as the victim's body is "read" and seems to acquire "the sturdiness and vibrancy of presence" (280). From this perspective, Lavinia acquires "presence," what Scarry terms evidence of sentience, when she is mutilated and because her family and the audience see her hurt. Her body in pain inscribes her.

WORKS CITED

Barker, Francis. *The Tremulous Private Body: Essays on Subjection.* London: Methuen, 1984.

Bergeron, David. *Shakespeare's Romances and the Royal Family.* Lawrence: Kansas UP, 1985.

Berry, Philippa. *Of Chastity and Power: Elizabethan Literature and the Unmarried Queen.* London: Routledge, 1989.

Braden, Gordon. *Renaissance Tragedy and the Senecan Tradition: Anger's Privilege.* New Haven: Yale UP, 1985.

Brathwait, Richard. *The English Gentlewoman, drawne out to the full Body: Expressing,*

What Habillments doe best attire her, What Ornaments doe best adorne her, What Compliments do best accomplish her. London, 1631.

Carducci, Jane S. "Shakespeare's *Titus Andronicus:* An Experiment in Expression." *Cahiers Elisabethains* 31 (1987): 1–9.

Crane, Mary Thomas. *Framing Authority: Sayings, Self, and Society in Sixteenth Century England.* Princeton: Princeton UP, 1993.

Cressy, David. "Kinship and Kin Interaction in Early Modern England." *Past & Present* 113 (1986): 38–69.

———. *Literacy and the Social Order: Reading and Writing in Tudor and Stuart England.* Cambridge: Cambridge UP, 1980.

Docherty, Thomas. *On Modern Authority: The Theory and Condition of Writing, 1500 to the Present.* Sussex: Harvester P; New York: St. Martin's, 1987.

Eisenstein, Elizabeth. *The Emergence of Print Culture in the West.* New York: Cambridge UP, 1983.

Fawcett, Mary Laughlin. "Arms/Words/Tears: Language and the Body in *Titus Andronicus.*" *ELH* 50 (1983): 261–77.

George, Margaret. *Women in the First Capitalist Society: Experiences in Seventeenth-Century England.* Urbana: U of Illinois P, 1988.

Goldberg, Jonathan. "Hamlet's Hand." *Shakespeare Quarterly* 39 (1988): 307–27.

———. *James I and the Politics of Literature: Jonson, Shakespeare, Donne and Their Contemporaries.* Baltimore: Johns Hopkins UP, 1983.

———. *Writing Matter: From the Hands of the English Renaissance.* Stanford: Stanford UP, 1990.

Green, Douglas E. "Interpreting 'her martyr'd signs': Gender and Tragedy in *Titus Andronicus.*" *Shakespeare Quarterly* 40 (1989): 317–26.

Heisch, Allison. "Queen Elizabeth I: Parliamentary Rhetoric and the Exercise of Power." *Signs* 1 (1975): 31–55.

Hicks, Jane. "A Margin for Error: Rhetorical Context in *Titus Andronicus.*" *Style* 21 (1987): 62–75.

Howard, Jean E. "Crossdressing, the Theatre, and Gender Struggle in Early Modern England." *Shakespeare Quarterly* 39 (1988): 418–40.

Hulse, S. Clark. "Wresting the Alphabet: Oratory and Action in *Titus Andronicus.*" *Criticism* 21 (1979): 106–18.

Jardine, Lisa. "Cultural Confusion and Shakespeare's Learned Heroines: 'These are old paradoxes.' " *Shakespeare Quarterly* 38 (1987): 1–18.

Jed, Stephanie. *Chaste Thinking: The Rape of Lucrece and the Birth of Humanism.* Bloomington: Indiana UP, 1989.

Kaufman, Gloria. "Juan Luis Vives on the Education of Women." *Signs* 3 (1978): 891–96.

Kendall, Gillian Murray. " 'Lend me thy hand': Metaphor and Mayhem in *Titus Andronicus.*" *Shakespeare Quarterly* 40 (1989): 299–326.

King, John, N. "Queen Elizabeth I: Representations of the Virgin Queen." *Renaissance Quarterly* 43 (1990): 30–74.

Kizer, Carolyn. "Pro Femina." *Norton Anthology of Literature by Women.* Ed. Sandra M. Gilbert and Susan Gubar. New York: Norton, 1985. 1973–75.

Levin, Carole. *The Heart and Stomach of a King: Elizabeth I and the Politics of Sex and Power.* Philadephia: U of Pennsylvania P, 1994.

Martin, Emily. *The Woman in the Body: A Cultural Analysis of Reproduction.* Boston: Beacon P, 1987.

Montrose, Louis A. "*A Midsummer Night's Dream* and the Shaping Fantasies of Elizabethan Culture: Gender, Power, Form." *Rewriting the Renaissance: The Discourses of Sexual Difference in Early Modern Europe.* Ed. Margaret W. Ferguson, Maureen Quilligan, and Nancy J. Vickers. Chicago: U of Chicago P, 1986. 65–87.

Mowat, Barbara. "Lavinia's Message: Shakespeare and Myth." *Renaissance Papers* (1981). Ed. A. Leigh Deneef and M. Thomas Hester. Southern Renaissance Conference. 55–69.

Newman, Karen. "Portia's Ring: Unruly Women and Structures of Exchange in *The Merchant of Venice.*" *Shakespeare Quarterly* 38 (1987): 19–33.

Orlin, Lena Cowen. "Familial Transgressions, Societal Transition on the Elizabethan Stage." *Sexuality and Politics in Renaissance Drama.* Ed. Carole Levin and Karen Robertson. Lewiston: Edwin Mellen P, 1991. 27–55.

Palmer, D. J. "The Unspeakable in Pursuit of the Uneatable: Language and Action in *Titus Andronicus.*" *Critical Quarterly* 14 (1972): 320–29.

Parker, Patricia. *Literary Fat Ladies: Rhetoric, Gender, Property.* London: Methuen, 1987.

Patterson, Annabel. *Censorship and Interpretation: The Conditions of Reading and Writing in Early Modern England.* Madison: U of Wisconsin P, 1984.

Puttenham, George. *The Arte of English Poesie.* Ed. Gladys Doidge Willcock and Alice Walker. Cambridge: Cambridge UP, 1936; rpt. 1970.

Rose, Mary Beth. "Women in Men's Clothing: Apparel and Social Stability in *The Roaring Girl.*" *Renaissance Historicism.* Ed. Arthur F. Kinney and Dan S. Collins. Amherst: U of Massachusetts P, 1987. 223–47.

Scarry, Elaine. *The Body in Pain: The Making and Unmaking of the World.* New York: Oxford UP, 1985.

Shakespeare, William. *Titus Andronicus. The Riverside Shakespeare.* Ed. G. Blakemore Evans. Boston: Houghton Mifflin, 1974.

Stallybrass, Peter. "Patriarchal Territories: The Body Enclosed." *Rewriting the Renaissance: The Discourses of Sexual Difference in Early Modern Europe.* Ed. Margaret Ferguson, Maureen Quilligan, and Nancy J. Vickers. Chicago: U of Chicago P, 1986. 123–42.

Stamm, R. "The Alphabet of Speechless Complaint: A Study of the Mangled Daughter in *Titus Andronicus.*" *English Studies* 55 (1974): 325–39.

Tennenhouse, Leonard. *Power on Display: The Politics of Shakespeare's Genres.* New York: Methuen, 1896.

Underdown, David. "The Taming of the Scold: The Enforcement of Patriarchal Authority in Early Modern England." *Order and Disorder in Early Modern England.* Ed. Anthony Fletcher and John Stevenson. Cambridge: Cambridge UP, 1985. 116–36.

Waith, Eugene M. "The Metamorphosis of Violence in *Titus Andronicus.*" *Shakespeare Studies* 10 (1957): 39–49.

Wynne-Davies, Marion. " 'The Swallowing Womb': Consumed and Consuming Women in *Titus Andronicus.*" *The Matter of Difference: Materialist Feminist Criticism of Shakespeare.* London: Harvester, 1991. 129–52.

3

"DOCUMENTS IN MADNESS"

Reading Madness and Gender in Shakespeare's Tragedies
and Early Modern Culture

CAROL THOMAS NEELY

IT HAS LONG been recognized that England in the period from 1580 to 1640 was fascinated with madness, although some aspects of this obsession have been overestimated or misreported. The signs of its fascination are to be found in the numerous treatises on the topic by Battie, Bright, Jorden, Wright, and Burton; in the many theatrical representations of madness in the plays of Kyd, Shakespeare, Dekker, Middleton, Fletcher, and Webster; in the large numbers of patients who consulted such well-known doctors as Richard Napier and John Hall (Shakespeare's son-in-law) with symptoms of mental distress; and in the numerous references to and representations of Bethlem, or Bedlam, the popular name for Bethlehem Hospital, the only institution in England in this period which confined the insane. Bedlam, according to a 1598 visitation report made a couple of years before *Hamlet* and *King Lear* were written, contained only twenty inmates: nine men and eleven women. The thirty-one inmates listed in a 1624 report caused overcrowding in the institution, which was tiny, "loathesomely and filthily kept," and badly mismanaged. The term "Bedlam" was in widespread use not because of the impact of the institution itself (which had been in existence as a hospital since about 1330 and may have started accepting disturbed patients sometime before 1403, when a report notes the presence of six men, "*mente capta*") but because it was becoming a code word in Elizabethan and Jacobean culture for the contested topic of madness.[1]

I

In the early modern period, the discourse of madness gained prominence because it was implicated in the wider transformation of the notion of what it meant to be human and was deeply intertwined with its medical, legal, theological, political, and social facets. Gradually, madness, and hence sanity, began to be secularized, medicalized, psychologized, and gendered. In the Middle Ages, madness was seen as the point of intersection between the human, the divine, and the demonic. It was viewed variously as possession, sin, punishment, and disease, and it confirmed the inseparability of the human and transcendent (Neaman 45–55; Doob chap. 1; MacDonald, *Mystical* 3–4). By theorizing and representing madness, the Renaissance gradually and with difficulty began to try to separate human madness from the spiritual (from doubt, sin, guilt, rational suicide, as does Timothy Bright in his *Treatise of Melancholy*); from the supernatural (from demonic and divine possession, as does Edward Jorden's treatise on hysteria, *The Suffocation of the Mother*); from witchcraft and bewitchment (as does Reginald Scot's *Discoverie of Witchcraft*); from frauds who imitated these conditions (as does Samuel Harsnett's *Declaration of Egregious Popish Impostures*); and from the sheerly physical (epilepsy and menstrual disorders, as do Jorden and doctors such as Richard Napier and John Hall), and to map the normal, "natural," and self-contained secular human subject.

Splitting the supernatural from the natural and categorizing what remained, the period began to separate mind from body, man from woman, and mental disorder from health and from other types of aberrance such as poverty, heresy, and crime. As madness began to be re-thought and re-gendered, certain kinds of disorders, particularly those associated with women, began to be discredited.[2] The two best-known theoretical works on madness, Michel Foucault's *Madness and Civilization* and Elaine Showalter's *The Female Malady*, have created misunderstandings about this gradual process. Each author fails to historicize carefully enough, neglects to challenge conventional periodization, distinguishes insufficiently between different modalities of representation, and fails to gender madness. For Foucault there are only madmen; for Showalter only madwomen.[3] Extending their analyses, I will examine the linked aspects of this multifaceted gendering of madness as it unfolds in treatises on melancholy, hysteria, and witchcraft, in medical and legal practice, and in the drama.

In his 1586 *Treatise of Melancholy* Timothy Bright (a doctor and subsequently an Anglican priest) provides elaborate classifications of madness and recommendations for treatment which serve, by complex distinctions between the spiritual and the psycho-physiological, to subordinate the former. The treatise is written in the form of a sympathetic letter to a male friend, M, who is suffering from what we would call depression. Designed to cure M, it advises him on how to distinguish between spiritual doubt and the disease of natural melancholy. Spiritual doubt, caused by the sense of sin and the "incomprehensible and inexpressible loss of God's favor" (185), is to be cured by penitence, prayer, and faith. Spiritual consolation is the subject of the longest chapter of the forty-one in the treatise (chap. 36, misnumbered 30, 201–41). The rest of the treatise outlines an etiology of melancholy which explicates the elaborate interactions between the soul, mind, passions, and body. Natural depression is caused by the unnatural excess or combustion of natural melancholy, the cold dry humor or black bile which, when burnt, goes berserk and causes such symptoms as passivity, unsociability, fury, stupidity, paranoia, lust, anger, mania, but especially sorrow and fear. *Its* recommended treatment (remarkably familiar) is healthy diet, exercise, sleep, and good friends.

But the careful distinctions between spiritual and physiological melancholy repeatedly collapse in the treatise. Both states are characterized by the same symptoms—hallucinatory terror and unreasonable sadness. Natural melancholy predisposes one to spiritual doubt, while spiritual doubt exacerbates the pathology of the black bile. Both the medical therapy, based on diet and rest, and the spiritual cure, dependent on faith and grace, are designed to relieve the loss of self-worth which characterizes equally both forms of the disease. The effect is to merge the two kinds of melancholy and to subordinate the spiritual causes and cure to the psychological ones. The gender of M, the respectful scholarly tone of Bright's letter/treatise, and the identification of the disease with spiritual doubt all point to the associations of melancholy with the fashionable, the upper class, the literate, the masculine, associations which reach back to Aristotle and are confirmed in Robert Burton's *Anatomy of Melancholy* (1621).

Bright's treatise strives unsuccessfully to distinguish spiritual guilt from natural melancholy. Edward Jorden's landmark treatise, *Brief Discourse of a Disease Called the Suffocation of the Mother* (1603), is composed to distinguish bewitchment from insanity (and, indirectly, to legitimize licensed physicians). It is directed at his fellow members of the College of Physicians, who, as trained and experienced doctors, are, he claims, "best able to discerne what is naturall, what is not naturall, what praeternaturall and what supernaturall" (fol.C1ʳ), and who might therefore be called upon, as Jorden had been, to testify to the status of the victim's symptoms in witch trials. If these are diagnosed as natural in origin, the result of hysteria, the accused witch is acquitted, as more than half were (Thomas 451–52); if they are found to be supernatural, she (or infrequently, he) is convicted. The diagnosis is difficult and often contested because the symptoms of bewitchment and hysteria are identical. The illness was caused, traditional medicine believed, by the pathology of the diseased and wandering womb, and hence it was primarily although not exclusively a disease of women: "The passive condition of womankind is subject unto more diseases and of other sortes and natures then men are: and especially in regard of that part from whence this disease which we speake of doth arise" (fol. B1ʳ), Jorden declares. One internal cause of the disease, Jorden claims with some reticence, is retention of menstrual blood or *sperma* (which women were believed to have) due to sexual frustration or the suppression of the flowers, the menstrual periods. The origin of the fantastic and disconnected symptoms of the disease—swoon, paralysis, choking, convulsions, numbness, delirium, epilepsy, headaches—is the wild peregrinations of the uncontrollable uterus and its capacity to corrupt all the parts of the body.[4] One recommended cure is marriage, which institutes regular sexual relations and thus aids in evacuation of fluids and brings the wild uterus under a husband's control (fols. F4ʳ and G3ᵛ). In spite of the tendency of such an analysis to identify hysteria as a disease of women, Jorden does not explicitly draw this conclusion and refers without comment (as do other writers) to men who suffer from the mother (Fol. F4ᵛ–G1ʳ, H1ʳ).

This association of hysteria with women, especially women of the upper classes, persists in Robert Burton's compendious *Anatomy of Melancholy*. As the all-male frontispiece of the book suggests, Burton associates melancholy especially with male scholars, philosophers, and geniuses such as Democritus and himself, although its causes and symptoms are multitudinous and its sufferers are everywhere. But when he defines the "Symptomes of Maids', Nuns' and Widows' Melancholy" (I, 414), a section new to the third edition of the text, he associates this type with "fits of the mother" (I, 415). It is linked with marital, sexual, and class status, associated with sexual frustration, and cured by sexual satisfaction: "For seldom should you see an hired servant, a poor handmaid, though ancient, that is kept hard to her work and bodily labour, a coarse country wench troubled in this kind." Those who are "prone to the disease" are "noble virgins, nice gentlemen women, such as are solitary and idle, live at ease, lead a life out of action and employment, that fare well in great houses and jovial companies, ill-disposed peradventure of themselves, and not willing to make any resistance, discontented otherwise, of weak judgment, able bodies, and subject to passions" (I, 417).[5] Like Jorden, Burton recommends marriage as a "remedy" (I, 417).

Jorden's *Discourse* aims not only to forestall mistaken diagnoses of bewitchment but also to expose "impostures" (Epistle Dedicatorie, fol. A3) who only pretend to have the symptoms. Reginald Scot's ironically titled and cogently argued *Discoverie of Witchcraft* (1584) is written by this justice of the peace to deny the supernatural powers of witches themselves, attributing their behavior, including their voluntary confessions, to the effects of melancholy or hysteria. This diagnosis, of course, has the effect of medicalizing witches' behavior and producing a category of menopausal melancholics. Witchcraft had already been secularized when its disposition was consigned to civil courts by a 1542 statute. Samuel Harsnett (an ambitious chaplin to Bishop Bancroft) joined the established church's coordinated campaign against Catholic and puritan exorcists in his *Declaration of Egregious Popish Impostures* (1603), which attacks illegal Catholic exorcism rituals, exposing both possession and exorcism as instigated insanity—fraud.[6] Witchcraft prosecutions continue to take place in England until 1680, but these treatises and others function to medicalize the behavior of witches and the bewitched and to call the trials into question by attributing pathologized forms of melancholy to women. In these areas, madness is becoming a psychological alternative to conditions formerly defined as supernatural in origin and treatment.

On the new stages of the public theaters, Shakespeare, in *Hamlet, Macbeth,* and *King Lear,* shapes a new language for madness and provides one important site for its redefinition.[7] The plays, by representing both madness and the process of reading madness, theatricalize and disseminate the complicated distinctions that the treatises theorize. In the drama as in the culture outside it, madness is diagnosed by observers—both specialists and laypersons. Their readings enable the drama's audience to participate with them in distinguishing madness from sanity and from its lookalikes: loss of grace, bewitchment, possession, or fraud. Since madness, like its imitations, is illusory, extreme, dislocated, irrational, alienated—separated from both the self who performs and the spectators who watch—the diagnosis is difficult. In making it, Shakespeare's plays represent madness as a special sort of speech and construct it as secular, socially enacted, gender- and class-marked, and medically treatable.

II

Although the importance of madness in the period's drama, especially in that of Shakespeare, has long been acknowledged, and critics such as Babb, Reed, Lyons, and Feder have traced its occurrences, there have been few recent attempts to understand its rhetorical structure and dramatic function in Shakespeare's tragedies, or its wider cultural significance. Take, for example, responses to Ophelia and to Lear. A. C. Bradley in *Shakespearean Tragedy* sums up, at the beginning of the twentieth century, two centuries of views of and visual representations of Ophelia in madness as beautiful, sweet, lovable, pathetic, and dismissible (138–39). More recently, feminist critics, challenging this interpretation, have replicated the polarity in feminist analysis of the association between women and madness in the nineteenth and twentieth centuries, reading Ophelia's madness as either her liberation from silence, obedience, and constraint or her absolute victimization by patriarchal oppression.[8] In responses to *King Lear*, traditional critics such as Heilman (chap. 6) and Jorgensen (78–82) interpret Lear's madness as a means to illumination and self-knowledge. Significant contemporary analyses, in opposing the humanist optimism of these earlier interpretations, oddly pass over Lear's madness without notice. Stanley Cavell's influential monograph "The Avoidance of Love: A Reading of *King Lear*" bypasses the long period when Lear is, as he puts it, "stranded in madness" (77, 50, 74). Stephen Greenblatt's important new historicist essay, "Shakespeare and the Exorcists," reinterprets Edgar's feigned madness but ignores Lear's actual madness. Jonathan Dollimore, in *Radical Tragedy*, rather than seeing radical theatrical or social implications to Lear's madness, dismisses it as "demented mumbling" (193). None of these critics, representing various current theoretical approaches, reads madness closely in the plays. None asks, as I do here, how its linguistic construction, its gender coding, and its dramatic functions participate in cultural needs, practices, and attitudes.[9]

Shakespeare, prefiguring Foucault's analysis,[10] dramatizes madness primarily through a peculiar language more often than through physiological symptoms, stereotyped behaviors, or iconographic conventions. This characteristic speech is both something and nothing, both coherent and incoherent. Spectators, on stage and off, read this language, trying to make "sense" of it and translating it into the discourse of sanity. It is characterized by fragmentation, obsession, and repetition, and, most important, by what I will call "quotation," and which might be called, following Luce Irigary and Nancy K. Miller, "bracketing" or "italicization."[11] The mad are "beside themselves"; their discourse is not their own. But the voices which speak through them are not (even in the case of Edgar's parody of possession) supernatural voices but gendered human ones—cultural remnants. The prose that is used for this mad speech (although it includes embedded songs and rhymes) implies disorderly shape,[12] associates madness with popular tradition, and contributes to its colloquial, "quoted" character. These quoted voices, however, have connections with (or can be interpreted to connect with) the mad characters' pre-mad, gendered identity and history, their social context and psychological stresses—as well as with larger themes of the plays and of the culture. The alienated speech allows psychological plausibility, thematic resonance, cultural constructions, and social critique. Using it, Shakespeare represents distinctions between female hysteria and feigned male melancholy in *Hamlet,* between supernatural female witchcraft and natural alienation in *Macbeth,* and between feigned demonic possession, natural madness, and theological despair in *King Lear.*

Onstage characters mediate this pregnant, mad discourse, showing us how to translate it in ways made explicit by the anonymous Gentlemen in *Hamlet* who prepares the audience for the entrance of Ophelia, Shakespeare's first extended "document in madness":[13]

> She . . . speaks things in doubt
> That carry but half sense. Her speech is nothing
> But the unshaped use of it doth move
> The hearers to collection; they yawn at it,
> And botch the words up fit to their own thoughts,
> Which, as her winks and nods and gestures yield them,
> Indeed would make one think there might be thought,
> Though nothing sure, yet much unhappily.
>
> (4.5.6-13)

The speech here described is painful, unshaped un-sense that can be "botched" up into shape by an audience's readings. Ophelia's alienated discourse invites a psychological, thematic, and gendered interpretation. It resituates sacred material in a secular, psychological context, and she and Hamlet act out distinctions between feigned and actual madness and between rational and mad suicide which the culture was gradually establishing.

Ophelia's madness is represented almost entirely through fragmentary, communal, and thematically coherent quoted discourse. Through it, the rituals elsewhere involving the supernatural are appropriated and secularized. She recites formulas, tales, and songs which ritualize passages of transformation and loss—lost love, lost chastity, and death. These transitions are alluded to in social formulas of greeting and leavetaking: "Well, God dild you," "Good night, ladies, good night"; in religious formulas of grace and benediction: "God be at your table!" "God 'a' mercy on his soul! / And of all Christian souls I pray you" (4.5.42, 73, 44, 198–99); in allusions to folk legends or tales of daughters' metamorphic changes in status: tales of the "owl who was a baker's daughter" (4.5.42–43) and the master's daughter stolen by the steward.

Her songs likewise enact truncated rites of passage. Love and its loss are embodied in the song of the "truelove," imagined with a cockle hat, staff, and sandals, icons of his pilgrimage. She sings of Valentine's Day loss of virginity when a maid crosses a threshold both literal and psychological: "Then up he rose and donned his clothes / and dupped the chamber door, / Let in the maid, that out a maid / Never departed more . . . Young men will do't if they come to't / By Cock they are to blame" (4.5.52–55, 61–62). This imagined deflowering preempts and precludes a marriage ritual. The other songs mourn a death and represent the concrete markers of a spare funeral ritual—a flaxen poll, a bier, a stone, no flowers. They enable Ophelia to mourn her father's death, enact his funeral, encounter his dead body, and find consolation for her loss: "He is gone, he is gone. / And we cast away moan" (4.5.196–97). Into this central loss and its rituals, Ophelia's other losses or imagined losses—of lover, of virginity, of "fair judgement"—are absorbed. Her distribution of flowers to the court is an extension of her quoted discourse, an enacted ritual of dispersal, symbolizing lost love, deflowering, and death. A secularized cultural ritual of maturation and mourning is enacted through Ophelia's alienated speech.[14]

Ophelia's madness, as the play presents it, begins to be gender-specific in ways which later stage representations of Ophelia and of female hysterics will exaggerate (Showalter, *Female*). Her restlessness, agitation, shifts of direction, "winks and nods and gestures" (4.5.11) suggest the spasms of the mother and show that madness is exhibited by the body as well as in speech: gesture and speech, equally convulsive, blend together: "[she] beats her heart, / Spurns enviously at straws" (4.5.5–6). The context of her disease, like that of hysteria later, is sexual frustration, social helplessness, and enforced control over women's bodies. The content of her speech reflects this context. Laertes's anguished response to Ophelia as a "document in madness"—"Thought and affliction, passion, hell itself, / She turns to favor and to prettiness" (4.5.187–88)—shows how the reading of madness's self-representation aestheticizes the condition, mitigating both its social critique and its alien aspects. Likewise Gertrude narrates Ophelia's death as beautiful, natural, and eroticized, foreshadowing later representations of it and of female hysterics as sexually frustrated and theatrically alluring. Ophelia's representation implicitly introduces conventions for reading madness as gender-inflected.

Gender distinctions likewise take shape in the contrasts between Hamlet and Ophelia. Ophelia in her mad scenes serves as a double for Hamlet during his absence from Denmark and from the play.[15] His madness is in every way contrasted with hers, in part, probably, to emphasize the difference between feigned and actual madness. His discourse, although witty, savage, and characterized by non sequiturs and bizarre references, almost never has the "quoted," fragmentary, ritualized quality of Ophelia's—as we are instructed: "Nor what he spoke, though it lacked form a little, / Was not like madness" (3.1.164-65). Significantly, the one time it is "like madness," that is, like Ophelia's speech, is after the encounter with his father's ghost, when Hamlet must abruptly re-enter the human, secular world of his friends. The "wild and whirling words" (1.5.33) that he utters to effect this transition are quoted truisms and social formulas for parting which are incoherently deployed:

And so, without more circumstance at all,
I hold it fit that we shake hands and part:
You, as your business and desire shall point you,
For every man hath business and desire
Such as it is, and for my own poor part,
Look you, I'll go pray.

(1.5.127-32)

After this moment of dislocation, Hamlet announces a plan to feign madness, "put an antic disposition on," and is able to "go in together," with his friends, reuniting with the world of human fellowship and sanity, although he is himself marked by the remembrance of the Ghost's "commandment" (1.5.172, 186, 102).

The stylistic distinction between Hamlet's feigned madness and Ophelia's actual madness is emphasized by other distinctions. Henceforth in the play, Hamlet is presented as fashionably introspective and melancholy, while Ophelia becomes alienated, acting out the madness he only plays with. Whereas her madness is somatized, its content eroticized, his melancholy is politicized in form and content. It is caused by Claudius's usurpation of the throne and by his father's commandment; it manifests itself in social criticism, and it is viewed as politically dangerous. Ophelia must be watched, contained within the family, within the castle; Hamlet must be expelled to England to be murdered. By acting out the madness Hamlet feigns and the suicide that he theorizes, the representation of Ophelia absorbs pathological excesses which threaten Hamlet and enables his reappearance as an autonomous individual and a tragic hero in the last act. There he is detached from family and from sexuality; apparently freed from passivity and loss of control, he is capable of philosophical contemplation and revenge, proving himself worthy of a spiritual epitaph and a soldier's funeral. His restored identify is validated—symbolically as well as literally—over Ophelia's grave: "This is I, / Hamlet the Dane" (5.1.257–58).

This contrast between Ophelia's mad suicide and Hamlet's contemplated one represents in drama the complicated distinction the period was required to make between calculated suicide, a religious sin and a civil crime (*felo-de-se*), and insane self-destruction (*non compos mentis*). If the act was adjudged self-murder, the deceased's property was seized by the state and Christian burial was not encouraged. Madness, however, rendered suicide innocent and permitted conventional inheritance and burial. The secularization of suicide and that of madness reinforced each other.[16] The play enacts these distinctions without choosing sides. Whereas Hamlet's calm contemplation of suicide would render the act on his part a crime and a sin (as he recognizes with his reference to the "canon 'gainst self-slaughter"[1.2.132]), Ophelia's suicide is depicted by Gertrude as accidental ("an envious sliver broke" [4.7.173]), passive, involuntary, mad. In England in the period, drowning was the most common cause of suicide deaths of women and the cause of death which made distinctions between accident and volition most difficult (MacDonald, "Ophelia's" 311 and "Inner" 566–67). The play keeps various possibilities in suspension. Gertrude's representation of Ophelia's death neither condemns it on religious grounds nor explicitly condones it on medical/legal grounds. Instead she narrates it without interpretation, as a beautiful, "natural" ritual of passage and purification, the mad body's inevitable return to nature:

> Her clothes spread wide,
> And mermaidlike awhile they bore her up,
> Which time she chanted snatches of old lauds,
> As one incapable of her own distress,
> Or like a creature native and indued
> Unto that element
>
> $$(4.7.175-80)^{17}$$

Later the issue of Ophelia's death is reopened when the lower-class gravedigger and priest skeptically challenge the "crowner's" warrant and aristocratic prerogative which permit Ophelia's Christian burial.

In *Macbeth*, Lady Macbeth's suicide has none of the purifying and involuntary aspects of Ophelia's, and its meaning is not interrogated. But it occurs following a state of alienation represented through quoted discourse with similarities to Ophelia's. The alienation of Lady Macbeth in sleepwalking is, like

Ophelia's, psychologized, represented by means of quoted speech, read by representatives of the community, associated with symbolic purification, and culminates in suicide. Her breakdown embodied in sleepwalking is feminized and passive, in contrast with Macbeth's excessive, enraged, bloody ambition ("Some say he's mad" [5.2.13]). But the division between her powerful will in the early acts of the play and her alienated loss of it in the sleepwalking scenes, her connections with and dissociation from the witches, and their bifurcated representation all construct—and blur—other distinctions associated with madness: those between supernatural and natural agency, diabolic possession and human malevolence.

Lady Macbeth's sleepwalking, like Ophelia's madness, occurs after an absence from the stage, is presented as a sharp break with earlier appearances, and is introduced by an onstage onlooker. When sleepwalking, Lady Macbeth quotes, in the form of proverbial commonplaces ("Hell is murky" [5.1.38]) and chilling pseudo-nursery rhymes ("The Thane of Fife had a wife. Where is she now?" [5.1.44–45]), her own earlier words (or perhaps thoughts) and Macbeth's. She refers to Duncan's murder, Banquo's ghost, and the death of Lady Macduff, all in the mode of advice and comfort to Macbeth ("No more o' that, my lord, no more o' that" [5.1.46]). She narrates Macbeth's bloody acts, talks directly to him although he is not present, and acts out her own complicity by "washing" her hands to remove the smell and sight of the blood which taints them. This "quotation" has the effect of distancing this alienated discourse from its speaker and inviting a reading. But it is less communal and thematic, more personal and psychological than Ophelia's. The doctor explicitly reads Lady Macbeth's state as religious despair, not as demonic possession or physical breakdown—in Bright's terms, as spiritual rather than natural melancholy: "More needs she the divine than the physician" (5.1.77).

The witches and Lady Macbeth, as Peter Stallybrass has argued (189–209), are indirectly identified with each other by their gender, by the structure and symbolism of the play, and by their parallel role as catalysts to Macbeth's actions. They function as cultural scapegoats for the unnaturalness, disorder, and violence let loose. But the play also implies contrasts between Lady Macbeth and the witches, and these produce disjunctions between the natural and the supernatural. The witches' supernatural ambiguity is contrasted with the "natural" ambiguity of Lady Macbeth's sleepwalking scene. In their early appearances, they are described as ambiguously male or female, as on the earth but not of it; they speak equivocally (but not madly). Lady Macbeth, when sleepwalking, is in a state which combines "the benefit of sleep" with "the effects of watching" (5.1.11); "Her eyes are open," "but their sense is shut" (5.1.26–27). The witches are dramatized in connection with some of the conventional accouterments of witchcraft belief: familiars, submission to Hecate, spells, potions, fortunetelling, and successful conjuring. But Lady Macbeth's attempted (and unsuccessful) invocation is to spirits that seem more natural than supernatural: they "tend on mortal thoughts" and "wait on nature's mischief" (1.5.41, 50). She does not ask directly for help to harm others as witches typically do, but only for a perversion of her own emotions and bodily functions: "fill me . . . top-full of direst cruelty"; "Make thick my blood" (1.5.42–43). In contrast, the witches plot to cause the kinds of harm to others conventionally associated with witches' maleficium: interference with livestock, weather, male sexuality.

The witches are then ambiguously associated with and dissociated from Lady Macbeth.[18] Their own representation is likewise bifurcated. They are ambiguously "natural" and supernatural. They are represented partly as the disgruntled outcasts of Scot's *Discoverie*, partly as the agents of harmful activities such as those charged in English witch trials, and partly as devil-possessed like the witches described by continental witchmongers in the *Malleus Maleficarum*. In the opening scenes, they seem to invite Scot's psychological interpretation (statistically supported by Alan Macfarlane's social, structural analysis); they are frustrated, melancholic women who, on the margins of society, get back at those who have disregarded them by muttering curses and plotting revenges—"I'll do and I'll do and I'll do" (1.3.10)—and hence attract blame and punishment. However, they do have familiars and seem capable of preternatural travels, so are not represented merely as social misfits. In their later appearances (3.5 and 4.1), the witches are endowed with all the paraphernalia of demonic possession from continental witchlore. They serve Hecate (in what may be a later addition), use illusion to influence Macbeth, mix a "charm" made from the noxious parts of animals (and humans).[19] Macbeth "conjures" them by their "profess[ed]" supernatural powers (4.1.50–61). The effect of these representations of an alienated Lady Macbeth and divided witches, ambiguously connected with each other, is to create a continuum of alienation and malevolence in the play which blurs the boundaries between natural and supernatural agency, between witchcraft of English or continental sorts, between antisocial behavior and madness. This continuum has made it tempting to put to the play the questions the period (through witchcraft prosecutions and through reading madness) was wrestling with—who is to blame for Duncan's murder, Macbeth's fall, Scotland's decline? Who or what is the source of harm and evil? The questions produce no simple answers. The continuum of malevolence blurs the question of agency in the play as it blurs the question of the ontological status of "witches." It reproduces the period's "hovering" between contradictory belief systems and conflicting attributions of causality and agency: God and the devil, madwomen and witches, castrating wives and ambitious tyrants.

III

To understand the complicated responses and flexible practices which such uncertainty created and to place Shakespeare's tragedies within his contemporaries' attempts to categorize madness, it is helpful to look briefly at the medical practice of Richard Napier and at the 1598 and 1624 Bedlam censuses. Napier was a doctor, minister, and astrologer who from 1597 to 1634 treated about sixty thousand patients in Great Linford in northern Buckinghamshire, taking notes on each consultation. Two thousand and thirty-four of these patients from all social classes consulted him for mental disorders, and these cases are analyzed in the epidemiology of mental disorder constructed by Michael MacDonald in *Mystical Bedlam: Madness, Anxiety, and Healing in Seventeenth Century England.* Thanks to MacDonald's superb, detailed, and gendered analysis, Napier's practice becomes a site where definitions, distinctions, and gender coding in mental ailments can be explored. Like theorists and playgoers, Napier strove to distinguish between the similar symptoms caused by possession, bewitchment, mental or physical disorders; he worked hard to do so but was often at a loss.[20] His cures, designed to fit the disorder, were eclectically magical, medical, astrological, and spiritual; to some patients he gave advice, to most purges, to a few amulets or prayers or exorcisms.

Women consulted Napier for all causes more often than did men (a ratio of 78 men to 100 women, similar to the ratio of visits to physicians today); they consulted him more for mental disorders than men (the sex ratio is 58.2 men to 100 women, similar to that in England today) and reported suffering almost twice as much stress as men (the ratio is 52.3 men to 100 women; MacDonald, *Mystical* 35–39). Most of Napier's female and male patients alike suffered mental distress and depression from the same causes: courtships (23.6%), marital problems (17.6%), bereavements (17.5%), and debt (12.9%) (ibid. 75). The reasons why women are overrepresented in Napier's practice, especially in consultations for mental distress, are as complex and difficult to analyze as why women visit doctors more than men do today and report more depression. Then as now it may be connected with their vulnerability to diseases of the reproductive system, to their need therefore to see doctors more, or to the extra stress that family life in patriarchy places on women.[21]

However, although more women come to Napier with symptoms of mental distress, there is not much difference in the percentages or even the numbers of men and women identified as suffering extreme forms of mental disturbance—madness. Likewise, recent findings by medical historians and sociologists show that while today women see doctors more for depression, insomnia, and other imprecisely identified disorders, they do not suffer from extreme pathological states such as schizophrenia more often than do men and, contrary to earlier claims, are not more likely than men to be institutionalized for mental disorders.[22] MacDonald's raw statistics show a similar pattern. Patients who report extreme symptoms—symptoms associated with mania as opposed to melancholy and designated by terms such as "mad," "lunatic," "mania," "frenzy," "raging," "furious," "frantic"—are rare. There are more cases for women in almost every category (because there are so many more women in the sample), but the percentages are virtually identical and the absolute numbers not that different. For example, of the 2,039 patients, 34 of the men (or 5%) and 54 of the women (or 4%) are designated "mad"; 25 of the men (3%) and 21 of the women (2%) as lunatic. There is 1 man with mania and 7 men and 3 women with frenzy. Men are more likely to be designated melancholy or "mopish," a milder form of melancholy in accord with the early modern period's male coding of this disease—which will be re-gendered female in the nineteenth and twentieth centuries. Women more often "take grief," "grieve," and are "troubled in mind"; men and women are tempted to and attempt suicide in about equal rates, but women are more often tempted to kill their children or, uniquely, their children or themselves.[23] Napier never identifies the fits of the mother as mental disturbance, but connects it with strictly physical symptoms such as menstrual cramps. And "sexual urges" are a symptom of only 1 (male) patient (244).

In Napier's report of his practice, while women suffer more mental disturbance than men, the identification of women or men with certain sorts of madness is much less apparent than in the drama. What stands out is Napier's attempts to categorize madness, to distinguish it from supernatural visitations and from physical maladies. Another set of documents of the period also shows movement toward division by gender, but here too the reading must be cautious. These are the 1598 and 1624 censuses of Bedlam, included in visitation committee reports to Bridewell Hospital, which administered the facility (reproduced in Allderidge, "Management" 152–53, 158–60). The reports give the names of the inhabitants and some of the following data: source of admission (from Bridewell, the Lord Mayor of London, or private parties); length of stay (from Neme Baker, 25 years in 1598, to Tho. Denham, 14 days in 1624); source of maintenance (guilds, individuals, parishes, colleges, other hospitals); indications of social class and context (in the 1598 census, when such information was more frequently noted, inhabitants included "Welch Elizabeth"; "Rosse, an Almswomen"; "Edmond Browne, one of the Queenes Chappel"; and "Anthoney Greene, fellow of Penbrooke Hall in Cambridge"). Both reports usually list patients with the longest tenure before those with less, but the first census is divided between Bridewell admissions and others, and the second is divided up into men (18) and women (13), and comments are made on the seriousness of the condition (probably because the place was overcrowded and the committee wished to lower the census). The designations for the men speak to their administrative status; they are termed "fitt to bee kepte," "not fitt to bee kepte," or "to bee sent to . . . some other hospital," "home to his wife," "to Hull from whence he came." Only two of the men who are "Idiots" have their illness specified, and none are called "mad," but many of the women are; they are explicitly characterized as "very ill," "madd," "very madd," "a mad woman," "something idle-headed," "fell madd." Eight of the 18 men are designated fit to be kept, and 9 are to be sent elsewhere; 7 of the 13 women are to be kept, and 4 are to be removed to other care (the dispositions of 1 man and 1 woman are not specified).[24] These unconsciously chosen designations suggest a tendency to identify the women with their illness and the men, instead, with their institutional disposition.

IV

While the stage does not associate madness exclusively with men or women, its representations begin to gender the signs of the condition and its cures. In *King Lear*, as in the records of Richard Napier and of Bethlehem Hospital, madness and distress are conceived of as treatable illnesses with mental and physical components. By underlining the distinction between Lear's natural madness and Edgar's feigned supernatural possession and by including two cures—one physical, administered by a doctor, and one mental, administered by a layperson—the play contributes to the secularization, psychologizing, and medicalization of madness and extends conventions for representing it. The context and speech of the disordered characters in *King Lear* further reveal how different symptoms, diagnoses, and cures of madness become associated with men and women.

Edgar, victimized by his bastard brother, Edmund, assumes the speech of demonic possession as a role—as a disguise.[25] Quotation in his speech is, in effect, quadrupled. Disinherited Edgar speaks in the voice of Poor Tom, the Bedlam beggar, who speaks in the voice of the devil, who quotes Samuel Harsnett's melodramatic exposure of the drama of bewitchment and exorcism.[26] Tom's mad speech, like Ophelia's, is made up of "quoted," culturally and psychologically resonant fragments, but his discourse incorporates differently inflected cultural voices. His speech embeds song fragments—"Through the sharp hawthorn blows the cold wind"—bits of romance—"But mice and rats and such small deer, / Have been Tom's food for many a year"—formulaic commandments and proverbial sayings—"obey thy parents; keep thy word's justice" (3.4.45, 136–37, 79–80). These quotations transmit a theological/moral discourse of sin and punishment in which Poor Tom is an emblematic fallen Christian, a "servingman, proud in heart and mind," "hog in sloth, fox in stealth, wolf in greediness, dog in madness" (3.4.84, 92–93). Embodying the seven deadly sins, especially those of pride and lust, he represents, like traditional madmen, guilt and punishment; he is led by the "foul fiend" "through fire and through flame, through ford and whirlpool, o'er bog and quagmire," and "eats the swimming frog, the toad, the todpole, the wall-newt and the water" (3.4.51–52, 127–28). Although Edgar's betrayal and exile have nothing to do with women, Poor Tom's feigned madness, like Hamlet's, is laced with misogyny. His introductory monologue identifies women's lust as the catalyst to his own catalogue of sins: "A servingman . . . that served the lust of my mistress' heart and did the act of darkness with her. . . . One that slept in the contriving of lust and waked to do it." His first commandment is avoidance of women's seductions: "Let not the creaking of shoes or the rustling of silks betray thy poor heart to women. Keep thy foot out of brothals, thy hand out of plackets . . . " (3.4.84–96). In Tom's fantasies of possession as punishment, the male demon Flibbertigibbet curses the products of women's wombs with deformities and then metamorphoses into the female nightmare (or incubus) and her offspring, a monstrous image of female sexual and reproductive power which is represented as well, Adelman claims, by the storm itself (*Suffocating* 110–14).

This mad discourse functions variously. It provides Edgar-as-Tom with a coherent characterization by permitting him to express and conceal his victimization and (as Adelman has argued) his suppressed desire for self-punishment and revenge.[27] It functions dramatically to trigger, mark, and counterpoint the specific moment of Lear's own break with sanity, which occurs decisively at his emotionally apt but logically groundless identification with Poor Tom at 3.4.62: "What, has his daughters brought him to this pass?"[28] The disguise allows the disinherited Edgar, by identifying with the middling or lower sorts and taking on their speech and beliefs, to participate with the fool and naked Lear in the reversals of class and status which pervade the play.

But always Edgar's quoted religious discourse is rendered theatrical, both because the discourse is feigned and because it is constructed through quotation of Samuel Harsnett, who himself narrates possession as theatrical roleplaying instigated by the suggestion and rehearsal of the exorcists. By appropriating for Poor Tom a "documented fraud" (Greenblatt 117), the spuriousness of Edgar's madness is emphasized, possession and divine retribution are mocked through mimicry, Lear's contrasting madness is marked as "natural," and the church's attempt to outlaw exorcism is furthered. At the same time, surviving belief in possession, perhaps especially prevalent among middle and lower ranks, is represented onstage. While Greenblatt (119) sees these rituals as "*emptied out*," I argue rather that in this mad discourse, their sacred meaning is resituated: morality, guilt, suffering, and punishment are understood within human, psychological, and gendered parameters.

In stark contrast to Edgar's feigned delirium of sin, guilt, and divine punishment, Lear's madness is staged as "natural," as psychologically engendered and obsessed with secular punishment, revenge, and justice. It is rooted in obvious physical and psychological causes: his exposure to the cold and storm in old age, his mistaken banishment of Cordelia, his other daughters' betrayals, his encounter with Poor Tom. His alienation is rendered on a continuum with his sanity from which it gradually emerges. He is metaphorically described by Kent as "mad" in the first scene, notes the onset of delirium himself, specifies his malady somewhat oddly, as "*hysterica passio*," the fits of the mother, defined, ingeniously, as his rising heart rather than his wandering womb (2.4.55–56). As he loses his kingdom, his children, his house, his robes, he feels weak, vulnerable, a victim of feminine and feminizing hysteria which attacks from within; he fears madness as he fears tears, as a sign of breakdown.[29] But once he is beside himself and seeks out Poor Tom as his philosopher (3.4.152), his madness grows self-authorizing, aggressive, and satiric. He is subsequently restored to sanity by conventional remedies, conventionally applied by a doctor—herbal medicine, sleep, clean garments, music, and the presence of Cordelia.

The construction of Lear's mad discourse, like that of Ophelia and Tom, involves fragmentation, formula, depersonalization, the intersection by communal voices, and secularized ritual. Like Ophelia, he uses tags of social formulas incongruously: "We'll go to supper i' the morning," "Give the word," "Pull off my boots: harder, harder: so" (3.6.83; 4.6.92, 173) to reestablish his shattered world. But more often, rather than being transected by quoted voices, Lear envisages hallucinatory cultural dramas in which he is both narrator and participant. Whereas Poor Tom acts out victimization and guilt by presenting himself as poor and persecuted, Lear defends himself against guilt by acting as persecutor: "cry / These dreadful summoners grace" (3.2.58–59). His hallucinations of the rituals of secular trial and judgment expose their fraudulence just as Edgar's feigned possession implicitly exposes demonic punishment as fraud. In the enacted mock trial on the heath (in Quarto), Lear plays the judge who "arraigns" (3.6.20) his absent daughters, Goneril and Regan, for their crimes against him, while Edgar, Kent, and the fool serve as jury. But the ritual, like those in Ophelia's songs, is aborted, the trial collapses, and the judge is humiliated, barked at by dogs (3.6.61–62).

During Lear's encounter with Gloucester on the heath, his identification with the persecutor and demonizing of women's sexuality continue to protect him from a sustained realization that he is not "ague-proof" (4.6.105). He fantasizes scenarios of justice undone by the corruption of women's "riotous appetite" (123) and the complicity of the judge. In his first fantasy, Lear as judge will "pardon that man's life" because all are guilty of copulation centered in the "sulphurous pit" of female sexuality, the domain to which the fiend is metaphorically confined in Lear's discourse (4.6.126–29). Whereas Edgar's feigned supernatural madness locates lust in himself, Lear's natural madness displaces it onto women and their judges. In Lear's second fantasy, following a series of reversals, the punisher and the punished become indistinguishable: the constable who whips the whore "hotly lusts to use her in that kind / For which thou whip'st her" (4.6.162–63). These fantasies expose Lear's habit of persecuting others to conceal his own guilt and provide a critique of a class-determined system of justice. Social status and the costumes which the period prescribed to mark it control guilt, judgment, and punishment: "Through tattered clothes small vices do appear; / Robes and furred gowns hide all. Plate sin with gold, / And the strong arm of justice hurtless breaks; / Arm it in rags, a pygmy's straw does pierce it" (4.6.164–67). Justice, like demonic possession, is theatrical, a matter of costumes, and hence fraudulent.

In this way, the impertinent madness of Lear, like that of Edgar and the fool, serves, as Robert Weimann suggests, to provide satiric "disenchantment" of conservative values and hierarchies supported by those in power: "The Prince of Darkness is a gentleman" (3.4.141). Ophelia's madness, although Weimann ignores it, functions similarly to disenchant domestic values: she "marks" the falsehood of love, the emptiness of religious formula, the betrayal of men. She narrates the arbitrariness, instability, and corruption of love and the family as Lear narrates those of justice and the state.[30] Ophelia, like Lear and Hamlet, speaks impertinently, proverbially, bawdily, disturbingly; she too is both actress and character, partly an object of the audience's gaze, partly a spokesperson for their contempt for Claudius and his court. Ophelia, as much as (or perhaps even more than) Lear, "disrupts the authority of order, degree, and decorum" (Weimann, "Bifold" 417). But because Lear, like Hamlet, speaks from a tradition of articulate, illuminating melancholia, his madness is credited. In contrast, Ophelia's madness remains underread, both by spectators in the play and by critics and playgoers outside. It does not open itself as easily as Lear's to producing "universal" truths; it is angry at male betrayal, not female sexual corruption, and is obsessed with Christian mercy and human mourning rather than with male authority and secular judgment.

Edgar in disguise not only provides critique and counterpoint but is the vehicle of another inversion as he becomes a "philosopher" to King Lear and cares for his father, Gloucester. With each, Edgar employs a traditionally recommended remedy for delusion and despair, a strategy which Burton and others record and which Foucault calls "continuing the delirious discourse" (154). The delusions of the mad are complied with and extended through theatrical representation in order to undo them. This strategy further naturalizes madness and brings it under human control while testifying to the power of illusion and the theatricality of madness. Doctors and friends fraudulently extend the delusions of the mad to manipulate them toward a cure. The most frequently cited example of this is a story of a melancholic man who, believing himself dead, refused to eat. Friends costumed themselves as dead men and consumed a banquet in front of him to demonstrate that the dead eat; he then ate too and recovered. A more bizarre example is that of a man who refused to urinate, believing that if he did, he would drown the world; friends set fire to the house next door and prevailed on him to put it out lest the town burn. He "pissed, emptied his bladder of all that was in it, and was himselfe by that means preserved" (Laurentius 103).[31] Less ingenious strategies reported involve physicians or friends curing patients who complain of toads or snakes in their bellies by administering emetics and slipping the animals into the vomit basin. Typically, as these cases get revised in the Early Modern period, men's bodily boundaries are protected and women's are breached. In treatises and plays, this is mainly a homosocial cure for men by men. In the play, when Lear imagines himself barked at by dogs, Edgar exorcises them for him through a song in which he impersonates a dog (3.6.64–72). Later he more elaborately "trifle[s]" with his father's "despair" to "cure" it, engineering Gloucester's mock suicide and the mock exorcism of his (and Edgar's own) demons to save his father from actual suicide. In this performance of possession and exorcism, the rituals of the supernatural are appropriated and secularized and used by humans to reverse human self-alienation just as they are in Renaissance treatises on melancholy, medicine, exorcism, and witchcraft.

V

Edgar's uses of the illogic of madness in the service of logic and sanity demonstrate that one purpose of reading madness, propounding definitions and prescribing cures, is to keep oneself sane and regulate the disruptiveness of the mad. In these Shakespeare tragedies, as in medical treatises and practices, the representation of madness enables a restoration of normality. But madmen and madwomen participate differently. Men can be cured but women die mad, mourning their losses. Hamlet recovers his identity in Ophelia's grave. Edgar exorcises Poor Tom and goes on to recover his dukedom and, in the Folio text, the kingdom. Gloucester eschews suicide for a time, and Lear is lovingly nursed back to health by his good daughter. But Ophelia's madness can be immunized only through her death and Christian burial. Lady Montague in *Romeo and Juliet* dies, for "grief hath stopped her breath" (5.3.212); Portia in *Julius Caesar* "fell distract" and "swallowed fire" (34.3.152–53). Lady Macbeth's somnambulism culminates in a suicide that, abruptly announced in the play's final lines, naturalizes and vilifies her as a "fiend-*like* Queen, / Who, as 'tis thought, by self and violent hands / Took off her life" (5.8.69–71). The elimination of madwomen from the plays exorcises certain forms of psychic and social disorder and allows the restoration of male health and male authority.

Likewise in the culture, constructions of madness tended to support established institutions in preserving the status quo. Preferred treatments were those undertaken by Anglican ministers, not Catholic exorcists or Puritan enthusiasts, by licensed practitioners, not quacks. These practitioners tended to favor outcomes which sustained social hierarchies and had different impacts on men and women; Napier, for example, viewed wives who wanted to leave brutal husbands, children who resisted their parents, servants who did not obey their masters, as mentally unstable and was severe with them. But the mad could be reabsorbed because they were not seen as inhuman; hence they were not usually isolated, confined, or ostracized. They might be subjected to purges and bleeding (like all ill people), drugged sleep, or music therapy, or might be coaxed back, through their own delusions, into the rituals of everyday life.

If the discourse of madness, in the short run, promoted normalization and supported the status quo, in the long run it had the capacity to contribute to changing constructions of the human and hence to cultural change. The distinctions established in this discourse helped redefine the human as a secular subject, cut off from the supernatural and incomprehensibly unstable and permeable, containing in itself a volatile mix of mind and body, of warring and turbulent elements: "For seeing we are not maisters of our owne affections, wee are like battered Citties without walles, or shippes tossed in the Sea, exposed to all manner of assaults and daungers, even to the overthrow of our owne bodies" (Jorden G3ᵛ). Such images opened up a new range of questions about and possibilities for human beings.

The theater, by representing and disseminating madness, contributes to its destabilizing potential. Shakespearean tragedy, drawn to madness perhaps because of its inherent theatricality, invented for it a discourse which was successful (and imitated) by virtue of its excessiveness, its rich imagery and associations, its verbal inventiveness, its multiple functions: psychological, thematic, satiric, theatrical. By providing a language for madness, the theater contributed to the process whereby it gradually became a secular, medical, and gendered condition. The Elizabethan theater is, at its origin, as C. L. Barber has suggested, a place apart, a space where the sacred is reconstituted in the human (20ff.), and in the discourse of madness this reconstitution is especially visible. The secular human characters this stage represents are inevitably gender- and class-specific in ways which the hierarchical *dramatis personae* or "names of the actors," introduced in seventeenth-century editions, inscribe. Gender distinctions may be especially rigid because of the absolute division between adult actors who play men and boy actors who must self-consciously perform femininity, drawing on gender stereotypes to do so as the instructions to the page in the Induction of *Taming of the Shrew* suggest. This may be one reason why madness is distinctly gender-marked in the theater earlier than in medical treatises or in the visual arts. But the theater, even while producing stereotyped or conservative formations, may participate in change. As Steven Mullaney has shown (chap. 2), it is a place apart from the established state as well as from the established church, situated in the liberties alongside unruly neighbors: taverns, bearbaitings, brothels, and the empty leper houses which Foucault (wrongly) imagines will soon fill up again with madmen (1–7). By constructing a language through which madness can be represented, the popular theater facilitates the circulation of the discourse; by italicizing the language of madness, it encourages its interrogation and transformation.

Although these Shakespeare plays represent madness to treat, italicize, or purge it, and although the gender distinctions they initiate can still prove oppressive to women, performed madness can transgress through unsettling productions or indecorous interventions by actors. Hamlet's feigned madness and Lear's natural madness can be performed and read as social critique (as in Grigori Kozintsev's 1970 film of *King Lear* or in the Studio Theater of Moscow's 1989 production of *Hamlet*). Ophelia's madness can be politicized by an actress who might represent the hysterical female body now as an eroticized and aestheticized object of desire and repulsion and now as an agent of uncontrollable voice, desire, pain, and rage (as in Ange Magnetic's "Ophelie Song" [1989]), an "opera minimal" derived from her songs).[32]

The complexities of reading the discourse of madness in Shakespeare and his culture reveal the difficulty and necessity of historicizing: examining one's own position and that of one's subject(s) in contemporary culture in relation to the construction of those subject(s) which emerged in early modern culture, working to tease out disjunctions and connections. This project reveals that the shape of gender difference cannot be assumed but must always be reformulated in specific cultural and historical contexts. Reading the discourse of madness provides powerful lessons in the gradual and erratic progress of cultural change and in the complex and not fully retrievable interactions between dramatic texts and other cultural documents. The theater does not just reflect, contain, or subvert the cultural realities in which it is embedded. But finding the right metaphor for the relationship is hard. Perhaps, in the context of this essay, it is appropriate to note that the playwright, like the mad, expresses inner conflicts, quotes cultural voices, speaks through disguises, enacts emotions visually and verbally, performs for diverse audiences, and is protected from harm because playtexts are illusions. These playtexts, moreover, like other "documents in madness," both do and do not belong to the authors who generate them, and they are read, performed, and used by us in the service of our own sanity.

NOTES

This essay is a revised version of the one published with the same title in *Shakespeare Quarterly* 42 (Fall 1991): 315–48. I am indebted to the questions, comments, and suggestions of fellow participants in Shakespeare Association of America seminars and of audiences who heard versions of this essay at Dartmouth College, Illinois State University, the University of Illinois at Champaign-Urbana, the University of Wisconsin–Milwaukee, and at the conference "New Languages for the Stage" at the University of Kansas. I am especially grateful for the challenging questions raised by Peter Stallybrass, Steven Mullaney, Jean Howard, Richard Knowles, Richard P. Wheeler, and Michael Shapiro and by *Shakespeare Quarterly*'s anonymous readers. My revisions of the essay for this volume have benefited from the astute suggestions of Madelon Sprengnether and from stimulating discussions of gender and madness in *Hamlet* and *King Lear* with the students in my Spring 1994 graduate seminar.

1. I draw on Allderidge's essays, which correct the inaccuracies and fantasies of Bedlam scholarship, especially those of the standard history by O'Donoghue.

2. Schiesari analyzes how the discrediting of female grief and mourning helps construct the validated condition of male melancholy from the Renaissance to the twentieth century. Winfried Schleiner discusses a countertradition emerging in the fifteenth and sixteenth centuries which demoted melancholy, especially when associated with divination and prophecy.

3. Showalter looks mostly at representations of women's madness after 1830, and gender is not analyzed in Foucault's large intuitive canvas. His discussion of supposedly unmediated madness from the Middle Ages to the seventeenth century is the least compelling part of his book (at least in the English translation), for his concept of the modern centralized state misunderstands early modern institutions. Mental institutions such as Bedlam often developed early out of medieval hospitals; unlike leper houses, they attempted cures and declared patients recovered. Confinement of the mad is also more varied, more historically continuous, and more complicated in its representations, aims, and consequences than Foucault or Showalter allows. But Foucault's intuitions about the transformation of the madman from supernatural voyager to secular case study are useful, as are Showalter's analyses of the associations between women, madness, and sexuality which developed in nineteenth-century representations of madwomen. For criticism of Foucault's historical inaccuracies, see Midelfort. For criticism of Showalter by a feminist medical historian, see Tomes.

4. Jorden is the first to find the source of hysterical symptoms in the brain as well as in the uterus. See Veith 122–23.

5. In fact, according to MacDonald's statistics, although far larger numbers and percentages of women came to Napier to report distress in connection with courtship, love, sex, and marriage negotiations, most of these sufferers were untitled (*Mystical* Table 3.6, 95; see also 94). Perhaps aristocratic women suffered less stress in matters of courtship and marriage because they had little or no choice in the matter.

6. For discussion of the political climate that produced Jorden's and Harsnett's pamphlets in 1603, see Thomas 482–86; Greenblatt 94–128; MacDonald, *Witchcraft* Introduction.

7. Ascriptions of madness occur elsewhere in Shakespeare beginning with *Titus*

Andronicus, Comedy of Errors, and *Twelfth Night* and conclude with the extended portrait of the Jailor's Daughter in *Two Noble Kinsmen.* Her characterization has connections with Ophelia's and with that of the madwomen and groups of madpersons in other Jacobean plays, for example, Dekker's *Honest Whore, Part I,* Webster's *Duchess of Malfi,* Fletcher's *The Pilgrim,* Middleton's and Rowley's *The Changling.*

8. These interpretations of Ophelia replicate feminist theorists' polarized interpretations of the association between women and madness. For positive interpretations of the textual representations of the connection, see Gilbert and Gubar; of Ophelia, see Neely 103–104. For the negative aspects of the connection, see Showalter, *Female* and "Representing" 77–94, where she discusses how different periods represent Ophelia according to their own stereotypes of female insanity.

9. However, in a book which appeared after the first publication of this essay, Duncan Salkeld examines how madness functions in Renaissance drama as a sign of ideological contradictions.

10. For Foucault, language constitutes madness; "*Language is the first and last structure of madness*" (100). Since madness is unreason, the "*delirious discourse*" (99) which constitutes it is the inverse of reason but, in effect, identical with it. It involves "sedimentation in the body of an infinitely repeated discourse" (97), "the language of reason enveloped in the prestige of the image" (95). "It is in this delirium, which is of both body and soul, of both language and image, of both grammar and physiology, that all the cycles of madness conclude and begin" (100–101).

11. Miller extends Irigary's analysis of women's special relation to the mimetic, defining italics as a modality of intensity, intonation, and emphasis which characterizes women's writing (343).

12. Bradley 336–37 notes that Shakespeare invariably uses prose to represent abnormal states of mind such as madness or Lady Macbeth's somnambulism. I am indebted to Lars Engle for bringing this discussion to my attention.

13. (4.5.178) Later mad characters are given equally precise and explicit introductions: see the conversation between Lady Macbeth's waiting woman and the doctor (5.1.1–20) and Edgar's commentary as he disguises himself as Poor Tom in *Lear* (2.3.1–21).

14. Klein reads Ophelia's madness closely and attends to its cultural lore. But whereas she sees Ophelia's role as providential, as a minister to Hamlet, I see religious references as split off from their theological context in her mad speech. Much of the attention devoted to Ophelia's speeches has been to determine who the referents of her songs are, especially the "true love," and to which characters they are addressed. My analysis suggests that it is not possible to pinpoint a single referent or audience since the discourse's referents are multiple and are both personal and cultural. In her madness, she does enact a ritual of mourning, the work which Schiesari argues has been culturally allotted to women. See Seng 131–56 for a summary of commentary.

15. Klein analyzes Ophelia as Hamlet's surrogate, and Lyons 11–12 claims that she mirrors aspects of Hamlet's melancholy. I see her rather as a "dark double," in Gilbert's and Gubar's sense (360), who acts out what is repressed in Hamlet.

16. Some form of Christian burial might be possible, even in cases of suicide. See MacDonald, "Ophelia's" 314–15. For discussions of suicide and mental disorder, see MacDonald, *Mystical* 132–38; "Inner" 566–67; "Secularization" 52–70; and *Sleepless.*

17. Immersion is conventionally a sign of madness and a cure for it. See Foucault 162, 166 and Clarke 229–30.

18. I see the relationship between the witches and Lady Macbeth as more ambiguous and unstable than does Adelman, *Suffocating* 130–47. I do not read their relationship as a literal or symbolic "alliance" (134, 136), nor do I find the witches or Lady Macbeth unstintingly malevolent and powerful. In fact, the witches wish Macbeth to fail while Lady Macbeth wishes him to succeed, and their relation to the supernatural is quite different from hers. Furthermore, both the witches and Lady Macbeth lose what power they have by the end of the play, though Adelman never discusses the implications of Lady Macbeth's somnambulism and suicide. Whatever power each has exists only contingently; neither the witches nor Lady Macbeth has agency or control except through Macbeth.

19. Thomas chap. 14 discusses how continental views of witchcraft conceived as a heresy centered in a pact with the devil were only gradually filtered into England, where witchcraft was more often defined as harmful activities. The fact that the witches are also called "weird women" (3.1.2) and compared with "elves and fairies" (4.1.42) emphasizes their shifting (and shifty) representations. If Hecate and the songs from Middleton's *The Witch* were later interpolations at odds with the earlier portrayal, this supports my claim that the witches' representations reflect contested notions of witches in the period. For arguments that act 3, scene 5, and act 4, scene 1, lines 39–43 and 125–32, are interpolations, see Muir, *Macbeth,* xxxii–xxxv. That the witches are dramatically more powerful early in the play when presented more naturalistically also may be connected to the weakening of beliefs in possession and witchcraft in England.

20. MacDonald, *Mystical* 189–217. John Hall, a successful doctor who practiced at the same time (1600–1635) as Napier in nearby Warwickshire and who appears to have been more puritan in his religious beliefs, and more of an apothecary and less of an astrologer than Napier, treated a similar range of disorders. Analysis of his casebooks shows that his patients presented similar symptoms of mental disorder in similar ratios. In his published cases (included in Joseph), Hall treated 70 men and 109 women; 13 of the men, or 7 percent, and 39 of the women, or 22 percent, showed signs of emotional disorder as analyzed by Howells and Osborn. These figures are based on only a small sample of Hall's cases which were published to disseminate his recipes for purges, not to explicate his patients' symptoms, and "emotional disorder" is more broadly defined by Howells and Osborn than by MacDonald.

21. MacDonald, *Mystical* 35–40 and Tomes 145–46. For a discussion of the gender distribution of psychiatric illnesses in twentieth-century London, see Shepherd et al. 164–66; for American statistics, see essays cited in note 22. The self-reporting and diagnosis of women's mental distress depend on a difficult-to-unravel conjunction of factors including vulnerability to gynecological ailments, women's self-images, gender-role socialization, medicine's construction of diseases, the social practice of diagnoses, and wider cultural trends.

22. Tomes 146–47 and her numerous sources, especially Goldman and Ravid 31–55 and Belle and Goldman 21–30.

23. Cf. MacDonald, *Mystical* 243–45. Selected comparisons:

symptoms	Males		Females		Totals	
	number	%	number	%	number	%
melancholy	177	24	287	22	465	23
mopish	160	21	187	15	347	17
troubled in mind	257	34	458	36	717	35
tpt kill child	9	1	31	2	40	2
tpt kill chd/self	0	0	20	2	20	1
tpt kill self	37	5	102	8	139	7
attempted suicide	17	2	29	2	46	2
suicidal act	17	2	30	2	47	2

24. The removal of more men could simply indicate that the distribution of space in the facility makes the confinement of similar numbers of men and women patients a convenience; hence more men are designated removable. I cannot tell whether Bedlam was sex-segregated as it and other asylums would come to be later.

25. This use of madness as disguise derives perhaps from Kyd's *Spanish Tragedy* and is common in other Jacobean plays, for example *The Changling* and *The Pilgrim.* Carroll analyzes the period's identifications of Tom o' Bedlams as feigning lower-class con men, revealing another association between Edgar's role-playing and feigning.

26. See Greenblatt and Muir, who finds over fifty separate fragments from Harsnett embedded in the play, many of them connected with the role of Poor Tom.

27. Adelman, *Twentieth* 8–21 has a fine discussion of how the role of Poor Tom turns blame inward and preserves Edgar. In contrast, Carroll 436 argues that the disguise is a source of pain and suffering for Edgar as well as a release from them.

28. Feder 132 and Jorgensen 80 concur. Lear's breakdown via his identification with Edgar is emphasized by his four-times-repeated claim that Tom's daughters are to blame for his state: "Didst give all to thy daughters?" "What, has his daughters brought him to this pass?" "Now . . . plagues . . . light on thy daughters!" "Nothing could have subdued nature / To such a lowness but his unkind daughters" (3.4.48, 62, 66–67, 69–70). Theatrically, this misogynistic iteration marks Lear's crossing of the boundary between sanity and madness.

29. Kahn argues that Lear's madness results from his rage at maternal deprivation and his suppression of the mother, his maternal side, and that through madness he

comes to accept his own vulnerability. Adelman, *Suffocating* 112–14 extends Kahn's argument by analyzing the suffocating maternal sexual monstrousness of the storm that engulfs him. In contrast, I see Lear's identification with the storm and subsequent madness as partially forestalling tears and restoring him to power underwritten by his misogyny and his fantasies of bringing judgment. His acceptance of vulnerability after recovering is deeply compromised, as Adelman 121–25 shows, by his unchanged need to love Cordelia "all" without consideration of her needs.

30. Weimann, *Shakespeare* 120–35, 215–20, uses the range and scope of Hamlet's and Lear's mad speech to exemplify the flexible alternation possible in Renaissance popular theater between the dialogue of naturalistic character staged from the illusionistic *locus* position and the nonrealistic monologue staged from the nonillusionistic *platea* position which draws on popular tradition, induces audience identification, and permits social critique. This flexibility also reveals "the twofold function of *mimesis* ('enchantment' and 'disenchantment'), which we have seen to be so fundamental a part of popular drama" (132). More recently, Weimann again uses the "impertinent" language of Hamlet and Lear to define the "bifold authority" generated by the Elizabethan theater (410, 416). I would not want this highly particularized mad discourse to stand as the theatrical norm, but Weimann's analysis does uncover the blend of individual psychology and cultural discourse which characterizes mad speech.

31. Clarke 222–23, 226 discusses such ingenious cures, dubbing them "part of the folk-lore tradition of the profession" (222). See also Burton II, 114–15, and Jorden chap. 7. Schleiner (152–57, 274–86) discusses revisions of these cases, including Luther's and Shakespeare's.

32. The Studio Theater performed this *Hamlet* at the University of Illinois at Urbana-Champaign, February 12, 1989. "Ophelie Song" was a coproduction by *Ange Magnetic* and *Mon Oncle d'Amerique* collaborated on by French director Antoine Campo and American choreographer Clara Gibson Maxwell and produced in 1989 in Paris, in New York, and at the Edinburgh Fringe Festival.

WORKS CITED

Adelman, Janet. Introduction. *Twentieth Century Interpretations of "King Lear."* Englewood Cliffs, N.J.: Prentice Hall, 1978. 1–21.

———. *Suffocating Mothers: Fantasies of Maternal Origin in Shakespeare's Plays, "Hamlet" to "The Tempest."* New York and London: Routledge, 1992.

Allderidge, Patricia. "Bedlam: Fact or Fantasy?" *Anatomy of Madness.* 3 vols. Ed. W. F. Bynum, Roy Porter, and Michael Shepherd. London: Tavistock, 1985. Vol. 2, 17–33.

———. "Management and Mismanagement at Bedlam, 1547–1633." *Health, Medicine, and Mortality in the Sixteenth Century.* Ed. Charles Webster. Cambridge: Cambridge UP, 1979. 141–64.

Babb, Lawrence. *The Elizabethan Malady.* East Lansing, Mich.: Michigan State UP, 1951.

Barber, C. L., and Richard P. Wheeler. *The Whole Journey: Shakespeare's Power of Development.* Berkeley: U of California P, 1986.

Belle, Deborah, and Noreen Goldman. "Patterns of Diagnosis Received by Men and Women." *The Mental Health of Women.* Ed. Marcia Guttenberg, Susan Salasin, and Deborah Belle. New York: Academic Press, 1980. 21–30.

Bradley, A. C. *Shakespearean Tragedy.* Greenwich, Conn.: Fawcett, n.d.

Bright, Timothy. *A Treatise of Melancholy.* London: Thomas Vautrollier, 1586. Facsimile rpt. Theatrum Orbis Terrarum, 1969.

Burton, Robert. *The Anatomy of Melancholy.* Ed. Holbrook Jackson. New York: Vintage Books, 1977.

Carroll, William C. " 'The Base Shall Top th' Legitimate': The Bedlam Beggar and the Role of Edgar in *King Lear.*" *Shakespeare Quarterly* 38 (1987): 426–41.

Cavell, Stanley. "The Avoidance of Love: A Reading of *King Lear.*" *Disowning Knowledge in Six Plays of Shakespeare.* Cambridge: Cambridge UP, 1987. 58–144.

Clarke, Basil. *Mental Disorder in Earlier England: Exploratory Studies.* Cardiff: U of Wales P, 1975.

Dollimore, Jonathan. *Radical Tragedy.* Brighton: Harvester Press, 1984.

Doob, Penelope. *Nebuchadnezzar's Children: Conventions of Madness in Middle English Literature.* New Haven: Yale UP, 1974.

Feder, Lillian. *Madness in Literature.* Princeton, N.J.: Princeton UP, 1980.

Foucault, Michel. *Madness and Civilization: A History of Insanity in the Age of Reason.* Trans. Richard Howard. New York: Random House, 1973.

Gilbert, Sandra, and Susan Gubar. *The Madwoman in the Attic.* New Haven: Yale UP, 1979.

Goldman, Noreen, and Renee Ravid. "Community Surveys: Sex Differences in Mental Illness." *The Mental Health of Women.* Ed. Marcia Guttenberg, Susan Salasin, and Deborah Belle. New York: Academic Press, 1980. 31–55.

Greenblatt, Stephen. "Shakespeare and the Exorcists." *Shakespearean Negotiations: The Circulation of Social Energy in Renaissance England.* Berkeley: U of California P, 1988. 94–128.

Harsnett, Samuel. *A Declaration of Egregious Popish Impostures.* London: James Roberts, 1603.

Heilman, Robert B. *This Great Stage: Image and Structure in "King Lear."* Seattle: U of Washington P, 1963; originally published 1948.

Howells, John G., and N. Livia Osborn. "The Incidence of Emotional Disorder in a Seventeenth Century Medical Practice." *Medical History* 14 (1970): 192–98.

Irigary, Luce. *This Sex Which Is Not One.* Trans. Catherine Porter with Catherine Burke. Ithaca: Cornell UP, 1985.

Jorden, Edward. *Brief Discourse of a Disease Called the Suffocation of the Mother.* London, 1603. Facsimile rpt. London: Theatrum Orbis Terrarum, 1971.

——. *Brief Discourse.* Rpt. MacDonald, *Witchcraft.*

Jorgensen, Paul A. *Lear's Self-Discovery.* Berkeley: U of California P, 1967.

Joseph, Harriet. *Shakespeare's Son-In-Law: Man and Physician.* Hampton, Conn.: Archon Books, 1964.

Kahn, Coppélia. "The Absent Mother in *King Lear.*" *Rewriting the Renaissance: The Discourses of Sexual Difference in Early Modern Europe.* Ed. Margaret W. Ferguson, Maureen Quilligan, and Nancy J. Vickers. Chicago: U of Chicago P, 1986. 33–49.

Klein, Joan. " 'Angels and Ministers of Grace': *Hamlet,* IV, v-vii." *Allegorica* 1.2 (1976): 156–76.

Laurentius, M. Andreas. *A Discourse of the Preservation of the Sight; of Melancholic Diseases.* Trans. Richard Surphlet (London, 1599). Ed. S. V. Larkey. Humphrey Milford, Oxford UP, 1938. Shakespeare Association Facsimile no. 15.

Lyons, Bridget Gellert. *Voices of Melancholy: Studies in Literary Treatments of Melancholy in Renaissance England.* London: Routledge, 1971.

MacDonald, Michael. "The Inner Side of Wisdom: Suicide in Early Modern England." *Psychological Medicine* 7 (1977): 565–82.

——. *Mystical Bedlam: Madness, Anxiety, and Healing in Seventeenth Century England.* Cambridge: Cambridge UP, 1981.

——. "Ophelia's Maimed Rites." *Shakespeare Quarterly* 37 (1986): 309–17.

——. "The Secularization of Suicide in England, 1660–1800." *Past and Present* 111 (1986): 50–100.

MacDonald, Michael, with Terence R. Murphy. *Sleepless Souls: Suicide in Early Modern England.* Oxford: Clarendon P, 1991.

MacDonald, Michael, ed. and Intro. *Witchcraft and Hysteria in Elizabeth London: Edward Jorden and the Mary Glover Case.* London: Routledge, 1991.

Macfarlane, Alan. *Witchcraft in Tudor and Stuart England.* London: Routledge, 1970.

Midelfort, H. C. "Madness and Civilization in Early Modern Europe: A Reappraisal of Michel Foucault." *After the Reformation: Essays in Honor of J. H. Hexter.* Ed. Barbara C. Malament. Philadelphia: U of Pennsylvania P, 1980. 247–66.

Miller, Nancy K. "Emphasis Added: Plots and Plausibilities in Women's Fiction." *Feminist Criticism: Essays on Women, Literature, Theory.* Ed. Elaine Showalter. New York: Pantheon, 1985. 339–60.

Muir, Kenneth. "Samuel Harsnett and *King Lear.*" *Review of English Studies* 2 (1951): 11–21.

Muir, Kenneth, ed. *Macbeth,* The Arden Shakespeare. London: Methuen, 1951.

Mullaney, Steven. *The Place of the Stage.* Chicago: U of Chicago P, 1988.

Neaman, Judith S. *Suggestion of the Devil: Insanity in the Middle Ages and the Twentieth Century.* New York: Octagon Books, 1978.

Neely, Carol Thomas. *Broken Nuptials in Shakespeare's Plays.* New Haven: Yale UP, 1985. Rpt. Urbana: U of Illinois P, 1993.

O'Donoghue, E. G. *The Story of Bethlehem Hospital.* New York: Dutton, 1914.

Reed, Robert Rentoul. *Bedlam on the Jacobean Stage.* Cambridge, Mass.: Harvard UP, 1952.

Salkeld, Duncan. *Madness and Drama in the Age of Shakespeare.* Manchester and New York: Manchester UP, 1993.

Schiesari, Juliana. *The Gendering of Melancholia: Feminism, Psychoanalysis, and the Symbolics of Loss.* Ithaca: Cornell UP, 1992.

Schleiner, Winfried. *Melancholy, Genius, and Utopia in the Renaissance.* Wiesbaden: Otto Harrassowitz, 1991.

Scot, Reginald. *The Discoverie of Witchcraft.* (1584) Rpt. Carbondale: Southern Illinois UP, 1964.

Seng, Peter. *The Vocal Songs in the Plays of Shakespeare.* Cambridge: Harvard UP, 1967.

Shakespeare, William. *The Complete Signet Classic Shakespeare.* Gen. ed. Sylvan Barnet. New York: Harcourt Brace Jovanovich, 1972.

Shepherd, Michael; Brian Cooper; Alexander Brown; and Graham Kalton. *Psychiatric Illnesses in General Practice.* London: Oxford UP, 1966.

Showalter, Elaine. *The Female Malady: Women, Madness, and English Culture, 1830–1980.* New York and London: Penguin, 1987.

———. "Representing Ophelia: Women, Madness, and the Responsibilities of Feminist Criticism." *Shakespeare and the Question of Theory.* Ed. Patricia Parker and Geoffrey Hartman. London: Methuen, 1985. 77–94.

Sprenger, James, and Heinrich Kramer. *Malleus Maleficarum* or *The Witch Hammer.* (c.1486) Trans. Montague Summers, 1928. Rpt. New York: Benjamin Blom, 1970.

Stallybrass, Peter. "*Macbeth* and Witchcraft." *Focus on Macbeth.* Ed. John Russell Brown. London: Routledge, 1982. 189–209.

Thomas, Keith. *Religion and the Decline of Magic.* New York: Scribners, 1971.

Tomes, Nancy. "Historical Perspectives on Women and Mental Illness." *Women, Health, and Medicine in America: A Historical Handbook.* Ed. Rima D. Apple. New York: Garland, 1990. 143–71.

Veith, Ilza. *Hysteria: The History of a Disease.* Chicago: U of Chicago P, 1965.

Weimann, Robert. "Bifold Authority in Shakespeare's Theatre." *Shakespeare Quarterly* 39 (1988): 401–17.

———. *Shakespeare and the Popular Tradition in the Theater: Studies in the Social Dimension of Dramatic Form and Function.* Ed. Robert Schwartz. Baltimore: Johns Hopkins UP, 1978.

4

"BORN OF WOMAN"

Fantasies of Maternal Power in *Macbeth*

JÁNET ADELMAN

IN THE LAST moments of any production of *Macbeth*, as Macbeth feels himself increasingly hemmed in by enemies, the stage will resonate hauntingly with variants of his repeated question, "What's he / That was not born of woman?" (5.7.2–3; for variants, see 5.3.4, 6; 5.7.11, 13; 5.8.13, 31).[1] Repeated seven times, Macbeth's allusion to the witches' prophecy—"none of woman born / Shall harm Macbeth" (4.1.80–81)—becomes virtually a talisman to ward off danger; even after he has begun to doubt the equivocation of the fiend (5.5.43), mere repetition of the phrase seems to Macbeth to guarantee his invulnerability. I want in this essay to explore the power of these resonances, particularly to explore how Macbeth's assurance seems to turn itself inside out, becoming dependent not on the fact that all men are, after all, born of woman but on the fantasy of escape from this universal condition. The duplicity of Macbeth's repeated question—its capacity to mean both itself and its opposite—carries such weight at the end of the play, I think, because the whole of the play represents in very powerful form both the fantasy of a virtually absolute and destructive maternal power and the fantasy of absolute escape from this power; I shall argue in fact that the peculiar texture of the end of the play is generated partly by the tension between these two fantasies.

Maternal power in *Macbeth* is not embodied in the figure of a particular mother (as it is, for example, in *Coriolanus*); it is instead diffused throughout the play, evoked primarily by the figures of the witches and Lady Macbeth. Largely through Macbeth's relationship to them, the play becomes (like *Coriolanus*) a representation of primitive fears about male identity and autonomy itself,[2] about those looming female presences who threaten to control one's actions and one's mind, to constitute one's very self, even at a distance. When

Macbeth's first words echo those we have already heard the witches speak—"So fair and foul a day I have not seen" (1.3.38); "Fair is foul, and foul is fair" (1.1.11)—we are in a realm that questions the very possibility of autonomous identity. The play will finally reimagine autonomous male identity, but only through the ruthless excision of all female presence, its own peculiar satisfaction of the witches' prophecy.

In 1600, after the Earl of Gowrie's failed attempt to kill James VI, one James Weimis of Bogy, testifying about the earl's recourse to necromancy, reported that the earl thought it "possible that the seed of man and woman might be brought to perfection otherwise then by the *matrix* of the woman" ("Gowries Conspiracie" 196). Whether or not Shakespeare deliberately recalled Gowrie in his portrayal of the murderer of James's ancestor,[3] the connection is haunting: the account of the conspiracy hints that, for Gowrie at least, recourse to necromancy seemed to promise at once invulnerability and escape from the maternal matrix.[4] The fantasy of such escape in fact haunts Shakespeare's plays. A few years after Macbeth, Posthumus will make the fantasy explicit: attributing all ills in man to the "woman's part," he will ask, "Is there no way for men to be, but women / Must be half-workers?" (*Cymbeline* 2.5.1–2).[5] The strikingly motherless world of *The Tempest* and its potent image of absolute male control answer Posthumus's questions affirmatively: there, at least, on that bare island, mothers and witches are banished and creation belongs to the male alone.

Even in one of Shakespeare's earliest plays, male autonomy is ambivalently portrayed as the capacity to escape the maternal matrix that has misshaped the infant man.[6] The man who will become Richard III emerges strikingly as a character for the first time as he watches his brother Edward's sexual success with the Lady Grey. After wishing syphilis on him so that he will have no issue (a concern that anticipates Macbeth's), Richard constructs his own desire for the crown specifically as compensation for his failure at the sexual game. Unable to "make [his] heaven in a lady's lap," he will "make [his] heaven to dream upon the crown" (*3 Henry VI* 3.2.148, 169). But his failure to make his heaven in a lady's lap is itself understood as the consequence of his subjection to another lady's lap, to the misshaping power of his mother's womb:

Why, love forswore me in my Mother's womb;
And, for I should not deal in her soft laws,
She did corrupt frail nature with some bribe

To shrink mine arm up like a withered shrub;
To make an envious mountain on my back.

(3.2.153–57)

Richard blames his deformity on a triad of female powers: Mother, Love, and
Nature all fuse, conspiring to deform him as he is being formed in his mother's
womb. Given this image of female power, it is no wonder that he turns to the
compensatory heaven of the crown. But the crown turns out to be an unstable
compensation. Even as he shifts from the image of the misshaping womb to
the image of the crown, the terrifying enclosure of the womb recurs, shaping
his attempt to imagine the very political project that should free him from
dependence on ladies' laps:

I'll make my heaven to dream upon the crown
And, whiles I live, t'account this world but hell
Until my misshaped trunk that bears this head
Be round impalèd with a glorious crown.
And yet I know not how to get the crown,
For many lives stand between me and home;
And I—like one lost in a thorny wood,
That rents the thorns and is rent with the thorns,
Seeking a way and straying from the way,
Not knowing how to find the open air
But toiling desperately to find it out—
Torment myself to catch the English crown;
And from that torment I will free myself
Or hew my way out with a bloody axe.

(3.2.168–81)

The crown for him is "home," the safe haven. But through the shifting meaning
of "impaled," the crown as safe haven is itself transformed into the dangerous
enclosure: the stakes that enclose him protectively turn into the thorns that
threaten to impale him.[7] Strikingly, it is not his head but the trunk that bears
his head that is so impaled by crown and thorns: the crown compensatory for
ladies' laps fuses with the image of the dangerous womb in an imagistic nightmare in which the lap/womb/home/crown become the thorny wood from
which he desperately seeks escape into the open air. Through this imagistic
transformation, these lines take on the configuration of a birth fantasy, or more
precisely a fantasy of impeded birth, a birth that the man-child himself must
manage by hewing his way out with a bloody axe.[8] Escape from the dangerous
female is here achieved by recourse to the exaggeratedly masculine bloody axe.

This, I will argue, is precisely the psychological configuration of *Macbeth*, where dangerous female presences like Love, Nature, Mother are given embodiment in Lady Macbeth and the witches, and where Macbeth wields the bloody axe in an attempt to escape their dominion over him.

At first glance, Macbeth seems to wield the bloody axe to comply with, not to escape, the dominion of women. The play constructs Macbeth as terrifyingly pawn to female figures. Whether or not he is rapt by the witches' prophecies because the horrid image of Duncan's murder has already occurred to him, their role as gleeful prophets constructs Macbeth's actions in part as the enactments of their will. And he is impelled toward murder by Lady Macbeth's equation of masculinity and murder: in his case, the bloody axe seems not an escape route but the tool of a man driven to enact the ferociously masculine strivings of his wife.[9] Nonetheless, the weight given the image of the man not born of woman at the end suggests that the underlying fantasy is the same as in Richard's defensive construction of his masculinity: even while enacting the wills of women, Macbeth's bloody masculinity enables an escape from them in fantasy—an escape that the play itself embodies in dramatic form at the end. I will discuss first the unleashing of female power and Macbeth's compliance with that power, and then the fantasy of escape.

In the figures of Macbeth, Lady Macbeth, and the witches, the play gives us images of a masculinity and a femininity that are terribly disturbed; this disturbance seems to me both the cause and the consequence of the murder of Duncan. In *Hamlet*, Shakespeare had reconstructed the Fall as the death of the ideal father; here, he constructs a revised version in which the Fall is the death of the ideally androgynous parent. For Duncan combines in himself the attributes of both father and mother: he is the center of authority, the source of lineage and honor, the giver of name and gift; but he is also the source of all nurturance, planting the children to his throne and making them grow. He is the father as androgynous parent from whom, singly, all good can be imagined to flow, the source of a benign and empowering nurturance the opposite of that imaged in the witches' poisonous cauldron and Lady Macbeth's gall-filled breasts. Such a father does away with any need for a mother: he is the image of both parents in one, threatening aspects of each controlled by the presence of the other.[10] When he is gone, "The wine of life is drawn, and the mere lees / Is left this vault to brag of" (2.3.93–94): nurturance itself is spoiled, as all the play's imagery of poisoned chalices and interrupted feasts implies. In his absence male and female break apart, the female becoming merely helpless or merely poisonous and the male merely bloodthirsty; the harmonious relation of the genders imaged in Duncan fails.

In *Hamlet,* the absence of the ideal protecting father brings the son face to face with maternal power. The absence of Duncan similarly unleashes the power of the play's malevolent mothers. But this father-king seems strikingly absent even before his murder. Heavily idealized, he is nonetheless largely inef-fectual: even while he is alive, he is unable to hold his kingdom together, reliant on a series of bloody men to suppress an increasingly successful series of rebellions.[11] The witches are already abroad in his realm; they in fact constitute our introduction to that realm. Duncan, not Macbeth, is the first person to echo them ("When the battle's lost and won" [1.1.4]; "What he hath lost, noble Macbeth hath won" [1.2.69]). The witches' sexual ambiguity terrifies: Banquo says of them, "You should be women, / And yet your beards forbid me to interpret / That you are so" (1.3.45–47). Is their androgyny the shadow side of the king's, enabled perhaps by his failure to maintain a protective masculine authority? Is their strength a consequence of his weakness? (This is the configuration of *Cymbeline,* where the power of the witch-queen-stepmother is so dependent on the failure of Cymbeline's masculine authority that she obligingly dies when that authority returns to him.) Banquo's question to the witches may ask us to hear a counterquestion about Duncan, who should be man. For Duncan's androgyny is the object of enormous ambivalence: ideal-ized for his nurturing paternity, he is nonetheless killed for his womanish soft-ness, his childish trust, his inability to read men's minds in their faces, his reliance on the fighting of sons who can rebel against him. Macbeth's descrip-tion of the dead Duncan—"his silver skin lac'd with his golden blood" (2.3.110)—makes him into a virtual icon of kingly worth; but other images surrounding his death make him into an emblem not of masculine authority but of female vulnerability. As he moves toward the murder, Macbeth first imagines himself the allegorical figure of murder, as though to absolve himself of the responsi-bility of choice. But the figure of murder then fuses with that of Tarquin:

> wither'd Murther,
> . . . thus with his stealthy pace,
> With Tarquin's ravishing strides, towards his design
> Moves like a ghost.
> (2.1.52–56)

These lines figure the murder as a display of male sexual aggression against a passive female victim: murder here becomes rape; Macbeth's victim becomes not the powerful male figure of the king but the helpless Lucrece.[12] Hardened by Lady Macbeth to regard maleness and violence as equivalent, that is, Macbeth responds to Duncan's idealized milky gentleness as though it were evidence of his femaleness. The horror of this gender transformation, as well as the horror of the murder, is implicit in Macduff's identification of the king's body as a new Gorgon ("Approach the chamber, and destroy your sight / With a new Gorgon" [2.3.70–71]). The power of this image lies partly in its suggestion that Duncan's bloodied body, with its multiple wounds, has been revealed as female and hence blinding to his sons: as if the threat all along were that Duncan would be revealed as female and that this revelation would rob his sons of his masculine protection and hence of their own masculinity.[13]

In *King Lear*, the abdication of protective paternal power seems to release the destructive power of a female chaos imaged not only in Goneril and Regan, but also in the storm on the heath. Macbeth virtually alludes to Lear's storm as he approaches the witches in act 4, conjuring them to answer though they "untie the winds, and let them fight / Against the Churches," though the "waves / Confound and swallow navigation up," though "the treasure / Of Nature's germens tumble all together / Even till destruction sicken" (4.1.52–60; see *King Lear* 3.2.1–9). The witches merely implicit on Lear's heath have become in *Macbeth* embodied agents of storm and disorder,[14] and they are there from the start. Their presence suggests that the absence of the father that unleashes female chaos (as in *Lear*) has already happened at the beginning of *Macbeth*; that absence is merely made literal in Macbeth's murder of Duncan at the instigation of female forces. For this father-king cannot protect his sons from powerful mothers, and it is the son's—and the play's—revenge to kill him, or, more precisely, to kill him first and love him after, paying him back for his excessively "womanish" trust and then memorializing him as the ideal androgynous parent.[15] The reconstitution of manhood becomes a central problem of the play in part, I think, because the vision of manhood embodied in Duncan has already failed at the play's beginning.

The witches constitute our introduction to the realm of maternal malevolence unleashed by the loss of paternal protection; as soon as Macbeth meets them, he becomes (in Hecate's probably non-Shakespearean words) their "wayward son" (3.5.11). This maternal malevolence is given its most horrifying expression in Shakespeare in the image through which Lady Macbeth secures her control over Macbeth:

> I have given suck, and know
> How tender 'tis to love the babe that milks me:

I would, while it was smiling in my face,
Have pluck'd my nipple from his boneless gums,
And dash'd the brains out, had I so sworn
As you have done to this.

(1.7.54–59)

This image of murderously disrupted nurturance is the psychic equivalence of
the witches' poisonous cauldron; both function to subject Macbeth's will to
female forces.[16] For the play strikingly constructs the fantasy of subjection to
maternal malevolence in two parts, in the witches and in Lady Macbeth, and
then persistently identifies the two parts as one. Through this identification,
Shakespeare in effect locates the source of his culture's fear of witchcraft in
individual human history, in the infant's long dependence on female figures felt
as all-powerful: what the witches suggest about the vulnerability of men to
female power on the cosmic plane, Lady Macbeth doubles on the psychological
plane.

Lady Macbeth's power as a female temptress allies her in a general way with
the witches as soon as we see her. The specifics of that implied alliance begin
to emerge as she attempts to harden herself in preparation for hardening her
husband: the disturbance of gender that Banquo registers when he first meets
the witches is played out in psychological terms in Lady Macbeth's attempt to
unsex herself. Calling on spirits ambiguously allied with the witches themselves, she phrases this unsexing as the undoing of her own bodily maternal
function:

> Come, you Spirits
> That tend on mortal thoughts, unsex me here,
> And fill me, from the crown to the toe, top-full
> Of direst cruelty! make thick my blood,
> Stop up th'access and passage to remorse;
> That no compunctious visitings of Nature
> Shake my fell purpose, nor keep peace between
> Th'effect and it! Come to my woman's breasts,
> And take my milk for gall, you murth'ring ministers.
> (1.5.40–48)

In the play's context of unnatural births, the thickening of the blood and the
stopping up of access and passage to remorse begin to sound like attempts to
undo reproductive functioning and perhaps to stop the menstrual blood that
is the sign of its potential.[17] The metaphors in which Lady Macbeth frames the
stopping up of remorse, that is, suggest that she imagines an attack on the
reproductive passages of her own body, on what makes her specifically female.

And as she invites the spirits to her breasts, she reiterates the centrality of the attack specifically on maternal function: needing to undo the "milk of human kindness" (1.5.18) in Macbeth, she imagines an attack on her own literal milk, its transformation into gall. This imagery locates the horror of the scene in Lady Macbeth's unnatural abrogation of her maternal function. But latent within this image of unsexing is the horror of the maternal function itself. Most modern editors follow Johnson in glossing "take my milk for gall" as "take my milk in exchange for gall," imagining in effect that the spirits empty out the natural maternal fluid and replace it with the unnatural and poisonous one.[18] But perhaps Lady Macbeth is asking the spirits to take her milk *as* gall, to nurse from her breast and find in her milk their sustaining poison. Here the milk itself is the gall; no transformation is necessary. In these lines Lady Macbeth focuses the culture's fear of maternal nursery—a fear reflected, for example, in the common worries about the various ills (including female blood itself) that could be transmitted through nursing and in the sometime identification of colostrum as witch's milk.[19] Insofar as her milk itself nurtures the evil spirits, Lady Macbeth localizes the image of maternal danger, inviting the identification of her maternal function itself with that of the witch. For she here invites precisely that nursing of devil-imps so central to the current understanding of witchcraft that the presence of supernumerary teats alone was often taken as sufficient evidence that one was a witch.[20] Lady Macbeth and the witches fuse at this moment, and they fuse through the image of perverse nursery.

It is characteristic of the play's division of labor between Lady Macbeth and the witches that she, rather than they, is given the imagery of perverse nursery traditionally attributed to the witches. The often noted alliance between Lady Macbeth and the witches constructs malignant female power both in the cosmos and in the family: it in effect adds the whole weight of the spiritual order to the condemnation of Lady Macbeth's insurrection.[21] But despite the superior cosmic status of the witches, Lady Macbeth seems to me finally the more frightening figure. For Shakespeare's witches are an odd mixture of the terrifying and the near-comic. Even without consideration of the Hecate scene (3.5), with its distinct lightening of tone and its incipient comedy of discord among the witches, we may begin to feel a shift toward the comic in the presentation of the witches: the specificity and predictability of the ingredients in their dire recipe pass over toward grotesque comedy even while they create a (partly pleasurable) shiver of horror.[22] There is a distinct weakening of their power after their first appearances: only halfway through the play, in 4.1, do we hear that they themselves have masters (4.1.63). The more Macbeth claims for them,

the less their actual power seems: by the time Macbeth evokes the cosmic damage they can wreak (4.1.50–60), we have already felt the presence of such damage, and felt it moreover not as issuing from the witches but as a divinely sanctioned nature's expressions of outrage at the disruption of patriarchal order.
The witches' displays of thunder and lightning, like their apparitions, are mere
theatrics compared to what we have already heard; and the serious disruptions
of natural order—the storm that toppled the chimneys and made the earth
shake (2.3.53–60), the unnatural darkness in day (2.4.5–10), the cannibalism
of Duncan's horses (2.4.14–18)—seem the horrifying but reassuringly familiar
signs of God's displeasure, firmly under His—not their—control. Partly because
their power is thus circumscribed, nothing the witches say or do conveys the
presence of awesome and unexplained malevolence in the way that Lear's
storm does. Even the process of dramatic representation itself may diminish
their power: embodied, perhaps, they lack full power to terrify: "Present
fears"—even of witches—"are less than horrible imaginings" (1.3.137–38). They
tend thus to become as much containers for as expressions of nightmare; to a
certain extent, they help to exorcise the terror of female malevolence by localizing it.

The witches may of course have lost some of their power to terrify through
the general decline in witchcraft belief. Nonetheless, even when that belief
was in full force, these witches would have been less frightening than their
Continental sisters, their crimes less sensational. For despite their numinous
and infinitely suggestive indefinability,[23] insofar as they are witches, they are
distinctly English witches; and most commentators on English witchcraft note
how tame an affair it was in comparison with witchcraft belief on the Continent.[24] The most sensational staples of Continental belief from the *Malleus Maleficarum* (1486) on—the ritual murder and eating of infants, the attacks specifically on the male genitals, the perverse sexual relationship with
demons—are missing or greatly muted in English witchcraft belief, replaced
largely by a simpler concern with retaliatory wrongdoing of exactly the order
Shakespeare points to when one of his witches announces her retaliation for
the sailor's wife's refusal to share her chestnuts.[25] We may hear an echo of some
of the Continental beliefs in the hint of their quasi-sexual attack on the sailor
with the uncooperative wife (the witches promise to "do and do and do," leaving him drained "dry as hay") and in the infanticidal contents of the cauldron,
especially the "finger of birth-strangled babe" and the blood of the sow "that
hath eaten / Her nine farrow." The cannibalism that is a staple of Continental
belief may be implicit in the contents of that grim cauldron; and the various

eyes, toes, tongues, legs, teeth, livers, and noses (indiscriminately human and animal) may evoke primitive fears of dismemberment close to the center of witchcraft belief. But these terrors remain largely implicit. For Shakespeare's witches are both smaller and greater than their Continental sisters: on the one hand, more the representation of English homebodies with relatively small concerns; on the other, more the incarnation of literary or mythic fates or sibyls, given the power not only to predict but to enforce the future. But the staples of Continental witchcraft belief are not altogether missing from the play: for the most part, they are transferred away from the witches and recur as the psychological issues evoked by Lady Macbeth in her relation to Macbeth. She becomes the inheritor of the realm of primitive relational and bodily disturbance: of infantile vulnerability to maternal power, of dismemberment and its developmentally later equivalent, castration. Lady Macbeth brings the witches' power home: they get the cosmic apparatus, she gets the psychic force. That Lady Macbeth is the more frightening figure—and was so, I suspect, even before belief in witchcraft had declined—suggests the firmly domestic and psychological basis of Shakespeare's imagination.[26]

The fears of female coercion, female definition of the male, that are initially located cosmically in the witches thus find their ultimate locus in the figure of Lady Macbeth, whose attack on Macbeth's virility is the source of her strength over him and who acquires that strength, I shall argue, partly because she can make him imagine himself as an infant vulnerable to her. In the figure of Lady Macbeth, that is, Shakespeare rephrases the power of the witches as the wife/mother's power to poison human relatedness at its source; in her, their power of cosmic coercion is rewritten as the power of the mother to misshape or destroy the child. The attack on infants and on the genitals characteristic of Continental witchcraft belief is thus in her returned to its psychological source: in the play these beliefs are localized not in the witches but in the great central scene in which Lady Macbeth persuades Macbeth to the murder of Duncan. In this scene, Lady Macbeth notoriously makes the murder of Duncan the test of Macbeth's virility; if he cannot perform the murder, he is in effect reduced to the helplessness of an infant subject to her rage. She begins by attacking his manhood, making her love for him contingent on the murder that she identifies as equivalent to his male potency: "From this time / Such I account thy love" (1.7.38-39); "When you durst do it, then you were a man" (1.7.49). Insofar as his drunk hope is now "green and pale" (1.7.37), he is identified as emasculated, exhibiting the symptoms not only of hangover but also of the greensickness, the typical disease of timid young virgin women. Lady Macbeth's argument is, in effect, that any signs of the "milk of human kindness" (1.5.17) mark him as more womanly than she; she proceeds to enforce his masculinity by demonstrating her willingness to dry up that milk in herself, specifically by destroying her nursing infant in fantasy: "I would, while it was smiling in my face, / Have pluck'd my nipple from his boneless gums, / And dash'd the brains out" (1.7.56–58). That this image has no place in the plot, where the Macbeths are strikingly childless, gives some indication of the inner necessity through which it appears. For Lady Macbeth expresses here not only the hardness she imagines to be male, not only her willingness to unmake the most essential maternal relationship; she expresses also a deep fantasy of Macbeth's utter vulnerability to her. As she progresses from questioning Macbeth's masculinity to imagining herself dashing out the brains of her infant son,[27] she articulates a fantasy in which to be less than a man is to become interchangeably a woman or a baby,[28] terribly subject to the wife/mother's destructive rage.

By evoking this vulnerability, Lady Macbeth acquires a power over Macbeth more absolute than any the witches can achieve. The play's central fantasy of escape from woman seems to me to unfold from this moment; we can see its beginnings in Macbeth's response to Lady Macbeth's evocation of absolute maternal power. Macbeth first responds by questioning the possibility of failure ("If we should fail?" [1.7.59]). Lady Macbeth counters this fear by inviting Macbeth to share in her fantasy of omnipotent malevolence: "What cannot you and I perform upon / Th'unguarded Duncan?" (1.7.70–71). The satiated and sleeping Duncan takes on the vulnerability that Lady Macbeth has just invoked in the image of the feeding, trusting infant;[29] Macbeth releases himself from the image of this vulnerability by sharing in the murder of this innocent. In his elation at this transfer of vulnerability from himself to Duncan, Macbeth imagines Lady Macbeth the mother to infants sharing her hardness, born in effect without vulnerability; in effect, he imagines her as male and then reconstitutes himself as the invulnerable male child of such a mother:

> Bring forth men-children only!
> For thy undaunted mettle should compose
> Nothing but males.
>
> (1.7.73–75)

Through the double pun on "mettle/metal" and "male/mail," Lady Macbeth herself becomes virtually male, composed of the hard metal of which the armored male is made.[30] Her children would necessarily be men, composed of her male mettle, armored by her mettle, lacking the female inheritance from the mother that would make them vulnerable. The man-child thus brought forth would be no trusting infant; the very phrase "men-children" suggests the presence of the adult man even at birth, hence the undoing of childish vulnerability.[31] The mobility of the imagery—from male infant with his brains dashed out, to Macbeth and Lady Macbeth triumphing over the sleeping, trusting Duncan, to the all-male invulnerable man-child—suggests the logic of the fantasy: only the child of an all-male mother is safe. We see here the creation of a defensive fantasy of exemption from the woman's part: as infantile vulnerability is shifted to Duncan, Macbeth creates in himself the image of Lady Macbeth's hardened all-male man-child; in committing the murder, he thus becomes like Richard III, using the bloody axe to free himself in fantasy from the dominion of women, even while apparently carrying out their will.

Macbeth's temporary solution to the infantile vulnerability and maternal malevolence revealed by Lady Macbeth is to imagine Lady Macbeth the all-male mother of invulnerable infants. The final solution, both for Macbeth and for the play itself, though in differing ways, is an even more radical excision of the female: it is to imagine a birth entirely exempt from women, to imagine in effect an all-male family, composed of nothing but males, in which the father is fully restored to power. Overtly, of course, the play denies the possibility of this fantasy: Macduff carries the power of the man not born of woman only through the equivocation of the fiends, their obstetrical joke that quibbles with the meaning of "born" and thus confirms circuitously that all men come from women after all. Even Macbeth, in whom, I think, the fantasy is centrally invested, knows its impossibility: his false security depends exactly on his commonsense assumption that everyone is born of woman. Nonetheless, I shall argue, the play curiously enacts the fantasy that it seems to deny: punishing Macbeth for his participation in a fantasy of escape from the maternal matrix, it nonetheless allows the audience the partial satisfaction of a dramatic equivalent to it. The dual process of repudiation and enactment of the fantasy seems to me to shape the ending of *Macbeth* decisively; I will attempt to trace this process in the rest of this essay.

The witches' prophecy has the immediate force of psychic relevance for Macbeth partly because of the fantasy constructions central to 1.7:

Be bloody, bold, and resolute: laugh to scorn
The power of man, for none of woman born
Shall harm Macbeth.

(4.1.79–81)

The witches here invite Macbeth to make himself into the bloody and invulnerable man-child he has created as a defense against maternal malevolence in

1.7: the man-child ambivalently recalled by the accompanying apparition of the Bloody Child. For the apparition alludes at once to the bloody vulnerability of the infant destroyed by Lady Macbeth and to the bloodthirsty masculinity that seems to promise escape from this vulnerability, the bloodiness the witches urge Macbeth to take on. The doubleness of the image epitomizes exactly the doubleness of the prophecy itself: the prophecy constructs Macbeth's invulnerability in effect from the vulnerability of all other men, a vulnerability dependent on their having been born of woman. Macbeth does not question this prophecy, even after the experience of Birnam Wood should have taught him better, partly because it so perfectly meets his needs: in encouraging him to "laugh to scorn / The power of men," the prophecy seems to grant him exemption from the condition of all men, who bring with them the liabilities inherent in their birth. As Macbeth carries the prophecy as a shield onto the battlefield, his confidence in his own invulnerability increasingly reveals his sense of his own exemption from the universal human condition. Repeated seven times, the phrase "born to woman" with its variants begins to carry for Macbeth the meaning "vulnerable," as though vulnerability itself is the taint deriving from woman; his own invulnerability comes therefore to stand as evidence for his exemption from that taint. This is the subterranean logic of Macbeth's words to Young Siward immediately after Macbeth has killed him:

Thou wast born of woman:—
But swords I smile at, weapons laugh to scorn,
Brandish'd by man that's of a woman born.
(5.7.11–13)

Young Siward's death becomes in effect proof that he was born of woman; in the logic of Macbeth's psyche, Macbeth's invulnerability is the proof that he was not. The "but" records this fantasied distinction: it constructs the sentence "You, born of woman, are vulnerable; but I, not born of woman, am not."[32]

Insofar as this is the fantasy embodied in Macbeth at the play's end, it is punished by the equivocation of the fiends: the revelation that Macduff derives from woman, though by unusual means, musters against Macbeth all the values of ordinary family and community that Macduff carries with him. Macbeth, "cow'd" by the revelation (5.8.18),[33] is forced to take on the taint of vulnerability; the fantasy of escape from the maternal matrix seems to die with him. But although this fantasy is punished in Macbeth, it does not quite die with him; it continues to have a curious life of its own in the play, apart from its embodiment in him. Even from the beginning of the play, the fantasy has not been

Macbeth's alone: as the play's most striking bloody man, he is in the beginning the bearer of this fantasy for the all-male community that depends on his bloody prowess. The opening scenes strikingly construct male and female as realms apart; and the initial descriptions of Macbeth's battles construe his prowess as a consequence of his exemption from the taint of woman.

In the description of his battle with Macdonwald, what looks initially like a battle between loyal and disloyal sons to establish primacy in the father's eyes is oddly transposed into a battle of male against female:

> Doubtful it stood;
> As two spent swimmers, that do cling together
> And choke their art. The merciless Macdonwald
> (Worthy to be a rebel, for to that
> The multiplying villainies of nature
> Do swarm upon him) from the western isles
> Of Kernes and Gallowglasses is supplied;
> And Fortune, on his damned quarrel smiling,
> Show'd like a rebel's whore: but all's too weak;
> For brave Macbeth (well he deserves that name),
> Disdaining Fortune, with his brandish'd steel,
> Which smok'd with bloody execution,
> Like Valour's minion, carv'd out his passage,
> Till he fac'd the slave;
> Which ne'er shook hands, nor bade farewell to him,
> Till he unseam'd him from the nave to th' chops,
> And fix'd his head upon our battlements.
>
> (1.2.7–23)

The two initially indistinguishable figures metaphorized as the swimmers eventually sort themselves out into victor and victim, but only by first sorting themselves out into male and female, as though Macbeth can be distinguished from Macdonwald only by making Macdonwald functionally female. The "merciless Macdonwald" is initially firmly identified; but by the time Macbeth appears, Macdonwald has temporarily disappeared, replaced by the female figure of Fortune, against whom Macbeth seems to fight ("brave Macbeth, . . . Disdaining Fortune, with his brandish'd steel"). The metaphorical substitution of Fortune for Macdonwald transforms the battle into a contest between male and female; it makes Macbeth's deserving of his name contingent on his victory over the female. We are prepared for this transformation by Macdonwald's sexual alliance with the tainting female, the whore Fortune;[34] Macbeth's identification as valor's minion redefines the battle as a contest between the half-female couple Fortune/Macdonwald and the all-male couple Valor/Macbeth. Metaphorically, Macdonwald and Macbeth take on the qualities of the unreliable female and the heroic male; Macbeth's battle against Fortune turns out to be his battle against Macdonwald because the two are functionally the same. Macdonwald, tainted by the female, becomes an easy mark for Macbeth, who demonstrates his own untainted manhood by unseaming Macdonwald from the nave to the chops. Through its allusions both to castration and to Caesarean section, this unseaming furthermore remakes Macdonwald's body as female, revealing what his alliance with Fortune has suggested all along.

In effect, then, the battle that supports the father's kingdom plays out the creation of a conquering all-male erotics that marks its conquest by its triumph over a feminized body, simultaneously that of Fortune and Macdonwald. Hence, in the double action of the passage, the victorious unseaming happens twice: first on the body of Fortune and then on the body of Macdonwald. The lines descriptive of Macbeth's approach to Macdonwald—"brave Macbeth . . . Disdaining Fortune, with his brandish'd steel . . . carved out his passage"— make that approach contingent on Macbeth's first carving his passage through a female body, hewing his way out. The language here perfectly anticipates Macduff's birth by Caesarean section, revealed at the end of the play: if Macduff is ripped untimely from his mother's womb, Macbeth here manages in fantasy his own Caesarean section,[35] carving his passage out from the unreliable female to achieve heroic male action, in effect carving up the female to arrive at the male. Only after this rite of passage can Macbeth meet Macdonwald: the act of aggression toward the female body, the fantasy of self-birth, marks his passage to the contest that will be definitive of his maleness partly insofar as it is definitive of Macdonwald's tainted femaleness. For the all-male community surrounding Duncan, then, Macbeth's victory is allied with his triumph over femaleness; for them, he becomes invulnerable, "lapp'd in proof" (1.2.55) like one of Lady Macbeth's armored men-children.[36] Even before his entry into the play, that is, Macbeth is the bearer of the shared fantasy that secure male community depends on the prowess of the man in effect not born of woman, the man who can carve his own passage out, the man whose very maleness is the mark of his exemption from female power.[37]

Ostensibly, the play rejects the version of manhood implicit in the shared fantasy of the beginning. Macbeth himself is well aware that his capitulation to Lady Macbeth's definition of manhood entails his abandonment of his own more inclusive definition of what becomes a man (1.7.46); and Macduff's response to the news of his family's destruction insists that humane feeling is central to the definition of manhood (4.3.221). Moreover, the revelation that even Macduff had a mother sets a limiting condition on the fantasy of a bloody masculine escape from the female and hence on the kind of manhood defined by that escape. Nonetheless, even at the end, the play enables one version of the fantasy that heroic manhood is exemption from the female even while it punishes that fantasy in Macbeth. The key figure in whom this double movement is vested in the end of the play is Macduff; the unresolved contradictions that surround him are, I think, marks of ambivalence toward the fantasy itself. In insisting that mourning for his family is his right as a man, he presents family feeling as central to the definition of manhood; and yet he conspicuously leaves his family vulnerable to destruction when he goes off to offer his services to Malcolm. The play moreover insists on reminding us that he has inexplicably abandoned his family: both Lady Macduff and Malcolm question the necessity of this abandonment (4.2.6–14; 4.3.26–28), and the play never allows Macduff to explain himself. This unexplained abandonment severely qualifies Macduff's force as the play's central exemplar of a healthy manhood that can include the possibility of relationship to women: the play seems to vest diseased familial relations in Macbeth and the possibility of healthy ones in Macduff; and yet we discover dramatically that Macduff has a family only when we hear that he has abandoned it. Dramatically and psychologically, he takes on full masculine power only as he loses his family and becomes energized by the loss, converting his grief into the more "manly" tune of vengeance (4.3.235); the loss of his family here enables his accession to full masculine action even while his response to that loss insists on a more humane definition of manhood.[38] The play here pulls in two directions. It reiterates this doubleness by vesting in Macduff its final fantasy of exemption from woman. The ambivalence that shapes the portrayal of Macduff is evident even as he reveals to Macbeth that he "was from his mother's womb / Untimely ripp'd" (5.8.15–16): the emphasis on untimeliness and the violence of the image suggest that he has been prematurely deprived of a nurturing maternal presence; but the prophecy construes just this deprivation as the source of Macduff's strength.[39] The prophecy itself both denies and affirms the fantasy of exemption from women: in affirming that Macduff has indeed had a mother, it denies the fantasy of male self-generation; but in attributing his power to his having been untimely ripped from that mother, it sustains the sense that violent separation from the mother is the mark of the successful male. The final battle between Macbeth and Macduff thus replays the initial battle between Macbeth and Macdonwald. But Macduff has now taken the place of Macbeth: he carries with him the male power given him by the Caesarean solution, and Macbeth is retrospectively revealed as Macdonwald, the woman's man.

The doubleness of the prophecy is less the equivocation of the fiends than Shakespeare's own equivocation about the figure of Macduff and about the fantasy vested in him in the end. For Macduff carries with him simultaneously all the values of family and the claim that masculine power derives from the unnatural abrogation of family, including escape from the conditions of one's birth. Moreover, the ambivalence that shapes the figure of Macduff similarly shapes the dramatic structure of the play itself. Ostensibly concerned to restore natural order at the end,[40] the play bases that order upon the radical exclusion of the female. Initially construed as all-powerful, the women virtually disappear at the end, Lady Macbeth becoming so diminished a character that we scarcely trouble to ask ourselves whether the report of her suicide is accurate or not, the witches literally gone from the stage and so diminished in psychic power that Macbeth never mentions them and blames his defeat only on the equivocation of their male masters, the fiends; even Lady Macduff exists only to disappear. The bogus fulfillment of the Birnam Wood prophecy suggests the extent to which the natural order of the end depends on the exclusion of the female. Critics sometimes see in the march of Malcolm's soldiers bearing their green branches an allusion to the Maying festivals in which participants returned from the woods bearing branches, or to the ritual scourging of a hibernal figure by the forces of the oncoming spring.[41] The allusion seems to me clearly present; but it serves, I think, to mark precisely what the moving of Birnam Wood is not. Malcolm's use of Birnam Wood is a military maneuver. His drily worded command (5.4.4–7) leaves little room for suggestions of natural fertility or for the deep sense of the generative world rising up to expel its winter king; nor does the play later enable these associations except in a scattered and partly ironic way.[42] These trees have little resemblance to those in the Forest of Arden; their branches, like those carried by the apparition of the "child crowned, with a tree in his hand" (4.1.86), are little more than the emblems of a strictly patriarchal family tree.[43] This family tree, like the march of Birnam Wood itself, is relentlessly male: Duncan and sons, Banquo and son, Siward and son. There are no daughters and scarcely any mention of mothers in these family trees. We are brought as close as possible here to the fantasy of family without women.[44] In that sense, Birnam Wood is the perfect emblem of the nature that triumphs at the end of the play: nature without generative possibility, nature without women. Malcolm tells his men to carry the branches to obscure themselves, and that is exactly their function: insofar as they seem to allude to the rising of the natural order against Macbeth, they obscure the operations of male power, disguising them as a natural force; and they simultaneously obscure the extent to which natural order itself is here reconceived as purely male.[45]

If we can see the fantasy of escape from the female in the play's fulfillment of the witches' prophecies—in Macduff's birth by Caesarean section and in Malcolm's appropriation of Birnam Wood—we can see it also in the play's psychological geography. The shift from Scotland to England is strikingly the shift from the mother's to the father's terrain.[46] Scotland "cannot / Be call'd our mother, but our grave" (4.3.165–66), in Rosse's words to Macduff: it is the realm of Lady Macbeth and the witches, the realm in which the mother *is* the grave, the realm appropriately ruled by their bad son Macbeth. The escape to England is an escape from their power into the realm of the good father-king and his surrogate son Malcolm, "unknown to woman" (4.3.126). The magical power of this father to cure clearly balances the magical power of the witches to harm, as Malcolm (the father's son) balances Macbeth (the mother's son). That Macduff can cross from one realm into the other only by abandoning his family suggests the rigidity of the psychic geography separating England from Scotland. At the end of the play, Malcolm returns to Scotland mantled in the power England gives him, in effect bringing the power of the fathers with him: bearer of his father's line, unknown to woman, supported by his agent Macduff (empowered by his own special immunity from birth), Malcolm embodies utter separation from women and as such triumphs easily over Macbeth, the mother's son.

The play that begins by unleashing the terrible threat of destructive maternal power and demonstrates the helplessness of its central male figure before that power thus ends by consolidating male power, in effect solving the problem of masculinity by eliminating the female. In the psychological fantasies that I am tracing, the play portrays the failure of the androgynous parent to protect his son, that son's consequent fall into the dominion of the bad mothers, and the final victory of a masculine order in which mothers no longer threaten because they no longer exist. In that sense, *Macbeth* is a recuperative consolidation of male power, a consolidation in the face of the threat unleashed in *Hamlet* and especially in *King Lear* and never fully contained in those plays. In *Macbeth*, maternal power is given its most virulent sway and then abolished; at the end of the play we are in a purely male realm. We will not be in so absolute a male realm again until we are in Prospero's island kingdom, similarly based firmly on the exiling of the witch Sycorax.

NOTES

This essay is reprinted from *Cannibals, Witches, and Divorce: Estranging the Renaissance* (Selected Papers from the English Institute, 1985, New Series, No. 11), ed. Marjorie Garber (Baltimore, Md.: Johns Hopkins University Press, 1987), 90–121. The essay is also incorporated in *Suffocating Mothers: Fantasies of Maternal Origins in Shakespeare, "Hamlet" to "The Tempest"* (London: Routledge, 1991).

1. All references to *Macbeth* are to the new Arden edition, edited by Muir.

2. I have written elsewhere about Coriolanus's doomed attempts to create a self that is independent of his mother's will; see my " 'Anger's My Meat': Feeding, Dependency, and Aggression in *Coriolanus*." Others have noted the extent to which both *Macbeth* and *Coriolanus* deal with the construction of a rigid male identity felt as a defense against overwhelming maternal power; see particularly Kahn, *Man's Estate*, whose chapter title "The Milking Babe and the Bloody Man in *Coriolanus* and *Macbeth*" indicates the similarity of our concerns (151–92). Bamber argues, however, that the absence of a feminine Other in *Macbeth* and *Coriolanus* prevents the development of manliness in the heroes, since true manliness "involves a detachment from the feminine" (20, 91–107).

3. Kozikowski argues strenuously that Shakespeare knew either the pamphlet "Gowries Conspiracie" (printed in Scotland and London in 1600) or the abortive play on the conspiracy, apparently performed twice by the King's Men and then canceled in 1604. Although I do not find his arguments entirely persuasive, it seems likely that Shakespeare knew at least the central facts of the conspiracy, given both James's annual celebration of his escape from it and the apparent involvement of the King's Men in a play on the subject. See also Mullaney's suggestive use of the Gowrie material as an analogue for *Macbeth* in its link between treason and magical riddle (32, 38).

4. After the failure of the conspiracy, James searched the dead earl's pockets, finding nothing in them "but a little close parchment bag, full of magicall characters, and words of inchantment, wherin, it seemed, that he had put his confidence, thinking him selfe never safe without them, and therfore ever carried them about with him; beeing also observed, that, while they were uppon him, his wound whereof he died, bled not, but, incontinent after the taking of them away, the blood gushed out in great aboundance, to the great admiration of al the beholders" ("Gowries Conspiracie" 196). The magical stopping up of the blood and the sudden return of its natural flow seem to me potent images for the progress of Macbeth as he is first seduced and then abandoned by the witches' prophecies; that Gowrie's necromancer, like the witches, seemed

to dabble in alternate modes of generation increases the suggestiveness of this association for *Macbeth*.

5. All references to Shakespeare's plays other than *Macbeth* are to the revised Pelican edition, *William Shakespeare: The Complete Works*, ed. Alfred Harbage.

6. Wheeler, Neill, and Kahn similarly understand Richard III's self-divided and theatrical masculinity as a defensive response to real or imagined maternal deprivation. See Wheeler, "History, Character and Conscience," esp. 314–15; Neill, esp. 104–106; and Kahn, 63–66.

7. "Impale" in the sense of "to enclose with pales, stakes or posts; to surround with a pallisade" (*OED*'s first meaning) is of course the dominant usage contemporary with *Macbeth*. But the word was in the process of change. *OED*'s meaning 4, "to thrust a pointed stake through the body of, as a form of torture or capital punishment," although cited first in 1613, clearly seems to stand behind the imagistic transformation here. The shift in meaning perfectly catches Richard's psychological process, in which any protective enclosure is ambivalently desired and threatens to turn into a torturing impalement.

8. Watson notes the imagery of Caesarean birth here and in *Macbeth* (see esp. 19–20, 99–105); the metaphors of Caesarean section and Oedipal rape are central to his understanding of ambitious self-creation insofar as both imagine a usurpation of the defining parental acts of generation (see, for example, 3–5). Though it is frequently very suggestive, Watson's account tends too easily to blur the distinction between matricide and patricide: in fantasies of rebirth, the hero may symbolically replace the father to re-create himself, but he does so by means of an attack specifically on the maternal body. In Shakespeare's images of Caesarean birth, the father tends to be conspicuously absent; indeed, I shall argue, precisely his absence—not his defining presence—creates the fear of the engulfing maternal body to which the fantasy of Caesarean section is a response. This body tends to be missing in Watson's account, as it is missing in his discussion of Richard's Caesarean fantasy here.

9. In an early essay that has become a classic, Waith established the centrality of definitions of manhood and Lady Macbeth's role in enforcing Macbeth's particularly bloodthirsty version, a theme that has since become a major topos of *Macbeth* criticism. Among the ensuing legions, see, for example, Proser; Taylor (unusual in its early emphasis on the extent to which the culture is complicit in defining masculinity as aggression); Harding (significant especially in its stress on women's responsibility for committing men to their false fantasy of manhood); Jorgensen, esp. 147ff.; Ramsey; Asp (significant especially for associating Macbeth's pursuit of masculinity with his pursuit of omnipotence); Berger, "Text against Performance," esp. 67–75; and Kimbrough. Virtually all these essays recount the centrality of 1.7 to this theme; most see Macbeth's willingness to murder as his response to Lady Macbeth's nearly explicit attack on his male potency. Biggins and Greene note particularly the extent to which the murder itself is imagined as a sexual act through which the union of Macbeth and Lady Macbeth is consummated; see also Watson 90. My account differs from most of these

largely in stressing the infantile components of Macbeth's susceptibility to Lady Macbeth. The classic account of these pre-Oedipal components in the play is Barron's brilliant early essay "The Babe That Milks." For similar readings, see Rosenberg 81–82, 270–72; and especially Kahn 151–55, 172–92, and Wheeler, *Shakespeare's Development* 144–49; as always, I am deeply and minutely indebted to the two last named.

10. Berger associates both Duncan's vulnerability and his role in legitimizing the bloody masculinity of his thanes with his status as the androgynous supplier of blood and milk ("The Early Scenes" 26–28). Schwartz (29) and Wheeler (*Shakespeare's Development* 145) note specifically the extent to which the male claim to androgynous possession of nurturant power reflects a fear of maternal power outside male control. My discussion of Duncan's androgyny is partly a consequence of my having heard at MLA in 1979 Erickson's rich account of the Duke's taking on a nurturant function in *As You Like It*; this account is now part of his *Patriarchal Structures*; see esp. 27–37.

11. Many commentators note that Shakespeare's Duncan is less ineffectual than Holingshed's; others note the continuing signs of his weakness. See especially Berger's brilliant account of the structural effect of Duncan's weakness in defining his (and Macbeth's) society ("The Early Scenes").

12. Many note the appropriateness of Macbeth's conflation of himself with Tarquin, given the play's alliance of sexuality and murder. See, for example, Robinson 104; Biggins 269; and Watson 100. Kirsch works extensively with the analogy, seeing the Tarquin of *The Rape of Lucrece* as a model for Macbeth's ambitious desire. Commentators on the analogy do not in general note that it transforms Macbeth's kingly victim into a woman; Rabkin is the exception (107).

13. Wheeler sees the simultaneously castrated and castrating Gorgon-like body of Duncan as the emblem of the world Macbeth brings into being (*Shakespeare's Development* 145); I see it as the emblem of a potentially castrating femaleness that Macbeth's act of violence reveals but does not create.

14. The witches' power to raise storms was conventional; see, for example, Scot 31; James I 46; and the failure of the witches to raise a storm in Jonson's *Masque of Queens*. Jonson's learned note on their attempt to disturb nature gives his classical sources for their association with chaos: see *Masque*, ll. 134–37, 209–20, and Jonson's note to l. 134, in Orgel, *Ben Johnson* 531–32.

15. Many commentators, following Freud, find the murder of Duncan "little else than parricide" (Strachey 14: 321); see, for example, Rabkin 106–109; Kirsch 276–80, 286; and Watson, esp. 85–88, 98–99 (the last two are particularly interesting in understanding parricide as an ambitious attempt to redefine the self as omnipotently free from limits). In standard Oedipal readings of the play, the mother is less the object of desire than "the 'demon-woman' who creates the abyss between father and son" by inciting the son to parricide (Jekels 240). See also, for example, Veszy-Wagner 242–57; Holland 229; and Hogan's very suggestive account of the Oedipal narrative structure (385–95). My reading differs from these Oedipal readings mainly in suggesting that the play's mothers acquire their power because the father's protective masculine authority is already

significantly absent; in my reading, female power over Macbeth becomes the sign (rather than the cause) of that absence.

16. For those recent commentators who follow Barron in seeing pre-Oedipal rather than Oedipal issues as central to the play, the images of disrupted nurturance define the primary area of disturbance; see, for example, Barron 255; Schwartz 29; Berger, "The Early Scenes" 27–28; Byles; Wheeler, *Shakespeare's Development* 147–48; and Kirsch 291–92. Although Madelon Gohlke (now Sprengnether) does not specifically discuss the rupture of maternal nurturance in *Macbeth*, my understanding of the play is very much indebted to her classic essay " 'I wooed thee with my sword': Shakespeare's Tragic Paradigms," in which she establishes the extent to which masculinity in Shakespeare's heroes entails a defensive denial of the female; in an unfortunately unpublished essay, she discusses the traumatic failure of maternal protection imaged by Lady Macbeth here. Willbern locates in Lady Macbeth's image the psychological point of origin for the failure of potential space that Macbeth enacts. Erickson, noting that patriarchal bounty in *Macbeth* has gone awry, suggestively locates the dependence of that bounty on the maternal nurturance that is here disturbed (116–21). Several critics see in Macbeth's susceptibility to female influence evidence of his failure to differentiate from a maternal figure, a failure psychologically the consequence of the abrupt and bloody weaning imaged by Lady Macbeth; see, for example, Bachmann, and particularly the full and very suggestive accounts of Barron 263–68 and Kahn 172–78. In the readings of all these critics, as in mine, Lady Macbeth and the witches variously embody the destructive maternal force that overwhelms Macbeth and in relation to whom he is imagined as an infant. Rosenberg notes intriguingly that *Macbeth* has twice been performed with a mother and son in the chief roles (196).

17. Despite some overliteral interpretation, Fox and particularly La Belle usefully demonstrate the specifically gynecological references of "passage" and "visitings of nature," using contemporary gynecological treatises (see Fox 129; and La Belle 382, for the identification of "visitings of nature" as a term for menstruation; see La Belle 383 for the identification of "passage" as a term for the neck of the womb. See also Barron, who associates Lady Macbeth's language here with contraception [267]).

18. "For" is glossed as "in exchange for" in the following editions, for example: *The Complete Signet Classic Shakespeare*, ed. Barnet; *The Complete Works of Shakespeare*, ed. Craig; *The Riverside Shakespeare*, ed. Evans; *William Shakespeare: The Complete Works*, ed. Harbage; *The Complete Works of Shakespeare*, ed. Kittredge. Muir demurs, preferring Keightley's understanding of "take" as "infect" (see the Arden edition, 30).

19. Insofar as syphilis was known to be transmitted through the nursing process, there was some reason to worry; see, for example, Clowes's frightening account (151). But Leontes's words to Hermione as he removes Mamillius from her ("I am glad you did not nurse him. / Though he does bear some signs of me, yet you / Have too much blood in him" [*The Winter's Tale* 2.1.56–58]) suggest that the worry was not fundamentally about epidemiology. Worry that the nurse's milk determined morals was, of course, common; see, for example, Phaire 18. The topic was of interest to King James, who claimed to have sucked his Protestantism from his nurse's milk; his drunkenness

was also attributed to her (see Paul 387–88). For the identification of colostrum with witch's milk, see Radbill 249. The fear of maternal functioning itself, not simply of its perversions, is central to most readings of the play in pre-Oedipal terms; see the critics cited in note 16 above.

20. Many commentators on English witchcraft note the unusual prominence given to the presence of the witch's mark and the nursing of familiars; see, for example, Rosen's introduction to the collection of witchcraft documents she edited (29–30). She cites contemporary documents on the nursing of familiars, for example 187–88, 315; the testimony of Joan Prentice, one of the convicted witches of Chelmsford in 1589, is particularly suggestive: "at what time soever she would have her ferret do anything for her, she used the words 'Bid, Bid, Bid, come Bid, come Bid, come Bid, come suck, come suck, come suck' " (188). Briggs quotes a contemporary (1613) story about the finding of a witch's teat (250); see also Notestein 36; and Kittredge, *Witchcraft* 179. Though he does not refer to the suckling of familiars, King James believed in the significance of the witch's mark, at least when he wrote the *Daemonologie* (see James I 33). Bradbrook notes that Lady Macbeth's invitation to the spirits is "as much as any witch could do by way of self-dedication" (43).

21. In a brilliant essay, Stallybrass associates the move from the cosmic to the secular realm with the ideological shoring up of a patriarchal state founded on the model of the family (esp. 196–98).

22. Sanders notes the extent to which "terror is mediated through absurdity" in the witches (277); see also Berger's fine account of the scapegoating reduction of the witches to a comic and grotesque triviality ("Text against Performance" 67–68). Goddard (512–13), Robinson (100–103), and Stallybrass (199) note the witches' change from potent and mysterious to more diminished figures in act 4.

23. After years of trying fruitlessly to pin down a precise identity for the witches, critics are increasingly finding their dramatic power precisely in their indefinability. The most powerful statements of this relatively new critical topos are those by Sanders (277–79), West (78–79), and Booth (101–103).

24. For their "Englishness," see Stallybrass 195. Macfarlane's important study of English witchcraft, *Witchcraft in Tudor and Stuart England*, frequently notes the absence of the Continental staples: if the witches of Essex are typical, English witches do not fly, do not hold Sabbaths, do not commit sexual perversions or attack male potency, do not kill babies (see 6, 160, 180, for example).

25. Macfarlane finds the failure of neighborliness reflected in the retaliatory acts of the witch the key to the social function of witchcraft in England; see Macfarlane 168–76 for accounts of the failures of neighborliness—very similar to the refusal to share chestnuts—that provoked the witch to act. Sprenger and Kramer, *Malleus Maleficarum*, is the *locus classicus* for Continental witchcraft beliefs: for the murder and eating of infants, see 21, 66, 99, 100–101; for attacks on the genitals, see 47, 55–60, 117–19; for sexual relations with demons, see 21, 112–14. Or see Scot's convenient summary of these beliefs (31).

26. The relationship between cosmology and domestic psychology is similar in

King Lear; even as Shakespeare casts doubt on the authenticity of demonic possession by his use of Harsnett's *Declaration of Egregious Popish Impostures,* Edgar/Poor Tom's identification of his father as "the foul Flibbertigibbet" (3.4.108) manifests the psychic reality and source of his demons. Characteristically in Shakespeare, the site of blessing and of cursedness is the family, their processes psychological.

27. Although "his" was a common form for the as yet unfamiliar possessive "its," Lady Macbeth's move from "while it was smiling" to "his boneless gums" nonetheless seems to register the metamorphosis of an ungendered to a gendered infant exactly at the moment of vulnerability, making her attack specifically on a male child. That she uses the ungendered "the" a moment later ("the brains out") suggests one alternative open to Shakespeare had he wished to avoid the implication that the fantasied infant was male; Antony's crocodile, who "moves with it own organs" (*Antony and Cleopatra* 2.7.42), suggests another. (*OED* notes that, although "its" occurs in the Folio, it does not occur in any work of Shakespeare published while he was alive; it also notes the various strategies by which authors attempted to avoid the inappropriate use of "his.")

28. Lady Macbeth maintains her control over Macbeth through 3.4 by manipulating these categories: see 2.2.53–54 (" 'tis the eye of childhood / That fears a painted devil") and 3.4.57–65 ("Are you a man? . . . these flaws and starts . . . would well become / A woman's story"). In his response to Banquo's ghost, Macbeth invokes the same categories and suggests their interchangeability: he dares what man dares (3.4.98); if he feared Banquo alive, he could rightly be called "the baby of a girl" (l. 105).

29. Willbern notes the extent to which the regicide is reimagined as a "symbolic infanticide" so that the image of Duncan fuses with the image of Lady Macbeth's child murdered in fantasy. Macbeth's earlier association of Duncan's power with the power of the "naked new-born babe, / Striding the blast" (1.7.21–22) prepares for this fusion. Despite their symbolic power, the literal babies of this play and those adults who sleep and trust like infants are hideously vulnerable.

30. See Kahn 173 for a very similar account of this passage.

31. Shakespeare's only other use of "man-child" is in a strikingly similar context. Volumnia, reporting her pleasure in Coriolanus's martial success, tells Virgilia, "I sprang not more in joy at first hearing he was a man-child than now in first seeing he had proved himself a man" (*Coriolanus* 1.3.15–17).

32. De Quincy seems to have understood this process: "The murderers are taken out of the region of human things, human purposes, human desires. They are transfigured: Lady Macbeth is 'unsexed'; Macbeth has forgot that he was born of woman" (335). Critics who consider gender relations central to this play generally note the importance of the witches' prophecy for the figure of Macduff; they do not usually note its application to Macbeth. But see Kahn's suggestion that the prophecy sets Macbeth "apart from women as well as from men" (187) and Gohlke's central perception that "to be born of woman, as [Macbeth] reads the witches' prophecy, is to be mortal" (176).

33. See Kahn's rich understanding of the function of the term "cow'd" (191).

34. Many comment on this contamination; see, for example, Berger, "The Early Scenes" 7–8; Hogan 387; Rosenberg 45; Biggins 265.

35. Watson notes the suggestion of Caesarean section here, though not its aggression toward the female. Barron does not comment specifically on this passage but notes breaking and cutting imagery throughout and relates it to Macbeth's attempt to "cut his way out of the female environment which chokes and smothers him" (269). I am indebted to Willbern specifically for the Caesarean implication of the unseaming from nave to chops.

36. The reference to Macbeth as "Bellona's bridegroom" anticipates his interaction with Lady Macbeth in 1.7: only the murderous man-child is fit mate for either of these unsexed, quasi-male figures.

37. To the extent that ferocious maleness is the creation of the male community, not of Lady Macbeth or the witches, the women are scapegoats who exist partly to obscure the failures of male community. For fuller accounts of this process, see Veszy-Wagner 244, Bamber 19–20, and especially Berger, "Text against Performance" 68–75. But whether or not the women are scapegoats insofar as they are (falsely) held responsible for Macbeth's murderous maleness, fear of the female power they represent remains primary (not secondary and obscurantist) insofar as the male community and, to some extent, the play itself define maleness as violent differentiation from the female.

38. A great many critics, following Waith (266–67), find the play's embodiment of healthy masculinity in Macduff. They often register some uneasiness about his leaving his family, but they rarely allow this uneasiness to complicate their view of him as exemplary. But critics interested in the play's construction of masculinity as a defense against the fear of femaleness tend to see in Macduff's removal from family a replication of the central fear of women that is more fully played out in Macbeth. See, for example, Wheeler, *Shakespeare's Development* 146, and Berger, "Text against Performance" 70. For these critics, Macduff's flight is of a piece with his status as the man not born of woman.

39. Critics interested in gender issues almost invariably comment on the centrality of Macduff's fulfillment of this prophecy, finding his strength here in his freedom from contamination by or regressive dependency on women: see, for example, Harding 250; Barron 272; Berger, "The Early Scenes" 28; Bachmann 101; Kirsch 293; Kahn 172–73; Wheeler, *Shakespeare's Development* 146; and Calef 537. For Barron and Harding, Macduff's status as the bearer of this fantasy positively enhances his manhood; but for many of these critics, it qualifies his status as the examplar of healthy manhood. Perhaps because ambivalence toward Macduff is built so deeply into the play, several very astute critics see the fantasy embedded in Macduff here and nonetheless continue to find in him an ideal manhood that includes the possibility of relatedness to the feminine. See, for example, Kahn 191 and Kirsch 294.

40. The triumph of the natural order has of course been a commonplace of criticism since the classic essay by Knight, "The Milk of Concord," esp. 140–53. The topos

is so powerful that it can cause even critics interested in gender issues to praise the triumph of nature and natural sexuality at the end without noting the exclusion of the female; see, for example, Greene 172. But Rosenberg, for example, notes the qualifying effect of this exclusion (654).

41. See, for example, Goddard 520-21; Jekels 238; Holloway 66; Rosenberg 626; and Watson 89, 106-16. Even without sensing the covert presence of a vegetation myth, critics often associate the coming of Birnam Wood with the restoration of spring and fertility; see, for example, Knight 144-45 and Greene 169. Only Bamber demurs: in her account Birnam Wood rises up in aid of a male alliance, not the Saturnalian disorder of the Maying rituals (106). My view coincides with hers.

42. When Malcolm refers to planting (5.9.31) at the play's end, for example, his comment serves partly to reinforce our sense of his distance from his father's generative power.

43. Paul attributes Shakespeare's use of the imagery of the family tree here to his familiarity with the cut of the Banquo tree in Leslie's *De Origine, Moribus, et Rebus Gesta Scotorum* (*Royal Play,* 175). But the image is too familiar to call for such explanation; see, for example, the tree described in *Richard II* (1.2.12-21).

44. As Wheeler notes, the description of Malcolm's saintly mother makes him "symbolically the child of something approximating virgin birth" (*Shakespeare's Development* 146)—in effect another version of the man not quite born of woman. Berger comments on the aspiration to be "a nation of bachelor Adams, of no woman born and unknown to women" ("Text against Performance" 72), without noting the extent to which this fantasy is enacted in the play; Stallybrass calls attention to this configuration and describes the structure of antithesis through which "(virtuous) families of men" are distinguished from "antifamilies of women" (198). The fantasy of escape from maternal birth and the creation of all-male lineage would probably have been of interest to King James, whose problematic derivation from Mary, Queen of Scots must occasionally have made him wish himself not born of (that particular) woman, no matter how much he was concerned publicly to rehabilitate her image. See Goldberg's account of James's complex attitude toward Mary and especially his attempt to claim the Virgin Queen, Elizabeth, rather than Mary as his mother as he moved toward the English throne (11-17, 25-26, 119); see also Goldberg's very suggestive discussions of James's poetic attacks on women (24-25) and his imaging himself as a man taking control of a woman in becoming king of England (30-31, 46). Orgel speculates brilliantly about the ways in which James's concerns about his own lineage and hence about the derivation of his royal authority are reflected in *The Tempest:* James "conceived himself as the head of a single-parent family," as a paternal figure who has "incorporated the maternal," in effect as a Prospero; the alternative model is Caliban, who derives his authority from his mother ("Prospero's Wife" 8-9). Perhaps *Macbeth* indirectly serves a cultural need to free James from entanglement with the problematic memory of his witch-mother (portrayed thus, for example, by Spenser in book 5 of *The Faerie Queene*), tracing his lineage instead from a safely distanced and safely male forefather, Banquo.

45. Although neither Berger nor Stallybrass discusses the function of Birnam Wood specifically, I am indebted here to their discussions of the ideological function of the play's appeal to cosmology in the service of patriarchy, Berger seeing it as "a collective project of mystification" ("Text against Performance" 64), Stallybrass as "a returning of the disputed ground of politics to the undisputed ground of Nature" (205–206). If, as Bradbrook suggests, witches were thought able to move trees (42), then we have in Malcolm's gesture a literal appropriation of female power, an act of making the unnatural natural by making it serve patriarchal needs.

46. See Erickson's fine discussion of this geographic dinstinction (121–22).

WORKS CITED

Adelman, Janet. " 'Anger's My Meat': Feeding, Dependency, and Aggression in *Coriolanus*." *Representing Shakespeare: New Psychoanalytic Essays*. Ed. Murray M. Schwartz and Coppélia Kahn. Baltimore: Johns Hopkins UP, 1980. 129–49.

Asp, Carolyn. " 'Be bloody, bold, and resolute': Tragic Action and Sexual Stereotyping in *Macbeth*." *Studies in Philology* 25 (1981): 153–69.

Bachmann, Susan. " 'Daggers in Men's Smiles'—The 'Truest Issue' in *Macbeth*." *International Review of Psycho-Analysis* 5 (1978): 97–104.

Bamber, Linda. *Comic Women, Tragic Men: A Study of Gender and Genre in Shakespeare.* Stanford: Stanford UP, 1982.

Barnet, Sylvan, ed. *The Complete Signet Classic Shakespeare.* New York: Harcourt, Brace, Jovanovich, 1972.

Barron, David B. "The Babe That Milks: An Organic Study of *Macbeth*." 1960. *The Design Within.* Ed. M. D. Faber. New York: Science House, 1970. 253–79.

Berger, Harry Jr. "The Early Scenes of *Macbeth*: Preface to a New Interpretation." *ELH* 47 (1980): 1–31.

———. "Text against Performance in Shakespeare: The Example of *Macbeth*." *The Forms of Power and the Power of Forms in the Renaissance.* Ed. Stephen Greenblatt. *Genre* 15 (1982): 49–79.

Biggins, Dennis. "Sexuality, Witchcraft, and Violence in Macbeth." *Shakespeare Studies* 8 (1975): 255–77.

Booth, Stephen. *"King Lear," "Macbeth," Indefinition, and Tragedy.* New Haven: Yale UP, 1983.

Bradbrook, M. C. "The Sources of *Macbeth*." *Shakespeare Survey* 4 (1951): 35–48.

Briggs, Katharine Mary. *Pale Hecate's Team.* New York: Arno Press, 1977.

Byles, Joan M. "Macbeth: Imagery of Destruction." *American Imago* 39 (1982): 149–64.

Calef, Victor. "Lady Macbeth and Infanticide, or 'How Many Children Had Lady

Macbeth Murdered?' " *Journal of the American Psychoanalytic Association* 17 (1969): 528–48.

Clowes, William. "A Brief and Neccessary Treatise Touching the Cure of the Disease Called Morbus Gallicus." London, 1585.

Craig, Hardin, ed. *The Complete Works of Shakespeare.* Chicago: Scott, Foresman, 1951. Rev. Ed. David Bevinton. 1973.

De Quincy, Thomas. "On the Knocking at the Gate in *Macbeth.*" *Shakespeare Criticism: A Selection, 1623–1840.* Ed. D. Nichol Smith. London: Oxford UP, 1946. 331–36.

Erickson, Peter. *Patriarchal Structures in Shakespeare's Drama.* Berkeley: U of California P, 1985.

Evans, G. Blakemore, ed. *The Riverside Shakespeare.* Boston: Houghton Mifflin, 1974.

Fox, Alice. "Obstetrics and Gynecology in *Macbeth.*" *Shakespeare Studies* 12 (1979): 127–41.

Goddard, Harold C. *The Meaning of Shakespeare.* Chicago: U of Chicago P, 1951.

Gohlke, Madelon. " 'I wooed thee with my sword': Shakespeare's Tragic Paradigms." *Representing Shakespeare: New Psychoanalytic Essays.* Ed. Murray M. Schwartz and Coppélia Kahn. Baltimore: Johns Hopkins UP, 1980. 170–87.

Goldberg, Jonathan. *James I and the Politics of Literature.* Baltimore: Johns Hopkins University Press, 1983.

"Gowries Conspiracie: A Discoverie of the unnaturall and vyle Conspiracie, attempted against the Kings Maiesties Person at Sanct-Iohnstoun, upon Twysday the Fifth of August, 1600." *A Selection from the Harleian Miscellany.* London: C. and G. Kearsley, 1793. 190–99.

Greene, James. "Macbeth: Masculinity as Murder." *American Imago* 41 (1984): 155–80.

Harbage, Alfred, ed. *William Shakespeare: The Complete Works.* Baltimore: Penguin, 1969.

Harding, D. W. "Women's Fantasy of Manhood: A Shakespearean Theme." *Shakespeare Quarterly* 20 (1969): 245–53.

Hogan, Patrick Colm. "Macbeth: Authority and Progenitorship." *American Imago* 40 (1983): 385–95.

Holland, Norman N. *Psychoanalysis and Shakespeare.* New York: Octagon Books, 1979.

Holloway, John. *The Story of the Night.* London: Routledge and Kegan Paul, 1961.

James I, King of England. *Daemonologie.* London, 1603.

Jekels, Ludwig. "The Riddle of Shakespeare's Macbeth." *The Design Within.* Ed. M. D. Faber. New York: Science House, 1970. 235–49.

Jorgensen, Paul A. *Our Naked Frailties: Sensational Art and Meaning in "Macbeth."* Berkeley: U of California P, 1971.

Kahn, Coppélia. *Man's Estate: Masculine Identity in Shakespeare.* Berkeley: U of California P, 1981.

Kimbrough, Robert. "Macbeth: The Prisoner of Gender." *Shakespeare Studies* 16 (1983): 175–90.

Kirsch, Arthur. "Macbeth's Suicide." *ELH* 51 (1984): 269–96.

Kittredge, George Lyman. *Witchcraft in Old and New England.* New York: Russell and Russell, 1956.

Kittredge, George Lyman, ed. *The Complete Works of Shakespeare.* Boston: Ginn, 1936. Rev. Ed. Irving Ribner. 1971.

Knight, G. Wilson. "The Milk of Concord: An Essay on Life Themes in *Macbeth.*" *Imperial Theme.* London: Methuen, 1965. 125–53.

Kozikowski, Stanley J. "The Gowrie Conspiracy against James VI: A New Source for Shakespeare's *Macbeth.*" *Shakespeare Studies* 13 (1980): 197–212.

La Belle, Jenijoy. " 'A Strange Infirmity': Lady Macbeth's Amenorrhea." *Shakespeare Quarterly* 31 (1980): 381–86.

Macfarlane, Alan. *Witchcraft in Tudor and Stuart England.* New York: Harper and Row, 1970.

Mullaney, Steven. "Lying Like Truth: Riddle, Representation and Treason in Renaissance England." *ELH* 47 (1980): 32–47.

Neill, Michael. "Shakespeare's Halle of Mirrors: Play, Politics, and Psychology in *Richard III.*" *Shakespeare Studies* 8 (1976): 99–129.

Notestein, Wallace. *A History of Witchcraft in England from 1558 to 1718.* Washington, D.C.: American Historical Association, 1911.

Orgel, Stephen. "Prospero's Wife." *Representations* 8 (1984): 1–13.

Orgel, Stephen, ed. *Ben Jonson: The Complete Masques.* New Haven: Yale UP, 1969.

Paul, Henry N. *The Royal Play of "Macbeth."* New York: Macmillan Co., 1950.

Phaire, Thomas. *The Boke of Chyldren.* 1545. Rpt. Edinburgh: E. and S. Livingstone, 1955.

Proser, Matthew N. *The Heroic Image in Five Shakespearean Tragedies.* Princeton: Princeton UP, 1965. 51–91.

Rabkin, Norman. *Shakespeare and the Problem of Meaning.* Chicago: U of Chicago P, 1981.

Radbill, Samuel X. "Pediatrics." *Medicine in Seventeenth-Century England.* Ed. Allen G. Debus. Berkeley: U of California P, 1974. 237–82.

Ramsey, Jarold. "The Perversion of Manliness in *Macbeth.*" *SEL* 13 (1973): 285–300.

Robinson, Ian. "The Witches and Macbeth." *Critical Review* 11 (1968): 101–105.

Rosen, Barbara. *Witchcraft.* London: Edward Arnold, 1969.

Rosenberg, Marvin. *The Masks of Macbeth.* Berkeley: U of California P, 1978.

Sanders, Wilbur. *The Dramatist and the Received Idea.* Cambridge: Cambridge UP, 1968.

Schwartz, Murray M. "Shakespeare through Contemporary Psychoanalysis." *Representing Shakespeare: New Psychoanalytic Essays.* Ed. Murray M. Schwartz and Coppélia Kahn. Baltimore: Johns Hopkins UP, 1980. 21–32.

Scot, Reginald. *The Discoverie of Witchcraft.* London, 1584. Intro. Hugh Ross Williamson. Carbondale: Southern Illinois UP, 1964.

Shakespeare, William. *Macbeth.* Ed. Kenneth Muir. Arden ed. London: Methuen, 1972.

Sprenger, James, and Heinrich Kramer. *Malleus Maleficarum.* Trans. Montague Summers. New York: Benjamin Blom, 1970.

Stallybrass, Peter. "*Macbeth* and Witchcraft." *Focus on "Macbeth."* Ed. John Russell Brown. London: Routledge and Kegan Paul, 1982. 189–209.

Strachey, James, trans. and ed. *The Standard Edition of the Complete Psychological Works of Sigmund Freud.* London: Hogarth P, 1957.

Taylor, Michael. "Ideas of Manhood in Macbeth." *Etudes Anglaises* 21 (1968): 337–48.

Veszy-Wagner, L. "Macbeth: 'Fair Is Foul and Foul Is Fair.' " *American Imago* 25 (1968): 242–57.

Waith, Eugene. "Manhood and Valor in Two Shakespearean Tragedies." *ELH* 17 (1950): 262–73.

Watson, Robert N. *Shakespeare and the Hazards of Ambition.* Cambridge, Mass.: Harvard UP, 1984.

West, Robert H. *Shakespeare and the Outer Mystery.* Lexington: U of Kentucky P, 1968.

Wheeler, Richard. "History, Character and Conscience in Richard III." *Comparative Drama* 5 (1971–72): 301–21.

———. *Shakespeare's Development and the Problem Comedies.* Berkeley: U of California P, 1981.

Willbern, David. "Phantasmagoric Macbeth." *ELR* 16, No. 3 (1986): 520–49.

5

"MAGIC OF BOUNTY"

Timon of Athens, Jacobean Patronage, and Maternal Power

COPPÉLIA KAHN

THIS ESSAY IS inspired by two approaches to Shakespeare: feminist criticism that employs psychoanalytic theory toward a critique of male subjectivity and social norms of masculinity, and "new historicism," which reads cultural practices and literary texts contiguously as representations of political structures and social differences. Both feminists and historicists have produced fresh, invigorating interpretations of Renaissance texts. They tend to work separately, the feminists writing about gender, sexuality, marriage, and the family; the historicists about power, ideology, and politics. Theoretically, however, they ought to share the same terrain, for questions of power cannot be separated from questions of gender, and vice versa. Feminists examine the patriarchal institutions and ideologies that construct gender, while historicists examine signifying practices—medicine, pageantry, fashion, for example—that are as important to the construction of gender as to the construction of power. Historicists, with their double focus on social practice and textuality, can refine a feminist criticism that has sometimes tended to see texts as either replicating a monolithic patriarchy or opposing it. Feminists, conscious of the political dimension in any sexual differentiation and alert to sites of power on the margins of discourse, can resist the tendency of historicist criticism to privilege power over gender. Feminists, especially if they work on Renaissance materials, are necessarily engaged with phallocentric discourse, even if they aim to identify a female voice distinct from it. By the same token, in recognizing the subversion and resistance that help constitute dominant discourse, historicists must take account of woman as other.[1]

My text is *Timon of Athens,* a curious play by any measure. Written between 1605 and 1608, it was printed only in the First Folio of 1623 and, so far as can be known, not performed during Shakespeare's lifetime.[2] Stuck incongruously between *Romeo and Juliet* and *Julius Caesar* in the Folio, it differs sharply from these two plays. Timon, Shakespeare's most solitary hero, has no family and holds no office; he is equally estranged from women and from politics. The play, it would seem, resists questions of both gender and power. Nonetheless, I believe, a deeply felt fantasy of woman and of power animates the play and provides a paradigm for its strikingly bifurcated action. In articulating this fantasy, moreover, Shakespeare draws upon the cultural forms that constituted patronage in the Elizabethan and Jacobean periods: gift-giving and credit finance, then known as usury. *Timon* explores the lethal ambiguities underlying the gifts and loans through which power was brokered in the courts of Elizabeth and James. It figures forth a Jacobean version of what anthropologists call in Melanesia, the Philippines, and the Pacific Northwest "the Big Man system."[3] But the play also gives that system a poignant psychological dimension through what I term its core fantasy. Without this fantasy of maternal bounty and maternal betrayal, the play's two disjunct halves would lack psychological coherence (as many critics maintain they do).[4] Through the grammar afforded by patronage, however, which is "an intermediate zone of symbolic social practice organized sufficiently like the literary text as to be almost continuous with it,"[5] the fantasy is made dramatically intelligible. In *Timon*, Shakespeare voices the appeal and the peril of largesse, magnificence, and royal gifts; of bounty experienced unconsciously as magical.

I

The play's core fantasy consists of two scenes in the course of which a male self is precipitated out of a profound and empowering oneness with the mother into a treacherous group of men in which he is powerless. It is the mother who betrays him, the whorish mother who singles him out and then spurns him. This fantasy is first presented in the opening scene by the Poet in a description of the offering he plans to make to Timon, and is then unconsciously acted out by Timon in the course of the play. The Poet's speech on Fortune is, as Maurice Charney says, "the central fable of the play" (1368).[6] First of all, it plainly describes Timon's rise and predicts his fall:

> *Poet.*   Sir,
> I have upon a high and pleasant hill
> Feign'd Fortune to be thron'd. The base o' th' mount
> Is rank'd with all deserts, all kinds of natures
> That labour on the bosom of this sphere

> To propagate their states. Amongst them all,
> Whose eyes are on this sovereign lady fix'd,
> One do I personate of Lord Timon's frame,
> Whom Fortune with her ivory hand wafts to her,
> Whose present grace to present slaves and servants
> Translates his rivals. . . .

Painter. This throne, this Fortune, and this hill, methinks,
> With one man beckon'd from the rest below,
> Bowing his head against the steepy mount
> To climb his happiness, would be well express'd
> In our condition.

Poet.   Nay, sir, but hear me on:—
> All those which were his fellows but of late,
> Some better than his value, on the moment
> Follow his strides, his lobbies fill with tendance,
> Rain sacrificial whisperings in his ear,
> Make sacred even his stirrup, and through him
> Drink the free air.

Painter.   Ay marry, what of these?

Poet. When Fortune in her shift and change of mood
> Spurns down her late beloved, all his dependants
> Which labour'd after him to the mountain's top
> Even on their knees and hands, let him sit down,
> Not one accompanying his declining foot.

> (1.1.64–90)[7]

The men that "labour on the bosom of this sphere" (the phrasing blends Fortune's body with that of mother earth) are dwarfed by Fortune. She is one and supreme, a "sovereign lady," and they are many—"all deserts, all kinds of natures," unindividuated, a mass. The one individual—Lord Timon—whom Fortune effortlessly "wafts to her" is a pygmy in comparison to her; his rivals are diminished to "slaves and servants." The image of him "bowing his head against the steepy mount" suggests a baby with its head on its mother's breast. Shakespeare gives this scene a dreamlike quality by infusing the medieval image of the goddess Fortuna with a sense of infantile dependency, and by portraying her as from an infant's or small child's point of view. Upon Timon's elevation by Fortune (ll. 80–85), however, the scene acquires the aura of a sovereign's presence chamber or great man's reception room. In this quasi-royal setting, the Timon figure is now but little lower than a god. He takes Fortuna's place and nurses his many worshippers, who "through him drink the free air." In the final movement, Fortuna is no longer nurturant mother but fickle mistress, who "Spurns down her late beloved," while his rivals, no longer either slaves or worshippers, rise above him, "the foot above the head" (l. 95).

This picture of Fortuna as the mother who first elevates and sustains the male child, then violently rejects him, resonates with two similar images associated with mothering figures in the tragedies: Lady Macbeth and Volumnia. When Macbeth shrinks from murdering Duncan, his wife taunts him for cowardice by holding up a verbal picture of herself as a nursing mother who, precisely at the height of trusting intimacy between her child and herself, would not scruple to snatch her nipple away and "[dash] the brains out" (*Macbeth*, 1.7.54–59).[8] When Virgilia expresses fears that her husband may be wounded in battle, Volumnia delivers a similarly brutal speech in which she gives priority of value to "Hector's forehead" spitting blood (wound turned to weapon) over "the breasts of Hecuba," who is nursing her heroic son.[9] In the action of both these plays, the mothering figure plays the same kind of dual role toward the hero that Fortuna plays toward Timon—she inspires him with the masculine ethos, whether it be ambition or killing (as Volumnia says, she "feeds" him "valiantness"), initiating him into a world of masculine competition, of combat, aggressiveness, and wounds, in which he meets his downfall through the treachery of those he holds as comrades. Aufidius, the unctuous lords of Athens, even, to some extent, Macduff: they all turn against their former friend, the hero. The first line of Randall Jarrell's "The Ball-Turret Gunner" contrasts—and also suggests a similar connection between—mothering and the state: "From my mother's sleep I fell into the state"—the state as the realm of men contending for power. The implicit logic of the fantasy in the Poet's fable, though, is *post hoc, ergo propter hoc:* because men first know the world as something separate from a mothering woman, she is held responsible for the outrages and terrors of the world men come to know.[10]

What is missing in this myth is the father: the male self is placed first in relation to a mother, then in relation to a single rival or a band of competitors. In *Macbeth*, Duncan the father-king has great symbolic resonance as an idealized figure of generous and just paternity, but he stands aloof from aggression and competition. The two aspects of oedipal authority, might and right, are split off from one another, leaving Duncan helpless under Macbeth's dagger. In *Coriolanus*, the hero's father is never even mentioned; his mother alone seemingly formed him in the mold of *virtus*. In *King Lear*, the hero is a father and a king, sole source of authority and power in the play's world—but the action moves so as to reveal his hidden dependency on mothering, and offers no comparable counterimage of mature, powerful male authority.[11] Nor does

Timon; and *Timon's* action similarly flows from the occluded primitive image of a mother.

The aesthetic coherence of the play derives from the emotional coherence of the feelings toward the mother articulated through the core fantasy and enacted by Timon and by the text.[12] In the first three acts, Timon plays the role of Fortuna, manipulating a form of social interaction central to the Renaissance court—gift-giving—so as to create for himself the kind of emotional setting he desires.

In Section II of this essay I will discuss the social mechanisms of giving in the context of the court; here I am concerned with its psychological nature. Even before Timon makes his first entrance or the Poet speaks his fable of Fortune, the hero is made to resemble this presiding deity of the drama. He looms like a giant above the "great flood of visitors" from "this beneath world," who, in the Poet's description of him (1.1.42–44), "embrace and hug" him:

> You see how all conditions, how all minds,
> As well of glib and slipp'ry creatures as
> Of grave and austere quality, tender down
> Their services to Lord Timon: his large fortune,
> Upon his good and gracious nature hanging,
> Subdues and properties to his love and tendance
> All sorts of hearts. . . .
>
> (1.1.53–59) ·

In the second scene of the play, "A great banquet [is] serv'd in," and Shakespeare sets Timon at the center of an Athens given wholly to the pleasures of eating and drinking. Hospitality flows from him, and waves of flattery wash back over him. As Minerva Neiditz comments: "Friends make Timon feel that he is magical, the housewife Nature, a container that is filled with nourishing roots. . . . In Timon's terms, either one is the bountiful breast which cannot be depleted, or one is the empty, powerless babe, the open mouth, the sterile moon."[13] Timon's bounty is magical: in his eyes, it needs no replenishment, it cannot be depleted, it has no limits.

Upon his entrance, Timon frees a debtor from prison, and confers a fortune and the bride he wants on a serving man—as easily as Fortune wafts her hand. As the Steward says, "Who is not Timon's?" (2.2.170); all flock to him, hang on him, fix their hopes on his generosity. The word "all," used three times in the speech quoted above (1.1.53–59), is double-edged. In its absoluteness and comprehensiveness, it bespeaks the charisma of his generosity: not just his wealth but his openhandedness toward anyone and everyone awakens their admiration. On the other hand, the lack of discrimination, ostentatiousness, and compulsiveness of his giving awakens our suspicions. Says one admirer:

> He pours it out. Plutus the god of gold
> Is but his steward. No meed but he repays
> Seven-fold above itself: no gift to him
> But breeds the giver a return exceeding
> All use of quittance.
>
> (1.1.275-79)

Insofar as his generosity is so great and so quick, it prevents reciprocity and makes others appear his dependents, his inferiors, "subdued" to his love. Regarding his gift to the servant Lucilius, Timon says, "To build his fortune I will strain a little, / For 'tis a bond in men" (1.1.146-47). But all his acts of giving belie the claim that he gives in order to make friends; instead of creating ties between himself and others, they set him apart, godlike and singular as the phoenix to which one senator compares him (2.1.32). When he rejects categorically any attempt to reciprocate his gifts, refusing to put himself and his beneficiaries on the same level, he puts them at a distance, and keeps them second to him in altruism.

> O by no means,
> Honest Ventidius. You mistake my love;
> I gave it freely ever, and there's none
> Can truly say he gives, if he receives.
> If our betters play at that game, we must not dare
> To imitate them; faults that are rich are fair.
>
> (1.2.8-13)

Giving is a one-way street on which only Timon can travel. (Ventidius has just attempted not only to return a loan but to emulate Timon by doubling the amount returned.) Timon calls his own giving a game and also a fault, yet it makes him, he implies, Ventidius's superior. His bantering courtesy belies an awareness of the manipulativeness, the bad faith, the obsessiveness of his behavior. But he wants to stay on top, the phoenix of generosity in Athens, renowned for a lavishness that, though it benefits all comers, keeps them in awe.[14] Thus he creates in the eyes of others the image of himself that he most enjoys, an image like that of Fortune, "Whose present grace to present slaves and servants / Translates his rivals" (1.1.73-74): Fortuna, the all-powerful woman on whom all men are dependent, while she remains aloof and unmoved.

During Timon's banquet scene, Apemantus, seated apart at a solitary table, relentlessly points out Timon's folly:

What a number of men eats Timon, and he sees 'em not! It grieves me to see so many dip their meat in one man's blood; and all the madness is, he cheers them up, too. I wonder men dare trust themselves with men. . . . There's much example for 't; the fellow that sits next him, now parts bread with him, pledges the breath of him in a divided draught, is the readiest man to kill him. 'T'as been proved. . . .

(1.2.39–43, 46–49)

We have moved from "magic of bounty" to cannibalism, from Timon's re-creation of the free-flowing breast to Apemantus's grim scenario of humanity preying on itself—as though the second scene of the core fantasy had been glimpsed through a scrim behind the first. Acts 2 and 3 will stage the truth embedded in this speech, when those Timon now feasts demand repayment of the loans he contracted in order to feast them, and he cries, "Cut my heart in sums . . . Tell out my blood" (3.4.91, 93). But at this point, it is Apemantus who, suggesting that Timon is not feeding others so much as being eaten by them, hints at a connection between the first scene of the fantasy—maternal bounty—and the second—fraternal betrayal.

Apemantus also comments on the most important dramatic irony of the play, Timon's obliviousness to the truth of his situation: "and all the madness is, he cheers them up, too." When Timon is later besieged by creditors (2.2), he seems bewildered and taken by surprise, yet as we learned earlier the Steward has often begged him to stop up his "flow of riot." The Steward's description of "drunken spilth" and "riotous feeders," braying minstrelsy and blazing lights, suggests that Timon pursues his reckless course in full knowledge of the consequences, yet hides that knowledge from his conscious thought. When, however, the Steward tells him that his land is either sold or forfeited, and that he cannot pay even half his debts, he stays calm; succumbing neither to rage nor fear, he declares serenely:

And in some sort these wants of mine are crown'd,
That I account them blessings; for by these
Shall I try friends. You shall perceive how you
Mistake my fortunes; I am wealthy in my friends.
(2.2.184–89)

Intentionally, but unconsciously, Timon pursues his philanthropy in such a way as to bring about his downfall.[15] It is as though he has acted out the first scene of the fantasy—being the bountiful mother—in such a way that betrayal and rejection by his "brothers" would inevitably follow, linked as in the core fantasy. The reversal of fortune that makes the play so disjointed fulfills Timon's deepest wishes, the wishes of a man who can deal with his idea of the mother only by total identification or total *dis*-identification, in the form of an undiscriminating hostility toward all things human (see Greenson).

II

Shakespeare consistently undercuts the "magic" of Timon's bounty by depicting it in terms of the same kinds of strategies that govern patronage, and thus creates a hero who, figuratively and literally, digs his own grave. By stripping the Athenian setting of any overt political reference—Timon hands out coursers, jewels, and cash rather than offices, titles, or monopolies—the playwright reveals the essential dynamic of social exchange through which the court and the entire kingdom operated.[16]

On a scale comparable to Timon's, Elizabeth's and James's royal gifts, through the trickle-down effect they had on the nobility and the nation, not only maintained and delineated the governing class but also carried on the administration of the government in its day-to-day, year-to-year operations. As Wallace MacCaffrey explains, the Tudors had centralized power in the sovereign, who ultimately made all decisions, but "without a professional army or paid bureaucracy, Elizabeth had to entice her courtiers into executing her will." She accomplished this through "the expert sharing of those gifts of office, prestige, or wealth. . . . By wide distribution of favour the Crown and its ministers sought to link to themselves the interests and the hopes of the great majority of the English governing class" (MacCaffrey 97–98).

Essentially, patronage was a form of the socially coded gift-giving that is termed prestation, defined by Louis Adrian Montrose as "a tacitly coercive and vitally interested process predicated on the fiction that it is free and disinterested" ("Gifts and Reasons" 454). Offices, ranging from embassies and lord-lieutenantships reserved for the nobility, down to clerkships for the lesser gentry; titles, from peerages to knighthoods; lucrative favors such as exemptions, annuities, monopolies, and leases; and outright presents of money and jewels—these were the gifts given and gotten in the great court round of prestation. Their cost to the recipient was attendance at court, service (real or delegated) to the sovereign, flattery, a lavish and ostentatious style of life, and in turn secondary patronage to other suitors for offices, favors, and gifts within his command.

Under James, the structure and function of patronage remained basically the same as under Elizabeth; only its magnitude, as is well known, increased. At her death, the queen left James enough to extinguish the outstanding debt and, allowing for funds to support a sovereign with a family, approximately £40,000 surplus. By 1608, after five years of peace, James had incurred nearly £600,000 in debt, six times that which Elizabeth had accumulated after fifteen years of war (Prestwich, "English Politics" 148). He ended his reign owing £1,000,000 (Tawney, *Business and Politics* 298). Historians in our century have analyzed the financial crisis inherited and increased by the Stuarts as a complicated cycle involving many factors, among them corrupt and wasteful administrators, the centralization of power at court, the inflation of honors by James, and an ethos of royal liberality and magnificence.[17] Wherever the individual historian's emphasis falls, all agree that the imbalance between revenue and expenditure that dogged James's reign can be traced mainly to the king's compulsive giving. Between 1603 and 1625, he gave the peerage alone more than £1,000,000 in Crown lands and rents (Stone, *Crisis* 225). These outright gifts, exclusive of the other kinds of magnificence James enjoyed, were in themselves a hallmark of his reign and a major cause of its financial dilemma. The ultimate source of bounty, throned at court like Fortune on her hill, was James.[18]

It is tempting to speculate that the king, separated at the age of ten months from a mother he never saw again, might have been coping with that loss in a fashion similar to Timon's. Both the king and Timon make gift-giving serve their emotional needs. Anthony Weldon, one of James's early biographers, observed that "in order to win a place in the king's circle, one had first of all to be the recipient of some royal benefit," rather than vice versa, and Queen Anne remarked, when Archbishop Abbot sought her support on behalf of an office for Villiers, "The King will teach him to despise and hardly entreat us all, that he may be beholden to none but himself."[19] Because of the king's position as Elizabeth's most likely successor, he was raised away from his mother, Mary, Queen of Scots, and we have few clues as to his true feelings toward her (see Willson 52, 54ff., 73ff., 79). But Jonathan Goldberg argues that, in the patriarchal ideology of the family with which James was so closely identified, representations of the father's power tended to absorb female creativity, making procreation an extension of male power and eclipsing the mother's role. In Jonson's *Masque of Queens* (1609), for example, Perseus as a parent figure is "a kind of male mother" (88). Goldberg describes an anonymous portrait of Sir Walter Raleigh and his son, in which the two figures are identical "in stance and expression," as a picture that represents sons as "the images of their fathers." In portraits of the royal family, Prince Charles appears as his father's word made flesh, and in portraits of the nobility and the gentry, the family line is represented iconographically as extending from father to children, the connection between father and mother interrupted and left as a gap (Goldberg 85–99, esp. 91). James's political rhetoric also affirms the male appropriation of the maternal function: in *Basilicon Doron*, James advises his son to be "a loving nourish-father to the Church," and in *The Trewe Lawe of Free Monarchies* he lists "nourishing" as the first "fatherly duty" of the sovereign to his subjects (see McIlwain 24, 55).

Whether or not James conceived his role of chief benefactor in filial or gender-linked terms, he pursued it on a scale previously unknown in England. Both apocryphal and documented stories of his prodigality abound. The following, from a Puritan history of his reign, is retold by G. P. V Akrigg, who regards it as "true in spirit if not in fact":

> . . . one day at Whitehall Sir Henry Rich, the handsome younger son of the Earl of Warwick, seeing three thousand pounds in coin being carried to the Keeper of the Privy Purse, whispered something to James Maxwell, a Scottish gentleman of the King's Bedchamber. King James overheard the sound and asked what had been said. He was told that Rich had wished that he had that much money. "Marry, shalt thou Harry," exclaimed King James, and at once ordered the bearers to carry the money to Rich's lodgings. Noting the amazed delight on the young man's face, he added, "You think now you have a great Purchase; but I am more delighted to think how much I have pleasured you in giving this money, than you can be in receiving it." (Akrigg, *Jacobean Pageant* 85)

The anecdote, in which James grants a barely voiced wish instantaneously, suggests that he thought of his power to give, at least on occasion, as magical. In a similar incident, Timon presents a lord with a horse he happens to admire (1.2.209–10); another lord, greeting a servant of Timon's, says: "One of Lord Timon's men? A gift, I warrant. Why, this hits right: I dreamt of a silver basin and ewer tonight" (3.1.4–6), expecting his patron to make the dream come true. Sir Francis Osborn reports that when Cecil tried to discourage his sovereign from giving £20,000 to a favorite by setting out the sum in coin so that he could actually see how large it was, "Thereupon the King fell into a passion, protesting he was abused, never intending any such gift: And casting himself upon the heap, scrabled out the quantity of two or three hundred pounds, and swore he should have no more" (Akrigg, *Jacobean Pageant* 91). Evidently, only the extraordinary sight of hard coin in such vast quantity could dissuade him from a dreamlike conviction of boundless wealth.

Unlike Timon, however, James could sometimes be persuaded by his ministers that severe economies were required. For example, in 1610 he issued a "Declaration of his majesties royal pleasure in the matter of bountie," forbidding any suits leading to "the diminution of Our Revenew and settled Receipts" (Akrigg, *Jacobean Pageant* 91–92). In a letter of 1617 he declares, "It is my pleasure that my charges be equalled with my revenue. . . . If this cannot be performed without diminishing the tables, diminished they must be," but, as he stipulates in a similar context elsewhere, "the honour, greatness and safety of the king and kingdom being always respected" (Akrigg, *Letters* 362, 291). For James, who "believed in the role of the ruler as the fountain of honour and reward," to decrease bounty was to lose honor (Akrigg, Introduction to *Letters* 18). He could suffer the dishes of meat served to him at dinner to be reduced from thirty to twenty-four, but he could not forgo giving £10,000 in jewels to the Lady Frances Howard upon her marriage to his favorite Carr, when his coffers were already drained by the sumptuous wedding he had given the Princess Elizabeth.

Intermittently, James allowed himself to realize just how limited his bounty was. Writing to Cecil in 1605, after the euphoric prodigality of his accession, he admits, "I cannot but confess that it is a horror to me to think upon the height of my place, the greatness of my debts, and the smallness of my means" (Akrigg, *Letters* 261). But as his language suggests, the very enormity of the situation created by his acts of bounty kept him from confronting it and, it would seem, drove him back into fantasies of inexhaustible supply and further acts of giving.[20]

What sustained the illusion of James's bottomless coffers (but finally exploded it) was the widespread, well-established practice of lending at interest. Though the Church had long banned interest-bearing loans, at the end of the Middle Ages they had become, by means of loopholes and hairsplitting interpretations, everyday transactions (see Ehrenberg 42). By the late sixteenth century, according to Keith Wrightson, lending at interest was not restricted to the court, the gentry, or the merchant class; rather, it was a "striking feature of English village society," and those who practiced it were "widows, single people, professional men and gentlemen. . . . In the absence of developed banking facilities, it would appear that people with spare money were ready to lend it to neighbours, doubtless knowing that they would borrow in their turn when need arose" (Wrightson 52). R. H. Tawney characterizes money-lending as a "bye-employment," pursued by "quite unpretending people . . . farmers, innkeepers, tailors, drapers, grocers, mercers, who have a little money laid by, [who] take to lending in order to eke out the earnings of their trade," and comments, "In such cases the very intimacy and informality of the relations makes oppression at once doubly easy and doubly scandalous" (Introduction to *Thomas Wilson* 22, 23).

The vast transactions of James and his courtiers stand in marked contrast to these modest dealings. Robert Cecil, Earl of Salisbury, one of the richest men in the kingdom, who followed his father as the sovereign's leading administrator, borrowed a total of £61,000 over a period of four years, and repaid only £36,000 of it. On his deathbed at the age of forty-nine, he owed £37,867—a large fortune in itself. His creditors included not only the great London merchants and financiers but his own household officials and personal friends, tellers in the Exchequer, lawyers, small merchants, and widows (Stone, *Family and Fortune* 25–26). Lawrence Stone compares the situation to "a gigantic merry-go-round, with the great moneyed men of London in effect paying each other off every six months or so" (*Crisis* 239). Not only James but Cecil and others resembled Timon, who could wield largesse in godlike fashion, succumb to flattery, and be sucked into a whirlpool of display and debt. Any large royal gift, especially an office or a monopoly, conferred in turn the power of patronage on its recipient, who in acting the part of magnifico invariably went into debt.

James's situation as debtor, however, differed from that of a courtier in that he enjoyed special kinds of privilege. The Crown was not subject to the legal sanctions lenders could seek in claiming redress from defaulting debtors; the king's creditors could not sue him and depended entirely on the royal word of honor for the repayment of any financial obligation. Many of James's borrowings, moreover, were not loans per se; they were secured through highly placed officials in disbursing departments who might pay out, from their own pockets, more than they received from the Exchequer, and let the amount be carried over to the next year's account. A similar practice was virtually institutionalized in the customs farmers, syndicates of wealthy men who purchased from James the right to collect customs duties, then made advances to him. What may well have supported the illusion of a limitless Exchequer most, though, was the Crown's power to grant titles. The lure of a baronetcy could induce creditors to take on greater financial risks in lending to the king than they faced with private borrowers.[21]

Whereas borrowing and lending among the "unpretending people" Tawney describes was a recourse in emergency or a way to supplement income, among the elite it was integral to the system of exchange that supported and in another sense constituted the social order. To attract James's favor, courtiers were obliged to garb and house themselves magnificently, which depleted their funds, plunged them into debt, and intensified their competitiveness for royal gifts. James, in need of talent and service to run the kingdom while he hunted and feasted, and ever susceptible to the importunings of his favorites, responded lavishly, fell into debt himself, and borrowed. But courtier and commoner alike might find their roles as creditor and debtor in conflict with their relations as friends and neighbors, as this anecdote told by Lawrence Stone suggests: "When in 1593 the Earl of Shrewsbury was trying to borrow £5000 from Sir Horatio Palavicino to clear off a debt to Thomas Sutton, the former remarked that 'Mr. Sutton was his neighbour and it had been his hap to be his paymaster many times' " (*Crisis* 239). Tawney, selecting from the personal correspondence of Burghley and Cecil during the last twenty years of the sixteenth century, cites numerous examples of nobles desperately seeking loans from each other. Lord Scrope, for instance, tells Cecil he cannot raise £300 from any other source, and begs a loan; the Earl of Southampton, already forced to surrender his estates to creditors, also pleads that "he scarce knows what course to take to live" (Introduction to *Thomas Wilson* 33).

When the king himself sought loans from his courtiers, though, a particular irony arose. Ashton comments that "those whom the king delighted to honour might sometimes find the wherewithal to provide for the Crown's needs out of purses which were already swollen with the royal bounty which itself had often been the chief factor out of which these needs had arisen" (17). In 1613, James accepted a sum of £22,000 from his favorite, Somerset, whose ability to supply it derived from the large gifts James had made to him.[22] Here Timon's Athens and James's court seem to mirror each other. The relationship of play text to social practice can be even more revealing, however, when the similarity is less exact. Though James enjoyed wider access to credit than his courtiers, he himself was the greatest source of bounty in the form of both wealth and honor and thus was subject to special pressures. Giving a detailed account to Cecil of the suit of Edmund Sheffield, Lord President of the Council of the North, James writes that when offered a lifetime pension of £1000, Sheffield replied "that this would do him no good, he was already ten thousand pounds in debt, and that he spent as much as that by the occasion of his presidentship every year beside all the gain that he could make of his office" (Akrigg, *Letters* 243). In this instance, James resists the considerable pressure Sheffield puts on him, and replies, "My liberality ought not to be measured by his want, for I was bound to be no man's banker."

The very contradictions of patronage on which Shakespeare draws in *Timon* appear here: the ruinous spending occasioned by high position, which exceeds even the profits of that position; the suitor's expectation of largesse from the patron to make up the difference; and, most relevant to the play, the slide from the discourse of patronage to that of credit, when James sees himself being used as a "banker" to bail a courtier out of the financial trap into which courtiership itself has led him. It is this irony, the commingling of two opposed registers of exchange, that Shakespeare exploits to the fullest. As early as the play's first scene, a lord describes Timon's gifts as profits realized on money lent at interest:

> No meed but he repays
> Seven-fold above itself: no gift to him
> But breeds the giver a return exceeding
> All use of quittance.
>
> (1.1.276–79)

(The last phrase means, according to the Arden edition, "all customary rates of repayment with interest.") In the second scene, Timon himself voices the idea that the bond of friendship includes the "use" to be made of his friends' fortunes. By means of rhetorical questions and apostrophes that appeal to his audience for confirmation of that which is presented as beyond doubt, Timon successively affirms that he expects his friends to help him, that he needs them, and that he will have use for them:

> O no doubt, my good friends, but the gods themselves have provided that I shall have much help from you: how had you been my friends else? Why have you that charitable title from thousands, did not you chiefly belong to my heart? I have told more of you to myself than you can with modesty speak in your own behalf; and thus far I confirm you. O you gods, think I, what need we have any friends, if we should ne'er have need of 'em? They were the most needless creatures living should we ne'er have use for 'em, and would most resemble sweet instruments hung up in cases, that keeps their sounds to themselves. Why, I have often wish'd myself poorer that I might come nearer to you. We are born to do benefits; and what better or properer can we call our own than the riches of our friends? O what a precious comfort 'tis to have so many like brothers commanding one another's fortunes. O joy's e'en made away ere't can be born! Mine eyes cannot hold out water, methinks. To forget their faults, I drink to you. (1.2.86–105)

"Help" and "need" here express a sense of dependency that is at variance with his previous declaration, at the beginning of the scene, that "there's none / Can truly say he gives, if he receives" (1.2.10–11). The idea of receiving help from friends is phrased piously, as something that the gods provide, something inherent in the very nature of friendship, which comes from the heart and is a matter of deep private satisfaction to Timon. But Timon's reference to "need"—"What need we have any friends, if we should ne'er have need of 'em?"—carries a different intonation. Friendship now seems less a matter of the heart than of practical necessity—one would prefer to do without friends, but unfortunately one cannot help needing them. Finally, "need" modulates into "use": "They were the most needless creatures living should we ne'er have use for 'em," a statement that makes the people Timon is addressing as friends seem people who have no value, no *raison d'être*, apart from what they can do for him. More important, in Shakespeare's world "use" always connotes usury, practiced widely though also disparaged as unethical. The implication is that Timon needs friends because he wants to borrow money from them. That is their "use" for him, a notion that he tries to prettify through resembling them to "sweet instruments," a comparison that only deepens the impression that Timon merely wants to play upon his friends, that he has no appreciation of them apart from his desire to make use of them, or rather of their money. And that is exactly the sentiment with which he climaxes the progression of his thought, from being helped by, to needing, and then to using friends: "What better or properer can we call our own than the riches of our friends?"

At this point Shakespeare evokes two conflicting registers of social exchange coexisting at this cultural moment: an ethos of disinterested friendship and diffuse reciprocity among peers inherited from Cicero and Seneca, and the legal contracts that made friends into creditors and debtors with fixed obligations for the purpose of profit, liable to penalties for forfeit. In John Harington's 1550 translation of Ciccro's treatise on friendship, known as *Laelius* or *De Amicitia*, explicit distinctions between giving to and profiting from friends are made: one should enter into friendship

> not of purpose to get thankes, (for in deede we make no usurie of our pleasures) but even of verie nature be geven to liberalitee ... we ought to covet freendship, not led therto by hope of rewarde, but because all the fruite thereof resteth in verie love selfe.

> For the veraie profite gotten by ones freend, doth not so muche like one, as his freendes very love doth delite hym ... freendship huntes not after profite, but profite foloweth freendeship. (Hughey 154, 162)

Seneca's *De Beneficiis* (translated by Arthur Golding in 1578), the most influential treatise of the Renaissance on gift-giving per se, similarly stresses the disinterestedness of benefits by contrasting them to loans:

> Onely have thou an eye too the faithfulnesse of the receyver. So shall benefytes keepe their estimacon, and continew honorable. Thou staynest them, if thou

make them a matter of Lawe. In dettes it is a most upright speeche and agree-able too the Lawe of all Realmes, too say, Pay that thou owest. But it is the foulest woord than [sic] can bee in benefiting, too say, Pay, for what shall he pay? . . . The estimation of so noble a thing should perish, if wee make a mer-chandyze of benefites. (3.14)

He that dooth men good freely, resembleth the Goddes: but he that lookes for recompence, resembleth the Usurers. (3.15)[23]

Timon's use of "use," then, at the climax of his speech, seems to sound the jarring note that soon becomes the keynote of the whole play, when his friends, either by calling in their loans or by refusing to loan further, refuse to be used by the patron through whose gifts they have profited.[24] Timon, though, veers away from the financial implications of his impromptu discourse on the uses of friendship, into a notion of fraternal communion that moves him so that he weeps: "O what a precious comfort 'tis to have so many like brothers com-manding one another's fortunes. O joy's e'en made away ere't can be born! Mine eyes cannot hold out water, methinks. To forget their faults, I drink to you." The melting of self-interest into communal love which he envisions here—and also experiences—recalls the blurring of ego boundaries, the blissful merger with the maternal source of bounty intimated in the Poet's speech when the Timon figure is singled out by Fortune. This kind of merger carries a heavy nostalgic charge for Timon, and unmans him into tears.

In the exchange that follows this speech, just such a moment of merger is enacted, between men:

Apem.	Thou weep'st to make them drink, Timon.
Second Lord.	Joy had the like conception in our eyes,
	And at that instant like a babe sprung up.
Apem.	Ho, ho: I laugh to think that babe a bastard.
Third Lord.	I promise you, my lord, you mov'd me much.
Apem.	Much.

(1.2.106–109)

It is at once the most intimate moment in the play and the most hollow, as Apemantus's jeering interjections suggest. According to the Arden edition, "to look babies in another's eyes" means "to see the small image of oneself reflected in another's eyes"—a common metaphysical conceit. As used here, it likens men sharing money with each other to lovers fondly gazing into each other's eyes, to the ecstatic fusion of sexual intercourse, and to conception: all in one image, notable for the intensity of heterosexual reference applied to sentiments experienced specifically by men.

This moment of homoerotic tenderness soon ends, however, decisively obliterated by the discourse of usury that takes over the play as Timon's fall begins. A senator, ready to call in his loans to Timon because he sees the great man's credit beginning to fail, refers to the gifts Timon received as investments:

> If I want gold, steal but a beggar's dog
> And give it Timon—why, the dog coins gold;
> If I would sell my horse and buy twenty moe
> Better than he—why, give my horse to Timon;
> Ask nothing, give it him, it foals me straight
> And able horses. . . .
>
> (2.1.5–10)

Timon's friends are making "use" of him, not he of them, as an investment banker; while he, captive to his fantasy of bounty, remains oblivious to their practices. The decline of his fortunes is marked by a trio of confrontations between Timon's servants and his friends that crisply voice the ironic collision of bounty and borrowing. When a friend of Timon's refuses his request for a loan, one servant comments:

> Timon has been this lord's father,
> And kept his credit with his purse;
> Supported his estate; nay, Timon's money
> Has paid his men their wages.
>
> (3.2.69–72)

Timon gave as a friend, and expects to borrow as a friend, but instead he is being treated like any debtor bound not by the ties of friendship but by the conditions of a legal contract.

III

In *King Lear*, Shakespeare generously distributes representations of the emotional symbiosis, loss, and rage that result from the king's attempt to make his daughters his mothers: in the hero's language, in his encounters with his daughters, in the storm on the heath. But in *Timon*, women are few and expressions of the hero's mother-identified self oblique, as though dependency and loss must be suppressed and denied. Yet a vivid sense of the family and of women in it erupts in Timon's tirades when he steps outside the traditionally feminine enclosure of the city walls, where the soliloquy that begins the play's second half is set (4.1). Now he no longer plays the bountiful mother; he hits back at her for the betrayal he suffered at her hands.

In the first part of this speech (not quoted here because of its length), he addresses apostrophes to a succession of emblematic figures that make up Athens: "matrons" come first, and "green virginity," "maid," and "mistress" follow, interspersed with references to slaves, fools, children, and "the grave and wrinkled senate." Suddenly women appear to be as integral to the social order as the senators and servants we have seen so far. As Timon vents his rage in sharply delineated curses, each one a mordant vignette of social corruption, he seems to have moved from the fantasy world of maternal bounty to an adult sense of people as objects. But as Richard Fly notes, the "magnificently stratified and variegated society" he depicts is still, after all, "a shadowy creation of Timon's increasingly solipsistic imagination" (136). When he reappears to give his next soliloquy, that imagination is possessed by the two scenes of the core fantasy, scenes defined by the whorish mother and the rivalrous man she has spawned:

> Twinn'd brothers of one womb,
> Whose procreation, residence and birth
> Scarce is dividant—touch them with several fortunes,
> The greater scorns the lesser. . . .
> Raise me this beggar, and deny't that lord,
> The senators shall bear contempt hereditary,
> The beggar native honor . . .
> . . . for every grise of fortune
> Is smooth'd by that below; the learned pate
> Ducks to the golden fool; all's obliquy. . . .
> (4.3.3–6, 9–11, 16–18)

Here Shakespeare represents as twinship an original state of unindividuated unity with the mother ("twinn'd brothers of one womb") compared to which all subsequent distinctions are invidious and all social relations hypocritical and competitive. In this vision, no differences occur originally in nature, and all subsequent differences amount to "obliquy," which seems to combine the senses of being oblique—devious or misleading—and slanderous (from "obloquy," slander). "Fortune" and "fortunes" are mentioned three times within sixteen lines, cueing us back to the Poet's picture of Fortune throned on a hill, a crowd of men laboring to climb it, one above the next, and the goddess beckoning one man forth, then letting him tumble down while the others climb above him. It is the fickle woman Fortune who creates differences simply for the sake of divisiveness, who sets men at odds with one another, who is responsible for alienated subjectivity and all social conflict. In another sense, though, the structures of desire in this play skirt sexual differences, which are overshadowed by the one difference that matters: enjoying maternal bounty (Fortune's favor) or being deprived of it. In *Timon*, otherness is not maleness as distinguished from femaleness by means of desire and the problematics of eros, but rather, identification with the mother as opposed to alienation from her, both of which are projected onto the entire dramatic landscape.

The embittered vision of society Timon voices in this second soliloquy is immediately confirmed by the play's boldest, most ironic moment. In total rejection of "All feasts, societies, and throngs of men!", muttering "Earth, yield me roots" (4.3.23), Timon turns to mother earth for natural sustenance, untainted by mankind, and finds—gold, the root of all evil. Nature is no better than society and the earth not a mother but a whore:

> Come, damn'd earth,
> Thou common whore of mankind, that puts odds
> Among the rout of nations, I will make thee
> Do thy right nature.
>
> (4.3.42–45)

Timon's discovery of gold articulates the movement from the first stage of the core fantasy to the second, through the associations between gold, whores, Fortune, and changeableness. Traditionally, "Fortune's an arrant whore"—capricious, incapable of fidelity; furthermore, she stands for "fortunes" in the monetary sense, which rise or fall according to the chances of the world. The whorishness of Fortune is next underscored by the entrance of Alcibiades (who has, like Timon, fallen from Fortune's favor) with his two whores, who will do anything for gold. Indeed, in Timon's eyes they embody the essential nature of money, which resonates, again, with the fickleness of Fortune. Gold, he says, will transform anything to its opposite:

> Thus much of this will make
> Black, white; foul, fair; wrong, right;
> Base, noble; old, young; coward, valiant.
>
> (4.3.28–30)

Timon's thinking in his tirades against gold is magical, in that he displaces human choice and responsibility for the use of gold onto the metal itself, an inanimate substance. His fall from fortune's heights has not jolted him into realizing that his own prodigality caused that fall. He is still stuck in the infantile fantasy of a mother who, in the same way that she supplies all, takes it away.

As his encounter with Phrynia and Timandra proceeds, the association between gold and whores intensifies, and then mutates into a further variation on the idea of the whorish mother. With his newfound gold, Timon coaxes the women to infect the populace of Athens with venereal disease. In his vision, matrons and virgins are whorish too, and something more than that:

> Strike me the counterfeit matron:
> It is her habit only that is honest,
> Herself's a bawd. Let not the virgin's cheek
> Make soft thy trenchant sword: for those milk-paps,
> That through the window-bars bore at men's eyes,
> Are not within the leaf of pity writ,
> But set them down horrible traitors.
>
> (4.3.114–20)

The image of breasts boring through window bars may have originated in the placing of prostitutes in windows to attract customers (as is still done today in Amsterdam), but it is the idea of the breast itself as a weapon that commands attention. It resonates with Lady Macbeth's vision of the nursing mother dashing her baby to the ground, and Volumnia's image of Hector's forehead superimposed on Hecuba's breasts, and "spitting forth blood." The breasts that Timon pictures are maternal "milk-paps," and they seem to be meeting a male gaze; they "bore at men's eyes." It is just when the babe is smiling in her face that Lady Macbeth envisions killing it. If the mutual gaze of mother and child constitutes the emotional nurture corresponding to the physical nurture of suckling, then in this image and the idea of the mother that looms behind it, Shakespeare portrays a radical mistrust of women in a male subject, which the male projects onto woman as her aggression toward him.[25] This aggression is all the more treacherous for being masked by an innocent appearance; those "milk-paps" belong to a virgin, and Timon says of Phrynia,

> This fell whore of thine
> Hath in her more destruction than thy sword,
> For all her cherubin look.
>
> (4.3.62–64)

A sense of woman as inherently deceptive is built into the design of the play through the correspondence of the Amazons in the first act with Phrynia and Timandra in the fourth. As Robert Fulton says, it is as though the "brave habits of the dancing ladies have fallen away to reveal a pair of poxy Amazons" (294). The masque of Amazons is offered at Timon's banquet as a testimony of love for him in return for his hospitality; he has gratified the senses of taste and touch in his guests, and the masque now hopes "to feast thine eyes," in the words of the presenter, whose language carries echoes of the Poet's language in the description of Fortune. Cupid says to Timon that the masque is intended "To gratulate thy plenteous bosom," and Lucullus remarks, "You see, my lord, how ample y're belov'd" (1.1.120–21, 126). In short, the masque responds to an image of Timon as one from whom, like Fortune, all bounties flow. But both masque and image are ostentatious and shallow, and the masque is a tissue of flatteries veiling a fantasy of female power, deceptiveness, and aggression.

Woman as object of erotic pleasure is represented in a highly formalized, mediated way, through the symbolic role of Cupid as presenter. Through him the idea of woman as inherently double is voiced; in Renaissance iconography, Cupid stands for the destructive and immoral force of love as much as for its sensual pleasures (Fulton 286). Visually, female doubleness resides in the spectacle of "Ladies as Amazons, with lutes in their hands, dancing and playing" (1.2.127, SD). If ladies can be dressed up as Amazons, then Amazons can be disguised as ladies, exchanging bows and arrows for lutes. Though Amazons carry some positive associations in Renaissance literature and spectacle, primarily they embody the idea that women, if they evade male control and form their own society, will assume the male role, become warriors, and turn ferociously cruel toward husbands and sons. In William Painter's *Novel of the Amazons,* they murder their husbands, and either send sons back to their fathers or break their arms and legs so as to fit them only for woman's work (2: 208–12). Tracing Amazonian mythology in *A Midsummer Night's Dream,* Louis Adrian Montrose comments that it "seems symbolically to embody and to control a collective anxiety about the power of the female not only to dominate or reject the male but to create and destroy him. It is an ironic acknowledgment . . . of the degree to which men are in fact dependent upon women" ("Shaping Fantasies" 66).

While the Amazons dance and play, Apemantus delivers a conventionally moralistic comment on the masque in his usual biting style:

Hoy-day!
What a sweep of vanity comes this way.
They dance? They are madwomen.
Like madness is the glory of this life,
As this pomp shows to a little oil and root. . . .
I should fear those that dance before me now

Would one day stamp upon me. 'T'as been done.
Men shut their doors against a setting sun.

(1.2.127–31, 139–41)

If we read Apemantus's lines in the context of Amazonian lore, the dancing
ladies represent more than the vanity or glory of "this life." They are emana-
tions of Fortune, of "the power of the female . . . to create and destroy" the
male. Here it is not Timon and his competitors who place "the foot above the
head," but women.

While this scene as a whole confirms Apemantus's judgment, it is clear that
in a sense Timon's lavish hospitality has solicited this hollow tribute. He refers
to the masque as "mine own device"; whether the word refers to the feast (as
the Arden editor believes) or to an idea of Timon's that his guests have executed, the feast has called forth the masque, and both are lavish but shallow—
travesties of love and admiration, not the real thing.

But Timon does not want the real thing—friendship, or reciprocated love.
Frozen in primitive identification with a powerful maternal woman, he cannot
cope with or even recognize the world of adult men. As Stephen A. Reid notes,
"Timon has no meaningful relations with other characters"; his misanthropy,
read psychologically, is a figure for his narcissism (443). He is Shakespeare's last
narcissist, and his predecessors are the young man of the sonnets and the
Adonis of the early narrative poem. Timon's curious death and burial seem to
literalize Shakespeare's metaphors for the self-destructive self-attachment of
the earlier figures. The young man who prefers "traffic with [himself] alone"
would consume himself in single life (Sonnet 4, 1.9), becoming "the tomb of
his self-love" (Sonnet 3, ll. 7–8): Adonis prefers to court death in the boar hunt
rather than let eros into his life. Shakespeare links Timon's narcissistic maternal identification with his death through a continuity between the oceanic imagery of his prodigality (the Steward refers to "the ebb of your estate, / And
your great flow of debts" [2.2.145–46]) and the imagery of his grave. Described
four times and then shown onstage, the tomb is located "on the very hem o' th'
sea." Its meaning and poetic appeal derive from its site:

Then, Timon, presently prepare thy grave;
Lie where the light foam of the sea may beat
Thy grave-stone daily. . . .

(4.3.380–82)

. . . say to Athens
Timon hath made his everlasting mansion

Upon the beached verge of the salt flood,
Who once a day with his embossed froth
The turbulent surge shall cover. . . .
                    (5.1.213–17)

More than the hero's misanthropy, Shakespeare stresses his desire to be wrapped
in a quasi-maternal embrace as the tide sweeps over him daily, weeping like a
mater dolorosa "for aye . . . on faults forgiven" (5.4.78–79). The impersonal but
rhythmically repeated caress of the tides parallels the systole and diastole of in-
trauterine life, and recalls Venus kissing Adonis, metamorphosed into a flower:
"My throbbing heart shall rock thee day and night; / There shall not be one
minute in an hour / Wherein I will not kiss my sweet love's flow'r" (ll. 1186–88).
Timon echoes *Lear* in its theme of ingratitude and its hero's rages against the
hypocrisy and corruption of mankind, but departs from it absolutely in focusing on a state of mind preceding the separation of self from world and the
development of object relations, a regression toward "abandonment in the primal boundless state."[26] The stony hardness of Timon's tombstone, repeatedly
contrasted with the tender sea foam touching it, suggests the paradox of the
narcissist who can carve out the identity he seeks only by the ultimate rejection
of all human contact, in death: "Here lie I, Timon, who, alive, all living men
did hate" (5.4.72).

In this play Shakespeare carries to the extremest verge of drama what I take
to be the underlying motif of *King Lear, Macbeth, Antony and Cleopatra,* and
Coriolanus: the attraction to and the fear of union with a seductively maternal
female presence.[27] However idiosyncratic to Shakespeare this motif may be, I
have tried to show that it nonetheless resonates strongly with some highly
visible social practices. Indeed, Shakespeare may have appropriated too readily
the discourse of Jacobean bounty; perhaps the play was never performed—and
as some critics believe, never finished—because it represented powerfully the
fears of courtiers caught up in the vortex of patronage and dependent on
James, who in 1607 lamented, in the oral imagery for patronage prominent in
Timon, "There are so many gapers and so little to be spared" (Akrigg, *Letters*
292). The Archbishop of York's respectful warning, "His Majesty's subjects
hear and fear that his excellent and heroical nature is too much inclined to giving, which in short time will exhaust the treasury of the kingdom and bring
many inconveniences," would not have seemed respectful onstage (Prestwich,
Cranfield 14). Given the crossover between Shakespeare's text and rhetoric
such as James's and the Archbishop's, it may not be coincidence that Timon

reflects James in other ways, as in his passion for hunting. (He receives presents of horses and greyhounds [1.2.179-81, 184-87] and gives away a bay courser [1.2.208-10]; he makes plans to hunt with Lucullus, and is shown returning from the chase with Alcibiades [1.2.188-89, 2.2.17].)[28]

Consensus holds, as noted earlier, that Shakespeare wrote *Timon* sometime between 1605 and 1608; it was in 1608 that Robert Cecil was appointed Lord Treasurer. James's "little beagle" immediately embarked on extensive measures to resolve his sovereign's financial crisis: drawing up budgets for branches of the royal household, investigating its financial abuses, persuading James to limit gifts, establishing new taxes, selling Crown lands, and, most promising of all, negotiating with Parliament for "The Great Contract," an annual subsidy of £200,000 in return for reduction of payments arising from certain feudal rights and tenures (see Akrigg, *Jacobean Pageant* 90-93). The Crown's financial problems were of concern to a wide circle of courtiers and their friends. John Chamberlain, for instance, through whose ample correspondence much court news circulated, wrote in 1607 that the king had undertaken £44,000 worth of debts owed by three prominent courtiers, while "in the meantime his own debts are stalled, to be paid the one half in May come two years, the residue in May following" (Thompson 40). In 1610 he reports of the Great Contract that "this proposition breeds much discontent already, and I am sorry to see us in this, as in all the rest, to grow so fast into the French fashion of loud-speaking and base suffering" (Thompson 42). In Parliament, Thomas Wentworth uses the same imagery as Timon's steward when, objecting to the proposed subsidy, he urges Commons to refuse "to draw a silver stream out of the country into the royal cistern, if it shall run daily out thence by private cocks."[29]

It is tempting to read *Timon* as a doubly topical play, linked to both the economic world and the fantasy world of the Jacobean court. It is tempting as well to see the congruence of unconscious fantasy with social practice in the play as suggesting a partial explanation for the baffling persistence of the Jacobean patronage system in the face of its sheer unworkability. One cannot but wonder at the capacity of Big Men and ordinary courtiers alike to spend far beyond their means, borrow heavily, then live in undiminished splendor while falling into enormous debt that they could never realistically hope to repay. It seems possible that the extreme dependency created by patronage, in which advancement or obscurity, prosperity or ruin, hung on the granting of a suit, could have reawakened anxieties stemming from infantile dependency on the mother, who it seems to the child, can give or take away all. A study of the intersection of Jacobean patronage with the fantasy life, individual or collective, of courtiers is beyond the scope of this essay. But my reading of *Timon* would suggest that they may have coped with the anxieties of dependency through an identification with the mother like Timon's—an idea of inexhaustible supply that found some ideological support in the aristocratic ethos and in James's particular enactment of royal largesse. In *Timon of Athens*, Shakespeare gives voice to such anxieties, drawing on the collective discourses of bounty and of usury, and coupling them with his own characteristic nexus of concerns—power, gender, and identity.[30]

NOTES

This essay has been reprinted from *Shakespeare Quarterly* 38.1 (1987): 34–57. Used by permission of the publisher.

1. For useful overviews of new historicism, see Dollimore; Howard; and Montrose, "Renaissance Literary Studies." For a description of feminist criticism as it pertains to culture and ideology, see Greene and Kahn. McLuskie argues persuasively for a feminist criticism that "[makes] a text reveal the conditions in which a particular ideology of femininity functions" (106).

2. When I wrote this essay, I was unaware that several scholars had persuasively argued that Thomas Middleton wrote substantial portions of *Timon* amounting to about one-third of the play. See Lake; Jackson; and Holdsworth, *Middleton and Shakespeare*. Holdsworth has since edited *Timon* in *The Complete Works of Thomas Middleton*, ed. Gary Taylor (forthcoming from Oxford). Some of the play's peculiarities of style and structure can be explained—at least partly—as the result of collaboration. While the probability that Middleton co-authored *Timon* doesn't lead me to change my interpretation, I regret not having been able to take account of his part in the play.

3. Gundersheimer suggests the analogy between the "Big Man" system and Jacobean patronage systems (13). Newman uses the "Big Man" system to discuss the role of Portia (20, 32–33).

4. Most critical responses to *Timon* either begin with or focus on the contrast between Timon's altruism in the first three acts and his misanthropy in the last two. In his introduction to the Arden edition, Oliver argues that the "constructional principle" of the play is dramatic counterpoint, setting opposite attitudes against each other (xlviii–xlix), but Levin faults Shakespeare for the "lightning change from one state of mind to its polar opposite" that characterizes the hero (89–94, esp. 92). Bradbrook explains *Timon*'s structural peculiarities as that of "no play but a shew," emblematic rather than dramatic, with distinct episodes flatly laid against each other and united by "rhythmic contrast" (2, 17). Similarly, Charney sees *Timon* as a "dramatic fable like an allegory or morality play, the structure of which is schematic, its episodes related analogically rather than causally" (1367). In an elegant, fascinating study, Fly holds that

the disparate, isolated structural units of the play mirror the misanthrope's refusal of the "dynamic interdependence" equally characteristic of society and of the dramatic medium (119).

5. Thomas Crow uses this phrase in describing the commensurability of literature (as opposed to the visual arts) with the surrounding social order, esp. p. 4.

6. The iconography of Fortuna in medieval and Renaissance drama has been treated by Patch, Farnham, Salingar, and Chew. With regard to *Timon*, critics see Fortune's role variously. Kiefer pairs *Timon* with *Antony and Cleopatra* as plays that "deal with the societal implications of Fortune," but he does not connect them with either a Jacobean social context or the hero's psychology (312). Soellner thinks that the dramatic action follows Fortune's cycle, with Timon falling from Fortune as Alcibiades ascends, and comments that Fortune's hill is a version of the traditional wheel on which man is either rising, at the top, falling, or dashed to earth (31–32). Walker argues that Timon's character is defined by his worship of Fortune: "Timon courts no human mistress . . . but has an intimate relationship with the supreme wanton of them all, who ultimately undoes him" (586). His reading touches mine at some points, but is more allegorical than psychological.

7. This and all subsequent quotations are taken from the new Arden edition, edited by H. J. Oliver (1959).

8. Schwartz comments, "I feel this violent interruption of a nurturant, communal interplay as a source of Shakespeare's recurrent preoccupation with betrayal and with feminine powers to create and destroy *suddenly*, and in the repeated desire of his male characters both to be that all powerful woman and to control the means of nurturance themselves, to the exclusion of the otherness of others" (29).

9. See Adelman's fine essay " 'Anger's My Meat.' "

10. Such scapegoating of the mother is virtually built into Freudian theory; see Rich and Dinnerstein for feminist critiques of Freud on this important point.

11. This is my interpretation in "The Absent Mother in *King Lear*."

12. As I was revising this essay for publication, I discovered Barber's interpretation of *Timon* in *The Whole Journey*, 305–309. Barber believes, as I do, that "Timon does without maternal nurturance by trying to be himself an all-providing patron" (305). He finds a more elaborate psychological rationale in the character than I do, however, maintaining that "Timon is engaged in a strategy of altruistic defense that joins potential rivals to him in apparent love; their threat to his security is denied in the precarious mutuality engendered by his feeding and giving" (306–307). Though he discerns an element of "social history" in the play, his interpretation remains at a purely psychological level. He views *Timon* in the light of Shakespeare's transition from tragedy to romance, and links it with *Coriolanus* on the one hand and *Pericles* on the other, noting that in all three plays Shakespeare moves "restlessly around a problematic center—the maternal presence crucial to sustain his hero's identity" (309).

13. Two somewhat similar psychoanalytic interpretations of Timon first enabled

me to understand how its language and action resonate with an infantile image of the mother. This quotation is taken from one of them, Neiditz's "Primary Process." She sees the play as centered on Timon's identification with a mother inseparable from himself as "the center of a world, the possessor of a breast which contains All" (32). Handelman thinks the play deals with Timon's refusal to mourn the loss of the first love object, "one's own body and that of the nurturant mother," and to accept any substitutes for that object (46); hence the virtual absence of women from the play and Timon's emotional isolation and misanthropy. See her powerful study "*Timon of Athens:* The Rage of Disillusion."

14. According to Mauss's theory, reciprocity is fundamental to the nature of the gift, and reciprocity involves power: "the mere fact of having the thing puts the *accipiens* in a condition of . . . spiritual inferiority . . . vis-à-vis the donor"; or, on the other hand, the recipient can humiliate the donor by failing to reciprocate (51). The power relations involved in a gift exchange, however, depend on the environment in which the exchange model is embedded—the sociocultural context, with which I will deal in the next section. For a useful review of theories of exchange, see Befu. I am indebted to Natalie Zemon Davis for helpful and stimulating discussion on Renaissance gift-giving and *Timon.*

15. Oliver (Arden edition xliv–xlv) summarizes an earlier critical tradition represented by Hardin Craig, J. W. Draper, and E. C. Pettet, who saw Timon's spending as a mark of his nobility, making him the symbol of a feudal ideal. Recently, critics perceive his spending as fault rather than ideal. Empson, for example, declares, "Timon's generosity was a sort of begging for affection, and it makes him the same kind of dog as the spaniels he could hire" (182). Scott remarks that Timon's giving "forces his superiority on others both by accepting no repayment and by more than reciprocating any gifts he receives" (295). In my view, Shakespeare is less interested in the morality of Timon's behavior per se than in the psychodynamics and the clash of social expectations resulting when bounty leads to indebtedness.

16. In this view, Lucian's dialogue, "Timon, the Misanthrope," could be a source for the play as important as Plutarch, for it is Lucian who portrays Timon's misanthropy as the direct result of his fall from riches to rags, while Plutarch merely sketches him as a man abandoned by his friends without explaining what he was before. Both Bullough (225–50) and Bulman, who believes that Shakespeare learned the outlines of Lucian's Timon story from a contemporary anonymous play, *Timon,* stress the importance of Lucian.

17. See Ashton; Prestwich's *Cranfield;* Stone's *Family and Fortune* and *Crisis;* and Tawney's *Thomas Wilson* and *Business and Politics.*

18. Symbolically both a virgin queen and the mother of her people, Elizabeth was also the source of all favors; in one portrait she wore a pendant shaped like a pelican, who wounds her breast to feed her young—an emblem of maternal bounty. Sir Robert Naunton characterizes her patronage as maternal when he describes Essex, eager for preferment, as "a childe sucking on an over-uberous nurse." In his imaginative, richly

documented study of Queen Elizabeth's "cultural presence" in *A Midsummer Night's Dream,* Montrose suggests that "virginal, erotic, and maternal aspects of the Elizabethan feminine" were variously combined in the royal cult ("Shaping Fantasies"). See 64 in particular, where Montrose quotes this phrase from Sir Robert Naunton's *Fragmenta Regalia* (51).

In Elizabeth's case, the iconography of the Virgin Mary assisted in the representation of a virgin as a bountiful mother. In James's case, a similar precedent (though of lesser cultural weight, perhaps) existed in Puritan usage. God was frequently figured in maternal language, the Word being His milk, flowing from the Preachers, His breasts. By 1656, drinking the Word had become such a common metaphor that John Cotton titled his standard catechism *Spiritual Milk for Boston Babes in either England. Drawn out of the Breasts of both Testaments for their souls nourishment.* Decades before, Thomas Playfere, preaching before King James at Whitehall in 1604, had declared, "The two breasts of the Church are the two testaments, out of which we that are the children of the church, suck the pure milke of the word of God." See Leverenz 1–5.

19. Akrigg quotes Weldon's *Court and Character* in the introduction to his edition of *Letters* (18). Lockyer quotes Queen Anne from Rushworth's *Historical Collections.*

20. To some extent, royal bounty was ritualized, and thus limited. The Earl of Huntingdon describes the custom of exchanging New Year's gifts with the sovereign as a succession of distinct financial transactions in precise locations, involving precise amounts. He advises the courtier to buy a new purse "of about v s. price," and put in it twenty pieces of new gold, each a 20 s. piece. At 8:00 A.M. on New Year's Day, he must deliver the purse to the Lord Chamberlain, then proceed to the Jewel-house for a ticket for 18 s. 6 d. to receive his gift from the king; then to another office to receive the money itself; then back to the Jewel-house to select a piece of plate of 30 oz. in weight. Finally, in the afternoon, the exchange is complete when he "may go and fetch it away." At each stage of the exchange, Huntingdon specifies the exact gratuity to be given to the official concerned. On the roll of New Year's gifts for 1605–1606, gifts to and from the king are listed on opposite sides, according to rank, from dukes down to knights and minor court officials, with the value of the gifts similarly coded: earls and viscounts gave £20 and received 30 to 32 oz. of gilt plate; barons, £10 in exchange for 15 oz., and so forth. Except for these annual standardized levies, however, royal gifts were circumscribed only by the king's sense of his own bounty. See Nichols 1: 471.

21. See Ashton, chap. 3, "The Problem of Inducement," especially 67–78; and Stone, *Crisis,* pt. 1, chap. 3, "The Inflation of Honours," passim.

22. Ashton 18; but compare Akrigg, *Jacobean Pageant* 95, who states the amount of the loan as £25,000.

23. Seneca sigs. 34^v, 35^r.

24. Wallace believes that Seneca's *De Beneficiis* is the immediate source of the ideas about giving that inform the play—but a source with which Shakespeare enters into "open dialogue." Wallace finds that "Timon is a martyr to profoundly held beliefs which

Shakespeare knew were inadequate but was powerless to change" (355, 363). See his subtly argued essay "*Timon of Athens* and the Three Graces."

25. See Gohlke's searching essay, " 'And when I love thee not.' "

26. Salomé 11. Now translated by Stanley Leavy, this essay was written in 1921. The "dual orientation of narcissism" means that the narcissistic person turns "on the one hand toward self-assertion and on the other toward abandonment in the primal boundless state," which suggests the contrast between gravestone and sea-foam I am discussing here.

27. In *Suffocating Mothers* Adelman argues that Macbeth enacts the will of women in such a way as to escape from that will. Her sense of Shakespeare's fascination with maternal power touches mine at many points.

28. Marcus notes that with regard to the masques performed at his court, "James had a broad tolerance for criticism *provided that the loyalty of the critic was not suspect,*" and raises the question, "If the Stuarts could tolerate criticism in masques, provided that it was tactfully managed, why not in plays as well?" (12, 13). According to my reading of the play, it is difficult if not impossible to regard any representation of James's patronage in *Timon* as tactful. Bergeron argues that the royal family headed by James and the attention paid to it constituted "a living text, writ large in the public consciousness," which Shakespeare then "represents" as the fictional royal families of the romances. Bergeron mentions in passing that "James's prodigality finds a literary analogue in Shakespeare's *Timon of Athens*" (45) but does not pursue the point.

29. Wentworth is quoted by Prestwich, *Cranfield*, from Gardiner 11–12. Compare the Steward:

When all our offices have been oppress'd
With riotous feeders, when our vaults have wept
With drunken spilth of wine, when every room
Hath blaz'd with lights and bray'd with minstrelsy,
I have retir'd me to a wasteful cock
And set mine eyes at flow

(2.2.162–67)

30. I wish to thank Samuel Crowl of Ohio University at Athens, Donald K. Hedrick of Kansas State University, and the Department of English at Brown University for giving me opportunities to present these ideas in a shorter version, and Jean E. Howard of Syracuse University for an astute reading of the longer version.

WORKS CITED

Adelman, Janet. " 'Anger's My Meat': Feeding, Dependency, and Aggression in *Coriolanus.*" *Representing Shakespeare: New Psychoanalytic Essays.* Ed. Murray Schwartz and Coppélia Kahn. Baltimore: Johns Hopkins UP, 1980. 129–49.

————. *Suffocating Mothers: Fantasies of Maternal Origin in Shakespeare's Plays, "Hamlet" to "The Tempest."* London: Routledge, 1992.

Akrigg, G. P. V. *Jacobean Pageant.* Cambridge: Harvard UP, 1962.

Akrigg, G. P. V., ed. *Letters of King James VI and I.* Berkeley: U of California P, 1984.

Ashton, Robert. *The Crown and the London Money Market, 1603–1640.* Oxford: Clarendon P, 1960.

Barber, C. L., and Richard Wheeler. *The Whole Journey: Shakespeare's Power of Development.* Berkeley: U of California P, 1986.

Befu, Harumi. "Social Exchange." *Annual Review of Anthropology* 6 (1977): 255–81.

Bergeron, David M. *Shakespeare's Romances and the Royal Family.* Lawrence: UP of Kansas, 1985.

Bradbrook, Muriel. *The Tragic Pageant of Timon of Athens.* Cambridge: Cambridge UP, 1966.

Bullough, Geoffrey, ed. *Narrative and Dramatic Sources of Shakespeare, VI.* New York: Columbia UP, 1966.

Bulman, James C. Jr. "Shakespeare's Use of the *Timon* Comedy." *Shakespeare Survey* 29 (1976): 103–16.

Charney, Maurice. Introduction to "Timon of Athens." *The Complete Signet Classic Shakespeare.* Ed. Sylvan Barnet. New York: Harcourt Brace Jovanovich, 1972.

Chew, Samuel C. *The Pilgrimage of Life.* New Haven: Yale UP, 1962.

Crow, Thomas. "Codes of Silence: Historical Interpretation and the Art of Watteau." *Representations* 12 (Fall 1985): 2–14.

Dinnerstein, Dorothy. *The Mermaid and the Minotaur: Sexual Arrangements and Human Malaise.* New York: Harper and Row, 1976.

Dollimore, Jonathan. "Introduction: Shakespeare, Cultural Materialism and the New Historicism." *Political Shakespeare: New Essays in Cultural Materialism.* Ed. Jonathan Dollimore and Alan Sinfield. Ithaca: Cornell UP, 1985. 2–17.

Ehrenberg, Robert. *Capital and Finance in the Age of the Renaissance.* Trans. H. M. Lucas. London: Jonathan Cape, 1928.

Empson, William. *The Structure of Complex Words.* Ann Arbor: U of Michigan P, 1967.

Farnham, William. *The Medieval Heritage of Elizabethan Tragedy.* Berkeley: U of California P, 1936.

Fly, Richard. *Shakespeare's Mediated World.* Amherst: U of Massachusetts P, 1976.

Fulton, Robert. "Timon, Cupid, and the Amazons." *Shakespeare Studies* 9 (1976): 283–99.

Gardiner, S. R., ed. *Parliamentary Debates in 1610.* London: Camden Society, 1852.

Gohlke, Madelon. " 'And when I love thee not': Women and the Psychic Integrity of the Tragic Hero." *Hebrew University Studies in Literature* 8, No. 1 (1980): 44–65.

Goldberg, Jonathan. *James I and the Politics of Literature: Jonson, Shakespeare, Donne and Their Contemporaries.* Baltimore: Johns Hopkins UP, 1983.

Greene, Gayle, and Coppélia Kahn. "The Social Construction of Woman." *Making A Difference: Feminist Literary Criticism.* London: Methuen, 1985. 1-36.

Greenson, Ralph. "Dis-Identifying from Mother: Its Special Importance for the Boy." *International Journal of Psycho-Analysis* 49 (1968): 370-74.

Gundersheimer, Werner. "Patronage in the Renaissance: An Exploratory Approach." *Patronage in the Renaissance.* Ed. Stephen K. Orgel and Guy Fitch Lytle. Princeton: Princeton UP, 1981. 3-23.

Handelman, Susan. "*Timon of Athens:* The Rage of Disillusion." *American Imago* 36 (1979): 45-68.

Holdsworth, Roger V. "Middleton and Shakespeare: The Case for Middleton's Hand in *Timon of Athens.*" U of Manchester dissertation, 1984.

Holdsworth, Roger V., ed. *Timon of Athens. The Complete Works of Thomas Middleton.* Ed. Gary Taylor. Oxford: Oxford UP, forthcoming.

Howard, Jean E. "The New Historicism in Renaissance Studies." *English Literary Renaissance* 16 (1986): 13-43.

Hughey, Ruth, ed. *John Harington of Stepney: Tudor Gentleman—His Life and Works.* Columbus: Ohio State UP, 1971.

Jackson, Macdonald P. *Studies in Attribution: Middleton and Shakespeare.* Salzburg, Austria: Institut für Anglistik und Amerikanistik, 1979.

Kahn, Coppélia. "The Absent Mother in *King Lear.*" *Rewriting the Renaissance: Sexual Discourses of Early Modern Europe.* Ed. Margaret Ferguson, Maureen Quilligan, and Nancy Vickers. Chicago: U of Chicago P, 1986. 33-49.

Kiefer, Frederick. *Fortune and Elizabethan Tragedy.* San Marino: Huntington Library, 1983.

Lake, D. J. *The Canon of Thomas Middleton's Plays.* Cambridge: Cambridge UP, 1975.

Leverenz, David. *The Language of Puritan Feeling: An Exploration in Literature, Psychology, and Social History.* New Brunswick: Rutgers UP, 1980.

Levin, Harry. "Shakespeare's Misanthrope." *Shakespeare Survey* 26 (1973): 89-94.

Lockyer, Roger. *Buckingham: The Life and Political Career of George Villiers, First Duke of Buckingham, 1592–1628.* London: Longmans, 1981.

MacCaffrey, Wallace. "Place and Patronage in Elizabethan Politics." *Elizabethan Government and Society: Essays Presented to Sir John Neale.* Ed. S. T. Bindoff, J. Hurstfeld, and C. H. Williams. London: U of London, 1961. 95-126.

Marcus, Leah S. "Masquing Occasions and Masque Structures." *Research Opportunities in Renaissance Drama* 24 (1981): 7-16.

Mauss, Marcel. *The Gift: Forms and Functions of Exchange in Archaic Studies.* Trans. Ian Cunnison. 1925. New York: Norton, 1967.

McIlwain, Charles Howard, ed. *The Political Works of James I.* Cambridge, Mass.: Harvard UP, 1918.

McLuskie, Kathleen. "The Patriarchal Bard: Feminist Criticism and Shakespeare—*King Lear* and *Measure for Measure.*" *Political Shakespeare: New Essays in Cultural Materialism.* Ed. Jonathan Dollimore and Alan Sinfield. Ithaca: Cornell UP, 1985. 88–108.

Montrose, Louis Adrian. "Gifts and Reasons: The Contexts of Peele's *Araygnement of Paris.*" *ELH* 47 (1980): 433–61.

———. "Renaissance Literary Studies and the Subject of History." *English Literary Renaissance* 16 (1986): 5–12.

———. " 'Shaping Fantasies': Figurations of Gender and Power in Elizabethan Culture." *Representations* 2 (Spring 1983): 61–94.

Naunton, Sir Robert. *Fragmenta Regalia.* 1641. Ed. Edward Arber. London, 1870. Folger ed. Ed. John S. Cerovski. Washington: Folger Books, 1985.

Neiditz, Minerva. "Primary Process Mentation and the Structure of *Timon.*" *Hartford Studies in Literature* 11, No. 1 (1979): 24–35.

Newman, Karen. "Portia's Ring: Unruly Women and Structures of Exchange in *The Merchant of Venice.*" *Shakespeare Quarterly* 38, No. 1 (Spring 1987): 19–33.

Nichols, John. *The Progresses, Processions, and Magnificent Festivities of King James I.* 4 vols. 1828. New York: AMS Press, 1969.

Oliver, H. J., ed. *Timon of Athens.* By William Shakespeare. Arden ed. London: Methuen, 1959.

Painter, William. *Novel of the Amazons.* Vol. 2 of *The Palace of Pleasure.* 4 vols. 1929. New York: AMS Rooks, 1967. 208–12.

Patch, Howard M. *The Goddess Fortuna in Medieval Literature.* Cambridge, Mass.: Harvard UP, 1927.

Prestwich, Menna. "English Politics and Administration in 1603–1625." *The Reign of James VI and I.* Ed. Alan G. R. Smith. New York: St. Martin's Press, 1973. 140–59.

———. *Cranfield: Politics and Profits under the Early Stuarts—The Career of Lionel Cranfield, Earl of Middlesex.* Oxford: Clarendon P, 1966.

Reid, Stephen A. " 'I am Misanthropos': A Psychoanalytic Reading of Shakespeare's *Timon.*" *Psychoanalytic Review* 56 (1969): 442–52.

Rich, Adrienne. *Of Woman Born: Motherhood as Experience and Institution.* New York: Harper and Row, 1976.

Rushworth, John. *Historical Collections.* 1721.

Salingar, Leo G. *Shakespeare and the Traditions of Comedy.* London: Cambridge UP, 1974.

Salomé, Lou Andreas. "The Dual Orientation of Narcissism." Trans. Stanley Leavy. *Psychoanalytic Quarterly* 31 (1962): 1-30.

Schwartz, Murray. "Shakespeare through Contemporary Psychoanalysis." *Representing Shakespeare: New Psychoanalytic Essays.* Ed. Murray Schwartz and Coppélia Kahn. Baltimore: Johns Hopkins UP, 1980. 21-32.

Scott, William O. "The Paradox of Timon's Self-Cursing." *Shakespeare Quarterly* 35 (1984): 290-304.

Seneca, Lucius Annaeus. *The woorke of the excellent Philosopher Lucious Annaeus Seneca concerning Benefyting, that is too say the dooing, receyving, and requyting of good Turnes.* Trans. Arthur Golding. London: John Day, 1578.

Shakespeare, William. *Timon of Athens.* Ed. H. J. Oliver. Arden ed. London: Methuen, 1959.

Soellner, Rolf. *"Timon": Shakespeare's Pessimistic Tragedy.* Columbus: Ohio State UP, 1978.

Stone, Lawrence. *Family and Fortune: Studies in Aristocratic Finance in the 16th and 17th Centuries.* Oxford: Clarendon Press, 1973.

———. *The Crisis of the Aristocracy, 1558-1641.* Abridged ed. London: Oxford UP, 1967.

Tawney, R. H. *Business and Politics under James I: Lionel Cranfield as Merchant and Administrator.* Cambridge: Cambridge UP, 1958.

Tawney, R. H., ed. *Thomas Wilson: A Discourse upon Usury.* 1925. New York: Augustus M. Kelley, 1963.

Thompson, Elizabeth McClure, ed. *The Chamberlain Letters: A Selection of the Letters of John Chamberlain concerning Life in England from 1597 to 1626.* New York: G. P. Putnam's Sons, 1965.

Walker, Lewis. "Fortune and Friendship in *Timon of Athens.*" *Texas Studies in Language and Literature* 18 (1977): 577-600.

Wallace, John. "*Timon of Athens* and the Three Graces: Shakespeare's Senecan Study." *Modern Philology* 83, No. 4 (1986): 349-63.

Weldon, Anthony. *The Court and Character of King James.* London, 1650.

Willson, David Harris. *King James VI and I.* New York: Oxford UP, 1956.

Wrightson, Keith. *English Society, 1580-1680.* Hutchinson Social History of England. London: Hutchinson, 1982.

PART TWO

IMPLICATING *OTHELLO*

❖ 6 ❖

DESDEMONA'S DISPOSITION

LENA COWEN ORLIN

MY TITLE FINDS its source in Othello's petition to the Duke of Venice as he accepts his commission for Cyprus: "I crave fit disposition for my wife," that is, "Due reference of place" for her in his projected absence.[1] From an immediate concern with Desdemona's proper (and improper) physical placements throughout *Othello*, I shall turn, second, to the relationship of those placements to the fitness of her disposition in another sense, that of her temperament or character. Then, third, I shall consider the ways in which both figure in her final disposition, her unfit death at Othello's hand. Throughout, I shall be occupied with how Desdemona can be and has been read, referring both to the sixteenth- and seventeenth-century domestic conduct books that serve as primary vehicles for interpretation and for judgment of her, and to the subsequent critical responses that have maintained their own continuity with a patriarchal philosophy that would have her complicit in her own tragedy. For all this, my overriding thesis is that while hers may be *a* tragedy of *Othello*, it is of course not *the* tragedy, and the latter is that with which I shall conclude: the tragedy of men-in-marriage that Othello personates and what it tells us of the incapacities of patriarchalism.

I

The implication of Othello's petition to the Duke of Venice is that Desdemona's disposition at the time of his request is unfit, or that it would be unfit in Othello's absence during the siege of Cyprus, or that it is unfit for any prolonged period—in any case, that it requires amendment. Our apprehension of its inadequacy is compounded by his overelaborated request for "Due reference of place, and exhibition" and "such accommodation and besort / As levels with her breeding" (1.3.236–39).[2] We have been given, with the odd insistence of designatory repetition, concrete information about Desdemona's location during her nuptial sojourn: Othello has been discovered at and she has been summoned from a building called the Sagittar in the first quarto, the Sagitary in the Folio. And so I shall begin with the problematic Sagittar/y and the import of this seemingly gratuitous act of naming.[3]

Iago's introduction of the name is resonant with signification:

> Though I do hate him, as I do hell's pains,
> Yet, for necessity of present life,
> I must show out a flag, and sign of love,
> Which is indeed but sign. That you shall surely find him,
> Lead to the [Sagittar/y] the raised search,
> And there will I be with him.
>
> (1.1.154–59)

On the literal level, this passage emphasizes the duplicity of Othello's ensign (or sign bearer). But his iteration of "flag," "sign," and "sign," a noun sequence culminating in "Sagittar/y" and punctuated by "*there* will I be with him,"[4] serves in addition the subliminal function of summoning up for the listener or reader a mental image of the sign with which an inn or tavern would have been identified—and in this provides some substantiating hint of what editors have generally concluded to be the public nature of the place. Editorial glosses frequently attempt an analogy to the "Centaur" of *The Comedy of Errors*,[5] although a more common related name for an inn in early modern England was undoubtedly the "Archer." This much is hinted in John Taylor's comic tour of the taverns of London in 1636, purportedly a search to record in their names the twelve signs of the zodiac and so to "imitate" the sun in its journey. He notes, "For Sagittarius, I was forced to make use of the sign of the Archer, near Finsbury-fields, or Grub-street end" (sig. A4ʳ).[6] Shakespeare may perhaps have reversed the Water Poet's linguistic process, latinizing a somewhat more common English name for his Venetian locale. As further suggested by Taylor, though, the identifying sign for an inn named the "Sagittar/y" would in any case have been itself a representation of a "celestial sign," the technical term in astrology for any one of the twelve elements of the zodiac. The "zodiacal man" of the English almanac—according to Ruth Samson Luborsky the most familiar secular image in Tudor England—fixed in universal currency the figurative nature of the Sagittarius as a centaur with drawn bow (see illustration).

The sign under which Othello and Desdemona institute their marriage is thus that of a monstrous being, half man, half horse. With "an old black ram / Is

The Anathomy of mans body, as the parts there-of are gouerned by the 12.fignes of the Zodiaque.

Aries the head and face.

Taurus Necke & throat

Cancer Breast stomak & ribs.

Virgo bowels & belly.

Scorpio Secret mem= bers.

Capri-cornus knees

Gemin Armes & fhoul-ders.

Leo Heart & backe.

Libra Reines & loines

Sagita-rius Thigh

Aquar. The legges

Pices thiese

♈ Aries ♉ Taurus ♊ Gemini ♋ Cancer ♌ Leo ♍ Virgo ♎ Libra ♏ Scorpio ♐ Sagitarius ♑ Capricorne ♒ Aquarius ♓ Pices.

The zodiacal man, from Richard Allestree's *Prognostication for this Present Year of Grace 1623*. Reproduced by permission of the Folger Shakespeare Library.

tupping your white ewe" (1.1.88–89), Iago has already initiated a network of allusions to the transformation of men into beasts (1.1.116; 2.3.256, 284, 297), horses (1.1.111–13), baboons (1.3.316), asses (1.3.400; 2.1.304), goats (3.3.184, 409; 4.1.259), toads (3.3.274), dogs (3.3.368; 5.1.62; 5.2.362), monkeys (3.3.409; 4.1.259), and wolves (3.3.410) that intersects with the zoologically transgressive nature of the centaur.[7] The Sagittar/y also participates in yet another ominous com-plex of images, the most notable elements of which are the figuration of Iago's scheme against Othello as a "monstrous birth" (1.3.402), his warning that jealousy is a "green-ey'd monster" (3.3.170), and Othello's eventual self-recognition that "A horned man's a monster, and a beast" (4.1.62).

Because illustrations of the "zodiacal man" typically depicted Sagittarius in profile, with the spines of both man and horse outlined, the creature is also in and of itself a "beast with two backs," the vivid image of bestial sexuality with which Iago torments Brabantio. The association of centaurs with sexual assault was located in the legends of their attempted rape of the Lapith women, to which Shakespeare refers in *Titus Andronicus* and *A Midsummer Night's Dream,* and of Nessus's rape of Deianeira, to which he alludes in *All's Well That Ends Well* and *Antony and Cleopatra.* To Brabantio's mind, Othello is just such a lustful kidnapper of his daughter; of Othello he might say, as does Parolles of Dumaine, "For rapes and ravishments he parallels Nessus" (4.3.251).

Finally, Sagittarius is particularized among centaurs by its weapon; its legendary association with military prowess (especially in the Trojan War) is corroborated in *Troilus and Cressida,* where "The dreadful Sagittary / Appalls our numbers" (5.5.14–15). It thus, of course, bears an affinity to the Othello who is described as "Horribly stuff'd with epithets of war," "warlike," and "a full soldier" (1.1.14; 2.1.27; 2.1.36) and who comes to Brabantio's house to tell the story of his life, "the battles, sieges, fortunes, / That I have pass'd":

> It was my hint to speak, such was the process:
> And of the Cannibals, that each other eat;
> The Anthropophagi, and men whose heads
> Do grow beneath their shoulders: this to hear
> Would Desdemona seriously incline;
> But still the house-affairs would draw her thence,
> And ever as she could with haste dispatch,
> She'ld come again, and with a greedy ear
> Devour up my discourse; which I observing,
> Took once a pliant hour, and found good means
> To draw from her a prayer of earnest heart,
> That I would all my pilgrimage dilate,
> Whereof by parcel she had something heard,
> But not intentively: I did consent,
> . . .
> She lov'd me for the dangers I had pass'd,
> And I lov'd her that she did pity them.
>   (1.3.142–68)

This passage, so often isolated for critical discussion that its central importance to the play cannot be doubted, establishes a telling dichotomy between, on the one hand, Othello's stories of sieges and monsters and, on the other, Desdemona's duties in managing Brabantio's wifeless household. The house exerts a socializing force that "ever" and "again" she attempts to frustrate, but her responsibilities repeatedly "draw her" away from Othello and, it is re-emphasized, prevent her from hearing anything other than interrupted "parcels." Finally, an "intentive dilation" initiates a movement from Brabantio's sphere to Othello's that culminates in her elopement. As she has hastened "house-affairs" for tales of monstrous men and battles, so she flees her father's house for a building named after a creature that is monstrously half man, half horse, and poised for attack.[8]

Until Desdemona confirms her willing translation to the Sagittar/y, Brabantio has entertained no doubts that his house represents the disposition that is fit for her. Iago and Roderigo play to this conventional understanding when they rouse him with their cry of thievery in the night. With "is all your family within?" and "Are all doors lock'd?" (1.1.84–85), they reinforce the notion that familial integrity requires the enclosure of the house around its members and (especially for female members) their confinement within. So confident is the first-scene Brabantio of his household security that Roderigo must challenge him to seek Desdemona "in her chamber, or your house" by vowing that the Venetian senator may "Let loose on me the justice of the state" (1.1.138–39) if the alarm is false. Even then only the correspondence of an obscure dream convinces Brabantio to test this challenge to his governance. When he finds that Roderigo has told "too true an evil," he demands, "Where didst thou see her?"; "how got she out?"; and "do you know / Where we may apprehend her, and the Moor?" "I think I can discover him," says Roderigo, and leads Brabantio to the Sagittar/y (1.1.160–79).

At his first opportunity to confront his daughter directly, Brabantio does not ask of her purported elopement, "Is this true?" Instead, because as before "Belief of it oppresses me already" (1.1.143), he speaks directly to the significance of her "escape": "Do you perceive in all this noble company, / Where most you owe obedience?" (1.3.179–80). Desdemona's "place" in a patriarchal familial and social structure is defined by the direction in which she tenders obedience; as already implied by the dereliction of household duties suggested in her "hasty dispatch" of them, her spatial displacement implicates her in a violation of the patriarchal hierarchy as well. The issue of her obedience has been skillfully mooted by Roderigo, twice interrupting his story of her elopement to ask Brabantio's forgiveness "If't be your pleasure, and most wise consent" or "If this be known to you, and your allowance" (1.1.121, 127). But, as

Roderigo says, "if you have not given her leave," then is it a "gross revolt" and a "treason of the blood" (1.1.133, 134, 169), and then can Brabantio accuse himself of insufficient "tyranny" (1.3.197) as the monarch in the little world of his house.

Thus, when, in response to Othello's petition, the Duke of Venice can suggest only that she return to "her father's," Brabantio jumps to restore the integrity of his house and reclaim his authority over it with the unhesitant declaration: "I'll not have it so" (1.3.240). With her flight to the Sagittar/y and the transposition of loyalties that it represents, Desdemona has rendered herself incapable of reintegration into Brabantio's household. Even as Brabantio has asked Roderigo, "Where didst thou see her?" he has also demanded, "How didst thou know 'twas she?" (1.1.163–65). Only enchantment, magic, "foul charms," drugs, minerals, "arts inhibited" (1.2.63–79), spells, medicines, witchcraft (1.3.61–64), "practices of cunning hell," "mixtures powerful," or "some dram conjur'd" (1.3.102–105) could have transformed beyond all recognition "A maiden never bold of spirit"; otherwise it is impossible that "perfection so would err / Against all rules of nature" (1.3.94, 100–101). In other words, in abandoning his house for the Sagittar/y, Desdemona has become as alien to her father as are the monstrous creatures of Othello's story, and as insusceptible of his welcome. She might be of the same order as Lear's daughters: "Down from the waist they are Centaurs" (4.6.124).[9]

In his *De sacramento matrimonii* (translated into English in 1540), the humanist philosopher Henricus Cornelius Agrippa von Nettesheim writes, "He that wanteth a wife hath no house, because he hath not settled a house. Yea, and if he have [that is, if he has a house but no wife], he tarrieth in it as a stranger in his inn" (sig. C8ʳ). With this he offers yet another indictment of the fitness of the Sagittar/y, a resort only for strangers and sojourners. But Agrippa also alludes to what was in the early modern period taken to be a natural corollary of marriage: the "settlement" of a household. In general, as Peter Laslett has demonstrated and as Agrippa here assumes, access to a house preceded any possibility of marriage.[10] That which is most peculiar about Desdemona's situation is not that her father's house is no longer fit for her, not that the Sagittar/y is unfit for more than temporary sojourn, but that no fit house, with its correspondent wifely role and responsibilities, has been established for her.

In this very absence of positional alternatives in Venice, Desdemona comes to accompany Othello to the besieged Cyprus. On the even more radical unfitness of this disposition, however, the contemporary prescriptive text (and the context for the unfolding of the tragedy of Othello) could not be more clear. "I deny not," writes William Whately, "that the service of the country and needful private affairs may cause a just departure for (even) a long time" (sig. A4ʳ), but he allows of nothing other than the husband's departure alone in these pursuits. Countless times repeated in the domestic conduct books is the rule that "God hath made the man to travail abroad, and the woman to keep home."[11] It goes unsaid—because it needed no saying—that these prescriptions presuppose that a house has been "settled" for the woman's occupation.

Desdemona's sojourn at the Sagittar/y is pivotal, on the one hand representing her determination both to deny the patriarchal text that has in Brabantio's house defined and confined her and to rescript her own story along the lines laid out by Othello's tales of monsters and battles; on the other, prefiguring her commitment to move outside the Venetian social order entirely by following Othello to a "warlike isle" and the "fortitude" of a Cypriot citadel (2.3.53; 1.3.222). The father whom she leaves embodies that social order: his faith in urban civility will not admit of "robbing" because "this is Venice, / My house is not a grange"; his comfortable certainty is that in calling at "every house" in Venice, he "may command at most"; his confidence in the fellowship of patriarchs holds that "any of my brothers of the state, / Cannot but feel this wrong, as 'twere their own" (1.1.105–106, 181–82; 1.2.96–97).[12] Offered the Duke's slight and aphoristic consolation on the loss of his daughter—"The robb'd that smiles, steals something from the thief, / He robs himself, that spends a bootless grief"—Brabantio retorts, "So let the Turk of Cyprus us beguile, / We lose it not so long as we can smile" (1.3.208–11). That is, even as the expectations of his world view are disappointed, he persists in his conviction of the fundamental symbiosis of political and familial structures of order, of the analogy of his displaced daughter to another vulnerable Venetian property that is besieged by infidels, of the relationship between the dis-positioned Desdemona and larger disorder. Even as this aging blocking figure is defeated, in short, he persists in maintaining for us the note of ominous irregularity with which Desdemona's marriage is inaugurated.

II

By speaking, above, of Desdemona's first-act "determination" and "commitment," I have already mooted the subject of her characterologic disposition. Her agency is an element of her character that the male characters would deny her. Brabantio, for example, first accuses Othello: "O thou foul thief, where has thou *stow'd* my daughter?" (1.2.62), figuring the movements of Desdemona as those of a kind of inanimate cargo. Roderigo, too, describes her as having been "*transported*" to the Moor (1.1.124); Othello admits that he has "*ta'en* [her] *away*" (1.3.78); the Duke commands, "*Fetch* Desdemona hither" (1.3.120). Later, Othello "crave[s] fit *disposition*" for her (1.3.236) and, for the journey to Cyprus, turns her over to Iago: "To his *conveyance* I *assign* my wife" (1.3.285); "My Desdemona must I *leave* to thee" (1.3.295).[13] In Cyprus, Cassio repeats that she has been "*Left* in the *conduct* of the bold Iago" (2.1.75) (emphasis added throughout). This verbal pattern is congruent with another (and widely recognized) set of images that characterize Desdemona as a (valuable) possession.[14]

Because it misrepresents Desdemona's actual first-act activity, however, this pattern exposes little more than the desire and denial of a patriarchal framework for female location. Desdemona in fact enacts her own preference for placement, unconfined by the passivity wished upon her by male language. As Roderigo indistinctly reveals, Othello has "ta'en her away" only metaphorically, through marriage. Physically, she has ta'en herself away to Othello:

> . . . your fair daughter,
> At this odd-even and dull watch o' the night,
> Transported with no worse nor better guard,
> But with a knave of common hire, a gondolier,
> To the gross clasps of a lascivious Moor. . . .
> (1.1.122–26)

Although Roderigo resorts to a passive voice that threatens to obscure the facts, they nonetheless disclose themselves. Desdemona has traveled unprotected not only by the "better" guardage of, say, Brabantio or one of his men but even by the "worse" guardage of, again, Othello or one of his. She has traveled only with a gondolier. To follow the pattern of Roderigo's evasion of active verbs is also to suspect that Desdemona herself has employed the "knave of common hire."[15] Brabantio, taking the point and echoing the diction, will later describe her as having herself "Run from her guardage to the sooty bosom" of Othello (1.2.70). The contrast between initial masculine construction and Desdemona's action fuels Roderigo's and Brabantio's respective characterizations of her elopement as a "gross revolt" and an "escape" (1.1.134; 1.3.197).[16]

Just as Desdemona's relocation to Cyprus is the most unfit of her physical dispositions, so her very request to accompany Othello there is the most troubling—and most portentous—instance of her agency. Before the Senate she has presumed to advance her own agenda, rejecting not only the Duke's assumption that she will return to Brabantio's house, rejecting even Othello's notion that accommodation should be found for her in Venice, proposing instead an alternative that no man in the play would have thought to assign her to: "let me go with him." She insists in "downright violence" and in "scorn of fortunes" that "I did love the Moor, to live with him." Her further statement that "my heart's subdued / Even to the utmost pleasure of my lord" scarcely obscures the fact that Othello has given no sign that it would be his pleasure for her to accompany him (1.3.248–51, 259).[17] In this intervention she goes some way toward justifying Iago's eventual remark of role inversion: "Our general's wife is now the general" (2.3.305–306).

The moral import of physical disposition is clear in the early modern prescriptive record. Henry Smith, for example, indicates why, if the husband goes abroad, the wife must stay home: "Paul biddeth Titus to exhort women that they be chaste, and keeping at home: presently after chaste, he sayeth, keeping at home, as though home were chastity's keeper." He moralizes that "a wife should teach her feet, go not beyond the door; she must count the walls of her house like the banks of the river which Shimei might not pass, if he would please the King" (sigs. F6ʳ–F7ʳ). His last analogy recalls the familiar Elizabethan proverb "Every man is King in his house." By her confinement a wife will please her husband, her proper lord; outside her house she strays into territory he cannot claim to control. Violations of positional limits expose her to suspicion of other violations, and in particular sexual violations.

That this conservative patriarchal ethos provides a text by which to read Desdemona is reinforced by the fact that a variation on it holds with respect to the other female characters in the play; Henry Smith's further advice that "As it becometh her to keep home, so it becometh her to keep silence" (sig. F7ʳ) might, for example, be the gloss for the responses of Cassio to Bianca and Iago to Emilia. These are precisely the ways in which Cassio finds Bianca unbecoming to him: her not keeping home and her not keeping silent. Nervous of being found "woman'd," he greets her at her first appearance on stage with "What make you from home?" and "I'faith, sweet love, I was coming to your house" (3.4.193, 167, 169); later, he complains that "she haunts me in every place" (4.1.131) instead of confining herself to her "proper" place, at home. He follows her because "I must, she'll rail i'the street else" (4.1.159). She offends not only as an unsilent woman but, more, by railing publicly rather than privately, in the street rather than behind the closed doors of her house. The association of female dislocation and loquacity then achieves its final significance when, for denying Desdemona's infidelity, Emilia, too, is accused by Iago of speaking out of place and is remanded to her "proper" place. Having previewed the issue in commanding her to "Speak within doors" (4.2.146), he in the last scene orders her first to "charm your tongue," then to "get you home." Her "I will not charm my tongue," "I am bound to speak," "let me have leave to speak," "I hold my peace sir, no," "I'll be in speaking, liberal as the air," and "yet I'll speak" are punctuated by " 'Tis proper I obey him, but not now: / Perchance, Iago, I will ne'er go home," and, in response to his repeated "Be wise, and get you home," "I will not" (5.2.184–224). As her articulation of insurrection escalates, so does his determination to control her, until he finally silences her tongue and sends her to her last home in the play's second uxoricide.[18]

Just as for Brabantio, then, for Cassio and Iago the "house" or "home" is the place where a woman belongs, and the notion of displacement elaborates or exaggerates other feminine trespasses against masculine notions of order and propriety. In the persons of Cassio and Iago, the world view of Brabantio survives the first act and informs the concerns of those critics who read a number of disturbing signals in Desdemona's character and actions. We have already heard testimony of her wish that "heaven had made her such a man" as Othello; Brabantio has drawn for us the further conclusion that such hints have made her "half the wooer" (1.3.163, 176) of Othello. There is, moreover, an earlier example of self-determination of which we are repeatedly reminded: she has been described by Brabantio as "So opposite to marriage, that she shunn'd / The wealthy curled darlings of our nation" (1.2.67–68). Iago exploits the unseemliness of her discrimination in the third act, when he argues the point of view that her decision "Not to affect many proposed matches" shows in her "a will most rank, / Foul disproportion; thoughts unnatural" (3.3.233–37), and her willfulness niggles again at our consciousness when in the fourth act Emilia recalls that Desdemona has "forsook so many noble matches" (4.2.127). Iago follows the same process of insinuation and condemnation when he reminds Othello of Brabantio's warning that "She has deceiv'd her father, may do thee" (1.3.293) by suggesting that "She did deceive her father, marrying you" (3.3.210).

Modern critics have, in addition, expressed discomfort with the wit and worldliness Desdemona displays in jesting with Iago upon her arrival in Cyprus. Her aside "I am not merry, but I do beguile / The thing I am, by seeming otherwise" (2.1.122–23) is insufficient to reassure them. It is particularly noteworthy here, and particularly vexing to them, that her banter belies her own endorsement of wifely obedience; she playfully urges Emilia, "do not learn of him, Emilia, though he be thy husband" (2.1.161–62). Critics have also fretted over her willow-scene speculation that "This Lodovico is a proper man. . . . He speaks well" (4.3.35, 37); it seems almost to confirm Iago's prediction that her affections will wander to some more appropriate man than Othello.[19]

And yet, she is chaste, and, at least in the last act of the play, she is so passive and submissive that she dies on a lie rather than condemn her husband:

Emilia.	O, who has done this deed?
Desdemona.	Nobody, I myself, farewell:
	Commend me to my kind lord, O, farewell!

(5.2.124–26)

Although she declares that "A guiltless death I die," she exonerates Othello of responsibility for it, characterizes him as "kind," and acknowledges him her proper "lord" (5.2.123, 126).

To many students of character-based criticism, what is finally most troubling about Desdemona is that she seems to represent some failure in Shakespeare, the failure of an inconsistency in portrayal: how can the woman who defends her love with such fearlessness and conviction in the Senate scene be reconciled with that woman who so effaces herself in death? But we have come to learn that there are dangers in overhumanizing dramatic characters, that the attempt of such reconciliation is a misguided interpretive strategy.[20] Another and more useful way of reading Desdemona is to think of her as not a being from whom we should demand consistency, but rather an artfully created embodiment of female behavior and feminine responses, in all the variety and ambiguity perceived by men. In this reading, she is a pattern rather than a personality, a pattern that serves a larger dramatic purpose than characterization.

This does not mean that her pattern does not have its own logic, but, let me suggest, it is a logic that may more usefully be found in the moral (or characterologic) significances of place than in human psychology. Although in the first part of the play insistent references to displacement seem engineered to impress upon us that the newly married Othello and Desdemona live as "strangers in an inn" rather than by "settling a house," gradually, in Cyprus, intimations of a settled domesticity accumulate. Upon his arrival there, Othello bids, "Come, let us to the castle. . . . come, Desdemona." He asks Iago to "disembark my coffers; / Bring thou the master to the citadel," and Iago advises Roderigo, "meet me by and by at the citadel: I must fetch his necessaries ashore" (2.1.201–11, 278–79); as late as the fifth act, Iago bids Emilia, "run you to the citadel, / And tell my lord and lady what has happ'd" (5.1.125–26). Through the association of Desdemona with the citadel, and especially given that personal possessions are twice mentioned in the same breath as the citadel, we seem clearly intended to apprehend that Othello and Desdemona will establish residence within its walls, the "fortitude" of which is "best known" to Othello (1.3.222–23). Now, a building designed for military fortification rather than domestic occupation is clearly no more fitting than an inn for the institution of marriage.

As the tragedy unfolds, however, this fix on Othello and Desdemona's residence slips, in a manner uniquely exploitable on the open and visually indeterminative stage of the English Renaissance. With the war "done," the military urgency of the first act relaxes. Othello, moreover, comes to tell Desdemona, "I shall not dine at home, / I meet the captains, at the citadel" (3.3.59–60)—as if their home is elsewhere. A motif of hospitality surfaces as Othello remarks that his wife "feeds well, loves company, / Is free of speech, sings, plays, and dances well"; as he invites "generous islanders" to dinner (3.3.188–89, 284–85); and as the couple welcomes Lodovico and Gratiano. One early crime against Desdemona, that she travels to Cyprus with no maidservant of her own, is redeemed as Emilia gradually resolves the conflict between her loyalties to mistress and husband by accepting a preeminent allegiance to Desdemona—and as Desdemona enjoys with her woman intensely private preparations for bed, idle chatter about Lodovico, intimate memories of her childhood maid, the willow song, a philosophy of marital fidelity. Othello, who has opposed himself to "chamberers," now finds himself imagining betrayal by his wife in "*my* chamber" (3.3.269; 4.1.139; emphasis added), and in the last scene, his distraught puzzling over whether to let Emilia "in" (5.2.95, 97, 105) underlines his own confinement within a "chamber" that now for the first time acquires visual definition through an aggregation of domestic props. The bed, its curtains, the wedding sheets, and the candle finally and concretely confirm the hints at an established household, so that Lodovico's closing judgment that Gratiano shall "keep the house, / And seize upon the fortunes of the Moor" does not jar at all (5.2.366–67).

The suggestions of a conventional domestic life intensify, in other words, even as Desdemona's unconventional independence of spirit fades, as if to confirm the power of place asserted by patriarchalists. Her discontinuous personal disposition in fact conforms to her variant physical dispositions.

III

The contradictions between Desdemona's initial agency and her final passivity are requisite to the dramatic purpose of Othello's tragedy. That is, while Desdemona's innocence is necessary, so too are the elements in her that raise doubts, that exonerate Othello of comic credulity, that enable her to exemplify all the tragic confusions about women that men hold, and that finally demonstrate the limits of patriarchalism as a text by which to read women. But even as the issue of Desdemona's complicity in her own victimization is moot to the dramatic ethos, the issue of Othello's part in his own tragedy is, according to the laws of genre, of the essence. How is it that this man, a man whom even Iago admits "is of a constant, noble, loving nature" and apt to "prove . . . A most dear husband" (2.1.284–86), comes to dispose of his beloved new wife by murder? To pursue the logic already proposed for Desdemona's dispositions is to recognize in turn the tragic consequences of the facts that Othello is dispositioned himself, that he is in addition the agent of her dis-positioning, and that he comes to see such meanings in displacement as Brabantio and Iago (and patriarchal philosophy) would find there.

To begin with the second phenomenon: for Desdemona's fateful displacements Othello must bear final responsibility, according to patriarchal convention. On this subject the prescriptive text is again unvarying. Othello is at fault for deferring domestic decision to the Senate, as the Duke intimates when with disinterest he dismisses the vexed matter of Desdemona's accommodation: "Be it, as you shall privately determine" (1.3.275). When Othello stoops to "beseech" and "beg" the duke to "let her will / Have a free way" (1.3.260–61) in the matter, he violates the fundamental counsel (here expressed by Edmund Tilney) that the new husband must set himself to "steal away [his bride's] private will"[21] so as to establish from the outset the preeminence of his own. John Dod and Robert Cleaver take it for granted that among the "dutie[s] of the Husband towards his Wife" are "to be ordinarily in a dwelling place," a "settled" house (sig. G7^r); Jean Bodin called it "the law of nature, which willeth, that every man should be master of his own house" (sig. C2^r). Othello flouts not only this residential imperative but also its variant, Dod and Cleaver's precept that

> For the first year after marriage, God would not have the husband go to war with his enemies, to the end that he and his wife might learn to know one another's conditions and qualities, and so afterwards live in godly peace, and not to war one with another. And therefore God gave and appointed that the new married husband that year is to stay at home and settle his love, that he might not war and jar after: for that God of peace dwelleth not in the house of war.[22]

This statement unifies two fundamentals of domestic prescription: the import of place is wed to the commonplace that the foundation and objective of a marital relationship is peace. Othello, unhappily, is apt for neither.

He is, first (and with this we return to the characterizing phenomenon of his displacement), a man of no fixed address. He defines himself in opposition to "chamberers" (3.3.269), as one who has made his residence instead in the "tented field" (1.3.85). Roderigo terms him "an extravagant and wheeling stranger, / Of here, and every where" (1.1.136–37); Iago, "an erring"—that is, wandering, vagabond—"barbarian" (1.3.356–57).[23] If Desdemona, "within" the Sagittar/y in the second scene, realizes escape from a delimiting household through her elopement there, Othello, standing outside it, anticipates only restriction in marriage:

> But that I love the gentle Desdemona,
> I would not my unhoused free condition
> Put into circumscription and confine
> For the sea's worth.
>
> (1.2.25–28)

Even despite this protest of willing translation, moreover, Othello continues to resist domestic confine. Iago, warning of the "raised father and his friends" which join the "three several quests" of the Senate in search of him, urges Othello, "You were best go in," but Othello says largely, "Not I, I must be found," that is, found outside, unhoused, and free (1.2.29–30, 46). Only a scene later, Othello will promise the Senate that marriage will not reduce the scope of his activity; if it does, then, worst of all fates, let him be wholly domesticated, "Let housewives make a skillet of my helm" (1.3.272), in his abhorrence revealing his unaccommodated inclination. He grieves at the notion that he may be made "A fixed figure, for the time of scorn / To point his slow unmoving fingers at" (4.2.55–56).

He is, second (with reference to Dod and Cleaver's insistence on peace as well as place in marriage), a man of war. He calls himself, inauspiciously, "little blest with the set phrase of peace" (1.3.82). His profession is a jealous mistress. Asking the bridegroom to "slubber the gloss of your new fortunes" by accepting a commission to Cyprus, the Duke admits that Othello's command is not of the absolute essence: "we have there a substitute of most allowed sufficiency"; mere "opinion, a sovereign mistress of effects"—nothing more tangible—"throws a more safer voice on you." Yet Othello defers to this "sovereign mistress" and to a "tyrant custom" that he cannot alter overnight, even despite the night this is. The ruling metaphor of his acceptance—that this custom "Hath made the flinty and steel couch of war / My thrice-driven bed of down" (1.3.223–31)—indicates at least a dim recognition that his "new fortunes" properly involve the marriage bed, the "right and lawful use" of which William

Perkins defines as "an essential duty of marriage" (424). Othello's muddled attempt to assure the Senate that his "appetite" will not interfere with their commission further suggests his apprehension of the tension between marital consummation and martial occupation (1.3.261–74). Repeated figurative commingling of the military and the marital—" 'tis the soldiers' life, / To have their balmy slumbers wak'd with strife," he will tell Desdemona in Cyprus (2.3.249–50)—highlights the incompatibility of Othello's occupation with the universally understood goal of marriage.[24] And the prevalence and suggestive power of linguistic links between love and violence in the play offer another hint of Othello's susceptibility (through his occupation) to domestic murder.

Despite the twin values of place and peace put forth in the idealizing literature of marriage, for Othello marriage itself is in fact psychologically displacing, profoundly disquieting, and far more dangerous than his martial occupation. He is defeated by the doubts of sure domestic ownership that are nurtured by Iago rather than by the Turkish challenge to the Venetian title to Cyprus. The fact that it is marriage that instead will subjugate him is hinted in the reference to Desdemona as "our great captain's captain" (2.1.74) and in Iago's remark that "His soul is so infetter'd to her love . . . her appetite shall play the god / With his weak function" (2.3.336–39). Othello seems to encourage his own overmastering when he tells Desdemona that he has given her a handkerchief that did "subdue my father / Entirely" to the love of his mother (3.4.57–58) and when he muses that Desdemona "might lie by an emperor's side, and command him tasks" (4.1.180–81). Further, marriage initiates him into the sexuality of the centaur,[25] under the sign of which he commences it, and so disorders his self-image that he who had celebrated his free condition is finally reduced to the cry of pathos, "Where should Othello go?" (5.2.272).

The cumulative signs of domestic instantiation that modulated our understanding of Desdemona's disposition also can be seen to participate in Othello's fatal jealousy: his acquisition of the trappings of a household reverberates with his discovery of the anxiety of possession:

> O curse of marriage,
> That we can call these delicate creatures ours,
> And not their appetites!
>
> (3.3.272–74)

Here Othello elucidates a key problematic of the patriarchal system as a text; it both asserts possession and finds possession always uncertain. In this, the psychology of jealousy is compounded by the patriarchal logic of place.

Members of *Othello*'s audience are invited to collude in Othello's jealousy and experience his tragedy. They witness all Desdemona's violations of domestic prescription: her willfulness in half-wooing Othello, in fleeing her father's house, in electing to accompany Othello to Cyprus. But then there are patterns of doubt that work independently of character and plot, suspicions that can resonate only in the minds of the audience. Desdemona's banter with Iago at the dockside, her advice to Emilia not to learn from her husband, her vow to make Othello's bed "a school, his board a shrift" (3.3.24), her willow-scene speculation about Lodovico—all of these hints at impropriety that have so troubled critics of the play are unseen, unheard, unknown by Othello, incapable of fueling his jealousy. In fact, they may trouble critics precisely because they work only upon the audience, inviting each (male) member of it to share Othello's doubts, to associate himself with Othello in questioning the nature of this woman and the nature of women. And some critics, even knowing Desdemona's chastity with a certainty unavailable to first viewers or readers of the play, have succumbed to the temptation thus offered and placed upon Desdemona the burden of responsibility for her victimization. How much more easily were members of the play's first audience infected with suspicion— and then brought to a terrible self-recognition at the denouement, when confronted with Desdemona's unimpeachable innocence. Those so snared have also shared Lodovico's shuddering response to "the tragic lodging of this bed": "the object poisons sight, / Let it be hid" (5.2.364-66).[26]

In this they experience in full the double-edged nature of patriarchalism: that is, that the absolute responsibility asserted for the husband carries its own jeopardy. As Dod and Cleaver admit, if a woman errs, "it is for the most part through the fault, and want of discretion, and lack of good government in the husband" (sig. L6ʳ). For this reason uxoricide is among the most heinous of crimes. Because a woman's nature is weak and susceptible, her behavior is the responsibility of her husband, and the husband who finds in his wife a fault grave enough to warrant her death admits of the gravest failure in himself. Those who are implicated in Othello's tragedy by sympathy with his suspicions may discover proportionate self-blame.

Othello's own self-condemnation for his action is stern: "nothing extenuate," he says (5.2.343). If they wish, however, members of the audience can find their own extenuation. Too terrible a process of audience identification with Othello can be subverted by his very distinctions and peculiarities: his race, his occupation, his extravagant otherness. Further, according to the tragic paradigm of *Othello*, this man has no "place"; this man is dedicated to war; and this man is subjected to the practices of the evil intelligence of an Iago; thus is this man, unlike other men, even other jealous men, a wife murderer. This distancing from him is the only amelioration of a tragedy based on the everyday relationships of male and female, on the essential unknowableness of the female to the male, and on man's ability to do such violence. The process of restoration that generally concludes Shakespeare's tragedies of state is aborted here, where only this amelioration offers any relief from confrontation with the tragic possibilities in human relationship.

This is the tragedy that *Othello* realizes in gender—the notion of gender, that is, that is constructed by patriarchalism. In Desdemona we find all the warning signals of unchastity that would have been recognized by Henry Smith, John Dod, Robert Cleaver, and a score of their fellow authors. But here all those signs are wrong. The patriarchal logic of place and its moral import works its way through the plot of *Othello* but is defeated by so simple and unarguable a fact as Desdemona's innocence. Her innocence exposes the predictive incapacity of patriarchalism and is in this respect subversive of its conceptual power.

NOTES

I would like to thank Leeds Barroll, who in 1980 asked what the significances of the "Sagittar/y" might be; Shirley Nelson Garner, who invited me to prepare the first draft of this essay for a 1987 seminar of the Shakespeare Association of America; and Michael Bristol, Alan Dessen, Barbara Mowat, Alan Sinfield, and (again) Leeds Barroll for their encouraging responses to that early version. A later version of this work has been published in chapter 4 of my *Private Matters and Public Culture in Post-Reformation England* (Ithaca: Cornell UP, 1994).

1. Although I have found Ross's edition of *Othello* particularly useful, for the convenience of the reader all citations to the play are from the New Arden Shakespeare, edited by Ridley. Citations from plays other than *Othello* are from the Riverside Shakespeare.

2. Ridley notes that "the passage seems overloaded with words expressing 'suitability' " (34). Ross provides the glosses "assignment to some appropriate residence and allowance of money for maintenance" and "such befitting arrangements [for her] . . . as corresponds with her upbringing" (37). Elliott also finds "anxiety" in Othello's overloaded language (6).

3. Ross first raised the question of the significance of the naming of the Sagittar/y in "The Shakespearean Othello" (566–71). For other views of the relevance of the centaur image to *Othello*, see Hansen, and also Elliott (252–53).

4. I except "love" from this noun sequence because it participates in a different sequence, the hate-love dichotomy.

5. See especially the notes in the New Variorum (25-26), and see Ridley (13) and the Ross edition (12). In *Errors*, the Centaur is explicitly identified as an inn (1.2.14, 23). While the Sagittar/y is never so identified, it *is* distinguished from more familiar forms of residence by the many references to Brabantio's house, Bianca's house, and the military quarters of Iago, Roderigo, and Cassio.

6. See also Larwood and Hotten, who record seventeenth-century public houses named "Arrow," "Archers," and "Sheaf of Arrows" (197).

7. Spurgeon concludes that "more than half the animal images in the play are Iago's, and all these are contemptuous or repellent" (335).

8. McAlindon terms this "her first dissociation from the world of domestic reality and common duties" (115); Erickson also recognizes that "through Othello's story she gains access to a larger world beyond the domestic realm that presently confines her" (91); and Stallybrass remarks how she "is drawn from 'house affairs' (1.3.147) to tales of an undomesticated landscape 'of antres vast and deserts idle.' . . . And her withdrawal from house affairs and the government of her father marks her out as 'untamed' " (136). Greenblatt pursues another set of analogies between Othello's tales ("the Cannibals, that each other eat") and Desdemona's behavior (she would "with a greedy ear / Devour up my discourse") in order to suggest that Othello "has a dim intimation of his fate" (238). In this regard the association of the centaur with cannibalism in Chester may be of interest. I differ from Knight, who suggests that reference to the "house affairs" establishes "a certain domestic feminity about" Desdemona (107-108).

9. Lear's association is glossed by Topsell: "Centaurs . . . are described by the poets to have their forepart like men, and their hinder part like horses, the occasion whereof is thus related by Pindarus: that Centaurus the son of Ixion committed buggery with the mares of Magnetia, under the mountain Pelius, from whence came that monstrous birth in the upper part resembling the father and in the nether the mother" (sig. Gg1^r). The association of the centaur with sexuality was undoubtedly reinforced by the fact that the part of the body governed by the sign of Sagittarius is the thigh, that almanac illustrations served to make Sagittarius and the thigh synonymous, and that the thigh has a long tradition as a code word for the seat of sexuality.

10. The necessity of housing helps account for the relatively late age at marriage in the early modern period, according to Laslett: "marriage could not come about unless a slot fell vacant and the aspiring couple was able to fill it up. It might be a cottage . . . which became available" (101).

11. Whately (sig. A4^r); see also, for example, Smith (sig. E2^r); Dod and Cleaver (sigs. M4^v-M5^r); Dillingham (sig. I6^v); Gainsford (fol. 101^v). In *The Comedy of Errors*, Adriana asks, "Why should their liberty than ours be more?" and Luciana answers, "Because their business still lies out a' door" (2.1.10-11).

12. Neill suggests that "the importance of Venice as the metropolitan center of the

play world is that it supplies, or offers to supply, each individual with a clearly defined and secure position within an established social order" (118).

13. In his edition, Ross notes that "other Shakespearean meanings of this word ['conveyance'] support the audience's anticipatory qualms about the meaning of this plan—particularly: (1) removal; (2) document by which transference of property is effected; (3) underhand dealing" (42).

14. See, for example, Burke and Snow (386).

15. The common notion that Cassio escorts Desdemona to Othello is undoubtedly read back from the later description of him as intermediary between the two during their courtship. It is explicitly contradicted by this passage as well as by Cassio's more immediately relevant scene 2 ignorance of the marriage and of Othello's location, so that in the first act at least (and perhaps only) we are given to understand Desdemona's independence of movement.

16. Greenblatt writes, "The safe passage of the female from father to husband is irreparably disrupted, marked as an escape" (240).

17. Ridley also notes that Othello does not hint that Desdemona might accompany him, "with whatever alacrity he welcomes the suggestion when she makes it" (35).

18. Bianca's loquacity has often been noticed in the criticism; her dislocation has been noted by Stallybrass (127), who also observes that "silence and chastity are, in turn, homologous to woman's enclosure within the house" and that "Emilia must open the closed mouth, the locked house" (127, 142).

19. Garner addresses both Desdemona's reference to Lodovico and her character in more complex ways than is common. For a review of prevailing critical trends (and some responses to them), see also Neely, Adamson, and Cook.

20. In "When Is a Character Not a Character? Desdemona, Olivia, Lady Macbeth, and Subjectivity," chapter 3 of *Faultlines*, Alan Sinfield provides a more detailed review of the perils of "character criticism." He concludes that "Desdemona has no character of her own; she is a convenience in the story of Othello, Iago, and Venice" (54). I am grateful for his sympathetic reading of this essay in its earlier stages. On this subject, see also Adelman (chapter 3), Belsey, and Stallybrass (141).

21. Of particular interest is the link between sexual possession and conquest of the will. Tilney writes in full: "In this long and troublesome journey of matrimony, the wise man may not be contented only with his spouse's virginity, but by little and little must gently procure that he may also steal away her private will and appetite, so that of two bodies there may be made one only heart" (sig. B6^r). Dod and Cleaver echo: "The husband ought not to be satisfied that he hath robbed his wife of her virginity, but in that he hath possession and use of her will" (sig. M4^r). Both continue that this advice is essential to marital peace.

22. Dod and Cleaver (sig. P4^r). They repeat with small variation a passage included in Smith (sig. F1^v); Perkins's marginal note to a similar statement reveals that the ultimate source is biblical, Deuteronomy 24:5: "When a man hath taken a new wife, he

shall not go out to war, neither shall he be charged with any business: *but* he shall be free at home one year, and shall cheer up his wife which he hath taken." Perkins says that marital duties are "principally two: cohabitation and communion" (423).

23. For "erring," see the OED. Neill suggests that Othello's "account of himself as a placeless wanderer" "awakened" Desdemona's "romantic response" (126).

24. This figurative encroachment of the military upon the marital is a motif that recurs also when Iago suggestively describes the "opposition bloody" of Cassio and Roderigo as having begun with them "In quarter, and in terms, like bride and groom, / Devesting them to bed" (2.3.171–75). McAlindon notes that the interruption of the nuptial night "confirms that the precarious balance between the domestic and the military worlds has broken down" (103).

25. On this subject see Snow and also Cavell.

26. Bradley seems relieved that "the bed where she is stifled was within the curtains [an arguable assumption], and so, presumably, in part, concealed," for he finds the play characterized by "a violence or brutality the effect of which is unnecessarily painful and rather sensational than tragic" (183–85). Davison notes the intense reactions that the play provokes: "What is surprising, perhaps, is the degree of acrimony, *personal* acrimony, betrayed by some critics towards one another or even towards Othello, in their discussions of this play" (10).

WORKS CITED

Adamson, W. D. "Unpinned or Undone? Desdemona's Critics and the Problem of Sexual Innocence." *Shakespeare Studies* 13 (1980): 169–86.

Adelman, Janet. *Suffocating Mothers: Fantasies of Maternal Origin in Shakespeare's Plays, "Hamlet" to "The Tempest."* New York: Routledge, 1992.

Agrippa von Nettesheim, Henricus Cornelius. *The Commendation of Matrimony* (1526). Trans. David Clapham. London, 1540.

Belsey, Catherine. "Alice Arden's Crime." *Renaissance Drama* n.s. 13 (1982): 83–102.

Bodin, Jean. *The Six Bookes of a Commonweale* (1576). Trans. Richard Knolles, 1606. Ed. Kenneth Douglas McRae. Cambridge: Harvard UP, 1962.

Bradley, A. C. *Shakespearean Tragedy: Lectures on "Hamlet," "Othello," "King Lear," "Macbeth."* 1904; rpt., London: Macmillan, 1967.

Burke, Kenneth. "*Othello:* An Essay to Illustrate a Method." *Hudson Review* 4 (1951): 165–203.

Cavell, Stanley. "Othello and the Stake of the Other." *Disowning Knowledge in Six Plays of Shakespeare.* Cambridge: Cambridge UP, 1987. 125–42.

Chester, Robert. *Love's Martyr.* London, 1601.

Cook, Ann Jennalie. "The Design of Desdemona: Doubt Raised and Resolved." *Shakespeare Studies* 13 (1980): 187–96.

Davison, Peter. *Othello*. The Critics Debate, series ed. Michael Scott. Houndmills: Macmillan, 1988.

Dillingham, Francis. *A Golden Key [containing] Christian Oeconomy, or Household Government*. London, 1609.

Dod, John, and Robert Cleaver. *A Godly Form of Household Government*. London, 1598.

Elliott, Martin. *Shakespeare's Invention of Othello: A Study in Early Modern English*. Houndmills: Macmillan, 1988.

Erickson, Peter. *Patriarchal Structures in Shakespeare's Drama*. Berkeley: U of California P, 1985.

Gainsford, Thomas. *The Rich Cabinet Furnished with Variety of Excellent Descriptions*. London, 1616.

Garner, S. N. "Shakespeare's Desdemona." *Shakespeare Studies* 9 (1976): 233–52.

Greenblatt, Stephen. *Renaissance Self-Fashioning from More to Shakespeare*. Chicago: U of Chicago P, 1980.

Hansen, Abbey Jane Dubman. "Shakespeare's *Othello*." *Explicator* 35 (1977): 4–6.

Knight, G. Wilson. *The Wheel of Fire: Interpretations of Shakespearian Tragedy with Three New Essays*. 4th ed. 1930; London: Methuen, 1949.

Larwood, Jacob, and John Camden Hotten. *English Inn Signs*. Rev. ed. of *History of Signboards*. 1866; rev. ed., London: Chatto and Windus, 1951.

Laslett, Peter. *The World We Have Lost—Further Explored*. 3rd ed. London: Methuen, 1983.

Luborsky, Ruth Samson. "What Tudor Book Illustrations Illustrate." Talk at the Folger Shakespeare Library, 20 March 1987.

McAlindon, T. *Shakespeare and Decorum*. London: Macmillan, 1973.

Neely, Carol Thomas. "Women and Men in *Othello*: 'What should such a fool / Do with so good a woman?' " *Shakespeare Studies* 10 (1977): 133–58.

Neill, Michael. "Changing Places in *Othello*." *Shakespeare Survey* 37 (1984): 115–31.

Perkins, William. *Christian Oeconomy* (1609). *The Work of William Perkins*. Ed. Ian Breward. Appleton: Sutton Courtenay P, 1970. 411–39.

Ross, Lawrence. "The Shakespearean Othello." Unpublished Ph.D. dissertation, Princeton University, 1956.

Shakespeare, William. *The Riverside Shakespeare*. Ed. G. Blakemore Evans. Boston: Houghton Mifflin, 1974.

———. *Othello*. Ed. Horace Howard Furness. *The New Variorum Shakespeare*. Philadelphia: J. B. Lippincott, 1986.

———. *Othello.* Ed. M. R. Ridley. *The New Arden Shakespeare.* London: Methuen, 1958.

———. *The Tragedy of Othello, the Moor of Venice.* Ed. Lawrence Ross. Indianapolis: Bobbs-Merrill, 1974.

Sinfield, Alan. *Faultlines: Cultural Materialism and the Politics of Dissident Reading.* Berkeley: U of California P, 1992.

Smith, Henry. *A Preparative to Marriage.* London, 1591.

Snow, Edward A. "Sexual Anxiety and the Male Order of Things in *Othello.*" *ELR* 10 (1980): 384–412.

Spurgeon, Caroline F. E. *Shakespeare's Imagery and What It Tells Us.* Cambridge: Cambridge UP, 1935.

Stallybrass, Peter. "Patriarchal Territories: The Body Enclosed." *Rewriting the Renaissance: The Discourses of Sexual Difference in Early Modern Europe.* Ed. Margaret W. Ferguson, Maureen Quilligan, and Nancy J. Vickers. Chicago: U of Chicago P, 1986. 123–42.

Taylor, John. *Taylor's Travels and Circular Perambulation through, and by more than Thirty Times Twelve Signs of the Zodiac, of the famous Cities of London and Westminster. . . . with an Alphabetical Description of all the Tavern Signs.* London, 1636.

Tilney, Edmund. *A Brief and Pleasant Discourse of Duties in Marriage, Called the Flower of Friendship.* London, 1568.

Topsell, Edward. *The History of Four-Footed Beasts.* London, 1607.

Whately, William. *A Bride-Bush, or a Wedding Sermon.* London, 1617.

7

"THE MOOR OF VENICE," OR THE ITALIAN ON THE RENAISSANCE ENGLISH STAGE

MARGO HENDRICKS

A NUMBER OF critics have read *Othello* principally with an eye toward illuminating the moral sense of the problematic racial and sexual politics engendered not only by the play's depiction of what is viewed as an interracial marriage but also by Othello's sensationalized murder of his wife, Desdemona.[1] The obstacle facing all such critical readings, as Michael Neill astutely points out, is that the play itself conspicuously denies us (even as it denies Othello) an opportunity to enact "the funeral dignities that usually serve to put a form of [moral] order upon such spectacles of ruins," creating an "ending [that is] perhaps the most shocking in Shakespearean tragedy" (383–412). Neill concludes that it is the final tragic scene, where "white" Desdemona is murdered and her husband/murderer, "black" Othello, violently avenges her murder—"I took by th'throat the circumcised dog / And smote him thus" (5.2.351-52)[2]—which most "articulate[s] the [racial] anxiety evident almost everywhere in the play's history—a sense of scandal that informs the textual strategies of editors and theatrical productions as much as it does the disturbed reactions of audiences and critics" (384).

Feminist scholars have made clear that this "scandal" actually begins long before this most "unnatural" ending to the marriage of Othello and Desdemona. For example, Patricia Parker sees the "simultaneously eroticized and epistemological impulse to open up to show" the " 'fantasies' of race and gender" in *Othello* as an anxiety-ridden linkage of female sexuality and the exotic narratives of "African or New World discovery" (92), while Janet Adelman argues that the "whole of his exchange with Desdemona demonstrates Othello's terrible conflict between his intense desire for fusion with the woman he idealizes as the nurturant source of his being and his equally intense conviction that her participation in sexuality has contaminated her and thus contaminated the perfection that he has vested in her" (66–67). What has become obvious in these recent studies of *Othello*, as Valerie Traub contends, is that "Othello's anxiety is culturally and psychosexually overdetermined by erotic, gender, and racial anxieties, including . . . the fear of chaos [usually] associate[d] with sexual activity."[3] In what follows, I wish to reconsider the possibilities of reading the racial and sexual anxieties latent in Shakespeare's *Othello*. The focus of my discussion is not so much the personal relationships represented in the play as it is the cultural assumptions which may be coincident with the notion of race in *Othello*; in particular, I want to argue the possibility that the social site of Shakespeare's tragedy, Venice, is a much more significant *player* in the construction of early modern English racialist ideology than critics have hitherto illuminated. Simply stated, my purpose is to show that Venice is a crucial yet often critically neglected racial persona in *Othello*.[4]

My reading builds upon and diverges from studies that examine Shakespeare's use of Italian city-states, in particular Venice, in his dramatic works—a usage which, according to these critics, highlights an Elizabethan "fascination" with Italian culture.[5] In the case of Venice, this fascination is rooted in, as David C. McPherson terms it, the "myth of Venice," wherein the city is perceived as a state whose wealth, political stability, justice, and civility set it above all others (27). This image, of course, has its origins in early modern Italian political theories whose principal goal was to conceptualize a model civil society that "was to be paradigmatic for [Italian] civic humanism" (Pocock 271). In these theories Venice is represented as an uncorrupted, tranquil, and stable state; in fact, "Venice appears, both physically and politically, 'rather framed by the hands of the immortal Gods, than any way by the arte, industry or inuention of men.' "[6] Ultimately, as J. G. A. Pocock has shown, this "myth of Venice (at its most mythical) was to lie in the assertion that the Venetian commonwealth was an immortally serene, because perfectly balanced, combination of the three elements of monarchy, aristocracy, and democracy" (102).

It is my contention that this myth inheres in Shakespeare's *Othello* and exercises a "compulsive force on the imagination," of both the characters within the play and the audience watching events unfold. But, because it is a mythology, "framed by the hands, . . . arte, industry, [and] invention of men," the ideal of Venice is also a paradox which ultimately subverts its illusion of perfection by drawing attention not only to the dichotomies (pure/impure, black/white) it constructs but also to the interiority that the myth and its dichotomies seek to conceal (Pocock 102). In other words, while the myth extols an image of Venice as the idealized feminine body, beautiful, desirable, and virginal, it also vicariously projects an image of Venice as the imperfect body—corruptive, desiring, and easily violated. If, as Patricia Parker argues, "the gaze is a vicarious gaze, a substitution of narrative" (89), then our attempt to discern how this paradox works racially must make use of this vicarious perspective.

"The Cunning Whore of Venice"

Lewes Lewkenor's 1599 translation of Gasparo Contarini's *De Magistratibus et Republica Venetorum* (along with Thomas Coryat's *Crudities*) did much to circulate this particular variant of the "myth of Venice" in Elizabethan and Jacobean England. In his dedication to the reader, Lewkenor writes that visitors to Venice, at least those "of a grauer humor,"

> would dilate of the greatnes of their Empire, the grauitie of their prince, the maiesty of their Senate, the vnuiolablenes of their lawes, their zeale in religion, and lastly their moderation, and equitie, wherewith they gouerne such subiected prouinces as are vnder their dominion, binding them therby in a faster bond of obedience then all the cytadels, garrisons, or whatsoeuer other tyrannicall inuentions could euer haue brought them vnto. (A2)

Lewkenor uses the dedication to set the context for his dilation of the greatness of Venice and to encourage his readers to gaze upon the book as if it were the city itself. Characterized as a "pure and vntouched virgine, free from the taste or violence of any forraine enforcement," Venice is laid open for the "admiration" and entertainment of the book's English readers. Though not often viewed as a narrative of discovery, Lewkenor's text might well be included in that genre, as it has in common with other narratives of discovery what Patricia Parker calls "the language of opening, uncovering or bringing to light . . . what had been secret, closed or hid" from the majority of the English reading public whose travels were limited to environs of London (87).

Of course, Venice is neither Africa nor the "New World," and Lewkenor's dedication to the reader of *The Commonwealth and Gouernment of Venice* is intended merely to set the stage for his translation of a work of political philosophy. Even so, the edition circulates conflicting images of the republic known as *La Serenissima*. In contrast to Lewkenor's praise of Venice's "unblemished" status, the commendatory poems written in praise of Lewkenor's endeavor convey a somewhat different vision of Venice. For example, one poem compares Venice to the "antique" cities of Babel, "fallen" "with the weight of their own furquedry." In another poem, though her "virgins state ambition nere could blot," the "swarmes" from "forrein nation[s]" prompt the writer to proclaim Venice's "ruinous case" which, of course, is reflected in the city's "painted face." Ironically, what is intended to honor the celebrated myth of Venetian stability and invulnerability, Lewkenor's dedication and the commendatory poems, actually draws attention to what stands behind the myth—Venice's notoriety as a site of illicit sexuality, dangerous passions, violence, and extraordinary cunning.

Thomas Coryat's *Crudities* exhibits a similar ambivalence toward Venice. In the account of his travel to Italy in 1608, Coryat begins with a description of Venice as "the fairest Lady," a "noble citie" (311). After a rather detailed description of the magnificence of Venice's architecture, Coryat interrupts his narrative to warn his readers to be wary of the city's gondoliers, who are "the most vicious and licentious varlets about all the City" (311). Coryat's warning is typical of his tendency to juxtapose an image of Venice as "this thrice worthie city . . . yea the richest Paragon" with an image of Venice as a city whose blatant acceptance of sexuality (the seeming valorization of the courtesans and the touted infidelity of Venetian wives) and violence denotes the "Virgin's" corruptibility. Coryat's maneuver serves strategically, as Ann Rosalind Jones suggests, as both a lure and an admonition: "Coryat writes with a double agenda: to thrill his readers and to protect their morals, to sell his book with the promise of titillation and to dignify it by setting his ethical seriousness as an Englishman against the variety of 'Ethnicke' types he encounters" (104). Jones rightly observes that the Venice "of English [writers such as Coryat] from the 1580s on was not a geographer's record but a fantasy setting for dramas of passion, Machiavellian politics, and revenge—a landscape of the mind" (110). For Coryat and others, within this "landscape of the mind" it is the "interplay of pleasure and danger" (Jones 102) posed by Venice's gendered and Janus-like status within European culture that must be castigated and the city reclaimed as the paradigm of cultural perfection.[7] And it is this gendered "interplay" that Shakespeare distills in *Othello*, coupling the metaphoric blackness of Venice's reputation as a site of feminine sexual corruption and the literalness of Moorish Othello's black skin with the unstained honor of the Venetian military commander Othello and the symbolic whiteness of an uncorrupted Venice. Shakespeare's *Othello* joins these other early modern English texts in presenting a perspective of Venice that satisfies the desire to see encompassed in one racialized body, even if vicariously, both the virgin and the whore. And that body belongs, of course, to a woman.

"Desdemona's Choice"

From the play's inception, when Brabantio reprimands Iago for his indecent language and both Roderigo and Iago for their disruption of Brabantio's peace—"What, tell'st thou me of robbing? this is Venice, my house is not a grange" (1.1.105–106)—the paradoxical "myth of Venice" is instantiated as a paradigm for reading the play's presumed sexual and racial deviances. Brabantio's words obviously are intended to correct what he perceives to be a misperception on the part of Iago, namely that there are no farm animals in his house. Significantly, Brabantio's rebuke conjures images of the Venice, *La Serenissima*, extolled in Lewkenor's translation, as the tone of Brabantio's declaration suggests that such a crime could never take place in Venice, and, more important, that Roderigo's and Iago's accusations of a barnyard theft would not have been brought surreptitiously to the victim's door in the middle of the night. Brabantio's reprimand indicates that he is a man possessed of the judicious gravity praised in Lewkenor's preface: a man whose "moderation and equitie" will lead him to behave rationally when confronted by what appears to be the irrational pranks of a spurned suitor.

Once he understands the implication of Iago's salacious words, however, Brabantio begins to exhibit the stereotypical irrationality which came to be a metaphoric staple of Jacobean dramatic depictions of Italians. Governed by his fury, Brabantio accuses Othello of sorcery or witchcraft even before the marriage is confirmed by the couple: "is there not charms, / By which the property of youth and maidhood, / May be abused? Have you not read, Roderigo, / Of such a thing?" (1.1.171–74) When we consider Brabantio's grave "This is Venice," the sight of the rational "senator's" descent into illogic is somewhat surprising as he attempts to explain what he perceives to be unexplainable:

> My daughter, O my daughter, . . .
> She is abus'd, stol'n from me and corrupted,
> By spells and medicines, bought of mountebanks,
> For nature so preposterously to err,
> (Being not deficient, blind, or lame of sense,)
> Sans witchcraft could not.
>
> (1.3.60–64)

Brabantio's "My daughter, O my daughter" poignantly recalls Solanio's account of Shylock's pained cry at Jessica's elopement with Lorenzo—"My daughter! O my ducats! O my daughter!—" and Shylock's own descent into irrationality (*MV* 2.8.15). Given Desdemona's position as only child and heir to Brabantio's estate, a situation analogous to Jessica's in *The Merchant of Venice*, it is not without significance that Shakespeare alludes to this earlier work in depicting a father's reaction to the news that his daughter has married without his approval and apparently to someone outside his ethnic community.

Shakespeare draws one other parallel between Brabantio and Shylock, in that both men seek to exploit the strict terms of Venetian law to extract justice from their perceived enemies. When he finally confronts Othello, Brabantio tells the general, "I therefore apprehend and do attach thee" (1.2.77).[8] In this moment, the rational Venetian has displaced the irrational father who has roused his "kindred" to pursue the couple. Once he has Othello in custody, Brabantio is confident that he will be able to prove Othello guilty of witchcraft and that the Venetian legal institution will prove "pure and uncorrupted" as it evaluates the truth of his accusation. And, not unexpectedly, when Venetian law appears, in the persona of the Duke, it reaffirms Brabantio's faith in its exactitude:

> Whoe'er he be, that in this foul proceeding
> Hath thus beguil'd your daughter of herself,
> And you of her, the bloody book of law
> You shall yourself read, in the bitter letter,
> After its own sense, though our proper son
> Stood in your action
>
> (1.3.65–69)

No matter the cost, Brabantio is being guaranteed that the "penal Lawes [will be] most unpardonably executed" (Pocock 325).

Whatever Brabantio's cause, when Othello is named the guilty party, the senators who have accompanied the Duke respond to Brabantio's accusation in a rather cryptic fashion: "We are very sorry for't" (1.3.73). This comment can, of course, be interpreted in one of two ways. First, it can be seen as an expression of regret that Othello's service will be lost to Venice, given the political tensions that exist between Venetians and Turks. Or it can be read as an expression of compassion for Brabantio and the loss of his daughter in the manner he has described. I would propose that the former reading (regret at the loss of Othello's service to Venice) is the more likely intent behind the senators' words. When Othello and Brabantio first come into the presence of the Duke and senators, one senator refers to Othello as "the valiant Moor." More telling of the esteem Othello has in Venice is the Duke's reaction after hearing

Othello's narrative, when the Duke exhorts Brabantio to "Take up this mangled matter at the best; / Men do their broken weapons rather use, / Than their bare hands" (1.3.172-74). Brabantio's refusal to comply with the Duke's admonition is, as Lynda Boose argues, a refusal to "act out," to ritualize the symbolic transfer of his daughter to her husband not because Othello is necessarily unworthy but because the selection of Desdemona's husband was not Brabantio's: that right had been usurped by his daughter ("Father and Daughter" 327).

Desdemona's choice of a husband has been the object of critical gaze ever since Thomas Rymer first questioned Shakespeare's use of a "Blackamoor" as the tragic protagonist in *Othello*: whether in M. R. Ridley's introduction to the Arden edition of *Othello*, where Ridley writes, "It is the very essence of the play that Desdemona in marrying Othello—a man to whom her 'natural' reaction should (her father holds) have been fear, not delight—has done something peculiarly startling" (liii), or in Stanley Cavell's careful explanation that, in choosing Othello, Desdemona has "overlooked his blackness in favor of his inner brilliance": in effect, "that she saw his visage as he sees it, that she understands his blackness as he understands it, as the expression (or in his word, his manifestation) of his mind" (129).

Complicating these, and other, critical attempts to explain Desdemona's choice is the fact that Shakespeare's play presents a world whose very social codes are frequently contradictory and conflicting, thus enabling Desdemona to act as she does. On one level, Venice is a place where the contagious rhetoric of racialism can easily destroy lives and careers, as Iago's manipulation so aptly illustrates. Yet it seems that early modern Venice is also a society where a man such as Othello can achieve success and fame to such a degree that a duke is moved to declare, "I think this tale would win my daughter too" (1.3.171). Othello's status and position, that is, his "honours and valiant parts" (1.3.253), prove as desirable to Desdemona as the narratives for which "She gave . . . a world of sighs" (1.3.159) and " . . . lov'd [Othello] for the dangers [he] had pass'd" (1.3.167).

Though a Moor, Othello is perceived as a valuable member of Venetian society and his action as nothing more than "a *mischief* that is past and gone" [emphasis mine] (1.3.204). Emily Bartels rightfully argues that Othello's acceptance includes Iago, who "even as he attempts to prove Othello the outsider, . . . represents him as an authorizing insider."[9] As Lewkenor's translation of Contarini work documents and J. G. A. Pocock's study substantiates, Venice was often cited by early modern political theorists as a state to be commended for its successful handling of its imperial aims through the hiring of foreign nationals to provide its military force and to police the city. This long-standing practice, plus the city's mercantile zeal, created a cosmopolitan environment where "one sees in this city an infinite number of men from different parts of the world" (McPherson 30). Furthermore, according to Lewkenor, it was apparently not unusual for "forreyn mercenarie souldiers" to be "enabled, with the title of citizens & gentlemen of Venice" (S2).

Brabantio's cultivation and acceptance of Othello, therefore, may very well reflect this custom, so that when Othello explains that Desdemona's "father lov'd me, oft invited me" (1.3.128), we are reminded that it was Brabantio himself, as a senator, who first acknowledged Othello an "insider."[10] It is the senator Brabantio, and thus by extension Venice, who sets up contradictory notions about racial identity and social place within Venetian society. Desdemona's marital choice, therefore, may very well enact not only adherence to assumptions about appropriate spouses (Othello is, by birth, a prince, by merit a general, and through patronage wealthy) but, in addition, the transference of the daughter's love for her father to another Venetian father figure and not an "outsider." Thus we may want to ask not why Othello drew her love but what is it in the *man that her father loved* that moves a woman "So opposite to marriage, that she shunn'd / The wealthy curled darlings of our nation . . . " (1.2.67–68) to set aside her reluctance to marriage and elope? And, whether Brabantio's reaction to the marriage, and Othello, is linked not to Othello's physical appearance but to that "thing . . . to fear, not to delight" in (1.2.71)—an incestuous desire for his daughter? If we view Desdemona's choice as being consistent with Shakespeare's characterization of her, of Othello, of Desdemona's willingness to perform her symbolic role in the ritual expression of marriage, and the myth of Venice, then perhaps it is Brabantio who continually refuses to participate in the ritual by subverting the activities which would require that he allow himself to be dispossessed of his daughter, that he permit another Venetian to sexually claim the one female body that he himself cannot sexually possess.[11]

Thus Brabantio's earlier rebuke of Iago becomes an ironic echo when Brabantio employs not only the language of theft to accuse Othello, "O thou foul thief," but also the language often associated with witchcraft, "chains of magic" and "foul charms," in an effort to destabilize the ritualized exchange of the female body that marks the institution of marriage. And Brabantio's charges, like his censure of Iago, allude to the complex and often contradictory social attitudes in Venice which allow for an Othello and a Desdemona but which also demand that they adhere to the customs and laws which govern that society.

Jacques Lacan has argued that "in our relation to things, in so far as this relation is constituted by the way of vision, and ordered in the figures of representation, something slips, passes, is transmitted from stage, to stage, and is always to some degree eluded in it—that is what we call the gaze" (73). I have been arguing that throughout *Othello*, this "something" is Venice, and I wish to conclude by looking briefly at the paradox that Shakespeare's play reveals Venice to be.

The Venetian Moor, or the Italian on the English Stage

One of the disturbing things about *Othello*, despite centuries of ideological intervention, is the play's ability to disrupt any attempt to make uneven the level playing field Shakespeare has created in his tragedy. This dilemma is further exacerbated by the crudely psychosexual dimensions engendered by Iago's rhetoric in the very first scene of the play:

> Zounds, sir, you are robb'd, for shame put on your gown,
> Your heart is burst, you have lost half your soul;
> Even now, very now, an old black ram
> Is tupping your white ewe. . . .
>
> (1.1.86–89)

Iago's words neatly transform what is an act of elopement into an imagined cuckoldry; that is, in the double reference to Brabantio's nakedness (he lacks both property and his "gown"), Iago sets the stage for a further shaming of Brabantio by subtly naming what is lost as if it were a wife ("half your soul") and luridly localizing this *pseudo-wife* in a pornographic fantasy. And though this fantasy is momentarily displaced by the intrusion (in the person of Othello) of Lewkenor's Venice, its affective power to create and sustain its image of perversion is not altered one whit.

Ironically, Iago's thematization of an imagined (and bestial) cuckoldry insinuates itself not only in Brabantio's imagination but in his later displacement of that anxiety onto Othello: "Look to her, Moor, have a quick eye to see: / She has deceiv'd her father, may do thee" (1.3.292–93). Predictably, Othello reenacts the violent passions that drove Brabantio to repudiate Desdemona, once again bringing to the surface the male anxiety about female sexuality (despite Desdemona's married state), considered the hallmark of "corrupt" Venice, that initiates the "tragedy of Othello." However, Othello's complete displacement of Brabantio can occur only when, I would argue, he takes to its ultimate, punitive conclusion (by killing Desdemona) Brabantio's disowning of his daughter.[12] In effect, it is the Venetian Othello who must see to it that

Venice's "penal Lawes [are] most unpardonably executed" when the virgin is shown to be a whore.[13]

Representations of early modern Venice were always gendered feminine: it was a city "so beautiful, so renowned, so glorious a Virgin" and, at the same time, a " 'Circe's court,' teeming with 'wanton and dallying' Calypsos and Sirens."[14] This allusion to the seductive women who delayed Ulysses' return to Ithaca finds its parallel in Desdemona's "supersubtle" seduction of the warrior Othello: "she thank'd me, / And bade me, if I had a friend that lov'd her, / I should but teach him how to tell my story, / And that would woo her" (1.3.163–66). Like Venice, Desdemona has the appearance of purity (and discretion) even as she boldly lays herself open to Othello's suit. Even so, when Iago calls into question Desdemona's virtue, Othello iterates his faith in his wife—"For she had eyes, and chose me" (3.3.193)—even as he leaves open the possibility of her infidelity: "No Iago, / I'll see before I doubt, when I doubt, prove, / And on the proof, there is no more but this: / Away at once with love or jealousy" (3.3.194–96).

Othello's insistence on "proof," of course, becomes the opening that Iago needs to "abuse Othello's ear" (1.3.393). It is not insignificant that both Othello and Desdemona initially are swayed by what is heard rather than what is seen. From its inception, the play luridly juxtaposes rumor and storytelling, on the one hand, and an emphasis on seeing, on the other. Brabantio must see for himself the truth of Roderigo's and Iago's report of Desdemona's elopement. Othello will not question Desdemona's virtue until he sees proof; but once rumor "abuses" his ear, Othello, as did Brabantio, begins the process of "bringing to light" the blackness of his Venetian wife.[15] If the first act of the play serves to displace Othello's blackness into his Venetian identity, then the remaining acts serve to dilate Desdemona's.

Iago is the first to constitute Desdemona black when, in response to her question "what wouldst thou write of me, if thou shouldst / praise me" (2.1.118), he reiterates a familiar trope of femininity:

> If she be fair and wise, fairness and wit;
> The one's for use, the other using it. . . .
> If she be black, and thereto have a wit,
> She'll find a white, that shall her blackness hit.
>
> (2.1.129–33)

Lines 132–33, not surprisingly, find their close interpretive echo in the adage "wash the Ethiop white." If Desdemona is "black" and possesses a "wit," Iago's advice to her is to seek that which will transform her, her opposite. Iago ends his "praise" of Desdemona by railing against even fair women, terming them "wight[s]" who "suckle fools, and chronicle small beer" (2.1.160).

This exchange, for all its seeming irreverence, finds its dramatic replay in act 4, scene 2. After a mournful lament for his "affliction," Othello turns his fury to Desdemona: "Turn thy complexion there; / Patience, thy young and rose-lipp'd cherubin, / I here look grim as hell" (4.2.63–65). Othello then goes on to say,

> O thou black weed, why art so lovely fair?
> Thou smel'st so sweet, that the sense aches at thee,
> Would thou hads't ne'er been born!
>
> (4.2.69–71)

Othello's language enacts the familiar Petrarchan opposition of fair/dark, yet it also perverts that rhetoric with its reluctance to further denigrate the object which it initially constitutes as undesirable (see Hall, esp. 178–79). More important, this semantic instantiation of Desdemona's desirability registers the allure traditionally associated with Venice, and which prompts Othello later to name Desdemona that which no Englishman who has read Coryat would have failed to understand, "that cunning whore of Venice."

Once again, despite the domesticity of this bedroom scene, it is Venice which becomes the object of our gaze as both the symbolic virgin that the warrior Othello defends and the corrupted bride he has wed.[16] In an emotionally charged accusation to Desdemona, Othello declares, "I took you for that cunning whore of Venice / That married with Othello" (4.2.91). Othello's words become a distorted projection of Brabantio's caution that the mask of virginity hid a corruption. It is Venice itself which suffers the "dilation" of its exterior to reveal the blackness inside. Othello's search for "proof" must begin "in" Venice, and thus with himself. What is revealed is the sameness of the interior and exterior: the Moor without is the Venetian within, and the Venetian within is the Moor without. And, in a remarkable mimicry of Brabantio's incredulity over Desdemona's willing participation in the marriage, Othello stages himself as the innocent seduced by the wiles of the Venetian whore—aided and abetted by the plot's initial and careful delineation of Othello as a Venetian. We see mirrored in Othello's rage that of Brabantio. Though born a Moor, in his irrationality Othello is very much a Venetian. And in an ironic though not surprising twist of fact, both the father and the husband, whose violations of the rites of marriage set into motion the tragic events of Shakespeare's tragedy, die as a result of their attempts to defend the illusion of perfection that is the myth of Venice.

"I took by th'throat the circumcised dog"

At the conclusion of *Othello,* Shakespeare leaves us with a disturbing dramatic tableau: the corpses of Othello, Desdemona, and Emilia upon the bed which has occupied (most likely) center stage for much of the final act; a (for once) silent Iago; and the Venetian lords as witnesses to this final tragic event. Just before he commits suicide, Othello says,

> And say besides, that in Aleppo once,
> where a malignant and a turban'd Turk
> Beat a Venetian, and traduc'd the state,
> I took by the throat the circumcised dog,
> And smote him thus.
>
> (5.2. 353–57)

This speech has often been read as, symbolically, a racialized confirmation of Othello's awareness of himself as an outsider—a Moor. But if my argument is valid, then such a reading is highly questionable and may point to the deployment of the "racial anxiety" that Michael Neill suggests is "everywhere" in the play's critical and cultural history rather than in Shakespeare's representation of Othello's self-consciousness.

I would argue that what Othello does is to draw upon the myth of Venice to re-create not just a racial image but also a political one where Venetian law is exact, swift, and inviolate—whether one is a Turk or, in the case of Othello, a Venetian. More important, as the symbol of Venetian law on Cyprus, it is Othello who must stand in for the Duke and affirm the "bloody book of law" against those who have violated that very law. It is Venetian Othello who judges and executes the Turk who assaulted a Venetian, and it's this same Othello who must judge and execute the murderer of another Venetian, Desdemona. The race of this judge cannot, therefore, be viewed in terms of his color but as identical to that of the Duke in whose stead Othello carries out Venetian law.

It seems imperative, therefore, not to overlook the complex history that the concept and the word *race* may project in early modern English discourses and its implications for interpretations of *Othello.* In a world where women were often described as a "race," where the word *race* signified aristocratic or noble lineage, where *race* was often used as synonymous with *nation,* to argue that issues of race in *Othello* are easily reducible to one matrix—color—is a problematic misreading of an emerging taxonomic shift in the process of classifying human beings. In early modern Venice and England, where racial and social identities are formulated as much in genealogy as in ethnicity or geography, in gender as in color, the "illusion of perfection" cannot sustain itself as its own discourse points to the almost yet not quite invisible fractures that inevitably occur in the process of mythologizing "race." And it is this paradox which must be recognized in *Othello* rather than, as Jack D'Amico suggests, the idea that "Shakespeare revealed how a man could be destroyed when he accepts a perspective that deprives him of his humanity, . . . Othello is debased by a role that he adopts and acts out on the *Venetian-Elizabethan* stage" (177). Ignoring, for the moment, the problematic collapsing of Venice and England, I want to call into question the implicit assumption that there is English identification with the Venetians as a homogeneous racial group. As I have suggested elsewhere, "the contours of race may not be as fixed, as transcendental, as universal as critical practices and postmodern social discourses seem to infer" ("Managing the Barbarian" 183). English writers, Shakespeare included, pointedly distinguished within the European community just as they did without (perhaps even more so given their more extensive knowledge of nations within Europe). One has only to recall Portia's mockery of her French, German, Scottish, and English suitors, or Shakespeare's depiction of the Welsh and French in *Merry Wives of Windsor* to know that D'Amico's "Venetian-Elizabethan" elides the powerful sense of national consciousness that encodes itself in the dramatic representation of other cultures (see Howard).

It seems to me that we might derive a better understanding of Shakespeare's tragedy if we recognize that the "lustful" Moor is the "whorish" Venetian. Behind Desdemona stands the duplicitous Venice, behind Iago the cunning "Machiavel," and behind Othello the irrationality of Italian masculinity. What sets into motion the tragic events in Shakespeare's tragedy, and what makes *Othello* an ideological quagmire, is the Venetian ambivalence that accepts Othello as a well-born, honorable, successful military commander and courtier even as it insists that he remain an outsider, an alien who must resort to sorcery or witchcraft to become a part of the world he inhabits already. In the end, our interpretive and critical imperative, in addition to tracing the overdetermined markings formalized by the racialist rhetoric figured by the references to the color of Othello, should be one of exploring the multifaceted and often subtly nuanced discourse of race that aligns color, gender, geography as it sees fit. In this vein, we might also want to pose another query that Shakespeare's tragedy seems to invoke and which has bearing for our understanding of racial discourse in early modern English contexts. Who, symbolically, comes to be racialized as the "cunning whore" of Venice capable of causing nature to err from itself? The answer, not surprisingly, is all in how one defines the concept of race.

NOTES

1. See Newman; Boose, "Othello's Handkerchief"; and Little. For a useful summary of critical responses to the play, see Neill, "Unproper Beds," particularly 391–95.

2. All *Othello* quotations are from the Arden edition, ed. M. R. Ridley.

3. Traub 36. See also Boose, "Othello's Handkerchief"; and Neill, "Changing Places."

4. Most references to Venice note either the city's significance in the Mediterranean political economy, its idealization as a model republic, or its exoticization as an international cultural site. See, for example, McPherson, esp. 27–50; Parker 95–96; Bartels; D'Amico 177; Cantor 296–319; and Braxton. In most other discussions of Shakespeare's tragedy, as I will argue, Venice appears to implicitly "stand in" for England.

5. See, for example, Levith, Partridge, McWilliam, Lievsay, Hale, and McPherson.

6. This panegyric appears in Lewes Lewkenor's 1599 translation of the Italian version of Gasparo Contarini's *De Magistratibus et Republica Venetorum*. Qtd. in Pocock 320.

7. Here I am referring to Stephanie Jed's brilliant argument in *Chaste Thinking.*

8. See Ruggerio, who argues that "in the Renaissance, ideally, the honor dynamic, with its threat of vendetta, was supposed to limit the level of violence in society. One did not cross the honor of another, one did not do violence to another, because that would require vendetta, that is violence and dishonor in return. Thus ideally, violence was avoided without formal institutions or additional violence within a community or group simply by maintaining a balance of honor." However, as Ruggerio further adds, if an individual "did not have the power to pursue vendetta, the support of threatened violence fell away, one's honor became problematic, and violent passions became easier to indulge, especially for the powerful."

9. Bartels 450. While Bartels's argument makes less of Othello's color than other critical essays, her reading succeeds in "making more" of the Moor-Venetian dichotomy than it makes of the racial ideology the play fashions. For similar discussions see Berry; D'Amico 177–96; Cantor; and Braxton.

10. Bartels cogently makes this argument in "Making More of the Moor" 435.

11. Garner argues that Shakespeare "keeps Desdemona off a pedestal and shows her to have a full range of human feelings and capacities. Yet he is careful not to allow her to fail in feeling or propriety" (238).

12. Snow notes that when Iago manipulates Othello's husbandly anxiety about Des-

demona's chastity, Othello "comes to see Cassio in his place" as Brabantio came to see Othello in his (Brabantio's). What also needs to be explored is the continual replay of the incestuous undertones created by Iago's words to Brabantio. See esp. 395.

13. It is not my intent to prove or disprove Desdemona's guilt or innocence, but to "dilate" her significance to Shakespeare's handling of the myth of Venice.

14. Roger Ascham, *The Schoolmaster,* quoted in Jones 102.

15. I am indebted to Parker's "Fantasies of 'Race' and 'Gender': Africa, *Othello* and Bringing to Light" for this analysis. What I would add to Parker's cogent discussion on the "visual" necessity of "bringing to light" that which is secret is the way aurality serves as a prefigurement to such dilation.

16. I am indebted to Adelman's excellent discussion in *Suffocating Mothers* for this idea.

WORKS CITED

Adelman, Janet. *Suffocating Mothers: Fantasies of Maternal Origin in Shakespeare's Plays, "Hamlet" to "The Tempest."* New York and London: Routledge, 1992.

Bartels, Emily C. "Making More of the Moor: Aaron, Othello and Renaissance Refashionings of Race." *Shakespeare Quarterly* 41 (1990): 433–54.

Berry, Edward. "Othello's Alienation." *Studies in English Literature* 30 (1990): 315–33.

Boose, Lynda E. "The Father and Daughter in Shakespeare." *PMLA* 97 (1982): 327.

———. "Othello's Handkerchief: 'The Recognizance and Pledge of Love.'" *English Literary Renaissance* 5 (1975): 360–74.

Braxton, Phyllis Natalie. "Othello: The Moor and the Metaphor." *South Atlantic Review* 55 (1990): 1–17.

Cantor, Paul A. "*Othello:* The Erring Barbarian among the Supersubtle Venetians." *Southwest Review* 75 (1990): 296–345.

Cavell, Stanley. *Disowning Knowledge in Six Plays of Shakespeare.* Cambridge: Cambridge UP, 1987.

Coryat, Thomas. *Crudities.* Glasgow: J. Maclehose and Sons, 1905.

D'Amico, Jack. *The Moor in English Renaissance Drama.* Tampa: U of South Florida P, 1993.

Garner, Shirley Nelson. "Shakespeare's Desdemona." *Shakespeare Studies* (1976): 235–39.

Hale, John R. *England and the Italian Renaissance.* London: Faber and Faber, 1954.

Hall, Kim F. "'I rather would wish to be a Black-Moor': Beauty, Race, and Rank in Lady Mary Wroth's *Urania.*" *Women, "Race," and Writing in the Early Modern Period.* Ed. Margo Hendricks and Patricia Parker. London and New York: Routledge, 1994. 178–94.

Hendricks, Margo. "Managing the Barbarian: *The Tragedy of Dido Queen of Carthage*." *Renaissance Drama* n.s. (1992): 165–88.

Howard, Jean E. "An English Lass amid the Moors: Gender, Race, Sexuality, and National Identity in Heywood's *The Fair Maid of the West*." *Women, "Race," and Writing in the Early Modern Period*. Ed. Margo Hendricks and Patricia Parker. London: Routledge, 1994. 101–17.

Jed, Stephanie. *Chaste Thinking*. Bloomington: Indiana UP, 1989.

Jones, Ann Rosalind. "Italians and Others: Venice and the Irish in Coryat's Crudities and *The White Devil*." *Renaissance Drama* n.s. (1987): 101–19.

Lacan, Jacques. *The Four Fundamental Concepts of Psycho-Analysis*. Ed. Jacques-Alain Miller. Trans. Alan Sheridan. New York: W. W. Norton and Co., 1978.

Levith, Murray J. *Shakespeare's Italian Settings and Plays*. New York: St. Martin Press, 1989.

Lewkenor, Lewes. *The Commonwealth and Gouernment of Venice. Written by the Cardinall Gasper Contareno, and translated out of Italian into English*. 1599. Facsimile copy, Amsterdam and New York: Da Capo Press, 1966.

Lievsay, John. *The Elizabethan Image of Italy*. Published for the Folger Shakespeare Library. Ithaca: Cornell UP, 1964.

Little, Arthur L. Jr. " 'An essence that's not seen': The Primal Scene of Racism in *Othello*." *Shakespeare Quarterly* 44 (1993) : 304–24.

McPherson, David C. *Shakespeare, Jonson, and the Myth of Venice*. Newark: U of Delaware P, 1990.

McWilliam, George W. *Shakespeare's Italy Revisited*. Leicester: Leicester UP, 1974.

Neill, Michael. "Changing Places in *Othello*." *Shakespeare Survey* 37 (1984): 115–31.

———. "Unproper Beds: Race, Adultery, and the Hideous in *Othello*." *Shakespeare Quarterly* 40 (1989): 383–412.

Newman, Karen. " 'And wash the Ethiop white': Femininity and the Monstrous in *Othello*." *Shakespeare Reproduced: The Text in History and Ideology*. Ed. Jean E. Howard and Marion F. O'Connor. New York and London: Methuen, 1987. 141–62.

Parker, Patricia. "Fantasies of 'Race' and 'Gender': Africa, *Othello* and Bringing to Light." *Women, "Race," and Writing in the Early Modern Period*. Ed. Margo Hendricks and Patricia Parker. London and New York: Routledge, 1994. 84–100.

Partridge, A. C. "Shakespeare and Italy." *English Studies in Africa* 4 (1961): 117–27.

Pocock, J. G. A. *The Machiavellian Moment: Florentine Political Thought and the Atlantic Republican Tradition*. Princeton: Princeton UP, 1975.

Ruggerio, Guido. *Binding Passions*. Oxford and New York: Oxford UP, 1993.

Shakespeare, William. *The Merchant of Venice*. New York: Viking, 1969.

———. *Othello.* Ed. M. R. Ridley. London and New York: Routledge, 1958.

Snow, Edward A. "Sexual Anxiety and the Male Order of Things in *Othello.*" *English Literary Renaissance* 10 (1980): 384–412.

Traub, Valerie. *Desire and Anxiety: Circulations of Sexuality in Shakespearean Drama.* London and New York: Routledge, 1992.

8

THE HEROICS OF MARRIAGE IN *OTHELLO* AND *THE DUCHESS OF MALFI*

MARY BETH ROSE

ENGLISH RENAISSANCE TRAGEDY can be characterized throughout its career by a relentless scrutiny of heroic energy; but that interrogation includes a major alteration in the conception of the heroic. Rooted in the connection between tragedy and history, the Elizabethan conception focuses on a heroism of public action, emphasizing the protagonist's will to power.[1] Centered on political and military struggles, tragic action consigns women, eros, and sexuality to the periphery of its concerns. In striking contrast, Jacobean plays emphasize a heroism of personal endurance, creating tragedies of private life that often focus on the consequences of unorthodox sexuality in a dark and narrow world, rapidly becoming devoid of possibility. The prominence of women as tragic heroes and/or eros as a tragic subject increases remarkably in Jacobean plays.

Two salient modes of conceptualizing women, love, and marriage can be identified in English Renaissance moral, religious, and tragic writing. The first is a dualistic, polarizing discourse that either idealizes or degrades women and eros. The logic of this dualistic sensibility often construes marriage as at best a necessary evil, the means by which a fallen humanity reproduces itself and ensures the orderly succession of property. This polarizing discourse usually emerges in Elizabethan tragedy as an irreconcilable conflict between desire and purity, love and duty, and can be associated with a heroism of public action. Women and eros are subliminally idealized or regarded as frivolous or potentially destructive; in either case they are peripheral to the represented action of a play.

Secondly, and in contrast, there is the Protestant idealization of "holy matrimony," which constitutes a coherent and self-conscious effort to construct a new ideology of the private life. Although Protestant sexual discourse retains much of the erotic skepticism of the polarizing sensibility just described, it nevertheless unites love with marriage and conceives of marriage with great respect as the foundation of an ordered society. Protestant discourse is not dualistic but complex and multifaceted, and one of its most significant and far-reaching changes is a shift in the prestige and centrality assigned to the institution of marriage. It is this sensibility that grants women and eros the kind of importance that allows them to become the primary subjects of a tragic action. Specifically this discourse compares marriage to the church and the state, drawing out the equation among spiritual, public, and private realms by analogizing the husband to God and the king, and the wife to the church and the kingdom.[2] The examination of Protestant sermons and conduct books about "holy matrimony" reveals that marriage is constructed in explicitly heroic terms, as the most critical endeavor of one's whole life, as a quest, or a "voyage on a dangerous sea," as the arena in which one pursues salvation or damnation, as inevitable destiny. Furthermore, the heroism being constructed is one of patient suffering rather than willful action; as such it is a heroism particularly suited to women. Within the terms of the heroics of marriage, I will argue, women begin to be represented in English Renaissance tragedy as powerful agents of cultural change.

Yet this attempt to grant new significance to private life by equating it with public and spiritual existence breaks down from the retention of domestic and political hierarchies that, issuing in a host of contradictions, subvert the attempted analogies and eventually result in the creation of separate spheres. By focusing on *Othello* and *The Duchess of Malfi* as particularly illuminating examples of this process, I will demonstrate that Protestant sexual discourse takes tragic form as a fatal deconstruction of the contradictions and paradoxes inherent in the Protestant marriage ideal itself. Specifically, by examining the deaths of Desdemona and the Duchess as symbolic foci of tragic experience, I will argue that tragedy functions paradoxically as both a radical and a conservative discourse in the representation of sexual and cultural change.

Evidence from the drama and from Renaissance sexual discourse indicates clearly both an emerging awareness of a growing sense of conflict between the demands of public and private domains, and a profoundly anxious cultural perception of that disjunction as problematic.[3] Jacobean tragedy centering on private life can be understood as an attempt to define and articulate this process of change, as well as an endeavor to arrest it.

This dramatic attempt at the definition and control of private life finds its analogue in Puritan sexual discourse. In their ideological campaign to promote the importance of the family, the Puritans continually define the family as a private institution which is nevertheless distinguished by its connections to political and spiritual life. With urgent solemnity all the Puritans argue, indeed insist upon, the public dignity and cosmic significance of marriage, viewing it as the arena in which salvation and damnation are determined for husband and wife. While the Puritan preachers express a wider variety of views and approaches than is commonly recognized, the crucial configuration on which all their arguments depend is the carefully and fervently constructed analogy between the family, the commonwealth, and the Church.[4] "Commonwealths I say," Alexander Niccholes declares of marriages, joining his colleagues in explaining that the husband is to the wife as the magistrate is to the subject, as Christ is to the Church (Niccholes 178). All the Puritans concur that the combination of cosmic and political as well as the individual stakes involved in marriage is momentous indeed. Choosing "a good Wife from a bad," Alexander Niccholes warns his readers, "is to cut by a thread betweene the greatest Good or Evill in the World"; while John Dod and Robert Cleaver assert that an irresponsible father who neglects the little commonwealth of his family is nothing less than the "murtherer of their souls, and cutthroats of their salvation" (Niccholes 156; Dod and Cleaver sig. A[4]).

As these emphases on the communal consequences of individual actions and on the connections between individual choice and public responsibility indicate, the Puritans develop from their idea of the family as a model of the church and state, containing within its private sphere multiple levels of significance and possibility, a conception of marriage as a heroic endeavor. To some, marriage presents the opportunity for self-knowledge and the glory of happiness: "the very name . . . should portend unto thee *merryage* . . . for marriage awaketh the understanding as out of a dream."[5] Others, more pronounced in their distrust of sexuality, view marriage as a solemn duty but happiness as a dangerous delusion: "Likely none doe meete with more crosses in marriage, or beare their crosses more untowardly, than those that most dreame of finding it a very Paradise," remarks William Whately, the Jacobean Vicar of Banbury (sig. A₄v). Yet, whether the Puritans stress the obstacles or the rewards inherent in marriage, the crucial point becomes their consensus that this relationship constitutes the arena in which the individual can struggle, meet death or defeat, triumph or salvation: "for marriage is an adventure, for whosoever marries, adventures; he adventures his peace, his freedom, his liberty, his body; yea, and sometimes his soul too." Furthermore, undertaking this quest, "the means either to exalt on high to preferment, or cast down headlong to destruction," becomes "this one and absolutely greatest action of a man's whole life," requiring the unwavering commitment characteristic of the hero and assuming the properties of inevitable destiny: "as thereon depending the future good or evil of a man's whole after-time and days." Marriage is a perilous odyssey, a voyage on a dangerous sea, "wherein so many shipwreck for want of better knowledge and advice upon a rock" (Niccholes 162, 159, 164, 159, 161).

Describing the perils involved in the heroic marriage and suggesting their remedies, commentators rely frequently on military metaphors of both conquest and self-defense: "for it is in this action as in a stratagem of war: 'Wherein he that errs can err but once, perisheth unrecoverably to all after-advice and relief' "; "a valiant souldier doth never repent of the battaile, because he meetes with strong enemies; he resolves to be conquerour, and then the more and stronger his foes, the greater his honour" (Niccholes 159–60; Whately 80). It should be stressed that the Puritans' use of military metaphors to construct the heroism of marriage is qualitatively different from poets' use of Petrarchan conceits that image love as the war between Venus and Mars. These tracts do not employ the vocabulary of the battle of the sexes—often frivolous, always self-defeating. Theirs is instead the language of epic endeavor. But the Puritans' use of "high astounding terms" to construct marriage does not function to clarify conflicting allegiances between duty and desire, public and private life, and to favor the former; rather, their urgent insight is that private life *is* public; love *is* a duty and marriage the conquest that must be achieved.

Indeed, the Puritans have not so much duplicated the military idiom in their idealization of marriage as absorbed and transformed it. Referring to bullying husbands, for example, William Gouge observes, "Their authoritie is like a swaggerers sword, which cannot long rest in the sheath, but upon every small occasion is drawne forth. This frequent use of commanding, maketh their commandements nought regarded."[6] The virtues required by the heroics of marriage are not those of magnificence—physical prowess and imperial will— but of the inner strength and courage required to act when necessary, but also to refrain from direct action, to suffer and endure. Husband and wife are frequently viewed as "yokefellows" in a struggle in which the inevitability of trouble must be acknowledged and prepared for: "Expectation of an enemy," warns Whately, "is halfe an arming; but suddennesse addes terriblenesse unto a crosse, and makes it insupportable" (74). The well-prepared soldier-spouse of either sex must be armed above all, then, with patience. As the rhetoric of armed struggle in this context makes clear, virtuous suffering, the extreme of which is victimization, is conceived not as passive but as a kind of action, requiring perhaps above all a dynamic obedience to God (see, e.g., Whately 83, 85).

Patience in the face of inevitable affliction; the moral prestige such affliction grants the sufferer, who is personally chosen by God to endure; obedience, humility, fortitude: the heroism of endurance has a multiplicity of sources, including Seneca and the Stoics, the lives of the Catholic saints, the continuing popularity of medieval treatises on the art of dying, Patient Griselda stories, and the careers and tribulations of both Protestant and Jesuit martyrs related to Renaissance audiences. The eclectic background of this tradition makes clear that it comprises a conception of heroism that includes both sexes among its protagonists. Yet the relevance that this construction of goodness and greatness has for women is peculiarly striking. For the terms that constitute the heroism of endurance are precisely those terms used to construct the Renaissance idealization of woman: patient suffering, mildness, humility, chastity, loyalty, and obedience.[7]

Given the fact that the properties of the heroism of endurance as established in the Puritan tracts coincide with the Renaissance idealization of women, it becomes clearer why women are able to assume a place of central importance in the drama of marriage, as well as to find a voice in which distinctly female experiences can be articulated. It is perhaps more accurate to state that this place and voice begin to be imagined in Puritan sexual discourse, which, like the drama, is produced almost exclusively by men.

Throughout the heroics of marriage, the conceptualization of women is riddled with ironies and paradoxes that are continually inscribed but inconsistently acknowledged. Although they are everywhere present, most of these unresolved logical discrepancies center on the issue of equality between spouses and the corollary tenet of wifely obedience and subordination. As is well known, the Puritans believed in a kind of spiritual autonomy, leading them to assert an equality before God between the sexes. This valued spiritual equality becomes the basis of the companionship between man and woman that the Puritans agree is fundamental to marriage. The problems come not when the preachers are formulating their vision of sexual equality, but when they turn to consider conduct, action. For example, rather than dwelling exclusively on female chastity, many of them argue against the sexual double standard, with some explicitly asserting equality of rights, expectations, and feelings in relation to sexual desire.[8] But having articulated that men and women have identical power in the realm of desire, Gouge, for example, immediately subverts this argument by declaring that the husband's power, and therefore his responsibility, are in fact greater in sexual as in other relations: "the more it apper-taineth to them [i.e., husbands] to excell in virtue, and to governe their wives by example" (219; also see Thomas 195–216).

Along with that of the spirit, the other conception of domestic equality that the Puritans urge and (with blithe inconsistency) undermine centers on class, status, age, and money, all areas in which, notably, private and public domains are linked by marriage in an affirmation of existing hierarchies. "An equall yoke-fellow would be taken, of due proportion in state, birth, age, education, and the like, not much under, not much over, but fit and correspondent. . . . The rich and noble will likely despise, or set light by the poorer and meaner: so will the younger do the aged," observes Whately, suggesting potential conflicts that do in fact become crucial in Jacobean tragedy (73). Yet when a marriage is socially unequal, it is always the husband's identity that determines the social status of the couple. Thus if a man "of meane place be maried to a woman of eminent place," she must nevertheless acknowledge him as her superior: "It booteth nothing what either of them were before marriage. . . . for in giving herselfe to be his wife, and taking him to be her husband, she advanceth him above her selfe, and subjecteth her selfe unto him" (Gouge 272). As is well known, this merging and transforming of a woman's identity into her husband's finds its correlative in the legal status of Renaissance wives, who lost all property, rights, and power upon marrying. As Lawrence Stone sum-marily reminds us, "By marriage, the husband and wife became one person in law—and that person was the husband."[9] Yet as Stone himself shows, the legal construction and cultural ideology of marriage in the Renaissance, including the status of wives, were far from being definite and clear. Nowhere do these inconsistencies manifest themselves more openly than in the Puritan doctrine of wifely subordination and obedience.

Like the analogy between family, church, and state, the requirement that wives be obedient commands the absolute consensus of these domestic ideal-ists. "By nature woman was made man's subject," Dod and Cleaver state baldly (149). Yet, while fervently proclaiming and defining the subjection of women, the Puritans provide the necessary material for its subversion. After lionizing obedience, for example (*"Let wives be subject to their husbands in everie thing"*), Gouge urges women never to obey husbands who want them to do what "is forbidden by God" (295, italics his; 328). In a similar vein, after demanding obe-dience and subjection (rising against husbands is the equivalent of rising against God), writers including Gouge, Cleaver, and Hieron urge women not only to disobey but actively to seek to correct erring husbands.[10] Furthermore, wives' subjection is merely temporal, temporary: "Her place is indeed a place of inferiority and subjection, yet the neerest to equality that may be," Gouge sums up, unhelpfully (356).

Absolute spiritual and social equality between the sexes, coexisting with the equally absolute subjection of women that is decreed and then subverted: the logical inconsistencies that now appear so glaring, particularly given their consequences, seem never to have occurred to the Puritans. I do not believe that the Puritans, busily seeking to separate the present from the past and participating in the abstract and visionary formation of an ideology, were aware of the contradictions they were articulating. The value of their discourse does not lie in its self-consciousness or its prescience. Rather, because of its historical position, Puritan marriage ideology in the Renaissance provides a remarkable index of the ways in which modern sexual values were being created, terms were being constructed, and conflicts were taking shape. The apprehension and exploitation of ideological inconsistencies becomes the task not of sermons but of the drama, in which a greater attachment to the concrete, obligation to action, and dependence on conflict bring paradox into the light of representation, giving visibility and significance to contradiction and seeking to resolve it through the operations of form.

In *Othello* the two predominant modes of English Renaissance sexual discourse described above meet and clash tragically. The two sensibilities and styles overlap as well as conflict throughout the play; but in the complex exploration of sexuality that *Othello* comprises, the dualizing mentality that simultaneously exalts and degrades women and eros also is clearly distinguished from the heroics of marriage, which comes painfully into being, defined and comprehended as a failed achievement. Yet as I will try to show, it is not simply the competition between distinctive modes of sexual apprehension that issues in violence; the heroics of marriage also collapses from within, dissolving inevitably from its own unresolved contradictions. As noted above, the requirements of the heroics of marriage resemble those of the Renaissance idealization of women; thus, while this discourse is concerned with both sexes, its materials have a particular relevance to women, allowing them a mode in which they can define themselves and be perceived as heroes. Accordingly in *Othello* the articulation and breakdown of the idealization of marriage are dramatized in the career of Desdemona.

In the scene (1.3) in which Desdemona and Othello seek to justify their marriage before the Venetian senate, she unwittingly articulates a conception of sexuality and its relation to public life that is antagonistic to Othello's. Openly and proudly acknowledging her love for her husband, Desdemona characterizes herself as a soldier-spouse, adopting the vocabulary of the epic quest (1.3.248–57).[11] By using a quasi-military idiom to insist that separation between spouses makes non-sense of marriage and associating herself with the Turkish wars, she also emphatically draws together public and private domains. In the paradoxically active submission that Desdemona describes herself as undertaking in her marriage, articulated in military terms, we can recognize the dynamic obedience and devotion idealized in the Puritan tracts. In short, Desdemona presents herself to the Senate as a hero of marriage.

As befits the major preoccupations of the play, the breakdown of the heroics of marriage is constituted in Desdemona's career as the breakdown of language.[12] The untenable position that she occupies in the action can best be described by noting that she makes three remarkable attempts to save her marriage in the play, and that each attempt is a lie. In examining her three lies, we can see that each issues from the paradoxical, contradictory materials that compose the idealization of marriage.

Desdemona's first lie involves not telling her father about her marriage. Strictly speaking, this lie of omission precedes the action and is responsible for generating the preliminary conflicts in the play. In defending her marriage before the Senate, Desdemona not only manifests courage and determination, she defines herself as a full-fledged subject, who assumes the legitimacy and priority of her independent desires and actions: "That *I did love* the Moor to live with him . . . "; "*My heart's subdued* / Even to the utmost pleasure of my lord"; "*I saw* Othello's visage in his mind; and to his honours, and his valiant parts / *Did I my soul and fortunes consecrate*"; "the rites for which *I love him* are bereft me" (1.3.248–57; italics mine). Scholars have demonstrated convincingly the ambivalence and narcissism of Othello's love for Desdemona, insights with which I fully agree.[13] Here I wish to stress, however, that whatever illusions are involved in Desdemona's and Othello's marriage, Desdemona, like Juliet, Rosalind, Portia, Viola, and Olivia, chooses freely to enter into them; at this point in the play she is not merely a victim and object of Othello's desires and fears, but a subject, with her own distinctive set of actions and priorities.[14] It is true that the terms in which Desdemona describes her own conflict in the Senate scene, picturing herself as bound to either father or husband, seem to undermine her assertions of independence and subjectivity: "My noble father / I do perceive here a divided duty . . . " (1.3.180–81); and as we will see, the unresolved paradoxes inherent in the ideals of female equality and wifely obedience contribute to her destruction. Yet, while these lines suggest the con-

tradictions inherent in Desdemona's assumption of autonomy, these potentially disturbing issues are deflected at the beginning of the play.

Indeed, no one at this point in the play, including Brabantio, questions the
well-established and accepted priority of wifely obedience or primary loyalty
to a spouse. Brabantio's bitter grievance lies instead with Desdemona's failure
to gain his consent for her marriage: it is this omission that constitutes her
deception. Rather than finding, as he had assumed, that chaste modesty is the
source of his daughter's opposition to marrying one of the "wealthy curled
darlings of our nation" (1.2.68), he discovers that she has been "half the wooer,"
determined to love the man she wants to love and to choose a spouse for herself
(1.3.176), a decision which she presents to her father as a *fait accompli*.

It is in the context of selecting her own mate that Desdemona inscribes herself in the heroics of marriage (1.3.248–59). And at this point it is useful to
recall the paradoxical view of parental consent to marriage embedded in that
discourse. Time and again the Protestant idealizers of marriage protest vehe-
mently the common phenomenon of parents' forcing children to marry against
their will; yet, inexplicably they are equally resistant to the idea of children
marrying *without* parental consent. "No man can passe away anothers right
without his liking," William Whately asserts in seeming defense of individual
choice of a spouse; yet he immediately adds that a couple marrying without
parental consent are living in sin until "they have procured an after-consent to
ratifie that, which ought not to have been done before" (34). It is precisely this
ambivalence in which Desdemona is trapped. Clearly her father's superstitious
abhorrence would have caused him to withhold his consent; indeed, Brabantio
himself admits that had he known his daughter's inclinations, he would have
gone to any lengths, including forcing her to marry the despised Roderigo, in
order to impede them (1.2.176). Desdemona's marriage to Othello consequently
requires elopement. Yet the fact that Brabantio remains permanently unre-
conciled to the match creates a lingering, negative resonance throughout the
play that is never overcome: "If you have lost him, / Why I have lost him
too" (4.2.47–48), Desdemona reminds Othello; and Gratiano's first reaction to
Desdemona's murder is to remark, "Poor Desdemona, I am glad thy father's
dead; / Thy match was mortal to him, and pure grief / Shore his old thread
atwain" (5.2.205–207). Thus the play keeps subtly alive the associations between Desdemona's independent act of choosing her own spouse with death
and sin. These associations explain her otherwise illogical deathbed response,
"They are loves I bear to you," to Othello's warning, "Think on thy sins"
(5.2.39–40). Thus Shakespeare dramatizes the contradictions inherent in indi-

vidual choice and parental consent in the heroics of marriage by establishing Desdemona's match as courageous and triumphant, while giving it the discursive status of a lie.

The unresolved dilemmas implied and hinted at in Desdemona's first lie explode into tragedy in the circumstances constituting the second and third. Once again Desdemona's predicament can be located in the contradictory terms in which female identity is constructed in the heroics of marriage. As we have seen, female equality and subjectivity are both asserted and denied by the Puritans. When focusing on the issue of individual choice of a spouse, the Puritans frequently ignore gender or, like Niccholes and Wing, address males exclusively. Yet many argue for the woman's need to choose and consent as well. Dod and Cleaver, for example, insist that a couple should spend as much time as possible together during courtship, observing each other: "It must be a mutual promise, that is, either party must make it to other, not the man only, nor the woman only, but both the man and the woman"; otherwise, "it is no true and perfect contract" (108–109; 122). At the same time that they argue for female independence in choosing a mate, however, the Puritans are constantly establishing the well-known if ambiguous hierarchy of domestic power, recommending that women help and advise their husbands while insisting on wifely obedience, silence, and subjection: "Hee is her head, and shee his glorie" (122–23).

We can recall that in the Senate scene Desdemona defines herself precisely in terms of choice and desire: "That I did love the Moor, to live with him" (1.3.248). Othello has responded to his wife's independence and self-conception during courtship with joyous pleasure, muted only by an ambivalence of which, at this point, he remains dimly aware. Yet it is precisely these qualities of self-assertion that combine with terrible irony to ruin Desdemona. When, after succumbing to Iago's temptation, Othello begins to confront Desdemona with his suspicions, the collapse of the heroics of marriage into its irreconcilable contradictions takes place, adding its force to the unyielding claustrophobia of the play. This process reaches a climax at Desdemona's second lie, which involves her loss of the handkerchief that was Othello's first gift to her.

As noted, Desdemona's self-presentation in the Senate scene is couched in a quasi-military idiom, by which she identifies herself with Othello's profession of soldier, an association reiterated in descriptions of Desdemona by herself and others throughout the play (e.g., 2.1.74, 2.1.75, and 3.4.149). In this same speech she establishes her identity as a wife in terms of the dynamic chosen submission defined in Protestant sexual discourse: "I saw Othello's visage in his mind, / And to his honours, and his valiant parts / Did I my soul and fortunes consecrate" (1.3.252–54). Desdemona's conflation of her desire and devotion with Othello's profession therefore unites public and private life in the analogous association idealized in Protestant sexual discourse. Othello's account of their courtship further clarifies his wife's identification with his heroic exploits; indeed, it is the "strangeness" of these endeavors, their legendary quality, that has enchanted her, thus making her self-assertion and their marriage possible (1.3.128–70). Yet when Desdemona lies to Othello about losing the handkerchief he gave her, it is precisely her allegiance to the exotic quality of his narrative reminiscences, the power of the discourse that had won her love, which recoils to overwhelm and terrify her.

> *Oth.*   That handkerchief
> Did an Egyptian to my mother give,
> She was a charmer, and could almost read
> The thoughts of people; . . .
> To lose, or give't away, were such perdition
> As nothing else could match.
> *Des.*   Is't possible?
> *Oth.*   'Tis true, there's magic in the web of it; . . .
> And it was dyed in mummy, which the skillful
> Conserve of maidens' hearts.
> *Des.*   I'faith is't true? . . .
> *Oth.*   Is't lost? is't gone? Speak, is it out o'the way?
> *Des.*   Heaven bless us!
> *Oth.*   Say you?
> *Des.*   It is not lost, but what an if it were?
> *Oth.*   Ha!
> *Des.*   I say it is not lost.
>
> (3.4.47–82)

Interestingly, Desdemona next attempts to respond to Othello's exotic tale of the handkerchief much as she had done during the legends of his courtship, with an act of self-assertion:

> *Oth.*   Fetch't, let me see it.
> *Des.*   Why, so I can sir, but I will not now,
> This is a trick, to put me from my suit,
> I pray let Cassio be receiv'd again.
>
> (3.4.83–86)

Aside from the fateful irony of her choice of subject, Desdemona's attempt to distract Othello, which persists for several more lines after the passage just quoted, now appears to him as willfulness, wifely disobedience. Endeavoring to declare her independence from Othello's discourse, she succeeds only in compounding the lie. Her identity as a subject, constituted by her active, chosen responsiveness to her husband's narrations, consequently begins to dissolve.

Initiated in the course of her second lie, this process of dissolution continues when Desdemona, overwhelmed by Othello's anguish, retreats from efforts to understand to fragile rationalizations of his behavior. Significantly, these rationalizations are expressed as an acknowledged division between public and private life, in which the latter is regarded as subordinate and inferior to the former:

> Something sure of state,
> Either from Venice, or some unhatch'd practice,
> Made demonstrable here in Cyprus to him,
> Hath puddled his clear spirit, and in such cases
> Men's natures wrangle with inferior things,
> Though great ones are the object.
>
> (3.4.137–42)

In this speech Desdemona reverses her conception of marriage as a heroic endeavor, uniting public and private domains and granting her status as a subject. As we have seen, this status is equivocal at best and is inscribed in a discourse that succumbs to its own contradictions. That wifely heroism is itself a contradiction becomes manifest in Desdemona's third lie. Attempting to protect Othello from being discovered as her murderer, Desdemona responds to Emilia's "O, who has done this deed?" with "Nobody, I myself, farewell" (5.2.124–25). Desdemona's final effort to identify with and absorb herself in her husband's actions (itself the definition of marriage in this play) becomes an act of self-assertion that is, simultaneously, an act of self-cancellation: "Myself" is the equivalent of "Nobody." Constituting the final dissolution of Desdemona's identity, the third lie is a dying voice. In this context Othello's outraged retort, "She's like a liar gone to burning hell, / 'Twas I that kill'd her" (5.2.130–31), could be read as a protest against his wife's destruction. But it is too late; the assertive and lively woman who "is fair, feeds well, loves company, / Is free of speech, sings, plays, and dances well" has disappeared, along with the troublesome contradictions of the heroics of marriage. Her chastity reestablished, Desdemona is rendered inert, removed from the realm of significant action. Brabantio's fantasy of "a maiden . . . So still and quiet, that her motion / Blush'd at herself" is consummated in the figure of the dead Desdemona as "monumental alabaster . . . one entire and perfect chrysolite," the "heavenly sight" with which *Othello* concludes (5.2.5; 146; 279).

The resolution of the action can be understood by examining the conjoined mechanisms of the play's complex treatment of language and sexuality. In her final martyrdom Desdemona returns, as it were, from the dead and lies in a self-sacrificing attempt to shield Othello; while both directly before and after the murder he idealizes her chastity as "whole," "entire," "perfect," and "alabaster," using terms that suggest virginity and stasis. Thus he denies her liveliness and wifehood and reveals both his longing and the desire to be released from that longing. In the process initiated by Desdemona's third lie, then, husband and wife in a sense conspire to retrieve the realm of autonomous discourse in which, discounting social and material circumstances, they had originally constructed their courtship and defined their marriage. Yet the power to create reality through language has increasingly become identified in the play with lying. Itself a lie, Desdemona's final self-abnegation initiates the resolution of the action and is essential to it, yet it is inadequate to bring the conflict to completion. What is needed to finish that process is not autonomous discourse but "a material limit before which the power of discourse is disarmed" (Eagleton 10). Thus it is not Desdemona's martyrdom that convinces Othello of her fidelity but Emilia's defiant self-assertion, rooted as it is in narrating the actual circumstances of Iago's deceptions.

Significantly, Emilia's revelations are couched entirely within the contradictory discourse of the heroics of marriage. Discovering that she has unwittingly contributed to her mistress's murder by adhering to wifely silence and obedience (i.e., in confidentially stealing Desdemona's handkerchief at her husband's request), she now realizes that her only recourse is to speak and disobey: "I am bound to speak," she replies to Iago's attempts to silence her, "Let heaven and men, and devils, let 'em all, / All, all cry shame against me, yet I'll speak" (5.2.185; 220–24). Here Emilia's declarations summon the paradoxical associations of speech throughout the play both with truth and with the incipient violation of established order; specifically, her linkage of her own courage and self-assertion with possible shame evokes the contradictions of the heroics of marriage. When we recall the Puritans' ambiguous injunction that a wife must obey her husband absolutely unless he commands "what God forbids," we can perceive Emilia's predicament as an irreconcilable conflict between the private obligations of a wife (loyalty, silence, and obedience) and the public duties of a citizen (revelation of a murder): "Good gentlemen, let me have leave to speak. / *'Tis proper I obey him, but not now:* / Perchance, Iago, I will ne'er go home" (5.2.196–98; italics mine).

Shakespeare thus distributes the components of female heroism between two characters. While the destinies of both Desdemona and Emilia issue in martyrdom, their heroic styles are distinct. The waiting-woman, subordinate in social status as well as integrity, at last courageously acknowledges and embraces through active conflict the contradictions of the status of wife that are inscribed in the heroics of marriage. The aristocratic Desdemona, on the other hand, dwindles, rather than grows, from a lively and courageous girl to a wife who is "half asleep," retreating, as we have seen, with little choice to fragile explanations that subvert the basis of her marriage and to a naive, insistent, and unhelpful purity, and recovering her courage only in a final act of self-cancellation.

Desdemona's unavoidable retreat to victimization, to passivity, and to the assumptions of a kind of premarital chastity correspond to Othello's final idealization of her as virginal, static, and inert. Removed from the heroics of marriage, she is also removed from action and conflict. The consignment of women and eros to inactivity is one of the solutions of the heroism of action. No longer distracted by the confusing, contradictory centrality that marriage has assumed in his identity, Othello ends his life by recalling his military achievements and devotion to public service. Thus the beautiful, immobilized Desdemona combines with the neighing steed, the plumed troop, the spirit-stirring fife, the royal banner, and all quality, pride, pomp, and circumstance of glorious war to evoke with unarguable lyric beauty the tremendous elegiac power of the lost past.

No Shakespearean tragedy focuses exclusively on a strong, central female figure. That in *Othello* Shakespeare should diffuse female heroism between two figures, distinguishing the sexual styles of waiting-woman and lady, has significant implications for determining his interests, as well as for assessing the tragic representation of sexuality. Before turning to these crucial issues, however, I would like to introduce a comparison with *The Duchess of Malfi* (c. 1613–14), written approximately ten years after *Othello*. Here it will suffice to note that it is, of course, Othello's heroism that assumes central importance in the earlier play. While Shakespeare clearly recognizes and explores the potential for female heroism in the qualities inscribed in the Protestant idealization of marriage, he remains primarily concerned to examine the decline of the heroism of action by dramatizing its inadequacy when faced with the challenges of private life. In his next tragedy of love, *Antony and Cleopatra* (1607), rather than elaborating his insights into the contradictions inherent in marriage itself, he chooses instead to focus on the conflict between eros and public service, continuing his intense scrutiny of the tragic obsolescence of the epic-chivalric heroic style.

In *The Duchess of Malfi* the process of decline characterizing the representation of the heroism of action in Jacobean tragedy is already complete, its logic manifest. As in *Othello,* the distinction between public and private domains demands scrutiny and redefinition. Conflicts centered on these issues are initiated by an aristocratic woman's decision to disobey her male relatives and to marry a man not her social equal, thus defying traditional social and sexual hierarchies and opening the way for their dissolution. Proud of her royal birth and stature, the widowed Duchess of Malfi is also in love with her steward and determined to disobey her brothers, woo Antonio, and marry him. Thus she is caught between classes, between sexes, between tenses: as a young widow, she has a past and seeks a future; as an aristocrat who is also royal, she is independent, politically central, a ruler; but as a woman she is marginal, subordinate, and dependent, a fact that her brothers' tyranny makes abundantly clear. With her conjoined, paradoxical attachments to present, future, and past, to status granted at birth as well as status gained by achievement, to female independence and female subordination, the Duchess is in a position as fluid and anomalous as the social conditions of Jacobean England. Viewed in this context, it becomes clear why Webster chooses an aristocratic woman as the figure that could represent most fully the irreconcilable conflicts of tragedy.

Understanding the play's class and sexual conflicts in terms of emergent and residual cultural modes allows us to connect the two dominant types of Renaissance sexual discourse examined in this study more firmly with historical process, with the shifting relations between present, past, and future, than is possible to do when exploring *Othello* (see Williams 122–23). Specifically, the polarizing mentality that idealizes or degrades women and eros is associated first with the decadent, tyrannical Aragonian brothers, particularly Ferdinand. While that villain conceives of women and sexuality as depraved, it is Antonio, in his role as obedient steward at the beginning of the play, who construes the Duchess as divine, an unattainable ideal, associated with rebirth, an exception to her sex (1.1.205–13). The Duchess recognizes both her brother's grotesque misogyny and Antonio's rapturous idealization as equally life-denying; indeed, she resists the dualizing sexual sensibility that would relegate her to aestheticized inactivity and permanent widowhood in terms and imagery that recall the destiny of Desdemona. "Why should only I, / Of all the other princes of the world / Be cased up, like a holy relic? I have youth, / And a little beauty," she protests to Ferdinand (3.2.137–40). And she exhorts Antonio to marry her by resisting in a similar vein immobilization as an icon, associating the widow's enforced chastity with stasis and death: "This is flesh, and blood, sir, / 'Tis not the figure cut in alabaster / Kneels at my husband's tomb" (1.1.459–61).[15]

The Duchess is inscribed instead in the heroics of marriage. As we have seen, in the Protestant conception of marriage as a heroic endeavor, a military idiom is absorbed and transformed from the heroism of action; while this idiom is sometimes applied exclusively to males, it frequently ignores gender or explicitly includes women as subjects as well. It is precisely this military vocabulary of conquest and defeat that the Duchess uses to define her marriage to her steward (1.1.348–56; 3.5.90, 140–41). Her conception of her marriage as a dangerous but necessary venture also takes on the lonely, absolutist commitment shared by the tragic hero and the hero of marriage ("I am going into a wilderness, / Where I shall find nor path, nor friendly clue / To be my guide" [1.1.367–68]), leading her inevitably to ponder her own condition in universal terms, as Desdemona never could, and to her prolonged encounter with death. It has been argued correctly that the Duchess's confrontation with "ultimate universal hostilities" distinguishes her as "the first fully tragic woman in Renaissance drama" (Whigham 174). I would add to this crucial point that it is the full recognition of the importance of private life, here claiming equal status with public concerns, that makes her tragic stature possible; in turn, as will be seen, the Duchess's heroism helps to define and clarify the heroics of marriage.

It has also been argued that the Duchess's metaphysical confrontation with the foundations of human identity "contain[s] the kind of speculation familiar from Shakespearean tragedy, where the elevated are crushed as they inaugurate new conceptual options" (Whigham 174). Despite her disclaimers to Ferdinand ("Why might not I marry? / I have not gone about, in this, to create / Any new world, or custom" [3.2.110–27]), this argument continues, the Duchess is in fact thoroughly committed to constructing a revolutionary future, viewing herself, like Tamburlaine, as a pioneer who, ignoring traditional class barriers, will chart a course through the wilderness to discover and colonize a new world, disdainful of the past and independent of it (see, for example, Whigham 172). There is, of course, no place within the absolutist neofeudal state of the Aragonian brothers to absorb and contain the Duchess's unusual marriage. The vision of the future cannot be amalgamated, put off, or distanced, as it can in a comic structure. In tragedy the future has arrived, and it is unquestionably violent, revolutionary.

Webster, then, clearly recognizes the radical potential of female heroism in the process of cultural change. Viewed in this context, distinct conceptual alliances and antitheses begin to take shape in our consideration of the play. The dualizing mentality that either idealizes or degrades women and eros becomes associated with an embattled and declining aristocracy, tyrannical political absolutism, an obsolete heroism of action, a receding past. In contrast, the heroics of marriage is associated with the bourgeois recognition of merit in determining status, rather than the aristocratic reliance on birth; with administrative rather than military skill; with upward social mobility and female independence; with an impending future.

Yet the Duchess's identity and greatness—her heroism—are grounded in the past as well as projected into the future. While on one level the dichotomy between a corrupt and decadent past and a more promising future is confidently formulated and supported in the play, on another the relation between past and future emerges in contrast as one of conflicting loyalties between two worthwhile modes of thought and being. This second, more subtle syndrome, which assigns not only corrupt power but sympathy and value to the past, can be perceived by locating the Duchess precisely within the heroics of marriage, the discourse that she creates and adheres to and which defines her.

Like Desdemona, the Duchess is forced to defy male relatives (i.e., authorities) in order to marry the man she wants. And, again like Desdemona, she becomes embroiled in the contradictory injunctions of the idealization of marriage that, as we have seen, both do and do not encourage woman to have a say in selecting her spouse, and do and do not demand familial consent to a match. Yet while Shakespeare dramatizes this issue as a subtle and significant but subordinate theme, Webster brings it to the very center of the action, embodying its consequences in the career of a female hero whose private life subverts the established order. While Desdemona's marriage matters to the established political order, its primary public importance rests in the state's need for her husband's services; Desdemona's and Othello's elopement precedes the action and takes place offstage. In contrast, the Duchess is a ruler; it is *her* marriage that has crucial importance to the state and shakes its foundations, a fact that, conjoined with her brothers' tyranny, makes the radicalism of her action at once more apparent, more urgent, and more sympathetic. Because the marriage between the Duchess and Antonio is fully dramatized onstage, the ambivalences conjoining family consent and female independence that are reduced in *Othello* to the receding residue of Brabantio's displeasure constitute the major, irresolvable tragic conflicts in the later play. The Duchess's and Antonio's marriage contract *per verba de presenti* itself has an ambiguous status. As historians have demonstrated, clandestine marriage, or vows made between consenting adults with a witness present, constituted a perfectly legal union in England until marriage laws were clarified in the eighteenth century. But the social status of such a marriage, contracted without banns, solemnized outside the church, and associated with both poverty and illicit sexual activity, was at best marginal (see Stone 35, 317, 629). All throughout her wedding ceremony, the Duchess both abjures and affirms the need for legitimating institutions and traditions, thus unwittingly emphasizing the problematic vulnerability of her marriage (1.1.489, 493–95; 3.5.39–40).

But the most powerful contradictions that work to undermine the Duchess's marriage are those centered on status and rank. While the inequalities that separate Othello and Desdemona (the Moor's age and blackness) are profound, they are nevertheless sufficiently intangible to be easily absorbed by the state: the marriage challenges prejudice rather than established, class-based social and political hierarchy.[16] In contrast, the discrepancies in rank between the Duchess and Antonio constitute officially institutionalized boundaries, not to be crossed: "Of love, or marriage, between her and me, / They never dream of," Antonio realizes (3.1.36–37), referring not only to the ruling elite but to the rest of the populace as well. By locating the foundation of identity in merit rather than birth, then, the Duchess drives a radical irreconcilable wedge between the natural and social orders, previously regarded as identical. Yet the Duchess does not adhere entirely to this commitment to achieved, rather than ascribed, status. While the greatest obstacles to her marriage take the form of the brothers' tyranny, an external impediment, it is important to note the extent to which the Duchess herself continues to rely on her royal birth. It is not simply that she takes the lead in the wedding scene (1.1.445–46); she also delivers a very mixed message on the question of rank. Thus she defines Antonio as a "complete man" and claims to "put off all vain ceremony," begging to be regarded not as a royal Duchess but merely as "a young widow / That claims you for her husband" (1.1.460–62). At the same time, however, she reminds him "what a wealthy mine / I make you lord of," and adds, in what is probably the clearest example of the double bind created by her superior power, "Being now my steward, here upon your lips / I sign your *Quietus est*. This you should have begged now" (1.1.433–34, 467–68).

Based in a problematic awareness of a wife's possible social superiority to her husband, the perception of a potentially severed relation between hierarchies of gender and power also constitutes a central issue in the heroics of marriage. "But yet when it hapneth, that a man marrieth a woman of so high a birth, he ought (not forgetting that he is her husband) more to honour and esteeme of her, than of his equall, or one of meaner parentage and not only to account her his companion in love, and in his life, (but in divers actions of publike appearance) hold her his superior," advise Dod and Cleaver. Yet they contradict themselves by adding, "She ought to consider, that no distinction or difference of birth and nobilities can be so great, *but that the league which both Gods ordinance and Nature, hath ordained betwixt men and women, farre exceedeth it: for by nature woman was made man's subject*" (1630, sigs. K and K2^V). What bond is more "natural," birth or marriage? Dod and Cleaver lean toward the radical position of granting greater importance to marriage, but continue perplexed. Their perception of the problem, which comes from the thwarted attempt to unite not only gender and power but public and private domains, is itself subversive; but it remains unresolved and, as such, sheds light on *The Duchess of Malfi*. The contradictions about rank, status, gender, and power that characterize the heroics of marriage perpetuate rather than resolve the conflicts between past and future. At the moment of the Duchess's death, the irreconcilable loyalties that are the source of tragic conflict become most clearly visible. On the one hand, the Duchess's rank plays a central role in the construction of her tragic heroism. "For know, whether I am doomed to live, or die / I can do both like a prince," she tells Ferdinand (3.2.70-71). Later, when Bosola, her murderer, confronts her with chaos and destruction, she asserts her identity in the play's most famous line, "I am Duchess of Malfi still" (4.2.142). Thus the Duchess's courage and dignity in facing death are indissolubly conjoined with her royal stature. On the other hand, the sociopolitical conditions that make heroism possible in the play unquestionably reside in the decay of and need to defy the order from which her stature derives. Antonio correctly defines the heroic response to the resulting untenable position as one of active, chosen suffering: "Contempt of pain, that we may call our own" (5.3.57).

As I have tried to show, with its background in stoicism, religious martyrdom, and medieval treatises on the art of dying, the heroism of endurance that Antonio defines is connected in Protestant moral treatises with the idealization of marriage and the elevation of the private life, a combination of elements particularly amenable to the construction of female heroism. Much recent scholarship has demonstrated that unstable social conditions often generate female heroism and creativity, which in turn plays a major role both in demolishing an old order and in constructing a future.[17] Viewed in this context, an interesting example of Shakespeare's relative conservatism in representing women emerges by contrasting the Duchess's death with Desdemona's. The two scenes offer a remarkable instance of a reverse parallel. Both women are unjustly strangled for misconceived sexual crimes; both die martyrs' deaths, accompanied by loyal and loving waiting-women. As we have seen, Desdemona's understanding of her own situation, along with her responsibility for it, recedes throughout *Othello*. At the moment of her murder, she begs for her life, an action which, however sensible it may appear in isolation, is definitely not characteristic of a tragic hero. While Desdemona's final act is one of self-cancellation, courageous self-assertion is instead assigned to the waiting-woman Emilia, who is given the noble lines "Thou hast not half the power to do me harm / As I have to be hurt" (5.2.163–64). By distributing the components of female heroism between the two women, Shakespeare confers independent selfhood on the subordinate character, while merging Desdemona's identity entirely with Othello's. Thus the stage is cleared for Othello's final, climactic consideration of his own, more active heroism, and the focus is entirely on the lost past. The emphases in the Duchess's death scene are, of course, different. The most prolonged moment in the play, the Duchess's death, is made to carry the full burden of tragic significance, as her debates with Bosola on the meaning of life and the effects of her death on the other characters make clear. Summoning all her princely dignity, the Duchess also dies thinking of her children's welfare, thus dissolving the distinction between "woman" and "greatness" that her waiting-woman Cariola makes after her marriage (1.1.505). The Duchess's dual role of agent and sacrifice is never simplified to an emphasis on her victimization. Instead her courage in facing death is emphasized, along with her acceptance of responsibility for her own actions (4.2.30–31, 211–14). A final contrast occurs when the waiting-woman Cariola provides a foil to the Duchess's heroism by begging for her life, the exact reverse of the situation in *Othello* (4.2.231–55).

Despite the Duchess's greater prominence, however, she is assigned precisely the same fate as Desdemona. She is removed from the active resolution of the conflicts of the play and granted instead the indirect role of inspiration. In one critic's useful terms, she ceases to be the maker, and becomes instead the bearer, of meaning (Laura Mulvey, qtd. in Vickers 109). Thus a varied range of crucial activities occupy the stage for an entire act after the Duchess's murder, when, like Desdemona, she returns from the dead as a disembodied voice, an echo and "thing of sorrow" meant to protect her husband (5.3.24). In order to clarify her permanent status as an unattainable ideal, Webster specifically constructs her death as a work of art, relegating her value to the state of bodiless, aestheticized inactivity that she had heroically resisted in life (4.2.31–35).

As the hero of the play, the Duchess embodies its major conflicts; thus in order to remove her from their active resolution, Webster has had, as it were, to rewrite her part. As we have seen, the Duchess is inscribed in the heroics of marriage, a discourse that inevitably breaks down from a combination of external opposition and its own internal contradictions that emerge as an irresolvable conflict of loyalties between future and past. At the end of the play, Webster resolves the conflict by discarding the future and reinscribing the Duchess in the dualistic discourse that idealizes (or degrades) women, thus placing her above and beyond the action, a position that she, pursuing the future, had specifically resisted and which, as we have seen, is unambiguously associated in the play with death and the disappearing past. As Bosola seeks to avenge her murder and the Cardinal and Ferdinand die, the associations of the past with pathology and corruption also recede, while the dead Duchess's elegiac role assumes greater prominence. Viewed in the context of the polarizing sexual discourse that defines her final position, the construction of the Duchess's death can be seen as reactionary: she is removed from the potentially radical conflicts of the heroics of marriage that had fully defined her, and the sympathy and value assigned to her life are unambiguously allied instead with a compelling tribute to the lost past.

Webster's removal of the hero from the last act of the play is so striking and bold a move that it raises important questions about the nature of English Renaissance tragedy. Indeed, given its pointed critique of political absolutism (the form of government favored, if not enacted, by James I), its recognition of the centrality of the private life, and its profound exploration of female heroism, *The Duchess of Malfi* becomes an excellent text from which to assess the nature and extent of radicalism in Jacobean tragedy. By embodying major tragic stature exclusively in a woman, Webster acknowledges the female hero's pivotal role in the process of historical change, exploring the workings of the contradictory components of female identity in Renaissance sexual ideology as Shakespeare never does.[18] Recalling the comparison between Tamburlaine's revolutionary career and the Duchess's role as a social pioneer who courageously disregards traditional class and rank barriers, one can perceive the impossibility of finding either figure in Shakespeare's plays, where shepherds who gain power turn out to be princes in disguise, while powerful, central women preside exclusively over the comic world, not the more elevated and prestigious tragic one. The figures of Malvolio and Antonio provide a similarly telling contrast. A Renaissance playwright creating an upwardly mobile steward clearly had options in his representation of that figure. Should he be a pompous ass, a vain, deluded buffoon, easily outwitted and finally expelled by the aristocracy? Or should he be able, competent, appealing, and, if perhaps also mediocre, nevertheless aware of his own limitations and capable of winning a Duchess's love? My purpose in making these comparisons is not to find fault with Shakespeare but to point out that, given the variety of conceptual options available in Jacobean culture, he often chooses the conservative ones, a pattern that becomes obvious when we view him not on his own but in relation to his fellow playwrights.

Because Shakespeare is indisputably the greatest writer of English tragedy, his conservatism relative to his contemporaries should have a great deal to tell us about the nature and purposes of that form of drama. Despite Webster's considerably greater interest in, and sympathy for, the future, for example, he nevertheless ends *The Duchess of Malfi* by diminishing the future and paying a powerful tribute to the past. Recent scholarship concerned with the relation of tragedy to history has emphasized the foundations of tragedy in the failures of the past.[19] With its relentless, subversive scrutiny of obsolete modes of heroism, tyrannical forms of government, unjust social systems, and inadequate sexual ideologies, tragedy is seen to play a radical role of negation, to clear the way for a new order by participating in the dissolution of archaic cultural formations. But in correctly emphasizing the function of tragedy as a social critique, these analyses have tended to assume that the tragic exposé of social injustice is more real than the focus on loss and death, thus underestimating tragedy's considerable allegiance to the past. As Webster's elegiac conception of the Duchess's death makes clear, no matter how pronounced the criticism of the past and sympathy for the future may be in a play, the separation between past and future that is the defining purpose of radicalism never occurs within Jacobean tragedy. Instead attention is focused on the radical act as one of sacrifice and extinction, and the future is diminished in deference to the past: "We that are young / Shall never see so much, nor live so long."[20] In this context Jacobean tragedy can be viewed not as radical but as conservative and nostalgic: a lament for a lost past from the point of view of the aristocracy. Seventeenth-century English tragedy tended increasingly to become a predominantly aristocratic form.

How can we reconcile the evident radicalism of Jacobean tragedy with its equally compelling nostalgia? As is well known, great tragedy, unlike comedy, has erupted in Western history in infrequent, irregular bursts, particularly in fifth-century Athens and sixteenth- and seventeenth-century Europe. Attempting to account for tragedy's simultaneous alliance with the past and future, Timothy J. Reiss has joined other scholars in pointing out that, in each of its major appearances, tragedy has accompanied the rupture of a familiar order, in which "the essential relationships between physical, social, and religious life are now losing their reference to any 'experience of totality.' " At the same time, however, in both ancient Greece and Renaissance Europe, the major developments in tragedy coincide with the rise of science, the struggle to realize an emergent rationality for which analytic, referential knowledge, rather than mystery and mythical thinking, becomes "the true expression of reality." Reiss argues that during this process of change, "a sense of injustice appears, compounded of ignorance, fear, unfulfilled desire, and suffering, the mark of an 'absence' which of necessity escapes organization"—i.e., meaninglessness. The function of tragedy is not simply to represent irreconcilable ambiguity, suffering, and injustice, but also to contain these ruptures precisely by defining them, giving them meaning and form: "the discourse of tragedy may be ambiguous internally, but that is just the point: it is an ordered and enclosed ambiguity. . . . It presupposes a knowledge." By clearly defining and finally immobilizing the destructive ambiguities of suffering and injustice, then, tragedy provides an affirmation that a future imposition of order is possible.[21] Reiss's formulations thus become particularly helpful for understanding the changing representation of love and sexuality in English Renaissance tragedy. In Elizabethan tragedy, created during a period of relative patriotism and optimism, the private life plays a marginal role in the representation of a heroism of action, to which it is at best subordinate, at worst destructive. In this context love and sexuality are constructed from a dualizing perspective that either idealizes or degrades women and eros, removing them from the significant center of action. While this dualistic sensibility is never superseded, and indeed still lingers as a conceptual option in our culture, during the late sixteenth and early seventeenth centuries it gradually recedes before the Protestant idealization of marriage, a more multifaceted sexual discourse that elevates the private life and grants greater centrality to women as necessary protagonists in its enactment. Conjoined with a complex of sociocultural factors, including both the absolutism and pacifism of the king and the attempt to halt and consolidate the social mobility of the sixteenth century, the heroics of marriage becomes the primary subject of Jacobean tragedy. While *Othello* dramatizes the beginnings of this process by scrutinizing the decline of the heroism of action, *The Duchess of Malfi* manifests its logic completely by granting full attention and distinction to the private life and making visible the pivotal role of the female hero in the process of cultural change. During the development of Jacobean tragedy, the dualizing sexual discourse becomes associated with the disappearing past, the heroics of marriage with the promise of the future. But, as we have seen, the heroics of marriage breaks down both from external (and reactionary) opposition and from its own unresolved contradictions. As these ambiguities assume greater centrality in tragic representation, they are immobilized within a final, elegiac tribute to the lost past, a process of containment clarified in the deaths of Desdemona and the Duchess of Malfi. In this way tragedy serves its complex function of articulating the need for a future by destroying the past and then mourning its disappearance. Once again this point becomes clear from examining the tragic representation of sexuality, in which no further development takes place. Either the scrutiny of the private life becomes increasingly involuted, focusing on corruption and extremes, as in the depictions of female villainy and incest in *The Changeling* and *'Tis Pity She's a Whore;* or the portrayal of endurance and suffering becomes increasingly static, as in *The Broken Heart.*

NOTES

This essay has been reprinted from Mary Beth Rose, *The Expense of Spirit: Love and Sexuality in English Renaissance Drama.* Copyright 1988 by Cornell University. Used by permission of the publisher, Cornell University Press.

1. For the emergence of tragedy from history, see Doran 112–47; Margeson 117; Mueller 8, 15, 20, 25, 46, 58. Mueller argues that Renaissance tragedy comprises "a shift from a collective to a private vision of tragedy" and from an emphasis on the fate of the community to an emphasis on individual psychology (18).

2. See Stone; and Schochet. Schochet argues that although the family was an established and frequently employed category in political philosophy prior to the seventeenth century, it was never consciously recognized as a standard category in political argument and did not acquire an overtly important status in the centuries before the Stuart period (54). See also Shorter, Wrightson, and Goody.

3. See Davis, "The Reasons of Misrule" and *The Return of Martin Guerre* 20–21; Stone 4, 6–7, 256, 484, 605; and Shorter 39–53.

4. See, e.g., Gouge 2, 17, 219–20, 260–61, 410; Perkins 669; Dod and Cleaver sig. A4;

Hieron 469; Whately 38. The Puritan analogies among the family, the state, and the church are discussed by Haller and Haller 235–72 and by Hill 443–81.

5. Niccholes 160. Cf. Dod And Cleaver, sig. K³; Gouge 225, 227; Wing 85, 98; and Smith.

6. Gouge 378. For other uses of the heroic/military idiom in constructing marriage, see Wing "To the Reader" and 63, 74, 125–33; and Whately 25–26, 42, 46–48, 58–59, 68, 72, 74, 76–77, 80.

7. For accounts of the association of female heroism with patient suffering, endurance, and martyrdom, see Warner, esp. 68–78. Also see Schulenburg; Lamb; and Rose, esp. 259–67.

8. See, e.g., Perkins 680; Gouge 217–19, 356, 425; Whately 25–26, 73; and Calvin 124.

9. Stone 195. Also see Todd 55; and T. E., *Lawes*, according to which the husband and wife "are but one person in Law, and the Feme taketh nothing but by agreement of the husband" (119). Also see 129–30.

10. Gouge 295, 328; Dod and Cleaver (1630) sig. o6ʳ; Hieron 411.

11. Ridley's choice of the Quarto's (Q₁) "utmost pleasure," rather than the Folio's "very quality," in line 251 of this passage in the Arden edition, which I accept, obviously serves to highlight Desdemona's eroticism.

12. Cf. Mueller, who argues in another context that in *Othello* "the destructiveness and destruction of grand language are the subject matter of the play" (6).

13. See Greenblatt, *Renaissance Self-Fashioning* 240–44; and Kirsch 33, 37, 39. Also see Erickson 80–103; Novy 125–49; Sprengnether 93; Gohlke; Wheeler; Dash 103–30; and Neely 105–35.

14. See Eagleton, who chastises Othello's "wholly 'imaginary' relation to reality; his rotund, mouth-filling rhetoric signifies a delusory completeness of being, in which the whole world becomes a signified obediently reflecting back the imperious signifier of the self. Even Desdemona becomes his 'fair warrior,' as though he can grasp nothing which he has not first translated into his own military idiom" (69–70). Desdemona does not simply accept such translations of her identity, however, but actively creates them herself; further, the military idiom, absorbed and transformed by domestic idealism, is part of the larger cultural vocabulary of the heroics of marriage.

15. Cf. *Othello* 5.2.3–5: "Yet I'll not shed her blood, / Nor scar that whiter skin of hers than snow, / And smooth, as monumental alabaster."

16. Interestingly, Othello justifies his marriage to Desdemona by alluding to his royal birth as well as his personal merit: "I fetch my life and being / From men of royal siege, and my demerits / May speak unbonneted to as proud a fortune / As this that I have reach'd" (1.2.21–24).

17. See Rose; Lamb; and Schulenburg. See also Gold. For a very interesting treatment of female heroism in Restoration and eighteenth-century tragedy, see Brown.

18. I do not regard Shakespeare's Cleopatra as an exception to this observation. Arguably, *Antony and Cleopatra* moves beyond tragedy and into romance. Certainly Cleopatra's "infinite variety" is unique, not characteristic; rather than embodying the contradictions of Renaissance sexual ideology, which becomes the central focus of the play, she provides an alternative ethos that is opposed to the public/political world: i.e., the conflict is between love and duty. Finally, Cleopatra is not the sole hero of her play, as Lear, Hamlet, Macbeth, Othello, Coriolanus, and the Duchess of Malfi are of theirs.

19. See especially Dollimore; Moretti; Whigham; Cohen; and Heinemann. For other scholars who have addressed the issue of subversion and authority in Tudor-Stuart drama, see Greenblatt, *Renaissance Self-Fashioning*, esp. 193–254, and "Invisible Bullets"; and Montrose.

20. I owe this point to Northrop Frye, who, quoting these lines, which are the last two lines of King Lear, comments that in Shakespeare the social contract that forms at the end of a tragedy is always a diminishment of the present and future: "the heroic and infinite have been; the human and finite are" (6).

21. Reiss 19, 36, 20, 21 (italics his), 24, 35 (see, in general, 1–39). He remarks that "the reaction to tragedy . . . would be at once the fear of a lack of all order and the pleasure at seeing such lack overcome" (36).

WORKS CITED

Brown, Laura. "The Defenseless Woman and the Development of English Tragedy." *Studies in English Literature* 22 (1982): 429–43.

Calvin, John. "The Form and Manner of Celebrating Marriage." *Tracts and Treatises on the Doctrine and Worship of the Church*. Trans. Henry Beveridge. Vol. 2. Grand Rapids, Mich.: Wm. B. Eerdmans, 1958. 123–26.

Cohen, Walter. *Drama of a Nation: Public Theater in Renaissance England and Spain*. Ithaca: Cornell UP, 1985.

Dash, Irene G. *Wooing, Wedding, and Power: Women in Shakespeare's Plays*. New York: Columbia UP, 1981.

Davis, Natalie Zemon. "The Reasons of Misrule." *Society and Culture in Early Modern France*. Stanford: Stanford UP, 1979. 97–123.

———. *The Return of Martin Guerre*. Cambridge, Mass.: Harvard UP, 1983.

Dod, John, and Robert Cleaver. *A Godlie forme of household Government*. London, 1598, 1600.

Dollimore, Jonathan. *Radical Tragedy: Religion, Ideology and Power in the Drama of Shakespeare and His Contemporaries*. Chicago: U of Chicago P, 1984.

Doran, Madeleine. *Endeavors of Art: A Study of Form in Elizabethan Drama*. Madison: U of Wisconsin P, 1954.

Eagleton, Terry. *William Shakespeare*. Oxford: Basil Blackwell, 1986.

Erickson, Peter. *Patriarchal Structures in Shakespeare's Drama*. Berkeley: U of California P, 1984.

Frye, Northrop. *Fools of Time: Studies in Shakespearean Tragedy*. Toronto: U of Toronto P, 1967.

Gohlke, Madelon. " 'I wooed thee with my sword': Shakespeare's Tragic Paradigms." *Representing Shakespeare: New Psychoanalytic Essays*. Ed. Murray M. Schwartz and Coppélia Kahn. Baltimore: Johns Hopkins UP, 1980. 170–87.

Gold, Penny Schine. *The Lady and the Virgin: Image, Attitude, and Experience in Twelfth-Century France*. Chicago: U of Chicago P, 1985.

Goody, Jack. *The Development of the Family and Marriage in Europe*. Cambridge: Cambridge UP, 1983.

Gouge, William. *Of Domesticall Duties*. London, 1622.

Greenblatt, Stephen. "Invisible Bullets: Renaissance Authority and Its Subversion." *Political Shakespeare: New Essays in Cultural Materialism*. Ed. Jonathan Dollimore and Alan Sinfield. Manchester: Manchester UP, 1985. 18–47.

———. *Renaissance Self-Fashioning: From More to Shakespeare*. Chicago: U of Chicago P, 1980.

Haller, William, and Malleville Haller. "The Puritan Art of Love." *Huntington Library Quarterly* 5 (1941–42): 235–72.

Heinemann, Margot. *Puritanism and Theatre: Thomas Middleton and Opposition Drama under the Early Stuarts*. Cambridge: Cambridge UP, 1980.

Hieron, Samuell. *The Sermons of Master Samuell Hieron*. London, 1635.

Hill, Christopher. *Society and Puritanism in Pre-Revolutionary England*. New York: Schocken, 1964.

Kirsch, Arthur. *Shakespeare and the Experience of Love*. Cambridge: Cambridge UP, 1981.

Lamb, Mary Ellen. "The Countess of Pembroke and the Art of Dying." *Women in the Middle Ages and the Renaissance: Literary and Historical Perspectives*. Ed. Mary Beth Rose. Syracuse: Syracuse UP, 1986. 207–26.

Margeson, J. M. R. *The Origins of English Tragedy*. Oxford: Clarendon, 1967.

Montrose, Louis Adrian. " 'Shaping Fantasies': Figurations of Gender and Power in Elizabethan Culture." *Representations* 1 (Spring 1983): 61–94.

Moretti, Franco. " 'A Huge Eclipse': Tragic Form and the Deconsecration of Sovereignty." *The Power of Forms in the English Renaissance*. Ed. Stephen Greenblatt. Norman, Okla.: Pilgrim, 1982. 7–40.

Mueller, Martin. *Children of Oedipus and Other Essays on the Imitation of Greek Tragedy, 1550–1800*. Toronto: U of Toronto P, 1980.

Neely, Carol Thomas. *Broken Nuptials in Shakespeare's Plays*. New Haven: Yale UP, 1985.

Niccholes, Alexander. *A Discourse of Marriage and Wiving*. London, 1615. Rpt. in Vol. 2 of *Harleian Miscellany*. Ed. William Oldys, 1808–13.

Novy, Marianne. *Love's Argument: Gender Relations in Shakespeare*. Chapel Hill: U of North Carolina P, 1985.

Perkins, William. *Christian Oeconomie; or, Household Government*. London, 1631. Vol. 3 of *Workes*.

Reiss, Timothy J. *Tragedy and Truth: Studies in the Development of a Renaissance and Neoclassical Discourse*. New Haven: Yale UP, 1980.

Rose, Mary Beth. "Gender, Genre, and History: Seventeenth-Century English Women and the Art of Autobiography." *Women in the Middle Ages and the Renaissance: Literary and Historical Perspectives*. Ed. Mary Beth Rose. Syracuse: Syracuse UP, 1986. 245–78.

Schochet, Gordon J. *Patriarchalism in Political Thought: The Authoritarian Family and Political Speculation and Attitudes, Especially in Seventeenth-Century England*. Oxford: Basil Blackwell, 1975.

Schulenburg, Jane Tibbetts. "The Heroics of Virginity: Brides of Christ and Sacrificial Mutilation." *Women in the Middle Ages and the Renaissance: Literary and Historical Perspectives*. Ed. Mary Beth Rose. Syracuse: Syracuse UP, 1986. 29–72.

Shakespeare, William. *Othello*. Ed. M. R. Ridley. London: Methuen, 1958.

Shorter, Edward. *The Making of the Modern Family*. New York: Basic, 1977.

Smith, Henry. "A Preparative to Marriage." *The Works of Henry Smith*. Vol. 1. Ed. Thomas Fuller. Edinburgh, 1866. 1–40.

Sprengnether, Madelon [Gohlke]. "Annihilating Intimacy in Coriolanus." *Women in the Middle Ages and the Renaissance: Literary and Historical Perspectives*. Ed. Mary Beth Rose. Syracuse: Syracuse UP, 1986. 89–111.

Stone, Lawrence. *The Family, Sex and Marriage in England, 1500–1800*. New York: Harper, 1977.

T. E. *The Lawes Resolutions of Womens Rights; or, The Lawes Provision for Woemen*. London, 1632.

Thomas, Keith. "The Double Standard." *Journal of the History of Ideas* 20 (1959): 195–216.

Todd, Barbara J. "The Remarrying Widow: A Stereotype Reconsidered." *Women in English Society, 1500–1800*. Ed. Mary Prior. London: Methuen, 1985. 54–92.

Vickers, Nancy J. "Diana Described: Scattered Woman and Scattered Rhyme." *Writing and Sexual Difference*. Ed. Elizabeth Abel. Chicago: U of Chicago P, 1980. 95–109.

Warner, Marina. *Alone of All Her Sex: The Myth and the Cult of the Virgin Mary*. New York: Random, Vintage, 1983.

Webster, John. *The Duchess of Malfi.* Vol. 2 of *Drama of the English Renaissance.* Ed. Russell A. Fraser and Norman Rabkin. New York: Macmillan, 1976. 476–515.

Whately, William. *A Care-cloth.* London, 1624.

Wheeler, Richard. "Since First We Were Dissevered: Trust and Autonomy in Shakespearean Tragedy and Romance." *Representing Shakespeare: New Psychoanalytic Essays.* Ed. Murray M. Schwartz and Coppélia Kahn. Baltimore: Johns Hopkins UP, 1980. 150–69.

Whigham, Frank. "Sexual and Social Mobility in *The Duchess of Malfi.*" *PMLA* 100 (March 1985): 167–86

Williams, Raymond. *Marxism and Literature.* Oxford: Oxford UP, 1977.

Wing, John. *The Crowne Conjvgall, or, The Spouse Royal.* London, 1632.

Wrightson, Keith. *English Society, 1580–1680.* New Brunswick, N.J.: Rutgers UP, 1982.

PART THREE

SHAKESPEARE OUR CONTEMPORARY?

9

THE FATAL CLEOPATRA

CAROL COOK

I

IN THE PREFACE to his edition of Shakespeare, Samuel Johnson ranked among Shakespeare's faults his susceptibility to "the quibble": "A quibble was to him the fatal Cleopatra for which he lost the World and was content to lose it" (Johnson, in Kermode 89). While Johnson introduces Cleopatra here simply as a local metaphor for what is seductive and subversive of Shakespeare's genius, we might pursue the comparison beyond Johnson's probable intentions to consider in larger terms what kind of subversion Cleopatra represents. Johnson's analogy linking Cleopatra with a subversive feature of Shakespearean language is curiously reminiscent of the work of certain French feminists who have sought to locate the feminine not in biology or psychology but in the operations of language. Ironically, Johnson's censorious comments on quibbles and Cleopatra may point the direction for a feminist consideration of *Antony and Cleopatra*.

Though the Cleopatra reference comes at the end of his paragraph on Shakespearean quibbling, Johnson introduces the subject in language that recalls the play in which Cleopatra appears:

> A quibble is to Shakespeare what luminous vapours are to the traveller; he follows it at all adventure; it is sure to lead him out of his way, and sure to engulf him in the mire. It has some malignant power over his mind, and its fascinations are irresistible. . . . A quibble . . . gave him such delight, that he was content to purchase it by the sacrifice of reason, propriety, and truth. (Kermode 86)

The irresistible fascination Johnson describes recalls the power that Cleopatra exercises in *Antony and Cleopatra*, leading Antony away from the sea battle where his Roman honor is at stake, a power "malignant" from the Roman point of view, as it undermines "reason, propriety, and truth"—Roman virtues to which Dr. Johnson, with his respect for the ancients, subscribes. But what is this "truth" that Cleopatra and the quibble so threaten—the truth of "reason" and "propriety"?

The grounds on which the quibble, or pun, is frequently dismissed as a low form of humor are that it relies on accidents of sound, the contingencies of language, in flagrant disregard of semantic proprieties, of the claims of the signified over the signifier. The play on words vulgarly obtrudes upon our notice the physicality of language, threatening to engulf us in a linguistic mire of materiality. Elsewhere in the preface, Johnson opposes "the stability of truth," which appears in "just representations of general nature," with "the customs of particular places . . . the peculiarities of studies or professions . . . the accidents of transient fashions or temporary opinions" (76, 77). The stability of Johnson's truth resides outside of history, of cultural difference, of the peculiar and accidental.

It may strike us as peculiar, though perhaps not accidental, that Cleopatra often appears, in theoretical discussions bearing on the subversive potential of language, as a figure for what destabilizes hierarchy and undermines system. Sigurd Burckhardt, for example, in the final chapter of his book *Shakespearean Meanings* (a chapter titled "The King's Language"), allusively identifies the disruptive force of poetic language with Cleopatra. Of the end of *Antony and Cleopatra*, he writes:

> Shakespeare here awakens in safely domesticated prosaists some sense of the capriciousness and infinite variety of this mistress, language, whom most of us tend to think of as a lawfully wedded, rather dull wife. Poetry, properly understood, will undermine our linguistic certitudes, call into question our faith in the verbal order as representing the order of reality, and in the social order as an adaquate guarantor of truth. (Burckhardt 283)

Hélène Cixous makes a similar identification between Cleopatra and the subversive effects of poetry in her essay "Sorties." Her essay begins with an ironic critique of phallogocentrism, the "Empire of the Selfsame," as she calls it, that exiles woman as a "dark continent" or appropriates her to its own uses. She then embarks on one of her controversial celebrations of the utopian potential of a "feminine practice of writing," which must "make up the unimpeded tongue that bursts partitions, classes, and rhetorics, orders and codes, must inundate, run through, go beyond the discourse [of phallogocentrism] with its last reserves" (Cixous 94–95). She finds something akin to this practice of writing in *Antony and Cleopatra*, exemplified by Cleopatra's enigmatic, insistent, playful otherness, and in the lovers' efforts to "struggle against all the forces of death and to change all the ancient and reductive means of thinking life that would threaten to enclose it, slow it down, deaden it" (128).

Jacques Lacan, my last example here, writes in "The Freudian Thing" that "Freud's discovery [of the unconscious] puts truth into question" (Lacan 118); that is, the truth of the unconscious puts Johnson's "stability of truth" in question. Lacan then ventriloquizes a long passage in which Freud's truth speaks— in a feminine voice:

> "So for you I am the enigma of her who vanishes as soon as she appears, men who try so hard to hide me under the tawdry finery of your proprieties! . . . I wander about in what you regard as being the least true in essence: in the dream, in the way the most far-fetched conceit, the most grotesque nonsense of the joke defies sense, in chance, not in its law, but in its contingence, and I never do more to change the face of the world than when I give it the profile of Cleopatra's nose." (121-22)

For all these writers, Cleopatra functions as a figure of an otherness conceived as feminine—an otherness also associated with disruptive operations of language, the contingencies of quibbles, of jokes, of farfetched conceits such as Lacan's farfetched metonymy of Cleopatra's nose (itself an allusion to Pascal's famous remark on contingency, that "had Cleopatra's nose been shorter, the face of the world would have changed"). In the cultural heritage out of which these writers, including Shakespeare, write, woman has always been the contingent, the particular and peculiar opposed to the "general nature," the "common humanity," of man. Cleopatra serves as a kind of synecdoche or epitome of the feminine and, like the concept of femininity itself, may be conceived as operating within the conventional parameters of a system (the system of binarily opposed genders, a system of representation) and also as a figure for what the system excludes or cannot contain.

Feminist criticism addresses itself to the impasse presented by a cultural order founded on the suppression, indeed the repression, of feminine difference. The search for a feminine voice, for reflections of a female identity or experience in literature, has repeatedly foundered on the repressions operating within representation itself, that is, on the conventions which always reclaim and subordinate what is gendered "feminine" within the terms of a system governed by the masculine norm. To psychologize Shakespeare's heroines, to celebrate the nobility of their "feminine" qualities, to identify with them as women, as some feminist critics of Shakespeare have tended to do, is not to address the issue of gender at the level of representation. As an alternative to the identificatory model of feminist criticism, we might argue that Shakespeare's plays appear to be at once deeply invested in the conventions of their culture, and at the same time keenly sensitive to them *as* conventions. Perhaps the plays go farthest toward challenging the underpinnings of patriarchy and its representations when they draw our attention to the conventionality of their cultural discourse, of gender, of representation itself.

If the passage from Lacan links the dream, the linguistic play of conceits and jokes, with an ever-elusive feminine enigma, it is because the proprieties of a phallocentric order of representation depend on the repression of differences such "nonsense" bespeaks, differences not between sense and nonsense, masculine and feminine, but within sense, within gender identity. In "The Power of Discourse and the Subordination of the Feminine," Luce Irigaray draws a parallel between the unconscious and femininity in Freud's work:

> Freud undermines a certain way of conceptualizing the "present," "presence," by stressing deferred action, overdetermination, the repetition compulsion, the death drive, and so on, . . . by indicating . . . the impact of the so-called unconscious mechanisms on the language of the "subject." But, himself a prisoner of a certain economy of the logos, he defines sexual difference by giving *a priori* value to Sameness, shoring up his demonstration by falling back upon time-honored devices such as analogy, comparison, symmetry, dichotomous oppositions, and so on. . . . In so doing, Freud makes manifest the presuppositions of the scene of representation: *the sexual indifference* that subtends it assures its coherence and closure.
>
> Thus one might ask whether certain properties [propriétés] attributed to the unconscious are not, in part, referable to the feminine sex censored by the logic of consciousness. Whether the feminine *has* an unconscious or *is* the unconscious. (Irigaray 72–73)

Freud did not invent, but only made explicit, a sexual mythology based on "analogy, comparison, symmetry, dichotomous oppositions" in which the little girl is "a little man," the woman a man manqué. Feminine difference, as distinguished from feminine *lack*, will always "vanish as soon as it appears"— when it appears at all—under the terms of the prevailing ideology.

Feminist critics are thus faced with the questions: How can woman represent herself, or be represented? And how can that feminine (Other) voice of the unconscious which Lacan "quotes" speak either in women or in men? Notwithstanding the phallocentric blindspot in his theories of sexual difference, it was

Freud who heard the voice of the unconscious in jokes and in dreams, heard it speaking through the bodies of female hysterics. In so doing, he "put in check a certain conception of 'present,' of 'presence.' . . . " The repressed Other makes itself known in what unsettles proprieties, categories, sense, the logic of identity and presence, which operate in representation, in language, in literature. Of special interest to feminist critics, then, are those moments when a work of literature gestures beyond the scene of representation to catch elusive echoes from an Other place.

Such a moment occurs in *Antony and Cleopatra,* perhaps the play in which Shakespeare struggled most to imagine the other, to represent the impossible—and struggled with the impossibilities of representation. In act 5 Cleopatra, recognizing the full extent of her entrapment by Caesar, chooses to stage her own theatrical death rather than be displayed in Rome as a spectacular symbol of Caesar's power, a humiliation which she imagines with revulsion:

> Saucy lictors
> Will catch at us like strumpets, and scald rhymers
> Ballad us out o' tune. The quick comedians
> Extemporally will stage us, and present
> Our Alexandrian revels: Antony
> Shall be brought drunken forth, and I shall see
> Some squeaking Cleopatra boy my greatness
> I' th' posture of a whore.
>
> (5.2.214–21)

We might describe this as a theatrical equivalent of the quibble—a kind of doubletalk which unveils the contingency of theatrical proprieties, of the convention which excludes women from the Renaissance stage. The stage serves as an apt emblem for the culture as a whole: it is a space from which women are absent, but where they are represented by men. The lines ring uncannily given the squeaking male voice with which this Cleopatra first spoke. The infinitely variable Cleopatra, steeling herself for absolute resistance to the domination of the conqueror, choosing to stage her own death to escape a scene of representation which would reduce her otherness to the limits of its own terms, speaks the impossibility of that escape. What we hear in these lines is impossible: a voice declaring, in effect, "I am not here. I am not speaking." The boy actor, speaking the lines of the male playwright, draws our attention to the absence of Cleopatra from this scene, the absence which constitutes Cleopatra, constitutes the unrepresentable woman, the unassimilable other.[1]

The problem enacted here in the tension between the constative dimension of the play, which requires Cleopatra's presence, and the performative, which demonstrates her absence, dramatizes the play's own entrapment within the culturally determined limits of its representation. *As* a representation, it is caught between its own investment in coherence and closure, and a subversion of that closure operating particularly in its style. This conflict, we might say, is precisely what is at stake in the contest between Egypt and Rome. I want to argue, on the one hand, that the play works through a structure of binary oppositions (Rome/Egypt, history/poetry, male/female) of which Cleopatra is a function, and, on the other hand, that Cleopatra and the play's own poetic language, which shares some of the qualities associated with Cleopatra, work to undermine or overflow systematicity and thereby to gesture toward something beyond the play's scene of representation.

Cleopatra seems an apt figure for a larger principle at work in the play, a fluid principle which destabilizes principles, overflowing the confines of categories as the Nile overflows its banks. While on the one hand Cleopatra and Egypt are hypostasized in diametrical opposition to Caesar and Rome, Cleopatra cannot be simply reduced to that specular symmetry.[2] The language of the play locates or creates Cleopatra in linguistic and logical gaps, in puns that tease us out of sense and paradoxes that tease us out of thought. While Caesar and Cleopatra stand as two poles between which Antony vacillates, and whose different energies he attempts to assimilate in some "visible shape" (4.14.14) he can call a self, he finds in Cleopatra finally not an Egyptian identity to replace his Romanness but an escape from the Roman principle of identity itself. Caesar succeeds in subduing the world to one imperial rule, but Cleopatra figures in the play a difference which eludes the Roman drive toward unification and control to testify that Rome's dominion is not all.

II

In Rome, in Caesar, we see the political operation of the drive toward coherence and closure which Irigaray characterizes as a presupposition of the scene of representation. Rome extends its power to subdue all cultural, political, and geographical difference to one rule. In the course of the play Pompey, the Parthians, Egypt, and the triumvirate itself—the heterogeneous political forces of the world—are subsumed by Caesar's political supremacy: he becomes the "universal landlord." The unwavering drive toward unification and control characterizes also the mental stricture by which Caesar rigorously subdues all impulse to the service of power.

The principle of Roman identity is founded on a premise of self-conquest, denial of the body, and creation of the self in the abstract image of the state. Caesar speaks of himself in the third person, as though he existed primarily as a conception of proper government: "It is not Caesar's natural vice to hate / Our great competitor" (1.4.2–3). Act 1, scene 4 is framed by two speeches in which Caesar implicitly sets forth the doctrine of Roman manhood. The first does so negatively by its condemnation of Antony's extravagant revelry:

> From Alexandria
> This is the news: he fishes, drinks, and wastes
> The lamps of night in revel; is not more manlike
> Than Cleopatra, nor the queen of Ptolemy
> More womanly than he . . .
>   Let's grant it not
> Amiss to tumble on the bed of Ptolemy,
> To give a kingdom for a mirth, to sit
> And keep the turn of tippling with a slave,
> To reel the streets at noon, and stand the buffet
> Of knaves that smells of sweat. Say this becomes him
> (As his composure must be rare indeed
> Whom these things cannot blemish); yet must Antony
> No way excuse his foils when we do bear
> So great weight in his lightness . . .
>   . . . to confound such time
> That drums him from his sport and speaks as loud
> As his own state and ours, 'tis to be chid
> As we rate boys who, being mature in knowledge,
> Pawn their experience to their present pleasure
> And so rebel to judgment.
>   (1.4.16–25, 28–33)

The "boy Caesar" speaks in the voice of the father here, pressed by the urgency of time, of history, which he would control and Antony "confounds." His censure of Antony repeatedly fixes on Antony's confounding of differences: temporal—Antony wastes the lamps of night and reels at noon; social— he drinks and jostles with slaves and sweating knaves; and sexual—he is not more manly than Cleopatra nor she more womanly than he. Antony's neglect

of proprieties, distinctions, and political priorities makes havoc of the hierarchies by which Rome exists at all.

The speech functions as much as a portrait of the quintessentially Roman
Caesar as of Antony in his Egyptian aspect. While the general accuracy of Caesar's account has been established by Antony himself in 1.1, the assessment that
goes with it reveals Caesar's own moral parsimoniousness and his recoil from
the flesh, his disgust with "waste," "indulgence," "voluptuousness," "sweat."
Roman virility demands the reining in of all excess and the complete subjugation of the body to the will. That Antony has proven himself worthy of this
heritage in the past, Caesar also attests in his apostrophe to him:

> Antony,
> Leave thy lascivious wassails. When thou once
> Was beaten from Modena, where thou slew'st
> Hirtius and Pansa, consuls, at thy heel
> Did famine follow, whom thou fought'st against
> (Though daintily brought up) with patience more
> Than savages could suffer. Thou didst drink
> The stale of horses and the gilded puddle
> Which beasts would cough at. Thy palate then did deign
> The roughest berry on the rudest hedge,
> Yea, like the stag when snow the pasture sheets,
> The barks of trees thou browsed. On the Alps
> It is reported thou didst eat strange flesh,
> Which some did die to look on. And all this
> (It wounds thine honor that I speak it now)
> Was borne so like a soldier that thy cheek
> So much as lanked not.
>
> (1.4.55–71)

Caesar's homage to Antony's soldiership stands in a remarkably symmetri-
cal opposition to his condemnation of Antony's voluptuousness: it focuses
almost exclusively on eating and drinking. The difference lies in a complete
inversion of the pleasure principle, and the implicit subjugation of the maternal function. The landscape in which Antony stoically struggles for survival is
no nurturing—and therefore seductive—maternal nature, but a place of horror
against which the soldier pits his will. The threat of desire, which Antony represents to Caesar in Caesar's first description of him, is here mastered by the
inversion which turns desire to disgust, "tippling with slaves" to drinking
horses' stale. The sparse sustenance provided by the barren Alps can be ingested
only by a violent repression of the instincts which make beasts "cough" at the

"gilded puddle"; nouriture is bodily waste, "strange flesh," a testament to the hideousness of all fleshly substance and an injunction to the soldier to dominate the impulses of his own. Roman identity is that abstraction of the will and that concentration of energies that consolidates the empire and the self in the service of power.

Singularly dedicated to control, rigorously abstract and impersonal in its ethic of duty, founded on the suppression of the heterogeneous, the feminine, the bodily, the maternal, Roman manhood is always threatened by the eruption of desire. Pompey counts on Cleopatra's allure and her cooks to undo the Oedipal repression which binds Antony to the fatherland "That sleep and feeding may prorogue his honor, / Even to a Leth'd dullness" (2.1.16–17). Pompey, like Caesar, conflates nurturance with seduction, appetite with destruction: Antony's Egyptian dish is really an emasculating Egyptian witch. Maternal seduction represents the most potent threat to Roman order and control. Roman womanhood, represented by Octavia, is not seductive but "holy, cold, and still." Octavia is "a piece of virtue" (3.2.28), a *piece* of Roman *virtus*, a man manqué. "A statue rather than a breather" (3.3.24), the petrified Octavia represents femininity as produced by Rome and submitted utterly to the imperatives of empire; she serves her brother as the currency which buys first Antony's return and then his defeat.

Roman virtue is the virtue of firmness, constancy, imperviousness: the cheek that "lanks not" in the face of ordeal and does not flush before temptation. The Roman ideal which relies on the suppression of internal heterogeneity, internal difference, turns out to be somewhat paradoxical, however, as does the logic of identity itself in the play, parodied by Antony in his whimsical description of the crocodile:

Antony   It is shaped, sir, like itself, and it is as broad as it hath breadth; it is just so high as it is, and moves with its own organs. It lives by that which nourisheth it, and the elements once out of it, it transmigrates.
Lepidus   What color is it of?
Antony   Of it own color too.
Lepidus   'Tis a strange serpent.   (2.7.43–50)

This tautological beast may serve, in its parodic way, as the model for Roman identity. Identity, from *idem*, "the same," implies a logic of resemblance: one's identity consists in being the same as oneself, *like* oneself. If similitude requires more than one term, identity is difference subsumed as equation, as exemplified by the crocodile, which is perfectly identical with itself. For Antony, however, the rigorous equation of identity proves an elusive ideal. Antony's name is spoken in the play as though it were an autonomous concept, a bounded space which the wavering man may or may not fill:

> ... sometimes when he is not Antony
> He comes short of that great property
> Which still should go with Antony.
>> (1.1.52–59)

> I shall entreat him
> To answer like himself.
>> (2.2.3–4)

> Had our general
> Been what he knew himself, all had gone well.
>> (3.10.25–26)

And Antony, despite his increasingly conflicted relation to the ideal of Roman selfhood, never ceases to conceive himself in its terms. He would be "the firm Roman" (1.5.43), but finds that solidity of self impossible to maintain. In 2.3 he wishfully tells Octavia:

> Read not my blemishes in the world's report:
> I have not kept my square, but that to come
> Shall all be done by th' rule.
>> (2.3.5–7)

But Antony continually finds himself drawn to a realm of experience which exceeds the straits of Roman rule. Insofar as he locates his identity within the Roman square, Antony is threatened by a loss of self in a flood of desire. We might then ask whether that loss is only the consequence of desire, or whether it is in some sense its aim.

III

Antony and Cleopatra is arguably the most schematic of Shakespeare's plays. Though Shakespeare uses schematic oppositions throughout his dramatic corpus—in Venice and Belmont, court and heath, Greek camp and Trojan palace—the detail with which the oppositions are worked out in *Antony and Cleopatra* is exceptional, as though binariness itself, and not simply the qualities contrasted, is offered to our attention. The language of the play sets up a detailed series of associations and oppositions whereby Caesar's Rome—cold, hard, sterile, ruled by the exigencies of time and history—is set against Cleo-patra's Egypt—lush, sensuous, fertile, a place less of time and history than of myth and dream.[3] Yet schematization, with its orderly symmetries, seems itself a Roman principle to which this extravagant play cannot be quite reduced. Cleopatra, in particular, eludes and undermines the stability of the play's cate-gories and the closure they would provide.

The passages from Irigaray quoted earlier in this essay concern the problem-atic relation between women and representation. Much of Irigaray's work examines the ways in which the discourses Western culture has relied upon to represent itself—scientific, psychoanalytic, philosophical—recognize woman only as the specular opposite, the reflection, of man, reducing all difference to an economy of the same. For Irigaray, "woman" is that which eludes the lan-guage we know, something known by its absence or as a "disruptive excess" which threatens systematicity itself (Irigaray 78). The importance of Irigaray's conception of the feminine is in its refusal to mirror the discursive practices she criticizes by defining woman or assigning her an identity or essence. The subversive power of the feminine has to do with its refusal of representation; it is that which signifies the existence of an "elsewhere," something beyond— or, in the language of the play, "past the size of dreaming."

Irigaray's concept provides a useful way to consider the operations of gender and the significance of Cleopatra in *Antony and Cleopatra*. The play's poetry, whose characteristic tropes are hyperbole and paradox, seems always to be straining at the limits of language, gesturing beyond what can be represented on the stage or in words.[4] As we saw at the beginning of this essay, Cleopatra calls explicit attention to her absence, her refusal of representation, in the "squeaking Cleopatra" lines. At another crucial moment in the play, a moment concerned with Cleopatra's representation, she eludes the language that at-tempts to capture her. Enobarbus's famous description of Cleopatra on her barge (2.2.197–224) is, perhaps more than any other single speech in the play, what creates Cleopatra for the audience. In this extravagant speech, lengthy and familiar enough that I won't quote it here, the richness of detail and the elaborate conceits of lovesick winds and waters suggest the speaker's effort to affect in his language the full impact of Cleopatra's presence. Yet Cleopatra not only threatens to make a gap in nature—she is a gap in the speech. Enobarbus has words for the barge, its trappings, the smiling Cupids and Nereides sur-rounding Cleopatra, but she herself "beggars all description," escaping the lan-guage that would fix her as spectacle. Of course, Enobarbus may be thought of here as simply employing the rhetorical strategy which best serves his purpose in asking his audience to imagine what words are insufficient to describe, but it must then be recognized that Enobarbus's strategy is also the play's. The rest of what he has to say about her can be expressed only in paradox:

> . . . she did make defect perfection,
> And breathless, pow'r breathe forth.
>
> Age cannot wither her, nor custom stale
> Her infinite variety; other women cloy
> The appetite they feed, but she makes hungry
> Where most she satisfies; for vilest things
> Become themselves in her, that holy priests
> Bless her when she is riggish.
>
> (2.2.237–38, 241–46)

The play consistently locates Cleopatra at the juncture where categories collide and cannot comprehend one another: defect/perfection, satiety/hunger, vileness/holiness. She is a space in which transformation occurs perpetually, defect is perfected, and vilest things become themselves in her—become *themselves* in her and also are becoming to, glorify, themselves. In her infinite variety, Cleopatra is always and never identical with herself: her identity is the refusal of identity, of essence, of the kind of stability which can be made property to serve Rome.

The mystique of Cleopatra *is* precisely her variety, her evasion of fixity. This infinite Cleopatra can be represented on stage because her presence, her demeanor, her role at any given moment, always signifies beyond itself to the infinity of other guises she *might* assume. The Cleopatra we see before us, as complex and changeable as she may be, is only the figure or sign of that infinite Cleopatra who cannot be represented in the finitude of the theater. The Cleopatra who could make a gap in nature could not be adequately embodied by a squeaking boy, and yet it is that unrepresentable Cleopatra who speaks through the squeaking boy to refuse his representation of her.

The Cleopatra that we see is most often engaged in running through the spectrum of feminine stereotypes: the seductress, the shrew, the catty gossip— roles which she plays with a certain exaggeration, as well as a certain self-consciousness, as though Cleopatra were always presenting herself in quotation marks. Irigaray writes that historically a single "field" has been assigned to the feminine: mimeticism. But to play the role(s) of the feminine deliberately, to affirm the subordination of the feminine, becomes a way to outmaneuver or elude that subordination:

To play with mimesis is thus, for a woman, to try to recover the place of her exploitation by discourse, without allowing herself be simply reduced to it. It means to resubmit herself—inasmuch as she is on the side of the "perceptible," of "matter"—to "ideas," in particular to ideas about herself, that are elaborated in/by a masculine logic, but so as to make "visible," by an effect of playful repetition, what was supposed to remain invisible: the cover-up [or recovery—recouvrement] of a possible operation of the feminine in language. It also means "to unveil" the fact that, if women are such good mimics, it is because they are not simply reabsorbed in this function. *They also remain elsewhere.* (76)

Cleopatra's "becomings," as she calls them, her repertoire of ephemeral fictions, expose all self-representation, her own and that of others, as charades. She mockingly coaches Antony in the postures of remorseful husband and dissembling lover, as she bids him to mourn Fulvia's death:

I prithee turn aside and weep for her;
Then bid adieu to me, and say the tears,
Belong to Egypt. Good now, play one scene,
Of excellent dissembling and let it look
Like perfect honor.

(1.3.76–79)

She recalls for her attendants her practical joke on sexual difference:

I laughed him out of patience; and that night
I laughed him into patience; and the next morn,
Ere the ninth hour, I drunk him to his bed;
Then put my tires and mantles on him, whilst
I wore his sword Phillipan.

(2.5.19–23)

Cleopatra's parodic assumption of Antony's sword, and her Omphalic transformation/castration of him, make sport of the code of sexual difference and masculine prestige in which Rome has such a stake. She knows that she can play at being a man as she plays at being a woman.

IV

To discuss Cleopatra in this way is to approach her less as a character, a psychology or personality, than as a figure for a certain kind of textual operation. *Antony and Cleopatra,* for all its vividness of characterization and its touches of realism, is in many ways closer to something like allegory or dialectic than to psychological drama, as critics have long recognized. John Danby, for example, writes about "the vast containing opposites of Rome and Egypt, the World and the Flesh . . . [in] which Cleopatra is the Flesh, deciduous, opulent, and endlessly renewable. . . . The Flesh is also the female principle. Cleopatra is Eve, and Woman . . . she is also Circe" (257, 262–63). Danby's discussion of the play as a "Shakespearean dialectic" posits that "Caesar and Cleopatra are simple and opposite" (259). His recognition of this opposition which casts Cleopatra as "Woman" is accurate, but raises the question of what "Woman" is. If we accept Irigaray's position that woman is not "simple," is not simply the specular reflection and opposite of Man, then we must look beyond such statically diametrical structures to locate the feminine.

Irigaray proposes to identify the feminine as an operation in language which "overflows" (déborder) the bounds of discursivity and "good sense," a feminine "style" or "écriture" which privileges not the look but the tactile, the simultaneous, the fluid. This "style," like the feminine sex, is never "one": it does not constitute any unity and "is never fixed in the possible identity-to-itself of some form or other" (Irigaray 79). The feminine " 'style' resists and explodes every firmly established form, figure, idea or concept" (79). Irigaray's language resonates suggestively with a larger metaphorical structure of the play. The Roman project of mapping out, penetrating, and conquering the world depends upon fixity of purpose, firmness, constancy, the consolidation of power. What is in flux threatens Roman control, particularly the varying tides of desire, whether it be Antony's "dotage," which "o'erflows the measure," or that of the fickle populace as Caesar describes it:

> This common body,
> Like to a vagabond flag upon the stream,
> Goes to and back, lackeying the varying tide,
> To rot itself with motion.
>
> (1.4.44–47)

Hoping to rely on Antony's leadership and soldiership, Caesar attempts to solidify their relations by means of Octavia, "the piece of virtue which is set / Betwixt us as the cement of our love / To keep it builded . . . " (3.2.28–30).

Egypt particularly is characterized by references to the flooding of the Nile, the burgeoning fertility of "Nilus' slime," and the "chance and hazard" of the sea, and part of Egypt's fluidity consists in the metonymic exchange of qualities between the nation and its queen, who is also called "Egypt." The qualities by which Cleopatra is represented exist "outside" her as much as they can be located in her person, and the qualities of Egypt are exemplified in her: "We cannot call her winds and waters sighs and tears," says Enobarbus, twitting Antony, "they are greater storms and tempests than almanacs can report" (1.2.149–52). The swelling of the Nile and the harvest that follows, which Antony describes in 2.7 ("The higher Nilus swells, / The more it promises"), is echoed in Cleopatra's pregnancies and childbirths:

> She made great Caesar lay his sword to bed;
> He plowed her and she cropped.
>
> (2.2.233–34)

While Caesar extends his power over provinces and territories, the language of the play—even that spoken in Rome—is permeated with the influence of Egypt. The style of the play suffuses the solid world of imperial politics with a fluidity which overflows and undermines its boundaries, its logic, its insistence on identity, as it creates a world not of being but of "becomings." Even the word "become," repeated throughout the play in its various forms, has a kind of quibbling duplicity and fluid transformative power over meaning. It is used both to describe transformation (Antony "is become the bellows and the fan / To cool a gypsy's lust") and to describe what is proper or flattering. "Say this becomes him," Caesar challenges Lepidus sarcastically after chronicling Antony's flamboyant debaucheries (1.4.21); "Look, prithee, Charmian, / How this Herculean Roman does become / The carriage of his chafe," Cleopatra taunts Antony (1.3.83–85), but later she apostrophizes him admiringly: "Be'st thou sad or merry, / The violence of either thee becomes, / So does it no man else" (1.5.59–61). Ledipus advises Enobarbus that it would "become [him] well" to entreat Antony to temper his speech (2.2.2), but when Enobarbus does not temper his own, Pompey compliments him: "Enjoy thy plainness, / It nothing ill becomes thee" (2.6.78–79). Cleopatra nominalizes the word:

> But, sir, forgive me,
> Since my becomings kill me when they do not
> Eye well to you.
>
> (1.3.95–97)

In this context the word can be glossed as "graces," yet it carries the connotations of mutability still, as Cleopatra's grace consists in her "infinite variety"; her "becomings" are the tempestuous but ephemeral passions which she displays to fascinate Antony ("If you find him sad, / Say I am dancing; if in mirth, report / That I am sudden sick"). The strategy proves effective; Antony calls her "wrangling queen! / Whom everything becomes," and when Enobarbus concludes that "vilest things / Become themselves in her," the very conception of vileness is transformed as it "becomes" Cleopatra.

The current of echoing "becomes" and "becomings" eddies through the play, gathering the worlds of Rome and Egypt into it, creating a sense of unending process and transformation. Political fortunes depend upon the "slippery people" and "the ebbed man, ne'er loved till ne'er worth love, / Comes deared by being lacked" (1.4.43–44). The lovers too seem "slippery" at times, to one another, at least; Antony accuses Cleopatra of having been a "boggler ever"; she describes him as a perspective picture "painted one way like a Gorgon, / The other way's a Mars" (2.5.116–17). Solid forms "melt" and "discandy":

Let Rome in Tiber melt . . .
          (1.1.33)

Melt Egypt into Nile . . .
          (2.5.78)

Authority melts from me . . .
          (3.13.89)

       . . . so
Dissolve my life!
     (3.13.161–62)

        The hearts
That spanieled me at heels, to whom I gave
Their wishes, do discandy, melt their sweets
On blossoming Caesar. . . .
       (4.12.20–23)

The crown o' th' earth doth melt.
      (4.15.63)

This linguistic deliquescence is not limited to scattered metaphors or verbal patterns; it flows through the logical boundaries, the categories and dichotomies that structure significance in the play in a way reminiscent of Irigaray's "feminine style." For Irigaray, recovery of the feminine, of an "elsewhere" not governed by a reductive discursivity, requires a "work of language" which undoes the repressions operating within representation:

How, then, are we to try to redefine this work of language that would leave space for the feminine? Let us say that every dichotomizing—and at the same time redoubling—break, including the one between enunciation and utterance, has to be disrupted. Nothing is ever to be *posited* that is not also reversed. . . .

This work of language would thus attempt to thwart any manipulation of discourse that would also leave discourse intact. Not, necessarily, in the utterance, but in its *autological presuppositions*. Its function would be to *cast phallocentrism, phallocratism,* loose from its moorings in order to return the masculine to its own language, leaving open the possibility of a different language. Which means that the masculine would no longer be "everything." That it could no longer, all by itself, define, circumvene, circumscribe, the properties of anything and everything. That the right to define every value . . . would no longer belong to it. (79–80)

Some such "work of language," for which Cleopatra, in the "sweating labor of her idleness," is the figure, is at work in this play, whose most characteristic quality is the way its oppositions and catagories tend to spill into, inhabit, and transform one another. Such reversals and subversions occur both on the microcosmic level of verbal figure and on a larger structural level. For example, in 1.4 Lepidus tempers Caesar's harsh censure of Antony thus:

I must not think there are
Evils enow to darken all his goodness;
His faults, in him, seem as the spots of heaven,
More fiery by night's blackness . . .

(10–13)

The conventional metaphor of evil darkness eclipsing or staining "goodness" is established only to be overturned: Antony's faults become the brilliant stars against a dark ground. The reversal does not immediately call attention to itself, for the second two lines sound as though they follow the conventional logic and metaphorical schema of the first, even as they undermine it. And yet the lines do not simply reverse the convention either, for when the faults become stars, it is not precisely "goodness" which becomes "night's blackness"; the signified of "blackness" is no longer something we can locate within the simple terms of the dichotomy. The metaphor does not lend itself to a systematic translation into the literal. The conventional associations which made the lines about evil's darkening goodness *signify* have been disturbed, thwarting the systematicity of rigid Roman moral discourse. The effect of Lepidus's description is to lift Antony outside the conventional categories by which Caesar would define him.

Similarly, the larger oppositions that structure the play begin to lose their "visible shape" and distinction to a larger process of transformation and exchange. Initially the play seems to pose Rome as the place of impersonal duty against Egypt's commitment to personal desire, yet it becomes difficult in the course of the play to see Caesar's rapacious pursuit of power as anything other than his own form of excessive self-gratification, however Caesar couches it in moral language; and Antony and Cleopatra's standards of "nobility" become the measure by which Cleopatra can conclude " 'Tis paltry to be Caesar" (5.2.2).

Roman commitment to steadfastness, constancy, the imperative to "possess" the time rather than to be its "child," establishes Rome as the place of stability as against Egyptian "variety" and flux. Yet Roman fortunes depend upon the contingencies of shifting political winds, as the language of the play constantly reminds us. Pompey feels that his "powers are crescent," but the crescent is only a phase of what Cleopatra calls the "fleeting moon," and the fate of crescent leaders is to become the "ebbed man." The references to the "slippery people" and the "varying tide" of popular loyalties make political change seem even less predictable than the orderly cycles of the moon, even more a matter of "chance and hazard." Egypt, on the other hand, claims for itself a kind of permanence, especially through what comes to seem the near-immortality of Cleopatra, when, for example, she languorously muses on the absent Antony and drifts into memories of lovers past:

> He's speaking now,
> Or murmuring, "Where's my serpent of old Nile?"
> (For so he calls me.) Now I feed myself
> On most delicious poison. Think on me,
> That am with Phoebus' amorous pinches black
> And wrinkled deep in time. Broad-fronted Caesar,
> When thou wast here above ground, I was
> A morsel for a monarch; and great Pompey
> Would stand and make his eyes grow in my brow;
> There would he anchor his aspect, and die
> With looking on his life.
>
> (1.5.24–34)

Here Cleopatra seems more ancient than Rome, older than time itself, elemental as the Nile and the sun; she loves and outlasts these men who conquer the world and die.

V

The desire that "o'erflows the measure" of Antony's Roman "square" seeks freedom from all bounds, all definition, even the boundaries of the body itself.

Philo's opening description of Antony suggests an energy impatient of containment:

> His captain's heart,
> Which in the scuffles of great fights hath burst
> The buckles on his breast, reneges all temper . . .
> (1.1.6–8)

Later, believing Cleopatra dead and looking to his own death to free him from the keenness of loss, Antony echoes the image:

> O, cleave, my sides!
> Heart, once be stronger than thy continent,
> Crack thy frail case!
> (4.14.39–41)

Antony's frequently reckless behavior in the play—his willful return to Cleopatra after the marriage to Octavia, his insistence upon giving himself to the "chance and hazard" of a sea battle when his advantage is on dry land—suggests a suicidal impulse, a drive to free himself from the struggle to "keep his square" between the conflicting pulls of Egypt and Rome. The end of this struggle is the dissolution that Antony describes to Eros:

Antony	Sometimes we see a cloud that's dragonish,
	A vapor sometime like a bear or lion,
	A towered citadel, a pendant rock,
	A forkèd mountain, or blue promontory
	With trees upon't that nod unto the world
	And mock our eyes with air. Thou hast seen these signs:
	They are black vesper's pageants.
Eros	Ay, my lord.
Antony	That which is now a horse, even with a thought
	The rack dislimns, and makes it indistinct
	As water is in water.
Eros.	It does, my lord.
Antony.	My good knave Eros, now thy captain is
	Even such a body: here I am Antony,
	Yet cannot hold this visible shape . . .
	(4.14.2–14)

Elegiac as Antony sounds here for the loss of his "visible shape," it is a loss which follows from the nature of his desire and seems requisite for its consummation (See Cantor 177). The annihilation of separateness comes to entail the annihilation of bodies. It is one of the play's many paradoxes that for Antony and Cleopatra, bodies, in their physical distinctness, their separateness and identity, come to represent obstacles to consummation rather than instruments of it; theirs is a desire impatient of the mediation even of the flesh. In his moment of triumph in 4.8, Antony invites Cleopatra:

> ... leap thou, attire and all,
> Through proof of harness to my heart, and there
> Ride on the pants triumphing.
>
> (14–16)

What this "means" cannot quite be translated either into visual image or into prose utterance. The jubilant eroticism of the language is partly a function of its ability to suggest a union that cannot be imaged or articulated, its ability to "o'erflow the measure" of common sense and ordinary experience.

It is consistent with their intolerance of bounds that both Antony and Cleopatra look to death to consummate their love; death is the "elsewhere" in which the play locates a possibility of pure fluidity, freedom from the confinement and obstacles of the "dungy earth." The homology of love and death, reflected in the familiar Renaissance play on the verb "to die," provides another instance of seeming opposites transforming one another, just as Enobarbus's sardonic pun is transformed into erotic lyricism when he says of Cleopatra, "I do think there is mettle in death, which commits some loving act upon her, she hath such a celerity in dying" (1.2.144–46). Antony, poised for suicide, calls to Cleopatra, "I come, my queen.—Eros!—Stay for me. / Where souls do couch on flowers . . . ," and prepares to "be / A bridegroom in my death, and run into't / As to a lover's bed" (4.14.50–51, 99–101).

The lovers' aspiration toward some unimaginable consummation, a union that could not be embodied or represented, may recall Troilus's exaltation of boundless desire and his denigration of the slavish "act" in *Troilus and Cressida;*[5] certainly Antony and Cleopatra are engaged with one another as fantasy objects, "past the size of dreaming." Antony even indulges in misogynistic fits of rage, reminiscent of Troilus's, when he believes himself betrayed, calling Cleopatra a "morsel" and "fragment" of leftover food, "the greatest spot / of all thy sex," and "monsterlike" (3.13.116, 117; 4.12.35–36). The rages are momentary, however. Unlike Troilus, Antony does not construct for himself an identity or integrity in opposition to a fragmented Cleopatra, does not seek to define himself as whole, pure, "truth's authentic author." Whatever notion of nobility the characters claim for themselves, it consists in an identification with one another, as Cleopatra suggests, when Antony's anger resolves into gaiety: " . . . since my lord / Is Antony again, I will be Cleopatra" (3.8.186–87). The mythic identities these lovers confer upon themselves can never be single or simple, as each is contingent upon the other, inhabited by the other. In this union, difference seems both exaggerated and annihilated, but it is never stabilized as hierarchy.

There is another way in which the desire represented in *Antony and Cleopatra* contrasts with that in *Troilus and Cressida*. In *Troilus*, both Helen and Cressida are objects of the desire, valuation, and fantasy of masculine subjects; the possibility of a feminine subjectivity is excluded from the world of that play, as it has historically been excluded from representations of patriarchal culture. *Troilus and Cressida* challenges the limitations of its ideology only insofar as it delineates and exposes them. If *Antony and Cleopatra* cannot get outside of its masculinist presuppositions either, it challenges them in a new way from within, gesturing toward some possibility which it can suggest if not realize. The play *plays* with gender, and does so in a more comprehensive way than even Shakespeare's cross-dressed romantic comedies. In the comedies, a Portia or Rosalind or Viola may adopt masculine dress in order to realign familial and sexual roles, to exchange a daughter's role for that of wife, to test a lover and achieve a liberty which is ultimately sanctioned by and reclaimed within existing structures of gender and power. The romantic comedies affirm the institutions of patriarchal societies by representing them as elastic enough to accommodate the lovers' personal desires, even when they initially conflict with the prerogatives of fathers. What is at stake in *Antony and Cleopatra* is something larger than its lovers, something the play characterizes repeatedly as "the world," and not simply the world of clay kingdoms which Antony and Cleopatra so frequently mock, much as they wish to control their shares of it; at stake in this play is not what can be possessed and governed but what can be imagined and articulated. Cleopatra plays with gender, not in order to overcome social or familial obstacles to her union with Antony, but precisely in order to transform conventional definitions, roles, and boundaries into objects of play. And unlike the male lovers of the romantic comedies, Antony too participates in this testing of limits, this play with gender roles; finding the square of Roman manhood confining, he gravitates toward the potentially emasculating East,[6] seeking some more fluid mode of being.

VI

What remains the most completely prohibited to woman, of course, is that she should express something of her own sexual pleasure. This latter is supposed to remain *a "realm" of discourse, produced by men*. For in fact feminine pleasure signifies the greatest threat of all to masculine discourse, represents its most irreducible "exteriority," or "extraterritoriality."

(Irigaray 157)

Antony and Cleopatra gestures more insistently than any play of Shakespeare's toward an extraterritoriality of feminine pleasure it cannot represent, and it does so partly by the way it calls attention to the limits of its representation. The play does depict Cleopatra's desire, Cleopatra's pleasure. When Antony is in Rome, all her language becomes sexually charged, as though to fill the vacancy:

Where think'st he is now? Stands he, or sits he?
Or does he walk? Or is he on his horse?
O happy horse, to bear the weight of Antony!

(1.5.19–21)

The arrival of a messenger from Italy provokes her voracious response: "Ram thou thy fruitful tidings in mine ears, / That long time have been barren" (2.5.23–24). In Antony's absence or finally after his death, Cleopatra is placed in the masculine position of desiring subject—another of the play's many reversals. In her "dream of Antony" speech, she wishfully constructs for herself her "man of men":

His legs bestrid the ocean: his reared arm
Crested the world: his voice was propertied
As all the tunèd spheres, and that to friends;
But when he meant to quail and shake the orb,
He was as rattling thunder. For his bounty,
There was no winter in't: an autumn 'twas
That grew the more by reaping. . . .

(5.2.83–88)

Here Antony becomes the kind of wonder that Cleopatra was in Enobarbus's barge speech, a creature of contraries and paradoxes, infinitely desirable. The reversal of the normative masculine and feminine positions within the subject/object relation is noteworthy, though it does not in itself subvert the norm or alter the terms of that relation. When Cleopatra appropriates the dead Antony to her desire, she is appropriated to the discourse of speaking (masculine) subjects. There is no other language she can speak, and she is not a "she" but a squeaking boy.

What the play cannot get outside of—the conventions of its representation—it points beyond by pointing *to;* it makes its limitations palpable. The squeaking Cleopatra speech discussed at the beginning of this essay is the play's articulation of an absence, the absence of a feminine voice, and to make that absence bespeak itself is to begin to recognize the possibility of an "elsewhere." Yet it is another of the play's acknowledgments of the limitations of its cultural discourse that that "elsewhere" can be represented only as death, the exteriority into which the lovers disappear. Death, like feminine pleasure, "has to remain inarticulate in language, in its own language, if it is not to threaten the underpinnings of logical operations" (Irigaray 77). The language of death in *Antony and Cleopatra* is the language of the Cleopatran quibble. Death's incongruous emissary, the clown who brings Cleopatra the fatal asp, speaks a riddling language of puns and paradoxes that reveals both more and less than it knows:

> Truly I have him; but I would not be the party that should desire you to touch him, for his biting is immortal: those that do die of it do seldom or never recover. . . . I heard of one of them no longer than yesterday; a very honest woman but something given to lie . . . how she died of the biting of it, what pain she felt; truly she makes a very good report of the worm . . . but this is most fallible, the worm's an odd worm. (5.2.245–58)

The clown seems at once privy to death's secrets and unconscious of his knowledge, garrulous in speaking them, and oblique in what he reveals. No subject can speak from beyond death or from the place of the feminine (though in the clown's report it is the honest lying woman who seems to); what the logic of discourse excludes can be spoken only as nonsense. Under the dominion of Rome, there is no place for an "elsewhere" except in death. After the sea battle in act 4, scene 12, Caesar becomes "sole sir o' th' world," and Cleopatra prepares to "rush into the secret house of death" (4.15.80).

  Cleopatra demonstrates another phase of her infinite variety when, after Antony's death, she seems to adopt the "high Roman fashion," disavowing the very variety and changeability that have constituted her difference from the Roman ethos. She wishes to "do that thing that ends all other deeds, / Which shackles accidents and bolts up change"; at the last she disclaims even her sex:

> My resolution's placed, and I have nothing
> Of woman in me; now from head to foot
> I am marble constant: now the fleeting moon
> No planet is of mine.
>
>   (5.2.238–41)

In one sense this appears to be a surrender to the dominion of Rome, an acceptance of the Roman version of "what's brave, what's noble"; the language suggests that Cleopatra is finally absorbed by the values of Roman culture as her kingdom is politically engulfed by its empire. Caesar's accession to world power has eliminated difference from the earth—or placed it in an exile beyond death. Yet there is much in the manner of Cleopatra's suicide to suggest that this is another of her "becomings," with an element of play and mockery in it—certainly it is theatrical.

Cleopatra's suicide is prompted by her wish to escape the grotesquely parodic representation of her in Caesar's triumph. Yet in her death, she also slyly turns the tables on Rome, becoming the parodist herself. Her luxurious death mocks the Roman ideal of stoic suicide. She "hath pursued conclusions infinite / Of easy ways to die" and chooses a method that "kills and pains not." She playfully adorns herself for another journey to "Cydnus, / To meet Mark Antony"; to her the waning of life is "as a lover's pinch, / Which hurts and is desired" (5.2.245–46). And part of her pleasure is the pleasure of mockery:

> Come, thou mortal wretch,
> With thy sharp teeth this knot intrinsicate
> Of life at once untie. Poor venomous fool,
> Be angry, and dispatch. O, couldst thou speak,
> That I might hear thee call great Caesar ass
> Unpolicied!
>
> (5.2.303–308)

Cleopatra makes of death not a conquest over feeling and the body but a culmination of eros and play. The ultimate gesture by which a Roman proves his manhood, his commitment to the abstract over the bodily, becomes for her an affirmation of feminine pleasure.

Cleopatra's death is the final paradox of the play. For while it marks Caesar's victory and leaves the Roman claim to universal power without a challenger, it is also a marking out of an "elsewhere" which announces that Rome and its empire are "not all."[7] In the final act of the play, Cleopatra retreats into her monument, and in her death becomes herself monumental, a spectacle presented for display. To become monumentalized is to become fixed, "marble constant" and objectified, subjected to interpretation, as the tableau of Cleopatra and her women is interpreted by Caesar and his men (5.2.335–55). Yet a monument also memorializes a loss, an absence. What Caesar has tried to exploit and subdue escapes him utterly and, at the last, mocks the limitations of his power.

NOTES

1. Sprengnether discusses the boy actor in similar terms: "Through the figure of the boy actor, Shakespeare stages the projection of a female 'otherness' (both threatening and subversive) and its neutralization, or reappropriation into the structure of masculinity and masculine power. The capacity of the boy actor to represent woman as 'other' and 'not other' allows Shakespeare to examine femininity both as an aspect of sexual difference and as an undeveloped potential within men" (203). I would agree with Sprengnether's incisive account of the double effect of the boy actor, adding only that this figure who both affirms and denies difference may be said to open an examination of femininity not only as "an undeveloped potential within men" but also as a disruption of representation, and perhaps an undeveloped potential within a cultural discourse founded on binary opposition.

2. For example, Danby: "the world . . . of Rome and Caesar . . . is radically opposed to the world of Egypt and Rome. . . . Caesar and Cleopatra are simple and opposite" (251, 259). Adelman argues, in her excellent book-length study of the play, that "both Cleopatra and Octavius are in a sense absolutes, untainted by their opposites" (130), though she goes on to complicate this argument by identifying Cleopatra with contradiction and by stressing the play's pattern of overflow and excess which tends to blur boundaries and definitions. My reading of the play follows hers closely at several points, but frames the issues in a somewhat different theoretical register.

3. Colie's chapter on *Antony and Cleopatra*, "The Significance of Style," in *Shakespeare's Living Art*, suggestively links the Roman and Egyptian qualities in the play with an ancient and long-standing debate about the relative virtues of "Attic" and "Asiatic" styles of expository prose, the "Attic" being "a simple, direct, relatively plain style" and the Asiatic "formally complex, ornate, decorated and elaborate" (171), qualities which took on moral as well as aesthetic implications. Colie summarizes the opposition between the Egypt and Rome of the play thus: "Rome is duty, obligation, austerity, politics, warfare, and honor: Rome is public life. Egypt is comfort, pleasure, softness, seduction, sensuousness (if not sensuality also), variety, and sport. . . . Rome is business, Egypt is foison; Rome is warfare, Egypt is love" (177).

An important qualification of this kind of schematizing is offered by Paul Cantor. Cantor argues that what critics have characterized as "Roman" in *Antony and Cleopatra* are qualities exemplified directly only in the Republican Rome of *Coriolanus* and in *Julius Caesar*, and felt in imperial Rome only as memories of a heroic past: "when critics speak about Roman qualities in [*Antony and Cleopatra*], they are talking of what is more absent than present in it, what is perhaps felt as a potentiality but not in fact seen as an actuality" (Cantor 27). Cantor's point is well taken, though we might argue that even in *Coriolanus* and *Julius Caesar* Rome's heroic identity as a state seems always lost or about to be lost. Coriolanus feels that Rome's virile integrity has been sacrified to political accommodation; Brutus and Cassius identify the true glory of Rome with the fraternity of their class and feel its impending loss as Caesar rises to imperial power. "Romanness" is in some sense an absence in these plays, which nonetheless operates as a structural principle within them.

4. Adelman gives specific attention to the rhetorical effects of paradox and hyperbole. Adelman argues, citing Peachum and Puttenham, that paradox and hyperbole enact a quasi-theological appeal to faith by asserting what we know to be impossible (111–13). See also Charney and Spenser.

5. See Cook.

6. "The Egyptian court is an idle, opulent, sensual, Asiatic place, where men are effeminate and women bold. Mardian the eunuch exists to remind us of what can happen to men in such an environment" (Colie 185).

7. I have in mind here Lacan's "pas-tout" from *Encore: Le Séminaire* XX, 1972–73 (Paris: Seuil, 1975).

WORKS CITED

Adelman, Janet. *The Common Liar: An Essay on Antony and Cleopatra.* New Haven: Yale UP, 1973.

Burckhardt, Sigurd. *Shakespearean Meanings.* Princeton: Princeton UP, 1968.

Cantor, Paul. *Shakespeare's Rome: Republic and Empire.* Ithaca: Cornell UP, 1976.

Charney, Maurice. *Discussions of Shakespeare's Roman Plays.* Boston: D. C. Heath and Co., 1964.

Cixous, Hélène. *The Newly Born Woman.* Trans. Betsy Wing. Minneapolis: U of Minnesota P, 1986.

Colie, Rosalie. *Shakespeare's Living Art.* Princeton: Princeton UP, 1974.

Cook, Carol. "Unbodied Figures of Desire." *Theater Journal* 38 (1986): 34–52.

Danby, John. "*Antony and Cleopatra:* A Shakespearean Adjustment." *Poets on Fortune's Hill.* Reprinted in The Signet Classic *Antony and Cleopatra,* ed. Barbara Everett.

Everett, Barbara, ed. The Signet Classic *Antony and Cleopatra.* New York: New American Library, 1964.

Holland, Norman; Homan, Sidney; and Paris, Bernard J. *Shakespeare's Personality.* Berkeley: U of California P, 1989.

Irigaray, Luce. *This Sex Which Is Not One.* Trans. Catherine Porter with Carolyn Burke. Ithaca: Cornell UP, 1985.

Kermode, Frank, ed. *Four Centuries of Shakespearean Criticism*. New York: Avon, 1965.

Lacan, Jacques. *Ecrits*. Trans. Alan Sheridan. New York: W. W. Norton, 1977.

Spenser, Benjamin T. "*Antony and Cleopatra* and the Paradoxical Metaphor." *Shakespeare Quarterly* 9 (1958): 3373-78.

Sprengnether, Madelon. "The Boy Actor and Femininity in *Antony and Cleopatra*." *Shakespeare's Personality*. Ed. Norman Holland et al. Berkeley: U of California P, 1989.

10

WHAT'S LOVE GOT TO DO WITH IT?

Reading the Liberal Humanist Romance in
Antony and Cleopatra

LINDA CHARNES

There's beggary in the love that can be reckoned.
—*ANTONY AND CLEOPATRA*[1]

What's love got to do, got to do with it?
—TINA TURNER, *WHAT'S LOVE GOT TO DO WITH IT*

BEFORE ADDRESSING WHAT love has to do and to do with it in Shakespeare's play, I want to consider what makes a question such as Tina Turner's intelligible in the first place. As a speech act, this song is a critical "intervention": a disruptive response to a narrative that precedes and exceeds it. Exactly what the question challenges is unimportant—for its rhetorical effectiveness depends not on the particular discourse it targets, but rather on our recognition of the strategic use of the word "love" with regard to it. In other words, what matters is not the matter but the form imposed on it "in the name of love."

That we understand instantly what the question does betrays our awareness of the use of the concept of love as an authoritative and sacralizing epistemology. Political rulers act "out of love" for their subjects; patriots "out of love" for their countries; fathers "out of love" for their families; mothers "out of love" for their children; spouses and lovers "out of love" for each other. Perhaps it goes without saying that political leaders have loved subjects, patriots countries, parents children, husbands wives, etc. But what doesn't go without saying are all the other narratives that seek, and find, refuge under such cover. The love story has been one of the most pervasive and effective—yet least deconstructed—of all ideological apparatuses: one of the most effective smoke-screens available in the politics of cultural production. One need think only of the historical popularity of crime stories purveyed as love stories: from the Trojan War—that paradigmatic "linkage" of love and genocide—to Bonnie and Clyde; from the subcultural Sid and Nancy to the hyperreal Ron and Nancy—we see the extent to which the concept of love is used as a "humanizing" factor, a way of appropriating figures whom we have no other *defensible* reason to want to identify with.[2] The popularity (and respectability—Julia Roberts was nominated for an Oscar) of the film *Pretty Woman*—a "Cinderella" story about a prostitute and a ruthless businessman who uses her to try to maneuver a hostile corporate takeover—is only the most recent example.[3] In these narratives, love is regarded as "content" rather than as something that influences our reception of other elements. I propose that we look at love as a genre or, in Bourdieu's terms, a re-structuring structure within other structuring structures: one whose coercive influence is camouflaged by its very obviousness. What we take as the love story aspect of other stories is exactly what enables us to *take* these other stories, period.

I

The coercive function of love stories has been analyzed by Tania Modleski, Janice Radway, Rosalind Coward, and others, who discuss the myths, functions, uses, and profits of "love" as it's been marketed in "women's novels," or popular romance fiction.[4] These important studies map the connections between the fantasies such texts encode and aspects of women's real social experience. In high-canonical critical circles, however, such texts have been (and continue to be) held in contempt for, among other things, their lack of "realism" and their blatantly fantastic representations of certain kinds of erotic and affective relations. It is easy to believe that the phenomenon of subjection, resistance, and displacement into "love" operates largely, if not entirely, in romance literature written for and/or by women. Much less obvious (but for that reason all the more infiltrative) are the ways in which a similar symptomology organizes criticism of male-authored texts of the "high" English canon and, in particular, has helped to consolidate Shakespeare's plays in the history of liberal humanist criticism.

There is little evidence that Shakespeare's *Antony and Cleopatra* was popular in his own day and much evidence that it was not. There were few critical statements about the play for several centuries after its first production in 1606–1607; and as Michael Steppat points out,

> though Chaucer about 1385 in his *Legend of Good Women* had spoken of Cleopatra's "passioun" and her "trouth in love," . . . most Elizabethan discussions focused on what were seen as her moral and political crimes. The Elizabethan writer Richard Reynoldes asserted that a "harlotte" like Cleopatra, who had committed "horrible murthers," [was] [in]capable of dying for love. (1–2)

In general, there doesn't seem to have been much critical interest in Shakespeare's version at all until, as Steppat says, "the early nineteenth century, when the Romantics showed an interest in *Antony* as a play to be read in the study" (1–2).

It is not an accident that the play caught the interest of "the Romantics." For writers such as Coleridge, Hazlitt, and Shelley, who, no matter what their professed social and political concerns, contributed more to the notion of "great individuals" than to anything else, have proleptically read that celebration into Shakespeare's play, finding their own cause in the play's effects. The very aspects of the play that Shakespeare's audience would have found most indecorous (Antony and Cleopatra's apparent indulgence of "self" over public duty, desire over public honor and reputation) are deemed liberatory. And it is not an accident that the intellectual legacy of Romanticism, liberal humanism, has also celebrated this play for its valorizing of Great-Individuals-in-Love.[5]

The increasing historical popularity of the play has been inseparable from a critical revisionism that has transformed it from what it was in Shakespeare's time—a notorious story about politics on every level—to what it is now: a "legendary" love story. And this transformation owes more to the ability of critics to misrecognize what love's got to do with it than with what love actually does in the play. This has been most true of the liberal humanist scholarship on the play, a way of reading that I would argue is always implicitly coded male (regardless of the anatomical sex of its practitioner) because it is a view—possible only from a position of total cultural entitlement—in which gender and class differences are "transcended" in great literature's embrace of a "universal" human nature.

There are, of course, many interpretive differences among liberal humanist critics; and it would be wrong to speak of them as a homogeneous group. However, there does seem to be a shared impulse regarding the concept of love. While much liberal humanist criticism of Shakespeare's play has been subtle and responsive to the social and the political discourses in the text, it tends to assume, in one way or another, explicitly or implicitly, that *in the last instance,* love (shared by autonomous human agents) is made of different stuff. Even certain critics who would not consider themselves liberal humanists commit the liberal humanist fallacy when it comes to love. What Flaubert said about himself vis-à-vis Emma Bovary is largely true of the way many critics have read Shakespeare's text: critics who have been either unwilling or unable to look at the cultural "work" being done by what they perceive, or construct, as the "love story."[6] In its compulsive drive to maintain love in a category all its own, a *deus ex machina* of affective experience, liberal humanist criticism of Shakespeare's play enacts the same interpretive symptomology Janice Radway has called "reading the romance." But it is a kind of masculine romance manqué, in which certain sociosexual anxieties, regarded as trivial in the "feminine" genre of "ladies' romance," are girded with (and ultimately hypostatized by) the status, dignity, and decorum of canonical drama.

This isn't to say that Shakespeare has written a Harlequin Romance or even anticipated it.[7] It is, rather, to talk about the way the play has been appropriated and understood; and in particular, the way it has been critically rewritten as a tale of epic, paradigmatic, and transcendent love. My concern is not to "rescue" the play, or to dismiss such criticism, but rather to look at what is *productive* about it—what it does—in a larger arena of cultural politics. In what follows, I want to put Tina Turner's question to the service of two other questions: how is reading Shakespeare's play like reading a Harlequin Romance? And what does this resemblance have to tell us about a certain symptomology of reading that is pervasive in Western culture?

II

I am aware that questioning the love of Antony and Cleopatra is in certain circles tantamount to slaughtering one of Shakespeare criticism's most sacred cows; but I for one have never found the play's rhetoric of love convincing. However, unlike those who reject their love as being morally offensive or untenable, critics who believe that such an attachment between the two figures couldn't be "real love" (usually supported with claims that he is misogynistic and she is manipulative), I don't have an alternative vision of what else love might mean in this play. The liberal humanist frequently sees it as Shakespeare's meditation on the pleasures of "mature love"; a ripened version of the passion we see in Romeo and Juliet; the "triumph" of Antony and Cleopatra's love over their mutual suspicions and political obstacles, etc. Regarded as transcendent *in the end*, the love of Antony and Cleopatra is reckoned "above" the politics in which the play's other power relations are mired.

Behind this, I believe, is an effort to retrieve or maintain a definition of love that will stand safely apart from politics—in fact, one in which love is defined precisely *as Other than* the political. But rather than regard the love of Antony and Cleopatra in such "bracketed" terms, I want to consider it precisely in terms of all the play's other power relations, and specifically its investigation of all representational strategies. Lest I seem too dismissive of the liberal humanist critic's (LHC) ability to read, I will acknowledge that his celebration of extraordinary-individuals-in-love is not solely a projection; for the play itself deploys such rhetoric. But it does so only to demonstrate that "transcendent love" is a discursive strategy—long recognized as such in courtly love poetry—with very public social and political aims. For as cultural historians, social theorists, feminist psychoanalytic critics, and materialist literary critics have shown us, the forms of affective relations are inseparable from the specific material, political, and social conditions which they constitute and which constitute them. And in early modern England, Love with a capital *L* (like Art with a capital *A*) would not have been thinkable apart from these conditions.[8]

It is (both for the protagonists and for most critics) the "love story" element that renders this historical narrative "mythic." As Hayden White has pointed out about interpretations of history, their comprehensibility tends to depend on their "figuration as a *story of a particular kind*." Drawing analogies between fictional and historical narratives, White claims that

> there are at least two levels of interpretation of every historical work: one in which the historian constitutes a story out of a chronicle of events and another in which, by a more fundamental narrative technique, he progressively identifies the *kind of story* he is telling—comedy, tragedy, romance, epic, or satire, as the case might be. It would be on the second level of interpretation that the mythic consciousness would operate most clearly. (59)

Shakespeare's *Antony and Cleopatra* tropes on each genre White lists above. But unlike Shakespeare's history plays or the other tragedies, its "comprehensibility," finally, seems always to boil down to this more "fundamental narrative"—the love story—a narrative that frequently disguises itself (qua narrative) or is taken as "natural" as opposed to the contrivances of other generic forms. In a recent essay significantly entitled "The Personal Shakespeare: Three Clues," William Kerrigan claims that it is the "worth" of Antony and Cleopatra's love, and their fidelity to it, that "inspires" their legend. Arguing that "as [Shakespeare] allied his dramatic art with the mythological greatness of his lovers, [he] struck against the designs of history" (189), Kerrigan's reading exemplifies precisely the kind of excision I have mentioned above, one in which "love" is universalized, naturalized, and, more important, essentialized in its separation from the discourses that construct other kinds of cultural experience.

But the "love story" in this play produces what Hayden White calls our "mythic consciousness" because it is a narrative that *pretends* to stand apart from and above other narratives; and it is the lovers themselves who alternately purchase, or jettison, the pretense. The legend effect that Kerrigan attributes to the love story "against the designs of history" I want to attribute to the love story *within* the designs of history. To situate a love story within a play that examines the implications of different forms of representation is to posit love "itself" as a crucial stratagem of ideological production. The central issue, then, must be regarded not as what the love story *is* apart from the play's other "designs" but rather as what it *does* in relation to them.

In this play, the politics of desire that motivate imperialist ambition are perfectly congruent with those that operate "privately" in the realm of love; and whatever Antony and Cleopatra feel for each other is composed of the same materials that constitute the rest of their world. "Naturally" Antony loves Cleopatra—she is exotic, mysterious, capricious, charismatic, charming, earthy—the characterological equivalent of the imagined terrain of Egypt, with which she is always synecdochized. "Naturally" Cleopatra loves Antony—he is magnanimous (in the Aristotelian sense), expansive, aggressive, powerful, manly, famous "in the word's report," like the imperial Roman terrain he both extends and is an extension of. "Naturally" they are drawn to each other; they are both so much larger than life. But to think of their love in these terms is to consent to Antony and Cleopatra's self-representations without paying adequate attention to Shakespeare's representations. It is to fall into what Bourdieu calls "the interactionist fallacy," or to assign to them "personally" the qualities that are in fact the metonymic extensions of their paradigmatic source: the "internalized" functions of their respective *habitus* (*Distinction* 169–74 passim). In a play that is simultaneously about legendary Roman expansionism and legendary lovers, it is not surprising that the play records (and produces) a confusion (and fusion) of persons with places. For the shared ideologies that construct Egyptian-ness and Roman-ness reproduce in subjects (as aspects of "self") the structures that structure, and therefore make sense of, their worlds. In this view, there can be no separation between the designs of history and the designs of persons.

Whatever love text these figures weave is repeatedly ruptured by political exigency. This is especially true of Antony, who can justify himself in his own eyes only by mystifying "this wrangling queen, whom every thing becomes" (1.1.49). But even the erotic rhetoric Antony uses is abandoned in those moments when he fears political betrayal, as he demonstrates in 3.13, when he calls Cleopatra a "morsel, cold upon / Dead Caesar's trencher" (116), a "boggler," a "fragment." That Antony can lapse so quickly into the debasing terms his fellow Romans use against Cleopatra (note Enobarbus's reference to her in 2.7.123 as an "Egyptian dish") reveals the extent to which his own construction of her as love object cannot be kept uncontaminated by that of his countrymen— such terms are ever-present in his mind, ready to be mobilized under the appropriate political conditions.

Antony's rhetoric of transcendence is apotropaic—a way of warding off an intolerable awareness of Rome's view of him as "a strumpet's fool" (1.1.13) who has "offended reputation" (3.11.48). In a play in which the political is set up as the "Real," Love becomes Antony's representation of his own "imaginary relationship to his real conditions of existence,"[9] a way of shoring up an identity grown blemished "in the world's report" (2.3.5). Unable to objectify the objectifications of himself produced in Rome, Antony feels "unqualitied with very shame" (3.11.44). Unable to escape his own constitution as a Roman (in the history of Augustus Caesar as Shakespeare's own sources wrote it), his heightened rhetoric of love for Cleopatra is, in Bourdieu's terms, his "attempt to reappropriate an alienated being-for-others" (*Distinction*, 207), to counter the "penetrative shame" that I would claim underlies every aspect of his character in this play. Using "love" to produce "distinction," Antony and Cleopatra themselves posit a transcendent rhetorical realm in which they can underwrite endangered reputations with the symbolic capital that transcendent love always lays claim to.

This is not to say that this is not love. But it can and must be regarded as inextricable from sociopolitical purpose. I have argued elsewhere that *Troilus and Cressida* (another legendary "love story") posits desire as a form of social production, inseparable in form and operation from the rest of the play's machinery of legend. A pervasive program of public desire (Helen and the War) underwrites what I have called myths of private desire.[10] Something similar happens in *Antony and Cleopatra*, insofar as the rhetoric of love is different from how it is practiced. Put more simply, Antony and Cleopatra talk about their love in ways that contradict what they actually *do* with it. In 1.1.14–18, we hear what amounts to a theory about love:

> Cleo.   If it be love indeed, tell me how much.
> Ant.   There's beggary in the love that can be reckon'd.
> Cleo.   I'll set a bourn how far to be belov'd.
> Ant.   Then must thou needs find out new heaven, new earth.

This language gestures toward a love that cannot be "reckon'd," that exceeds the supposed baseness of thinking in quantitative terms. But for these two figures, thinking in *any* terms other than those of an acquisitive expansionism seems to be impossible, as even their "alternative" terms of measurement rely on colonialist images of new territories: finding out a new heaven, a new earth. The "expansiveness" that critics attribute to Antony's love for Cleopatra (in a term that, like "misrecognition," refracts the truth of what it misspeaks) can be understood as a part of the play's lexicon of imperialism. This expansiveness is in fact expansionist. Here is not a love that cannot be reckon'd, but rather a love that requires even *more* territory, more, even, than that Octavius covets. Antony's claim of unwillingness to perform "exact bookkeeping"[11] is itself a kind of social performance, one that generates symbolic capital by observing in the realm of love what Castiglione describes as a "certain sprezzatura," a way of treating artfully acquired and socially useful skills (in this instance, a style of loving) as if they were intrinsic or "natural" (43).

This love story, then, far from providing a refuge from Rome's imperial project, a "distinction" from the world of Octavius Caesar, conceives imaginative space for itself in language that partakes of similar narratives, in similar terms. What has frequently been taken as the "alternative" world of Egypt and Cleopatra turns out to be not so different after all. While on one level the play beckons us with the allure of "difference" and its hold over Antony, on another level it demonstrates again and again that while Egypt and Rome may be the sites of different representational strategies, the stakes of their conflict are finally the same. And these are the ability to lay claim to authoritative space in which the acquired can be *appropriated* (in senses both personal and political) as *property*.

The connections, then, between the "epic" narrative of empire and the "timeless, mythic" narrative of love are imbricated, as Octavius's political defeat of Antony is figured in language similar to Cleopatra's sexual "conquest" of Antony: both are represented as strategic and in military terms. In 4.14, just before Mardian tells him, falsely, of Cleopatra's death, Antony informs Eros,

I made these wars for Egypt, and the queen,
Whose heart I thought I had, for she had mine:
Which whilst it was mine, had annex'd unto't
A million moe, now lost . . . (15–18)

Antony, here convinced that Cleopatra has betrayed him to "pack cards" with Caesar, explicitly reveals the connections between his love and his soldiership, passion and militarism, the conquest of one heart and the annexation of "a million moe." Antony and Cleopatra's mutual having of hearts gives them the ground and impetus for their own imperial project: theirs is literally a consuming passion insofar as the power it produces is the power to consume new territory. When Antony believes that Cleopatra no longer loves him, what he says is, "She has robb'd me of my sword." Falsely informed of her death by Mardian a few lines later, Antony makes it very clear that without Cleopatra, all that is left to do is "unarm, the long day's task is done" (35). If Antony is "No more a soldier" (42), it is because he is now no more a lover. Unlike Troilus, who renounces his role as lover in order to play the soldier, Antony cannot be the one without being the other.

To say this is not to abrogate the sense of love and loss Antony experiences at this moment. But it is to talk about that love as a constituent element of the power relations that inform every aspect of this play. Although the play encourages us to misrecognize Antony's love for Cleopatra as an alternative to the identity and project he bears for Rome, we see that in his role as Cleopatra's Antony, he is put to similar use. Except that now, in and from Egypt, he is misplaced in a representational *habitus* alien to his "original" constitution as "Antony," a constitution which requires the submission of self to the demands of legendary posterity. We can see this imperative at work in Antony's death scene, where he reverts to type, his dying words most concerned with how he will be narratively re-membered. Ever obsessed with "report," Antony narrates his own memorial, calling himself "the greatest prince o'the world," "a Roman valiantly vanquished" (4.15). After bungling his fall on his sword, this rhetoric exemplifies the split between what these figures do and what they say about what they're doing, a disjunction reinforced by Cleopatra, who is less concerned with the time Antony has left than with remaining in a secure position on her monument. Denying Antony's request that she descend to kiss him in his last moments, Cleopatra answers,

I dare not, dear,
Dear my lord, pardon: I dare not,

Lest I be taken: not the imperious show
Of the full-fortun'd Caesar ever shall
Be brooch'd with me, if knife, drugs, serpents have
Edge, sting, or operation. I am safe:
Your wife Octavia, with her modest eyes,
And still conclusion, shall acquire no honour
Demuring upon me: but come, come, Antony—
Help me, my women,—we must draw thee up:
Assist, good friends.

(22–30)

Ever obsessed with how she is staged, Cleopatra is more anxious about not being a "brooch" in Caesar's imperious show than in granting her dying lover's last request. Her foremost thoughts at this moment are on how to keep Caesar and Octavia from "acquiring honour" from her capture; and her references to suicide are prompted here, at least syntactically, not by Antony's impending death but by the prospect of being made Caesar's spectacle. For both Antony and Cleopatra, love—even at this most critical of moments—cannot transcend the particular textual material it operates in.

For many critics, the play affectively "ends" here in 4.15, with the death of Antony and Cleopatra's poetic eulogy to him. Her mythic language about her lover enables the liberal humanist critic to contrive the emotional "sense of an ending" that the play at once invites and refuses. Cleopatra says she will commit suicide, will die "after the high Roman fashion," will seek "the briefest end" (87–90). The problem, however, is that she doesn't, and still has the entire fifth act of the play to get through. We watch her efforts to secure resources, to position herself with regard to Octavius, to manuever her way out of her predicament, all to no avail. Does she at last commit suicide because she cannot imagine life without Antony, or because she cannot imagine the humiliation of watching "some squeaking Cleopatra boy [her] greatness / I'the posture of a whore" (5.2.218–19)? Somehow one suspects that not even her hairdresser knows for sure.

Of course, none of this is meant to indict Cleopatra for not loving "truly" or well enough. Quite the reverse. The play posits two versions of love: love as poetic construct or usable material for fiction, and love as *realpolitik*; love that is "to die for," and love that is to die for if nothing else can be worked out. Which leads us to speculate on why there has been such an abiding effort by liberal humanist critics to recuperate the story for transcendent love. In this play it is *Antony* who kills himself for love when he believes, wrongly, that Cleopatra is dead. And we should remember that it is Cleopatra herself who has had him falsely informed. As an effort to test his love? To make him regret his accusations against her? I suggest that Cleopatra does this because it never occurs to her that Antony might respond to this news by actually killing himself.

So there is a problem here. And I believe it's around how to recuperate Antony's epic masculinity—his "worth" and dignity as a legendary warrior-lover—when in this play he occupies a subject position almost always culturally reserved for women, and in relation to a Cleopatra who occupies a position almost always reserved for men. Here a few words about the rigid formula of the Harlequin Romance would be helpful. In *Loving with a Vengeance*, Tania Modleski explains that

> it is useful to see in each *Harlequin* two basic enigmas: the first, which is more or less explicitly stated (and often constantly repeated), has to do with the puzzling behavior of the hero: why does he constantly mock the heroine? Why is he so often angry at her? The second enigma, usually but not always implicit, concerns how the hero will come to see that the heroine is different from all other women, that she is not, in other words, a "*scheming little adventuress*." (39, my italics)

In the Harlequin Romance, the male lover is mocking and cynical directly in proportion to the feelings of love and attraction he represses for the heroine, who, unlike the reader, is unaware of the hero's "true" feelings.

In Shakespeare's play it is Cleopatra who presents an unreadable, impenetrable surface, the sphinx-like opacity that produces Antony's fascination and resentment. It is Cleopatra who mocks Antony repeatedly for his allegiances and attachments to Fulvia, Caesar, and Rome. And it is Antony who is left to waffle and wonder, Antony who feels the simultaneous humiliation and infatuation that in the *Harlequin* Romance is the designated preserve of the heroine. It is Antony who feels exposed and feminized, "his corrigible neck, his face subdued / To penetrative shame" (4.14.75). In this play it is Antony who is in thrall to love, Antony who leaves battle to follow Cleopatra back to Egypt, Antony who basically quits his job (working for Rome) and abandons everything for his obsession with this love object whom he cannot properly read.

All this breach of gender decorum does not a comfortable liberal humanist make. The tension, then, which the LHC must resolve is that between Antony's love for Cleopatra, who is "different from all other women" because of her extraordinary power, and his inability (shared by the critic) to eliminate lingering fears that she *is*, finally, a "scheming little adventuress." Of course, if by "scheming little adventuress" one means a woman for whom eroticism involves a conscious desire for power and property, then we must regard Cleopatra as just such an adventuress; but one whose "adventurism," then, is *like* Antony's, *like* Caesar's, in short, like that of most of the male lovers in Shakespeare's plays. Cleopatra is, erotically as well as theatrically, one of the boys. For Antony, this is precisely what makes her exciting. For the LHC, however, this thralldom can be tolerated only if the "proper" gender arrangement is finally restored. What makes *Antony and Cleopatra* recuperable as a legendary "love story" (in a way that *Troilus and Cressida* is not) is the fact that Cleopatra does finally "do the right female thing" and commit suicide. And with this final act, she seems to inscribe herself into the time-worn tradition of women who kill themselves "for love," providing the critic with the glue needed to cement his reading of this play.

Like the ways in which Harlequin romances are read, the LHC's reading is neither simplistic nor inconsequential. The Harlequin offers the female reader a way to imaginatively revise her real history, to make it come out "right," to provide a new epistemology for a form of cultural experience that has been humiliating and intolerable. In these texts, the cruelty, standoffishness, cynicism, and contempt of the male lover are proven in the end to be "about" his love for the heroine. His behavior, therefore, has not been a sign of his disregard and disrespect for her or about her social insignificance. On the contrary. The fantasy ensures her centrality. In these narratives, the heroine's humiliation becomes the very sign of her power; and the real female social experience of oppression and marginality is given a new history. This is the "payoff" that the Harlequin story line promises: that in the end "love" will proleptically revise and make emotional sense of all preceding experience, no matter how violent or disjunctive. What drives the reader to new Harlequins, in the repetition compulsion Modleski describes, is the fact that she keeps returning to a real world which belies the textual fantasy.

In the LHC's reconstruction of love in *Antony and Cleopatra*, we see a similar symptomology. Only in this version, whatever was undignified (unerect) about Antony is firmed back up as the story takes its place in the reified canonical ranks of legend. Unwilling fully to confront (or, one imagines, to identify with) this unstable representation of a seriously compromised masculine subject-in-love, the liberal humanist seeks transcendence. Faced with Cleopatra's ability, to paraphrase Cordelia, to love and be politic, the liberal humanist separates the two categories, for fear that the alternative must be an Antony who has been enthralled by a "scheming little adventuress." In a move that proves that the repetition compulsion is alive and well in canon formation, Cleopatra's suicide is read in the tradition of the "legend of good women," and Antony becomes a recuperable epic lover.

While I readily admit that the liberal humanist position I've been outlining here is something of a composite for the sake of argument, it is not inaccurate. Some critics occupy it fully and vociferously, others only obliquely and perhaps even unwittingly. Liberal humanism has, after all, taken a certain amount of critical fire over the last decade; and it is clear that such criticism has had to cede (or at least share) its position of academic centrality to more politicized and theorized kinds of approaches.[12] But the humanist way of reading has been the academy's most successful export into the culture at large, as Alan Bloom, William Bennett, and Lynne Cheney (to name only the most visible proponents) have demonstrated, a way to appeal to the "structures of feeling" that prompt reluctant taxpayers to continue to subsidize higher education in the liberal arts. In the current climate of "backlash" against multiculturalism, race politics, canon expansion, feminisms, gay and lesbian studies, and other foregroundings of "the political" in academic discourse, liberal humanism is once again set to position itself as the (now martyred) defender of the Faith (whether in Great Books, Genius Authors, Western Reason, or the Sovereign Individual). Outside academic circles, humanism reigns, among educated middle-class liberals and political conservatives alike, as the voice of centrist interpretive reason, setting the ideological agenda for "enlightened" individuals. In American culture, liberal humanism—in virtually every sphere of ideological production—is far more pervasive than poststructuralism.

What is at stake in all this is how both the consumers and the producers of cultural texts re-member histories, their own and those of others. We have seen with appalling clarity just how subject we still are to the uses of transcendent narratives ("just wars," prosecuted in the name of Freedom, Liberty, Democracy, Faith, the New World Order) when those in power live in terror of "the wimp factor." As Foucault has taught us, we must be very careful about how we talk about cause and effect with regard to power relations; and I certainly do not mean to link liberal humanism, or the defenders of the high canon, directly with the obscene events that have gutted the Persian Gulf. Surely there are many liberal humanists (and high-canonists) who were horrified by the alacrity and relish with which we pursued Operation Desert Storm. What profoundly disturbs me, however, is that try as I might, I cannot completely dissever what gets prosecuted in literary and cultural production in the name of

Love from what gets prosecuted in the New World Theatre in the name of Freedom and Democracy.[13] The degree of misrecognition needed to subsidize our investment in any notion of transcendent anything is matched only by the degree of violence that erupts when our real conditions of existence intrude on the fantasy.

In the rarefied ranks of Shakespeare scholarship, that most "legitimate" canonical field, we can see that the specious separation of love and politics that I've been discussing is not unlike that of high and low culture. Anyone who has seen the Taylor/Burton film version of the Antony and Cleopatra story will recall how easily it lent itself to a mass cultural treatment. And in the recent film *L.A. Story,* not only does Steve Martin's character (a weatherman with a Ph.D. in "Arts and Humanities") quote Shakespeare, but there is a parody of the graveyard scene in *Hamlet* (with Rick Moranis of *Honey I Shrunk the Kids* fame) playing the gravedigger. Martin knows that he is in love with his romantic object (the British Victoria Tennant) when she recognizes the allusion and recites the proper lines from the play. Unlike the Valley Girl shop clerk he is having casual sex with, this is someone he can take to meet Mother: this girl knows her Shakespeare. All this at the same time that Glenn Close and Mel Gibson are playing the "real thing" in Zeffirelli's version of *Hamlet* (suitably revised, through the elimination of Fortinbras and references to potential war, to hail U.S. moviegoers as Oedipalized Individuals rather than as social and political subjects).[14]

To what do we owe this upsurge in Shakespeare's mass-cultural visibility? I wish to suggest that it is due to Shakespeare's position as iconic guarantor of liberal humanism, at a time when as a society we desperately need to find ways to justify our moral authority as we throw our weight around. Like so many other products in American consumer culture, Shakespeare is used to reinforce our sense of "distinction": like the best cars, the best furnishings, or the best wine—Shakespeare: the best that's been thought, said, and felt.[15]

Shakespeare and Antony have both been *res-*erected by the liberal humanist fallacy; and in this consolidation that occurs behind "a kinder, gentler" patriarchalism, I believe we can read the same symptomology that produces *all* desire for legends. For a legend is the interpretive overkill designed to ensure the final stability of the Text—the concrete that bricks signifier to signified and arrests any slippage between effects and what are taken to be their acceptable causes. Legends are things that "stand the test of time." This cliché is true, but not in the way intended by those who still utter it. For transcendence is not about getting it up, but rather about *keeping* it up—freezing history in an essentializing of being that denies epistemological (and therefore historical) uncertainty and its threat of authoritative impotence. In the reification of meaning, that textual hardening that is always the aim of legend, Transcendent Love can be regarded as a monumental erection of the critical Phallus against any text that subversively insists on asking, What's love got to do, got to do with it?

NOTES

This essay first appeared in *Textual Practice* 6, No. 1 (Spring 1992), and I thank Terence Hawkes and Routledge for permission to reproduce it, in somewhat revised form, here. A short section of it also appears in chapter 3 ("Spies and Whispers: Exceeding Reputation in *Antony and Cleopatra*") of *Notorious Identity: Materializing the Subject in Shakespeare* (Cambridge, Mass., and London: Harvard University Press).

1. All references are to the Arden edition, M. R. Ridley, ed.

2. I refer here to the 1967 Warner Brothers film *Bonnie and Clyde* and to the 1986 Zenith Production of *Sid and Nancy,* the story of "Sid Vicious" and his American girlfriend Nancy Spungen, whom he murdered in a drug-induced rage. As for Ron and Nancy, their narrative is still undergoing revisions, the latest offering being Kitty Kelley's "unauthorized" biography of Nancy Reagan (Simon and Schuster, 1991).

3. Roberts did not win for Best Actress. But Whoopi Goldberg won Best Supporting Actress for her role in *Ghost*—another hugely successful American film in which love is *literally* transcendent.

4. The title of this essay is meant to recall Radway's *Reading the Romance.* See also Modleski, *Loving with a Vengeance;* Coward, *Female Desires;* and Snitow, "Mass Market Romance."

5. One must take into account Dryden's 1678 version, *All for Love,* in which political issues recede under the foregrounding of a more domesticated vision of the problems of love, jealousy, and fidelity. But despite its title, Dryden's treatment of love doesn't have the strongly individualist romance ethos that I would claim isn't fully developed or ideologically operative until the late eighteenth century.

6. Anyone who is at all familiar with Shakespeare criticism will recall how pervasive this way of reading the play has been and continues to be. My concern here is not to prove that this critical tendency exists by singling out particular critics and their readings of Shakespeare, but rather to examine the cultural "work" performed by the critically misrecognized text: to analyze how a certain attitude toward and construction of love (and Shakespeare) within liberal humanist criticism is congruent with (and even indirectly authorizes) the use of other, more overtly dangerous narratives of transcendence in mass culture and politics.

7. Modleski discusses the worldwide success of Harlequin Enterprises, LTD, and their chain of low-budget formulaic romance novels. According to the publishers,

> Harlequins are well-plotted, strong romances with a happy ending. They are told from the heroine's point of view and in the third person. There may be elements of mystery or adventure but these must be subordinate to the romance. The books are contemporary and settings can be anywhere in the world as long as they are authentic. (35-36)

Harlequin Romance is the generic name of the publisher's series; but because of its sales success it has also come to be a descriptive term for any kind of novel that corresponds to this particular formula. As Snitow points out in "Mass Market Romance,"

> Harlequin is 50 percent owned by the conglomerate controlling the Toronto Star. If you add to the Harlequin sales figures (variously reported from between 60 million to 109 million for 1978) the figures for similar novels by Barbara Cartland and those contemporary romances published by Popular Library, Fawcett, Ballantine, Avon, Pinnacle, Dell, Jove, Bantam, Pocket Books, and Warner, it is clear that hundreds of thousands of women are reading books of the Harlequin type. (262, note 1)

8. These are just a few of the many works that inform this claim: Elias, *The Civilizing Process;* Underdown, *Revel, Riot and Rebellion;* Adelman, *The Common Liar;* Stone, *The Family, Sex and Marriage in England, 1500–1800;* Michel Foucault, *The History of Sexuality;* Bourdieu, *Outline of a Theory of Practice;* Certeau, *The Practice of Everyday Life;* Rose, *Sexuality in the Field of Vision;* Sprengnether, "The Boy Actor and Femininity in *Antony and Cleopatra*"; Belsey, *Subject of Tragedy;* Dollimore, *Radical Tragedy;* Stallybrass and White, *The Politics and Poetics of Transgression.*

9. This phrase comes from Althusser's famous definition of ideology in "Ideology and Ideological State Apparatuses," in *Lenin and Philosophy.*

10. See Charnes, " 'So Unsecret to Ourselves': Notorious Identity and the Material Subject in *Troilus and Cressida,*" in *Notorious Identity.*

11. Aristotle defines this unwillingness as characteristic of the "magnificent man," in *Nichomachean Ethics* 90.

12. Although for some liberal humanist critics, not without a fight. I am thinking here of Levin, quixotic defender of Shakespeare and the values of humanist scholarship. See "Bashing the Bourgeois Subject" 76–86 (and Belsey's reply, 87–90) and "The Poetics and Politics of Bardicide" 491–504. Since this essay first appeared in *Textual Practice* 6, No. 1 (Spring 1992), Levin has published a rebuttal to my argument, and I, a reply. See Levin, "On Defending Shakespeare," and Charnes, "Near Misses of the Non-transcendent Kind."

13. Even taking into account Saddam Hussein's brutal treatment of the Kurds in 1988, one can only wonder how much of the ferocity of his latest crushing of rebellion is due to the humiliation Saddam and his army experienced at the hands of the U.S. and allied forces. After devastating Saddam's forces, we could not resist reveling in our

military, technological, and moral superiority. Wielding his usual Janus-faced rhetoric in response to the Kurdish refugee disaster, President Bush at once asserted that the New World Order is "a responsibility imposed by our successes," and "reaffirmed" the U.S. "policy" (such as it is after Chile, Nicaragua, Iran, El Salvador) of "non-interference" in the civil affairs of a nation-state. In a rhetorical move that has much in common with the strategies of liberal humanism, Bush first defined the tenets of the New World Order in universalist terms: "Peaceful settlements of disputes, solidarity against aggression, reduced and controlled arsenals, and just treatment of all peoples," before asserting that "the new world order [is] based on *American* ideals" (*New York Times*, April 14, 1991; my italics).

14. In both of these films the icon (and iconicity) of British high culture is adjusted to American popular culture and the cult of the individual. *L.A. Story* takes the Hamlet motif (well-read young man, too attached to mother and alienated by the rottenness of the state of Los Angeles) and transforms it into the ultimate Steve Martin comic fantasy: the *Lonely Guy/Jerk* finds love and hipness in L.A. And Zeffirelli's *Hamlet*, in terms of casting as well as cinematography, becomes an intimate story of unbalanced individuals: a *Fatal Attraction* leads to a *Mad Max*, who in turn becomes a *Lethal Weapon*. In both cases, we can see in the realm of popular "entertainment" the same relationship adumbrated between Bush's New World Order and particularly *American* ideals.

15. For an important discussion of the relationship between Shakespeare and American culture, see also Bristol.

WORKS CITED

Adelman, Janet. *The Common Liar: An Essay on Antony and Cleopatra.* New Haven and London: Yale UP, 1973.

Althusser, Louis. *Lenin and Philosophy and Other Essays.* London: New Left Books, 1971.

Aristotle. *Nichomachean Ethics.* Trans. Martin Ostwald. Indianapolis: The Liberal Arts Press, 1962.

Belsey, Catherine. "Reply to Richard Levin." *Textual Practice* 3, No. 1 (Spring 1989): 87–90.

———. *The Subject of Tragedy.* London and New York: Methuen, 1988.

Bourdieu, Pierre. *Distinction: A Social Critique of the Judgement of Taste.* London: Routledge and Kegan Paul, 1984.

———. *Outline of a Theory of Practice.* Cambridge: Cambridge UP, 1977.

Bristol, Michael. *Shakespeare's America, America's Shakespeare: Literature, Institution, Ideology in the United States.* London and New York: Routledge and Kegan Paul, 1990.

Castiglione, Baldasar. *The Book of the Courtier.* Trans. Charles Singleton. New York: Anchor Books, 1959.

Certeau, Michel de. *The Practice of Everyday Life.* Berkeley: U of California P, 1984.

Charnes, Linda. "Near Misses of the Non-transcendent Kind: Reply to Richard Levin." *Textual Practice* 7, No. 1 (Spring 1993): 56–59.

———. *Notorious Identity: Materializing the Subject in Shakespeare.* Cambridge, Mass.: Harvard UP, 1993.

Coward, Rosalind. *Female Desires: How They Are Sought, Bought, and Packaged.* New York: Grove Press, 1985.

Dollimore, Jonathan. *Radical Tragedy.* Chicago: U of Chicago P, 1984.

Elias, Norbert. *The Civilizing Process,* Vol. I: *The History of Manners.* New York: Pantheon, 1978.

Foucault, Michel. *The History of Sexuality, I: An Introduction.* New York: Pantheon, 1978.

Kerrigan, William. "The Personal Shakespeare: Three Clues." *Shakespeare's Personality.* Ed. N. Holland, S. Homan, and B. Paris. Berkeley: U of California P, 1989. 175–90.

Levin, Richard. "Bashing the Bourgeois Subject." *Textual Practice* 3, No. 1 (Spring 1989): 76–86.

———. "On Defending Shakespeare, 'Liberal Humanism,' Transcendent Love, and Other 'Sacred Cows' and Lost Causes." *Textual Practice* 7, No. 1 (Spring 1993): 50–55.

———. "The Poetics and Politics of Bardicide." *PMLA* 105, No. 3 (May 1990): 491–504.

Modleski, Tania. *Loving with a Vengeance: Mass-Produced Fantasies for Women.* London and New York: Methuen, 1984.

Radway, Janice. *Reading the Romance: Women, Patriarchy, and Popular Culture.* Chapel Hill: U of North Carolina P, 1984.

Rose, Jacqueline. *Sexuality in the Field of Vision.* London: Verso, 1986.

Shakespeare, William. *Antony and Cleopatra.* Arden ed. Ed. M. R. Ridley. London and New York: Methuen, 1965.

Snitow, Ann Barr. "Mass Market Romance: Pornography for Women Is Different." *Powers of Desire: The Politics of Sexuality.* Ed. Ann Snitow, Christine Stansell, and Sharon Thompson. New York: Monthly Review Press, 1983. 245–63.

Sprengnether, Madelon. "The Boy Actor and Femininity in *Antony and Cleopatra.*" *Shakespeare's Personality.* Ed. Norman N. Holland, Sidney Homan, and Bernard J. Paris. Berkeley: U of California P, 1989. 191–205.

Stallybrass, Peter, and Allon White. *The Politics and Poetics of Transgression.* Ithaca, N.Y.: Cornell UP, 1986.

Steppat, Michael. *The Critical Reception of Shakespeare's "Antony and Cleopatra" from 1607 to 1905*. Amsterdam: Verlag B. R. Grüner, 1980.

Stone, Lawrence. *The Family, Sex and Marriage in England, 1500–1800*. New York: Harper Colophon, 1979.

Underdown, David. *Revel, Riot and Rebellion: Popular Politics and Culture in England, 1603–1660*. Oxford: Oxford UP, 1987.

White, Hayden. *Tropics of Discourse: Essays in Cultural Criticism*. Baltimore: Johns Hopkins UP, 1978.

11

SHAKESPEARE IN MY TIME AND PLACE

SHIRLEY NELSON GARNER

> There's hell, there's darkness, there is the sulphurous pit,
> burning, scalding, stench, consumption.
> —*Lear* 4.6.128-29[1]

IN THE SEMINAR I teach on Shakespearean tragedy and gender, my students and I struggle to understand the linkage between the tragic heroes and their misogyny. It is as though Shakespeare puts them in situations in which they experience some form of madness so they can express their deepest hate and fear of women:

> Behold yond simp'ring dame,
> Whose face between her forks presages snow,
> That minces virtue and does shake the head
> To hear of pleasure's name.
> The fitchew, nor the soilèd horse, goes to't
> With a more riotous appetite.
> (*Lear* 4.6.118-23)

Wise men know well enough what monsters you make of them. . . . I have heard of your paintings, well enough. God hath given you one face, and you make yourselves another. You jig and amble, and you lisp; you nickname God's creatures and make your wantonness your ignorance. (*Hamlet* 3.1.139-47)

Where else in our traditionally canonized literature do we find lines like these? Unless we turn to *The Winter's Tale* and Leontes as he angrily denounces Hermione and women generally when he fantasizes that his wife is guilty of adultery (1.2.185-207) or Posthumus's shocking speech on the "woman's part" in *Cymbeline* (2.5.1-35).

How is it that we didn't notice or hear these lines earlier? Or if we did, why did we never speak about them? (And the "we" here is faculty members, graduate and undergraduate students, dramaturges, playgoers—everyone.) I remember reading Maynard Mack's article "The Jacobean Shakespeare: Some Observations on the Construction of the Tragedies" and his discussion of the coincidence of the hero's insight and his madness (38–40). Thinking about the union of wisdom and madness that is commonly found in the fool, I was struck by their disjunction in Shakespeare's tragic heroes, their terror and rage as they meditated on women. Why did Mack fail to see this? Surely he didn't think Hamlet's misogyny was part of his wisdom. Or did he?

But once I notice the tragic hero's misogyny, I am brought to contemplate my history as a woman student, teacher, and scholar. The tragedies engage my imagination more than the comedies or romances, but should they? Or is it a perverse taste that inevitably turns me against myself?

I tend to see Shakespeare's tragedies from the point of view of the women characters. I am alert to the notions of masculine and feminine and to the frequent suggestions in Shakespeare's plays that these categories are socially constructed, and the more fragile and vulnerable for that.

I think of a stunning production of *Richard III* I saw performed at the Guthrie Theatre, under the direction of Garland Wright. When I went a second time to participate in a discussion after the performance, I noticed that the audience was rapt. My mother, then in her mid-eighties, who often fell asleep at the Guthrie, was wide awake, attentive. My role as a "humanities scholar" was really to fill in, I suspect, until the actors shed their costumes and make-up and sauntered out onto the stage one by one in the clothes of ordinary life to take part in the discussion.

So I decided to risk something and talk mainly about the women. Margaret, for instance, was a wonderful shock. Vaguely witchlike and mad, she was a powerful actress, with an incredibly resonant voice. Her curse hovered over the action, and every character who met an untoward fate accepted it resignedly as Margaret's wish enacted on her or him. What intrigued me was that Margaret was an anachronism. She wasn't alive at the time *Richard III* took place. I told the audience that I thought Richard was mainly responsible for the evil in the play, though the other characters were complicit, that this was the ultimate end of what began in *Richard II*, the grand crescendo of moral collapse. Yet, I asked, why did Margaret and her curse hover over this world? Did Shakespeare need a witch, a female principle, whenever he presented evil on a colossal scale? Does this play presage *Macbeth* and its witches?

I had only ten minutes and could make only two points. My other one was that as a reader of Shakespeare I had always found *Richard III* hard. I could never understand why Anne and Elizabeth go along or seem to go along with Richard. I had seen only that though the women were players in a power game with high stakes, they were finally oppressed and dependent on men as the source of their power. What the production made clear to me was something psychologically plausible in all this. Byron Jennings, as Richard, was an incredibly attractive figure, physically and intellectually. Even ill-shaped, he was amazingly beautiful. His jet black hair, striped with a few snow-white strands extending from his widow's peak, swept just past his shoulders, falling in washboard waves as though it had just been unbraided, and gave him a wonderfully distinctive flair. I found myself looking at his hair, imagining running my fingers through it, forgetting about his humped back and his thickened crippled leg. I confessed this, wondering if the audience would be appalled that this was how a "humanities scholar" responded. I understood how his extravagant rhetoric drew Anne to him, how its very outrageousness promised that he would make good in the political world, where in this play *all* power is located. Later the actress who played Anne responded to my remarks describing how as she rehearsed and finally came to feel her role, she got in touch with the link between mourning and the erotic, Anne's dependency in the face of her father-in-law's and husband's deaths and her consequent vulnerability to Richard's attractions.

Elizabeth taught me something else. Richard's arguments that she should help him persuade her daughter to marry him are surely as audacious as Shakespeare ever framed. As she counters him at every turn with common sense, wisdom, her sense of moral outrage—how dare he presume to woo her daughter, much less try to enlist her help—he responds with the most absurd insistence. When he finally tells her that by placing new sons in young Elizabeth's womb, he will make up for the loss of Elizabeth's sons, make her a mother again, she looks at him stunned, *as though she is trapped by someone who is mad*.

I asked the audience to recall whether they had ever been in a conversation in which they had wisdom and common sense on their side while the other person persisted in maintaining a position that everyone would agree was untenable. Could they remember having to acknowledge that there were certain people with whom there was just no communicating? I felt easy assent coming from all around. A woman in the back of the theater, looking at me and nodding, began pointing to a man sitting next to her; I took him to be her husband and interrupted myself: "I see a woman in the audience pointing at her husband." Everyone laughed. And then women in the audience began to ask questions and comment. One wondered about the dependence of women on men in the play: Could the women have survived without allying themselves with whatever men were in power? Were they concerned about preserving their own histories?

As the actors joined us, I noticed that the men came to one side of the stage, the women to the other. Someone in the audience raised the question of Richard's conscience: Where does it come from? He implied a conscience from Richard's nightmares, in which all the people he has killed or is responsible for killing pass before him. I don't see this as a manifestation of conscience, but rather as nightmares come to haunt him. Yet the dramaturge and one of the actors explained this moment: In production, they saw Richard change after his mother denounced him. She had never loved him, and even after he became king she didn't love him. They believed that he realized that what he really wanted was to have her love rather than to become king. Once he knew he would never get it, he changed and began to see how he had gone after the wrong things. I thought about Macbeth and remembered what for me are his most moving lines:

> My way of life
> Is fall'n into the sear, the yellow leaf,
> And that which should accompany old age,
> As honor, love, obedience, troops of friends,
> I must not look to have; but, in their stead,
> Curses not loud but deep, mouth-honor, breath,
> Which the poor heart would fain deny, and dare not.
>
> (5.3.22–28)

But I was uncomfortable. We had somehow moved into a conversation that was all too familiar in its turn to blaming-the-mother. I didn't quite know how to take this up since I didn't want to arouse a feminist debate—somehow it didn't feel like the right context for it. The actor and dramaturge were actually affirming what I suggested only as a possibility, that Shakespeare may link rampant evil to women or a female principle. But the actress who played Richard's mother had come out on stage and had no trouble responding. With a slight edge in her voice, not enough to break the surface of politeness, she insisted that it would be a mistake to blame Richard's mother for his twisted personality, that surely one could not impute it to a simple cause. The men quickly retreated, saying, "No, no, of course not, we didn't mean to imply . . . " The manager of public relations, who conducted the panel, thanked me when it was over and told me that none of the other visiting scholars had raised issues pertaining to women, that she was pleased that so many women in the audience participated, that my response to the play seemed particularly to invite them into the conversation. But how have I come to this place?

I come from Texas, and though people in the South have an affinity for the Elizabethans and you will often meet Shakespeare buffs among them, I came to Shakespeare slowly. I remember studying *Hamlet* in high school, but I remember only the fact of it, nothing of the content. My college and graduate education took me through two phases of Shakespeare studies. The first was histrionic and appreciative; the second was based on the history of literature and ideas. The underpinning of the first was a knowledge of theater; of the second, a vast knowledge of Renaissance thought and literary history. Though the New Criticism, which focused on close reading and attention to detail, was becoming the generally accepted mode of English study as I began undergraduate school and had more or less edged out other critical practices by the time I reached graduate school, neither of my teachers of Shakespeare worked in that mode. Both teachers offered formidable examples, which, I think it is safe to say, none of their students would be able to follow.

When I went to the University of Texas in 1953, I, like many of the students I teach at the University of Minnesota, was starved for culture. Though I grew up among smart, lively people, almost none of my friends' parents read or had many books in their homes. My mother, an educated woman and an avid reader, worked at several jobs to support us while I was growing up, so she had time only for the newspaper. Only one family I knew had real paintings in their house, and I had never attended a symphony or an opera. I majored in something called "Plan II," a humanities program that enrolled only a hundred students each year. We had special classes with the best teachers and were encouraged to get a broad liberal arts background. Though Shakespeare was not a requirement, I took it anyway.

My first professor, I'm convinced, should have been an actor. Tom Cranfill, at the University of Texas, assumed that if he read Shakespeare's plays aloud, more or less acting them, we would *get* them. By osmosis. I first experienced Shakespeare as something to watch, mainly as my professor's performance. It was rumored that Dr. Cranfill (we were expected to call our professors "Dr.") was independently wealthy, and his manner confirmed the rumor. At a time when professors rarely entertained their students, at least at the University of Texas, he always invited his students to his home (which *did* have real paint-

ings) once during the semester. Evidently feeling no obligation to follow anyone's rules about teaching, he did just what he wanted: he read to us aloud every
day. Like many teachers of Shakespeare, he was a wonderfully dramatic reader;
he would even have been a great Lady Macbeth. But I remember nothing of
the Shakespeare I heard from him. I imagine that I was doing well to get the
plot. We were never encouraged to see a Shakespearean film or play. I came out
of the class feeling that Dr. Cranfill was a talented, friendly person and devoted to Shakespeare, but I had no idea what Shakespeare was about or why
Dr. Cranfill liked him. I think I was supposed to intuit that *this* was Culture;
that I was in the presence of greatness; that what was before me was too profound to need explanation.

I avoided Shakespeare at Stanford graduate school as long as I could. Virgil
Whitaker, a formidable presence who was generally reputed to be unpleasant
and difficult, taught the course; and though some graduate students got on
with him, none recommended his class. Myths of a retired Shakespearean
grande dame were part of the department history, handed down to us mainly
at cocktail parties. At Minnesota I still hear of Allen Tate, Robert Penn Warren,
Samuel Holt Monk, Joseph Warren Beach—many ghosts linger to haunt us. At
Stanford there was only Margery Bailey. Evidently the only woman faculty
member in the Stanford English Department's collective memory, either she
had so traumatized the faculty that they had been dead set against hiring
another woman after she retired, or she was cantankerous enough to justify a
disinclination already deeply ingrained. But "Marge" Bailey, as she was called,
was said to have been a beautiful reader, just like Tom Cranfill.

She apparently delighted in embarrassing Virgil Whitaker. Once when he
tried to join in a conversation with her and others at a cocktail party and asked
innocently what they were talking about, legend had it that she hissed, "Sex,
Virgil, sex!" A socially reticent bachelor, he never forgave her. Herbert Merritt,
the Anglo-Saxon scholar, recalled with a mischievous laugh trying to ingratiate
himself with Miss Bailey (no one ever referred to her as "Professor") when he
was new on the faculty. At a professional meeting, when she had happily de-
molished the author of a paper, Merritt whispered to her, "Miss Bailey, you
really gave him his comeuppance!" Looking down on this small, merry man
who had a slight overbite, she silenced him in a moment: "That's enough out
of you, rat tooth!"

When I heard that Madeleine Doran was coming to Stanford as a visiting
professor, I jumped at the chance to take her seminar. I had been impressed by
Endeavors of Art: A Study of Form in Elizabethan Drama, her best-known book,

and I imagined that studying Shakespeare with her would be better than taking it from Whitaker. Virgil Whitaker, who was on leave the year she visited, had been her dissertation director, and she gave the appearance of having mastered his formidable Latin background as well as bringing to bear on Shakespeare her own study of comparative drama and iconography. Steeped in intellectual and literary history, she suggested that the way you came to understand Shakespeare was to begin from outside. But it was never clear how you came to locate outside, and I supposed that she read everything in the original—Latin, Italian, French, German. This was not possible for any of us, even the most well educated and studious among us.

But the class turned out to be the bad experience I had hoped to avoid. Miss Doran (as we called her) held the seminar at her house, and one afternoon a week we arrived to find Miss Doran, tea, and home-baked cookies waiting. Miss Doran's mother, who lived with her but whom we never saw, evidently made the cookies. None of us wanted to arrive much before the class began. An oppressive silence was always filled with awkward conversation about the tea or the cookies or the weather until one of our number who was a former Rhodes scholar arrived. When he entered, Miss Doran brightened perceptibly and began to talk animatedly about the people they knew in common at Oxford. They reminisced until class began while the rest of us sat silent, at first feeling left out, but later only amused and bored. At each meeting of the seminar, they seemed to take up the conversation wherever it had left off, as though they had been speaking only minutes before and had been interrupted. This ritual always prefaced our discussions of *King Lear*. We studied only this one play, and lines that now command my attention were passed over. "There's hell, there's darkness, there is the sulphurous pit, burning, scalding, stench, consumption" (4.6.128–29), for example, went unnoticed. We were *assigned* seminar topics that had already been adequately and even too much published upon in the scholarly world. My topic was the fool. Only now, after years of experience, can I imagine saying something new on this subject, though I have no inclination to. All of us made "B's," except the Rhodes scholar, who made an "A."

So thoroughly mediated through my teachers' tastes, particular talents, and prodigious learning were these encounters with Shakespeare that, though it now amazes me to think it, nothing in the plays touched me. It is as though I never read them.

Though I couldn't have articulated it at the time, I felt myself to be an outsider in graduate school. I was one of a relatively few women in the English Department. We were so sufficiently marginalized that only one other in my beginning class completed her Ph.D., and she left the profession after just a short time in it. There were no women professors; I remember only one in the entire university, in psychology. As a Texan and a graduate of the University of Texas, I was an anomaly. I was not prepared for the academic snobbery of Stanford, and I felt it acutely at times. I was only later to recognize that the Stanford English Department's elitism rested on its own insecurity. Its eagerness to hire scholars from Oxford, Cambridge, or Harvard rather than, say, Berkeley was awakened more often by the source of their degrees than by their intelligence or achievements.

I chose for my dissertation another outsider, George Gascoigne. Because he stood on the edge of the sixteenth-century English court and had financial difficulties, his vision was different, and it interested me. Though I didn't recognize my kinship with him at the time, I'm sure it was responsible for drawing me to him. Literarily, my interest in his work waned fairly quickly because it could not sustain the kind of close reading that I had been taught to value. But because there wasn't a great deal written about him, I did considerable primary research and immersed myself in Elizabethan language, all of which has served me well. It would never have occurred to me to write on Shakespeare. Nothing in my training would have led me to be engaged with his work or confident enough to undertake this central figure.

So when I left graduate school and went to Minnesota, I was ill prepared to teach Shakespeare, though it was a requirement for English majors and a course I was expected to teach. In fact, one of the attractions of Minnesota was that I would have considerable freedom to teach courses in the Renaissance, to develop in my specialty. It was typical of most universities at that time, as it is still, that senior professors more or less owned the Shakespeare courses and that a beginner had no hope of teaching them.

By happy accident, I discovered Shakespeare for myself before I began to teach him. A colleague, Toni A. H. McNaron, asked me to respond to a paper on *Othello* to be presented at the annual meeting of the Midwest Modern Language Association that fall. Though I was flattered by the invitation, I was also anxious because I had little experience in attending scholarly conferences and none in responding to or presenting papers. I was puzzled when my colleague remarked that she especially wanted a woman to respond to the paper, but I didn't ask why. I had planned to proceed in typically thorough Stanford fashion: I would collect bibliography on *Othello*, read all of the criticism I could, read the play (I don't think I'd ever done so), read the paper to be presented,

and then write my response. But as the quarter wore on and I struggled to prepare three new courses and find my way in a strange city and new university,
it was clear I would have very little time to prepare for the MMLA. Frantically,
I revised my plans. I decided to read *Othello*, read the paper, prepare my response, and then review whatever criticism I could.

The only time I had for this work was at night, in bed, after I had finished
my daily preparations for teaching. Reading *Othello* in this unaccustomed
space, I read it differently—less as a scholar than as an ordinary reader. I
imposed on *Othello* less of my learning or my sense of the ways one *ought* to
read a literary text and read it as I might a novel or a mystery. Reading in this
posture, I was startled when I came to Desdemona's line "This Lodovico is a
proper man" (4.3.38), spoken as she is undressing to go to bed with Othello.
I began to meditate on her character, to try to understand the psychology
behind what I recognized as desire. Then I read through her character rather
than through Othello's, speculating about her place in Venice and in Brabantio's
household and what it meant for her to fall in love with a Moor in a racist society. This path took me to other issues in the play: the reasons Shakespeare
had chosen a black tragic hero; the significance of the homoeroticism among
Othello, Iago, and Cassio; and Shakespeare's possible motives for denying
Othello the fullness of tragic subjectivity that he allows Hamlet, Lear, or Macbeth.

When I read the paper I was to critique and began to read literary critics on
the play, I was shocked. Reasoning that Desdemona showed signs of sexual
experience that she could have come by only through a sexually experienced
man, the writer of the paper argued that Desdemona *did* in fact have an affair
with Cassio, that she more or less *was* "the cunning whore of Venice." On the
contrary, the major critics of *Othello* idealized Desdemona, seeing her as near
to divine, if not actually so. My explorations led me to write a piece of feminist
criticism, though I wouldn't have called myself a feminist or understood feminist literary criticism as a possibility.

What interests me most in all this is that for the first time I read from the
perspective of a woman character or the feminine when the text didn't invite
it. I recognized my own place as an outsider through Desdemona, who as a
woman is excluded from the world of male camaraderie so prominent in the
play as well as from the movement toward tragic subjectivity, which is finally
denied. I trace my engagement with Shakespearean tragedy, now more than
twenty years long, from this moment—an unexpected jarring into an awareness that blurred personal and professional boundaries. This encounter became
the source of "Shakespeare's Desdemona," my first published essay. Though I

did not know it consciously, what I wrote was informed by the women's movement, my own psychotherapy, and my experiences as a southern woman. Shakespeare was large enough to allow me to find myself in him, even if only in bits and pieces.

When I teach Shakespeare, I hope to create moments that will allow my students to enter the plays in the way this chance experience permitted me. For many, such a moment is born, as it was for me, when they read through gender.[2] And only as my students come to feel that they owe Shakespeare no allegiance, no unearned respect, do I find them able to engage with his work in a meaningful way. I want them to see that he does not speak for or to every man or woman; that his perspective is peculiar to his time and place; that his vision reflects his particular interests as a playwright, his experiences as a man and an artist. At the same time, Shakespeare isn't what one of my colleagues considers him, "just another writer." My students' responses often remind me of his power at moments when I am struggling with my own ambivalence.

I teach several courses in Shakespeare at the University of Minnesota: an introduction for beginning students; Shakespeare's early and late plays, both designed for upper-division students to meet the Shakespeare requirement for English majors; and a graduate seminar, the topic of which varies from year to year. The several undergraduate courses attract many who are not majoring in English. Seniors headed for careers in business, engineering, nursing, and law enroll in my large introductory lecture course as though they're grasping for their last chance at "Culture" (and surely Shakespeare is it, they believe). The graduate seminar draws a mix of students: some from English, others from theater and various languages, many interested in the Renaissance or Shakespeare, some curious about feminist criticism, and a few without definite aims but who think they mustn't take a Ph.D. without Shakespeare. As a teacher, I am still struck by the reverence with which many, in fact most, of my students approach him. Assuming that I demand this reverence, they have internalized our culture's general regard for Shakespeare without realizing it.

I think about an assignment I gave in an honors course two years ago. I asked my students to discover how our culture viewed Shakespeare. They were to choose a group of subjects—strangers on the street, students in their dormitories, professors, members of their family, any group would do—and learn about their acquaintance with Shakespeare. Though I didn't specify the questions, I suggested that class members ask how familiar their subjects were with Shakespeare: Had they studied him in high school or college? Had they seen his plays acted on the stage or on film? Which plays did they know, which ones did they like or not like? Did they currently read or see Shakespeare's plays? Our project was to understand what Shakespeare meant culturally at the end of the twentieth century to people living in Minneapolis. My pedagogical aim was to allow my students to "place" themselves and their academic work. I also expected to learn something myself.

I learned that the awe that has long surrounded "the bard" is still there. Many of my students reported that people wouldn't even talk to them about Shakespeare. Possible subjects continually demurred: "Oh, no! *I* can't talk about *Shakespeare!* Please find someone else; *I* wouldn't have anything useful to say!" We learned that in high-school English, Shakespeare is still a consistent part of the curriculum, though other writers move in and out of it. In colleges and universities, his work is usually required somewhere in the curriculum for most students; it goes without saying that English majors are generally expected to take a course in Shakespeare.

I also learned that to people in Minnesota, Shakespeare meant mainly tragedy: specifically, *Julius Caesar, Romeo and Juliet, Hamlet,* and *Macbeth,* in that order. It is hard for secondary-school teachers to deviate because the sophomore English teacher, for example, assumes that the freshman English teacher has taught *Julius Caesar;* the junior English teacher, that the sophomore has taught *Romeo and Juliet,* and so on. Shakespearean texts are often shortened and usually expurgated. While subjects interviewed had read or seen other tragedies and a few histories, comedies, and romances, almost none had read any of the sonnets.

One student recounted an unexpected experience with African exchange students. Having invited her next-door neighbors to tea, she decided to ask them about their experience of Shakespeare so as to learn something about his place in another culture. To her dismay, when she asked them whether they would mind spending a few minutes talking to her about their experience of Shakespeare, they became very annoyed and told her that the *last* thing they wanted to talk about was Shakespeare. They even began to make motions to leave. It turned out that they had learned to read and speak English by laboriously reading play after play and memorizing pages of Shakespeare. By now, they thoroughly hated him. Shakespeare's use as a "colonizing" tool had led to the opposite of its intended effect.

For so many, he is seen as the embodiment of all that is fine in white, Western, middle-class culture. He is still held up to such idealization that he daunts many of us. As a freshman in high school, my son got through *Julius Caesar* without too much difficulty, but in his sophomore year, *Romeo and Juliet* seemed to lay him low. From the prologue, he was mystified and impatient. He read to me aloud:

> From forth the fatal loins of these two foes
> A pair of star-crossed lovers take their life;
> Whose misadventured piteous overthrows
> Doth with their death bury their parents' strife.

"What does it *mean*?" he looked at me blankly. "Fatal loins"? "Misadventured piteous overthrows"? "What is it?" he glowered. Later, when I described to his teacher the difficulty he was having and complained about her demand that her students identify by act and scene any passage she gave them, she looked irritated. "But you *know* how hard it is!" as though it was and it needed to be. Suffering. Labor. The cost of the fruits of civilization.

I am often amazed at the way Shakespeare touches my women students. I remember teaching *Taming of the Shrew* and having a graduate student, who had never read the play before, remark that she was shocked that Shakespeare had written such a play.[3] Another said that it made her sad. She remembered liking it years earlier, but it disappointed her when she read it now. And she often had this experience, she said. Rereading a novel, hearing an opera, seeing a play, she would discover that something she remembered loving was so deeply sexist that it broke her bond with it, and she felt a sense of loss. It was as though she was continually finding her culture slipping away.

One undergraduate told me that she liked my class, that she hadn't expected to like being taught by a feminist, that she had enrolled in the class because she had to take the class at the hour I taught it. She had been surprised to discover that I wasn't angry. "Most feminists," she said, "are angry." I told her that most of my feminist friends were no angrier than anyone else, and I suggested that perhaps she was defining "feminists" so as to exclude anyone who wasn't angry. Then she added, "But why do you teach this stuff? Shakespeare has such an awful view of women!"

Over time, I have had to struggle with my own ambivalence when I read Shakespeare or teach Renaissance writers. In teaching Machiavelli's *Prince*, for instance, I was struck by a gratuitous comparison: "Fortune is a woman, and the man who wants to hold her down must beat and bully her. We see that she yields more often to men of this stripe than to those who come coldly toward her. Like a woman, too, she is always a friend of the young, because they are less timid, more brutal, and take charge of her more recklessly" (Machiavelli 72). Moments such as this kept coming up the whole quarter when I taught an introduction to the Renaissance. I even had to preface a discussion of *Volpone* by saying, "The assumptions that underlie *Volpone* are racist, sexist, anti-Semitic, and elitist" and hoping that would take care of it. Having said this, I could go on with the rest of the play. But I kept stewing over what I knew about the Renaissance and why and how I was teaching it. I thought of a moment at Stanford when I was the administrative assistant for a writing project and was "assigned" to have dinner with John Barth, who had come as a consultant. I remember his asking what my dissertation topic was. When I replied, "George Gascoigne," he asked, quite simply, "Why?" His question hovered over the next several years of my life. But as a teacher of the introductory course, I was interrogating myself. I kept a journal and wrote therapeutic poems all quarter. One for Machiavelli:

> The Secret in the Garden
> I've found you out,
> Caught you in my garden.
> You said you wanted
> To gather my rosebuds,
> Taste my berries.
>
> But all along you planned
> To mow down my flowers,
> Crush my fruit.
>
> Machiavelli told your secret,
> Winking at you across the page:
> "Fortune is a woman," he wrote,
> "And the man who wants to hold her down
> Must beat and bully her."
>
> I know you now.
> So beware:
> I've unleashed my dogs.

Another for Ben Jonson's Celia, who seemed to me the epitome of a desiccated, chaste woman. I wanted to give her a shocking voice:

> For Celia
> Board up the windows, lock up my loins,
> promise death if I cross your line.
> I will not weep,

or pine and die,
a chaste martyr to your jealous fears.

Disobedient, I will yell at passers by,
bribe your servant to steal the keys
(giving my body if I must).

But if you've made the walls thick
and the servant your man,
I will live in my mind.

And I will not have there a poet writing my praise,
a golden-haired prince scaling the wall
to touch me sleeping,
or Jove in golden rain.

I will have instead a dark gypsy lover
kissing my cunt,
his earring pressed against my thigh.

And I will weave my wish into a tapestry,
or carve it on the wall,
but like murder, Corvino,
it will out.

Poems such as this contained my rage, got me through the quarter.

Some ten years ago now, what I began to work out, though I didn't know it then, were some ideas about the connection between tragedy and gender. While preparing for a seminar at the International Shakespeare Association Congress in Stratford, I read for the first time Maynard Mack's "The Jacobean Shakespeare: Some Observations on the Construction of the Tragedies." The essay is so without an awareness of gender differences and so written for an exclusively male audience that it appalled me. In response to Mack's rhetorical question "Who would be Horatio if he could be Hamlet?" I wrote, only a little perversely, that I would prefer to be Horatio because he "loves, he survives, Shakespeare leaves him to tell Hamlet's story." I recall another member of the seminar, in response to something I said in our discussion, teasing me, "But after all, *you* want to be Horatio!"

Sitting on the lawn in Stratford after the seminar, Gayle Greene, Peter Erickson, Madelon Sprengnether, and I were eating cake and drinking tea, more or less continuing the discussion. Gayle wanted to go back to the Hamlet-Horatio question. I remember insisting that in some sense I meant it: I would rather be Horatio than Hamlet. I remember saying, "But I've *been* Hamlet, I've been neurotic and despairing, I don't ever want to be there again." Had I been an actor, however, I would have wanted to *play* Hamlet. What I knew was that everyday life, particularly everyday women's lives, are taken up with the ordinary. Perhaps that was part of my connection with Horatio. I wanted to rescue the life of everydayness and survival; I wanted a story that validated the ordinary, that even made it extraordinary.

Slowly I began to realize a notion of gender and tragedy that clarified what was missing in Mack. And finally I could see my way around "Who would be Horatio if he could be Hamlet?" What began to take shape in my imagination was a sense of how profoundly Shakespearean tragedy was gendered.

In the course of time, I have been fascinated to discover how unconventional and iconoclastic were Shakespeare's choices of tragic hero. Surely, Lear, Macbeth, Othello, Hamlet, and Antony undercut the usual notion that the hero must be noble; and Shakespeare goes to pains to reveal their weaknesses. Think of the difference between what we are shown of Oedipus and Lear, for example.

I think about Leslie Fiedler's argument in *The Stranger in Shakespeare*, in which he sees Shakespeare as taking a biased position, making women, Jews, and blacks "others" and reinscribing in his plays the status quo in his society. I recognize that set against other Renaissance playwrights, Shakespeare may be seen as making conservative choices of characterization, subjects, and themes.[4] If Shakespeare raised doubts in his audience, he never took them on in the way that Marlowe does in *Tamburlaine*, for example. He let them leave the theater with their values undisturbed if they so chose.

It is, of course, a commonplace that Shakespeare thrives on ambiguity and that when you try to fix meaning in his plays, like mercury it continually eludes your grasp. But I have felt drawn to the side of Shakespeare that anatomizes racism and anti-Semitism while recognizing that to some extent he participates in them. I have even been led to write about racism and anti-Semitism because of his portrayal of them.[5]

Sometimes the material seems intractable. On two occasions when I began my course "Shakespeare's Later Plays" with *Othello*, the few black students in the course dropped my class immediately. A colleague tells me that she doesn't teach it anymore because she feels that it isolates her black students. I still teach it, but I move it to later in the quarter so I can establish an atmosphere in which we can talk with some degree of openness and comfort about such things as the myth of black sexuality and miscegenation as a threat to whites in the United States.

The last time I taught *The Merchant of Venice*, I spent considerable energy discussing Elizabethan attitudes toward Jews and the fact that Venice, like America and Europe for Henry James, was a place in Shakespeare's mind. Venice, in fact, was much more liberal in its treatment of Jews than England. I referred students in the class to my article "Shylock: 'His stones, his daughter, and his ducats,' " which delineates the historical context against which Shakespeare wrote. In the course of the quarter, I had mentioned that my husband was Jewish and that my children went to religious school. Still my students wrote me unconsciously anti-Semitic papers. I realized that to teach the play adequately I would have to spend much more time on it than a quarter allows. I haven't had the energy for it again.

My classes are composed mainly of white students, roughly half women and half men. In Minnesota, whose population is predominantly Scandinavian in origin and Lutheran or Catholic, the university draws relatively few Jews or people of color. Only rarely do they speak about their personal responses to these plays. With gender, it's different.

Women in my classes are often outraged by the plays. Some are merely indifferent. The last time I taught my seminar "Shakespearean Tragedy and Gender," a woman told me that she enjoyed writing her paper, which led her into the history of women and property, until she got to the plays, and then her interest paled. At the same time, a man read through *Hamlet* his experience of gender for the first time. Growing up in a milieu where masculinity was negotiated through one's position in and relationship to cockfighting and in a family where he is the first man not to have shot or killed another man, he found Hamlet's struggle to fulfill the terms of the masculine code compelling. Clearly, Shakespeare had a resonance for him that he had found nowhere else.[6]

One of my principal avenues to understanding the cultural construction of gender is through Shakespeare, and my students are fascinated to encounter similar insights. He allows us a fuller understanding of the traditional meanings of "masculinity" than of "femininity." But what engages me and my students most now is the fact of the construction of these identities and Shakespeare's sense of that as well as his representation of a dynamic between them, particularly as it manifests itself in male characters. The representation of homoerotic desire or of a fluid and ambiguous gender identity, as in the figure of the fool, for example, suggests a freedom of imagination to which few writers give rein.

Much of my fascination with tragedy, I think, comes from watching the hero struggle with his gender identity. In most of the great tragedies, the hero grapples with what it means to be a man. These plays are filled with references to manliness or the lack of it. Most of the tragic heroes discover in themselves a feminine side that they resist but may ultimately let live, at least in some measure. In the shock of discovery, their resistance reveals itself in misogyny. In the plays where there are prominent couples—*Romeo and Juliet, Othello, Antony and Cleopatra*—the hero's love of a woman outside of himself often seems to mirror his incipient acceptance of the feminine, i.e., the "woman," inside of himself. In other plays, *Lear* and *Hamlet*, for example, the heroes' struggle against the feminine side of themselves is obvious. Lear calls on the gods:

> Touch me with noble anger,
> And let not women's weapons, water drops,
> Stain my man's cheeks.
>
> (2.4.273-75)

Hamlet condemns what he sees as his cowardice:

> This is most brave,
> That I, the son of a dear father murdered,
> Prompted to my revenge by heaven and hell,
> Must, like a whore, unpack my heart with words
> And fall a-cursing like a very drab,
> A stallion!
>
> (2.2.589-94)

Having suffered this conflict, the tragic hero is changed—how much may be debated—but some movement in his character seems apparent. The tragedy becomes the hero's inability to survive this experience. I do not think this is a case of learning too late to be wise. The world of the play is tragic because it cannot allow the hero to exist; it does not provide a place for him.

This gender issue is not the center of tragedies by other Renaissance dramatists. I think this engagement reflects cultural concerns apparent in other pieces of literature, such as Castiglione's *Courtier*, which reflects on what it means to be an aristocratic man. It is also Shakespeare's particular focus, which would seem to stem from an interest in bisexuality in his poetic imagination and probably in his life.

I like discussing the ways Shakespeare was radical in his time. Elizabethans were, after all, still struggling to believe that one really could write eloquently in English as well as in Latin. They were also struggling with considerable cultural insecurity. Witness Portia's merciless description of her English suitor:

"He is a proper man's picture, but alas, who can converse with a dumbshow? How oddly he is suited! I think he bought his doublet in Italy, his round hose in France, his bonnet in Germany, and his behavior everywhere" (*Merchant* 1.2.70–74). To see that Shakespeare intended in his Greek and Roman plays to counter the idealization of the ancients, that he could be iconoclastic and anti-authoritarian, is to see him differently. He becomes "modern" in the sense that he is poised on the edge of cultural upheaval and helps to create the overturning, the making of the world anew. I like pointing out how radical his notion of tragedy is, how he flaunts dramatic tradition by including among his tragic heroes a murderer who could be described as a "butcher" (*Macbeth* 5.8.69), a black "extravagant and wheeling stranger / Of here and everywhere" (*Othello* 1.1.133–34), an eighty-year-old man who "hath ever but slenderly known himself" (*Lear* 1.1.292–93), and a prince who was still struggling in his thirties to come of age.

Placing Shakespeare historically, seeing him and his work as particular, recognizing that his vision is not universal, not everyman's, and that it illuminates most clearly a white, middle-class, Western perspective, shaped by his time and place, has made him more rather than less interesting for me and, I think, for my students. They do not have to find themselves in his work, and nothing is wrong with them if they do not.

Over time, I have valued Shakespeare's work because it has helped me to understand my life. I remember a man's accosting me at a party one night to tell me about his unfaithful wife and to excoriate me as a woman. "It's the women, the women," he said, as my mind flashed to Leontes, and I thought, "I am in the presence of a cuckold." Knowing Shakespeare made it possible to place at once what would have been an enigmatic encounter.

Though I like the comedies and romances and have written on them, the tragedies have compelled me most strongly. I go to see them more often, I teach them most often, and they occupy my everyday imagination. Yet they awaken in me profound ambivalence: I can describe my relationship with them only as one of love-hate.

As a respondent at an MLA session called "Marriage and the Family in Shakespeare," I once commented:

> I often have the same experience in reading Shakespeare that I had the last time I heard *Don Giovanni*. I kept listening to it in all of its splendor and thinking, "All this beauty, all this energy—on this man! this story!" Perhaps

it's because the ERA is about to fail, or because it seems more likely than not that abortions will be made illegal, or because I read daily in the Minneapolis paper the trial transcript in a case of sexual abuse, rape, and murder of a University of Minnesota student, and the murderer's confession and remarks about her in particular and women in general sound too much like Othello's mad ravings—but I find myself wishing for other stories.

I think the love-hate is something that Shakespeare provokes; it doesn't arise simply from me. And it helps me to understand my feelings to remember that he chose as his profession the only place in which transvestism was allowed. Similarly, Shakespeare had a very great capacity to let the feminine inside himself live. Like D. H. Lawrence and Henry James, he could characterize women better than other writers of his time, and even than writers across time, and could draw male characters grappling with the feminine in themselves.

At the same time, the plays express a powerful misogyny. Though when looked at whole they do not affirm this feeling, they verbalize it more strongly than its opposite. At times I am oppressed by the woman-hating voices I hear even as I am caught up in the richness of the plays, and I think that one of the reasons Shakespeare has become a cultural icon is that he mirrors the culture's ambivalence toward women. Whether men weary of patriarchal impositions may find in Shakespeare a more hopeful ambivalence toward stereotypical masculinity, I cannot say. But as a woman, I find myself needing more comforting, assuring stories to set beside Shakespeare in order to continue reading and teaching him.

NOTES

1. All quotations of Shakespeare are from *The Complete Signet Classic Shakespeare,* ed. Sylvan Barnet (New York: Harcourt, 1972).

2. Though students occasionally read across gender rather than through it, this is less often the case.

3. As I suggest in my article "*Taming of the Shrew:* Inside or Outside of the Joke?" my students' responses to *Taming* serve as reminders of the harsher side of this "comedy."

4. Mary Beth Rose's discussion of Shakespeare's plays and other Renaissance dramas in *The Expense of Spirit: Love and Sexuality in English Renaissance Drama* makes clear how other dramatists often made more radical choices than Shakespeare.

5. See "Shakespeare's Desdemona" and "Shylock: 'His stones, his daughter, and his ducats.' "

6. His seminar paper was later published; see Dews.

WORKS CITED

Castiglione, Baldassare. *The Book of the Courtier.* Trans. Charles J. Singleton. Garden City, N.Y.: Doubleday, 1959.

Dews, C. L. Barney. "Gender Tragedies: East Texas Cockfighting and *Hamlet.*" *Journal of Men's Studies* 2, No. 3 (February 1994): 253–67.

Fiedler, Leslie A. *The Stranger in Shakespeare.* New York: Stein and Day, 1972.

Garner, S. N. [Shirley Nelson]. "Shakespeare's Desdemona." *Shakespeare Studies* 9 (1976): 233–52.

Garner, Shirley Nelson. "Shylock: 'His stones, his daughter, and his ducats.' " *The Upstart Crow* 5 (1984): 35–49.

———. " *Taming of the Shrew:* Inside or Outside of the Joke?" *Bad Shakespeare: Revaluations of the Shakespeare Canon.* Ed. Maurice Charney. Madison, N.J.: Fairleigh Dickinson; London and Toronto: Associated University Presses, 1988. 105–19.

Machiavelli, Niccolò. *The Prince.* Trans. and ed. Robert M. Adams. New York: Norton, 1977.

Mack, Maynard. "The Jacobean Shakespeare: Some Observations on the Construction of the Tragedies." *Jacobean Theatre.* Ed. John Russell Brown and Bernard Harris. Stratford-upon-Avon Studies 1. London: Edward Arnold, 1960. 11–41.

Rose, Mary Beth. *The Expense of Spirit: Love and Sexuality in English Renaissance Drama.* Ithaca: Cornell University Press, 1988.

Shakespeare, William. *The Complete Signet Classic Shakespeare.* Ed. Sylvan Barnet. New York: Harcourt, 1972.

12

LEAVING SHAKESPEARE

GAYLE GREENE

IT'S BY NO means clear what a girl like me, coming of age in the California suburbs in the 1950s, was doing with Shakespeare. When I think about high school—the homecoming games and proms, the local drag strip we cruised searching for action, the Mel's Drive-In where we hung out, boy-crazy, clothes-crazy, decked out in crinoline petticoats, charm bracelets, bobby sox, pony-tails—it seems a bizarre and eccentric attraction. It was an affair of the heart, I know that: for me, anything interesting or worth doing, anything that makes me do real work—is about love. Not all my loves have been happy or produc-tive, though—far from it: in fact some of the strongest have been tormented and destructive. This thing with Shakespeare —what was it?

I'd been intrigued by *Hamlet* in high school, but it wasn't until my freshman year at college that I was really bowled over by a Shakespeare play—*Richard II*. I was barely seventeen, at the University of Chicago, homesick and lost, and I read *Richard II* in a humanities course. Though this course had little to do with Shakespeare, or with much of anything else as far as one could tell, when I heard the language, really heard it, it was like a spell. I was hooked, caught, cathected, transfixed by that spectacle of ruined royalty, entranced by that sweet sound. I suppose there was something in Richard's adolescent self-pity that validated my own: I too was ready to sit upon the ground and tell sad sto-ries of the death of kings, sure as I was that all was vanity, and certain, also, that I'd been deprived of a birthright—what else could explain my unsatisfac-tory existence? I was not as critical of Richard as I'd later be, though I was not completely uncritical of him either—I sensed even then affinities between his problems and my own. I had read other plays, but it was Richard, Richard, that ravished me, that struck a chord so deep that it drew me back again and again.

When I think about what else drew me to Shakespeare in those early years,

I recall Laurence Olivier, stunningly blond and anguished in black tights; James Mason, looking distant and Roman in a toga: all that tortured nobility, so tragic, so eloquent—so *male*. I thrilled to Mark Antony's pronouncement over the body of Brutus, "this was a man" (5.5.75), and to Hamlet's words to Horatio, "give me that man that is not passion's slave, and I will wear him in my heart's core, ay, in my heart of heart, as I do thee" (3.2.72). It didn't occur to me that all this homosocial intensity was obliterating me: the men were grooving on the men and so was I, and it took me years to notice my own absence—such was my alienation from my experience. It was years before I thought about the women in the plays, riveted as I was on those dazzling men, and then it was only working on *The Woman's Part* that succeeded in focusing my attention on them. I suppose falling in love with those heroes was a version of falling in love with movie stars, which I did plenty of in those days—except that it was a more respectable passion, one that I sensed might get me further than a crush on Jimmy Dean. Doubtless that attraction to anguished and inaccessible masculinity was about my father, always a powerful and disturbing presence, or absence, in our so-called family, someone I hadn't a clue how to think about.

Our family went through what a lot of families in the suburbs in the fifties were going through—that suburban loneliness you could die of, that sense of not being connected anywhere, to anything. But our loneliness was exacerbated by my parents' unconventional arrangements and their politics. We were not a happy family: my parents were always in the process of separating, and when I was ten, they finally did, leaving my mother that most miserable of anomalies, a woman alone in the suburbs in the fifties, in her forties. My father was mainly away, even when he was around, and he was a womanizer, a philanderer, who was nevertheless oddly devoted to his children and in other ways a nice guy (it took some talent not to get rich as a doctor in those California boom years, but he was an old-style G. P. who didn't insist on collecting payment when his patients were poor, which they often were). He was Jewish, my mother was not, and when the marriage finally came apart and she changed our name, I was completely confused—I became aware of being Jewish at precisely the time it was denied that I was Jewish, whatever "Jewish" meant. Also, at the height of McCarthyism, my parents were lefties, the few friends they had living under shadows, some blacklisted; yet my parents didn't identify wholeheartedly with politics either—we were lefties and not lefties. We were quite simply without the consolation of any kind of group identity, even oppositional. In those years when everyone was conforming and when, as an adolescent, I wanted nothing more than to belong, conforming was never an option, since I'd been taught so thoroughly that everything out there—the ideology of happy families, of a greater America—was fucked. We were rootless, headless, godless, adrift, and there seemed no way of conceiving of alternatives, no way to imagine any other way of being or living.[1]

I turned, for a sense of other possibilities, to reading. But what I found there was not very helpful: the "tiresome, hysterical pretentious Jewess" of Durrell's *Justine;* Caddie of Faulkner's *Sound and the Fury,* "doomed and knew it"; Hedda Gabler, fatally fixated on the pistols of her father the general; doomed Brett; doomed Gudrun—all male-authored except for Scarlett O'Hara, whose spunkiness I found irresistible, but who also turned out to be doomed. I found myself, disastrously, in Madame Bovary and Anna Karenina. God knows why they were a comfort, these intense, fragile creatures living at the edge of experience—I suppose it was all that exquisitely expressed anguish: they did their despair so beautifully. I was also drawn to the women of Austen and Eliot, who had more interiority and were occasionally even allowed to survive, but I found their happy endings unlikely; I didn't mind the idea of marriage to Mr. Knightley, but it seemed implausible. By now we know about those death and marriage plots, where they get us, but at the time, in my teens and twenties, this was all there was.[2] The books I needed—the feminist fiction and theory that would help me make the connections between the confusions I was living through and something out there—were only then being written, and it was decades before I would find them (*Martha Quest* was published in 1952, *The Golden Notebook* in 1962; *The Second Sex* was translated into English in 1953. I did not read these until the late sixties).

There was never any doubt that I would study literature: it was the only thing I'd ever really—wholeheartedly, unequivocally—loved. I muddled through two undergraduate majors, in English and comparative literature, fulfilling requirements that didn't make much sense (it never occurred to me that they should be making sense), living in terror that the computer would spew me out at the last minute and keep me from graduating. (I had transferred to Berkeley my sophomore year, on account of a boyfriend; by October we'd broken up. This ought to have taught me more than it did.) I never got to know a professor, I never had a woman professor in the five years it took to the M. A., and "woman writer" wasn't a category in the curriculum. But in spite of the Berkeley English Department I continued to love reading, and in spite of two dreadful Shakespeare lecture courses I elected to take a senior seminar in Shakespeare, where, turned loose on a play of my choice, I turned to Richard, Richard again, and sunk once more into that sweet despair.

To this day, I don't know whether the decision to go with Shakespeare rather than the novels I lived on was a bad or a good choice—whether it was a choice that reflected (as many of my choices did) alienation from my deepest needs, or whether it actually expressed my deepest needs. Shakespeare seemed to be something I very badly needed to do, since when I found myself at Columbia a few years later (a move which was not, I'm happy to say, precipitated by a man), where I was surrounded by exciting activity in the nineteenth century and a vacuum in the Renaissance, it would have made more sense to work on the novel than to persist in a Shakespeare dissertation, which turned out to be self-directed. (No one wanted to touch it—the resident Shakespearean said it was "too modern and psychological" and that I "couldn't possibly master all the scholarship" and the resident Miltonist was afraid of offending the resident Shakespearean—though he eventually did read and rubber-stamp it and set up a defense committee and smuggle me out the back door.) It now strikes me as stubborn and perverse to have persisted in doing Shakespeare with everyone advising against it. Perhaps it had to do with Steven Marcus scaring me off George Eliot by naming every German philosopher she'd ever read and assuring me that I'd have to master all of them to write on her. Mastering the Shakespeare scholarship seemed like a piece of cake by comparison (and from what they all said, the dissertation was about "mastery"). Or perhaps there was a lurking fear that working on a woman writer would make me second-rate. Or perhaps it was a deeper fear of those doomed, desperate women that drove me away from those novels I nonetheless devoured.

I now think that my determination to work on Shakespeare had to do with power. Not in any simple or obvious way—not in the way E. M. Forster's Leonard Bast or Rita in the film *Educating Rita* latches on to culture as upward mobility. More in the sense of identifying with the male, wanting to be my father. The thing is, our family was so marginal, and I was on the losing side even of it. I knew I didn't want to be my mother, an abandoned wife, without resources, dependent on a man. Although she had stayed with us children, and although she was the more attractive of my parents, I felt complimented when people said I looked like my father: he was the doctor, he had the Yale degree, he had position, power, women—freedom; she had us. So it was inevitable that I identify with him, and perhaps also inevitable that I work on Shakespeare. Mind you, my father was never even remotely impressed by my doing graduate study in literature—"In all that time you could have been a real doctor" was his comment when I finally got my Ph.D.—so working on Shakespeare wasn't in any obvious way about pleasing him. It was just that I felt that doing Shakespeare would in some way validate me, would prove I was an intelligent person—and I had a fierce need to prove myself an intelligent person. One of the sad ironies of my life is that I expend enormous energies trying to get the attention of people who turn out not to have been looking, over what turns out not to have been the point.

But there was power of another sort that Shakespeare seemed to offer: it had to do with order, with the edifices built by his language, structures I found shelter in—his works seemed a tower of male strength, what Mrs. Ramsay calls the "admirable fabric of the masculine intelligence" (Woolf 159). I suppose it was understandable, given the shifting sands of my childhood, that I'd flee anything resembling postmodern uncertainties and seek a solid place. Oh, it was always already crumbling, this place, I knew that—that was part of its fascination. But it still seemed to represent something more certain, more clarifying, than anything around me, than the prospects of growing up female in the fifties, than the misery of my mother as she whittled herself down to the confines of her life. I've sometimes wondered how much my attraction to Shakespeare had to do with those wasteful, tormented affairs that consumed large parts of my twenties, thirties, and yes, even forties, where I sought validation in brilliant, articulate, narcissistic men who turned out to be using *me* to validate *them,* for whom I functioned mainly as an admiring audience. Still, as painful as much of that was, I did not make the usual mistakes: some sort of conditioning that was marching my friends—compulsively and often disastrously—through the steps of marriage, motherhood, divorce, seemed to have been left out of me. Though I thought I wanted to marry (someday, someone, never now), conventional domestic arrangements held a kind of horror for me—houses, entrapment, babies. I did feel an occasional twinge of envy for the matching dish sets and stemware of my married friends (this was how you could tell those of us who "lived together" from those who were married, in the middle classes in the sixties—by our mismatched dishware), but they didn't seem worth the price, those dishes.

One thing I knew, nothing was as it was claimed to be—and for this, I found corroboration in Shakespeare; for always in his plays, though I was drawn to the grandeur, the splendor, I was driven to ferret out the soft spots—to find the rifts and cracks in the structures. What fascinated me about Richard and Brutus and Othello was the way the fine language masked insecurity, the way those dazzling talkers used words to cheer themselves up, to shore up their realities, while in fact their self-delusions left them wide open to self-deceptions and the lies of others. The thing is, I always knew that people lied: the happy fifties masked insanity, a suicidal military stockpiling—the war in Vietnam came as no surprise, though what did surprise me was that people imagined their protests might halt it (this early cynicism combined with shyness to cut me off from sixties activism in a way I now regret). I always knew that my father lied, but, more importantly, I knew that my mother lied—in pretending to be okay when she was really coming apart, in telling us to love our father when she hated his guts, in trying to inculcate virtues of love and loyalty in us from a situation that travestied them. So I went for and found in Shakespeare's plays confirmation of my deepest sense of reality—that words were unreliable, that people could build facades and get trapped behind them, could get confused and ensnared by their own stories. I wrote on this, obsessively, in *Richard II*, in *Julius Caesar*, in *Othello*, in *Troilus and Cressida*. I was struck by the pairings of worders against worders—Richard and Bolingbroke, Brutus and Antony, Othello and Iago—winners and losers differentiated by their ability to wield words. I eventually wrote my (self-directed) dissertation on *Julius Caesar* and discovered that Shakespeare had homed in on something very big, as he so often does, and was intuiting a cultural moment—no less than the revolution in attitudes toward language that was occurring from the medieval to the modern world, the transition from sixteenth-century belief in language and rhetoric to seventeenth-century skepticism, nominalism, and the plain style.

I guess, in an odd way, "mastering" the master was a way of incorporating his power, harnessing (if not exactly understanding) some of the forces that were driving me, demystifying some of that male mystique. I think what I really needed was time and a safe place from which I could take stock—of myself and possibilities—before I could see what I needed to do next. Shakespeare gave me this. I got tenure off him, developed skills of writing and editing, used him to explore certain questions. I learned from him the way language functions in constructing identity and how this process has social (if not political) implications; I learned about systems (value systems, social systems, philosophical, epistemological, and aesthetic systems) and how at times of stress these are prone to come apart; and I learned a lot about power from him—and long before new historicists or poststructuralists or deconstructionists were naming these issues. His plays corroborated my sense—gleaned from a life on the margins—of the contingency of systems and the arbitrariness of convention, of language as a code to be broken: all of which turned out to be fundamental to feminism. I learned what I needed for my next move, to feminist theory and fiction, and when I learned this I left him.[3]

I now work on Doris Lessing, Margaret Drabble, Margaret Laurence, Margaret Atwood, Toni Morrison, Alice Walker, Paule Marshall—contemporary writers whose novels include me and speak to me as no other literary works do, and whose protagonists survive, often alone, to tell their tales. The route I've taken, from a canonized male writer to women writers, has been traveled by other feminist scholars—in fact it describes the trajectory of feminist scholarship, which began with the study of the canon and shifted to the study of women writers. I think for me it was related to recognizing the influence and importance of my mother, accepting my mother in me, realizing that it was okay to be her. It took me years to figure out that though my mother never finished a degree, she was really the smart one, the strong one, in ways that counted. It took me years to understand that I could never be my father, and more, that I didn't want to. I think this was necessary before I could turn to women writers with a sense that I wasn't doing something second-rate—could approach them with the love and intensity that I'd first brought to Shakespeare.

But in a way, Shakespeare has been the most lasting and stable relationship I've ever had with a man. It was a connection, a kind of wonder, a sort of faith—and faith was something sorely lacking in my life. Probably it was faith in some things I'd have been better off not believing in, but I wouldn't have traded it for a wilderness of critical theory: I wouldn't have wanted my Shakespeare parceled out in little "isms"—poststructuralism, new historicism, cultural materialism, Marxism, no, not even feminism. It seemed to offer something beyond what was available to me as an adolescent going through a confused coming of age in a demoralizing decade, and though I probably stayed with him too long, as I tend to do in relationships, it made certain things possible.

It may also, of course, have made other things impossible. Perhaps it did keep my lid on when it should have been blowing off—the study of literature did tend to produce political zombies in those days; perhaps if I'd written that George Eliot dissertation, I'd have found a faster route to feminism. I know that it took Simone de Beauvoir, Doris Lessing, Sheila Rowbotham, Juliet Mitchell, Kate Millett, Shulamith Firestone, and Adrienne Rich to show me the connections between the roles my mother and father had played out and the social and political structures out there in the world; it took feminist theory and fiction to make me understand the sexual politics of my interactions with lovers, professors, advisors (yes, even Shakespeare)—to make me see that the political was personal and was what hurt.

My mainstay writer now is Doris Lessing, and I know exactly why. What draws me to Lessing is her articulation of the problems of women and men in our time and her illumination of connections between those problems and the times; her ability to pierce the veil of hypocrisy, the veneer of official versions, and to deconstruct systems (colonialism, capitalism) and to demonstrate (my old theme) that "listening to the words people use is the longest way around to an understanding of what is going on" (*Ripple* 7). Here were women—Martha Quest, Anna Wulf—who were not only facing the sorts of problems I was facing, struggling with their sense of themselves, with commitments to work and to men, but who corroborated my deepest sense of reality: that the most important conversation going on is not usually the one that is being verbalized, that the "small ironical grimace" is what signifies—"you have to deduce a person's real feelings about a thing by a smile she does not know is on her face, by the way bitterness tightens muscles at a mouth's corner" (*Summer* 62, 1). Here was confirmation that if I was inhabiting "another room" (in Lessing's term), so too were others. It was, of course, the women's room, where the women were—at least the women I knew, who had always been having another conversation, inhabiting another culture, and whose relation to the dominant culture was just then being articulated by feminist theory. I still turn to books for validation—I think most people who study literature do—but it is validation of another sort, that has less to do with the "male approval desire filter"[4] and more to do with—what? Something closer to, something more like, what I can only call a center. Something less mediated by the law of the father.

But sometimes when I turn a corner I'm still surprised to find Shakespeare there, in places where I least expect him. When Lessing wants to intimate the existence of something wondrous at the end of *The Four-Gated City,* something miraculous that's survived the wreck of the world, she takes us to an island rich and strange and evokes the sound of a flute; when Drabble wants to suggest something infinitely mysterious, ineffable, and sad at the end of *The Radiant Way,* her language evokes "such stuff as dreams are made on"; and when Margaret Laurence wants to show the heroine of *The Diviners* growing into her own powers, she has her develop from a sense of herself as Miranda to a sense of herself as Prospero. When I find him there, in the hearts and minds of the women writers who are now my greatest loves, I feel that those years were a growing toward something I could have neither predicted nor resisted.

NOTES

"Leaving Shakespeare" is part of a longer piece entitled "Looking at History," published in *Histories: The Making of Feminist Criticism,* ed. Gayle Greene and Coppélia Kahn (London: Routledge, 1991).

1. Piercy captures this "isolation and dead-endedness" of the fifties: what was "lacking" was "a sense of possibilities"; "there was little satisfaction for me in the forms offered, yet there seemed no space but death or madness outside the forms"; "nowhere could I find images of a life I considered good or useful or dignified"; "I could not make connections" (208, 215, 207).

2. I did not realize it, but I was not alone in seeking in fiction for the meaning and connections missing from my life: Doris Lessing, Margaret Drabble, Gail Godwin, Marge Piercy, and Erica Jong write of characters growing up in these years who turned to reading this way.

3. It wasn't this simple, of course. I am omitting a good deal, making it all sound much clearer and cleaner than it was. I am leaving out the pain and confusion and lone-liness—what it was like to be plodding through a Ph.D. program with the certainty that what awaited me at the end (in the mid-seventies) was unemployment; what it was like to be buffeted by those strong sexual attractions against which there seemed no defense, that cooperated with the coldness of Columbia to leave me feeling unfit for life, let alone able to imagine a future. Perhaps this is what narrative does, looks back from an end and selects the steps leading to that end; or perhaps that pain is the subject of another story. The truth is that both stories are true—that despite the anguish of those years, there was this thinking, writing being struggling to survive and make sense of it. I write, therefore I am. Of course there was also a lot of luck (though there was a lot of bad luck too), and a lot of white middle-class support to fall back on—financial, even emotional, from a family that, despite its fuck-ups, had a way of coming through.

4. Which "instructs by quiet magic women to sing proper pliant tunes for father, lover, piper who says he has the secret." Honore Moore, quoted in Miller (36).

WORKS CITED

Beauvoir, Simone de. *The Second Sex*. New York: Vintage, 1952.

Drabble, Margaret. *The Radiant Way*. New York: Knopf, 1987.

Durrell, Lawrence. *Justine, a Novel*. London: Faber and Faber, 1957.

Faulkner, William. *The Sound and the Fury*. New York: Random House, 1956.

Flaubert, Gustave. *Madame Bovary*. New York: Random House, 1957.

Forster, E. M. *Howard's End*. New York: A. A. Knopf, 1921.

Hemingway, Ernest. *The Sun Also Rises*. New York: Grosset and Dunlap, 1926.

Ibsen, Henrik. *Hedda Gabler*. Introduction by H. L. Mencken. New York: Boni and Liveright, 1917.

Laurence, Margaret. *The Diviners*. New York: Knopf, 1974.

Lawrence, D. H. *Women in Love*. New York: T. Seltzer, 1923.

Lenz, Carolyn Ruth Swift; Gayle Greene; and Carol Thomas Neely, eds. *The Woman's Part: Feminist Criticism of Shakespeare.* Urbana: U of Illinois P, 1980.

Lessing, Doris. *The Four-Gated City.* New York: Knopf, 1969.

———. *The Golden Notebook.* London: Joseph, 1962.

———. *Martha Quest.* New York: New American Library, 1964.

———. *A Ripple from the Storm.* New York: New American Library, 1966.

———. *The Summer before the Dark.* New York: Bantam, 1974.

Miller, Nancy K. *Getting Personal: Feminist Occasions and Other Autobiographical Acts.* New York: Routledge, 1991.

Piercy, Marge. "Through the Cracks." *Partisan Review* 41 (1974): 202–16.

Shakespeare, William. *Hamlet.* In *William Shakespeare: The Complete Works.* Ed. Alfred Harbage. Baltimore: Penguin, 1969.

———. *Julius Caesar.* In *William Shakespeare: The Complete Works.* Ed. Alfred Harbage. Baltimore: Penguin, 1969.

———. *Othello.* In *William Shakespeare: The Complete Works.* Ed. Alfred Harbage. Baltimore: Penguin, 1969.

———. *Richard II.* In *William Shakespeare: The Complete Works.* Ed. Alfred Harbage. Baltimore: Penguin, 1969.

———. *Troilus and Cressida.* In *William Shakespeare: The Complete Works.* Ed. Alfred Harbage. Baltimore: Penguin, 1969.

Tolstoy, Leo. *Anna Karenina.* New York: Random House, 1939.

Woolf, Virginia. *To the Lighthouse.* New York: Harcourt, Brace, and World, 1955.

NOTES ON CONTRIBUTORS

Janet Adelman is Professor of English at the University of California, Berkeley. She is the author of *The Common Liar: An Essay on Antony and Cleopatra* and editor of *Twentieth-Century Interpretations of "King Lear."* Her most recent book is *Suffocating Mothers: Fantasies of Maternal Origins in Shakespeare, "Hamlet" to "The Tempest."*

Linda Charnes is Associate Professor of English, Renaissance Studies, and Cultural Studies at Indiana University, Bloomington. She is the author of *Notorious Identity: Materializing the Subject in Shakespeare* and has published articles and reviews in *Chaucer Review, Shakespeare Quarterly,* and *Textual Practice.* She is currently at work on a book-length manuscript entitled "Reading the Irrational: Logics of Cultural Unreason," and co-editing an anthology entitled *Early Modern/Post-Modern.*

Carol Cook has taught at Oberlin College, Vassar College, and Princeton University and has published essays on Shakespeare in *PMLA, Theatre Journal,* and various anthologies.

Sara Eaton is an Associate Professor of English at North Central College in Naperville, Illinois. Her essays on Shakespeare and Renaissance drama have appeared in *Ambiguous Realities: Women in the Middle Ages and Renaissance; Staging the Renaissance: Studies in Elizabethan and Jacobean Drama; The Matter of Difference: Materialist Feminist Criticism of Shakespeare;* and *Power and Punishment in Shakespeare* (forthcoming).

Shirley Nelson Garner is Professor and Chair of English at the University of Minnesota, Twin Cities. She has written articles on Shakespeare and women writers and is a co-editor of *The (M)other Tongue: Essays in Feminist Psychoanalytic Interpretation* and of *Interpreting Women's Lives: Personal Narratives and Feminist Theory.* She is a founder of *Hurricane Alice: A Feminist Quarterly* and on its editorial board.

Gayle Greene is Professor of English and Women's Studies at Scripps College, Claremont, California. She has co-edited *The Woman's Part: Feminist Criticism of Shakespeare; Making a Difference: Feminist Literary Criticism;* and *Changing Subjects: The Making of Feminist Criticism.* She has written *Changing the Story: Femi-*

nist Fiction and the Tradition and *Doris Lessing: The Poetics of Change* (forthcoming). She is currently at work on a book on conflict of interest in cancer research.

Margo Hendricks teaches at the University of California, Santa Cruz. Her essays have appeared in *Renaissance Drama; Women, Race, Writing in the Early Modern Period;* and *Changing Subjects: The Making of Feminist Literary Criticism.* She is completing a book on Aphra Behn and beginning a project on the philology of race in early modern England.

Coppélia Kahn, Professor of English at Brown University, is the author of *Man's Estate: Masculine Identity in Shakespeare,* and of articles on Shakespeare, Renaissance drama, and feminist theory. She has co-edited several anthologies: *Representing Shakespeare: New Psychoanalytic Essays; Making A Difference: Feminist Literary Criticism;* and *Changing Subjects: The Making of Feminist Literary Criticism.* She is currently writing a book on the sexual politics of Shakespeare's Roman plays.

Carol Thomas Neely, Professor of English and Women's Studies at the University of Illinois, Urbana-Champaign, is co-editor of *The Woman's Part: Feminist Criticism of Shakespeare* and author of *Broken Nuptials in Shakespeare's Plays* and of articles on Shakespeare, Sonnet sequences, feminist theory, and a recent piece on the fetishized feminist utopias of Margaret Cavendish and Gloria Anzaldúa. Her essay in this collection is part of her current project on the gendering of madness in early modern England.

Lena Cowen Orlin is Executive Director of the Folger Institute at the Folger Shakespeare Library. She is the author of *Private Matters and Public Culture in Post-Reformation England* and *Elizabethan Households: An Anthology* and co-editor of *The Fashioning and Functioning of the British Country House,* and has published articles on Elizabethan domestic tragedy, domestic architecture, and political thought.

Phyllis Rackin, Professor of English in General Honors at the University of Pennsylvania, is a past president of the Shakespeare Association of America. Her articles on Shakespeare and related topics have appeared in such journals as *Shakespeare Quarterly, PMLA,* and *Theatre Journal,* and in various anthologies. Her most recent book is *Stages of History: Shakespeare's English Chronicles.* She is presently working with Jean Howard on a feminist study of Shakespeare's English history plays, entitled *Engendering a Nation: Shakespeare's Chronicles of the English Past.*

Mary Beth Rose is Director of the Newberry Library Center for Renaissance Studies and Adjunct Associate Professor of English at Northwestern University. She is the editor of *Women in the Middle Ages and the Renaissance: Literary and Historical Perspectives* and the annual volume of essays *Renaissance Drama.* She is the author of *The Expense of Spirit: Love and Sexuality in English Renaissance Drama.*

Madelon Sprengnether is Professor of English at the University of Minnesota, Twin Cities. She is the author of *The Spectral Mother: Freud, Feminism and Psychoanalysis* and co-editor of *The (M)other Tongue: Essays in Feminist Psychoanalytic Interpretation.* She is also the author of a book of poetry, *The Normal Heart,* and a book of personal essays, *Rivers, Stories, Houses, Dreams.* She recently co-edited *The House on Via Gombito.*

INDEX

Adelman, Janet, 13, 19n.2, 49n.3, 90, 100–101n.29; on *Antony and Cleopatra*, 265n.2; on *Macbeth*, 99n.18, 163n.27; on *Othello*, 193–94
Akrigg, G. P. V., 144, 145
Anatomy of Melancholy (Burton), 77, 78
Anne (*Richard III*), 39–40
Antonio (*The Duchess of Malfi*), 224, 231
Antony (*Antony and Cleopatra*): death of, 277–78; identity of, 246, 247–48, 250, 260–61; as lover and soldier, 275–76; physical boundaries of, 258–61; recklessness of, 259; sociopolitical concerns of, 276; as subject, 278
Antony and Cleopatra (Shakespeare), 157, 174, 224, 235n.18, 241–66; becoming as concept in, 255–56; binary opposition in, 246, 250–51, 252; Caesar's supremacy in, 246–47; cross-dressing in, 15, 253, 261; death in, 263; desire in, 258–61; Egypt/Rome opposition in, 254–55, 258, 265–66n.3, 273–74; feminine language in, 242–43; Harlequin romance reading of, 15–16, 271, 278–79, 283n.7; liberal humanist romance in, 268–84; love and death in, 260; mass-cultural appeal of, 281; poetry in, 251; quibbles in, 241, 242, 245, 255, 263; reception history, 269–70; rhetoric of love in, 274–75; Roman identity in, 246–50; Rome in, 254–55, 256, 258, 265n.2, 265–66n.3; transcendent love and, 272, 274, 277; union in, 259–60
Apemantus (*Timon of Athens*), 141, 155–56
Audience, 35; feminization of, 41–42, 43, 48; as interpreter of madness, 79, 80, 81, 93; reaction to *Othello*, 186–87; seduction of, 41–42

Barber, C. L., 95, 160n.12
Barker, Frances, 66
Bartels, Emily C., 199, 206n.9
Belsey, Catherine, 18, 21n.10, 37, 43, 45, 49n.3
Berger, Harry Jr., 125n.10, 130n.44, 131n.45
Bianca (*Othello*), 179, 189n.18
Book of the Courtier, The (Castiglione), 62
Boose, Lynda, 199
Brabantio (*Othello*), 175–76, 197–98, 200, 201, 202, 207n.12
Bradley, A. C., 3–4, 8, 10, 17, 18, 80; on *Othello*, 190n.26
Bright, Timothy, 76–77
Brooke, Nicholas, 37

Burckhardt, Sigurd, 242
Burton, Robert, 77, 78, 93
Bushnell, Rebecca, 40

Caesar (*Antony and Cleopatra*), 246–47, 248, 258
Cassio (*Othello*), 179, 180, 189n.15, 207n.12
Castiglione, Baldassare, 62, 275
Cavell, Stanley, 80, 199
Cecil, Robert, 146, 147, 158
Character, 3, 5, 6. *See also* Hero; Heroine
Charnes, Linda, 15–16
Charney, Maurice, 136, 159n.4
Chiron (*Titus Andronicus*), 57, 58, 60, 63
Cixous, Hélène, 242–43
Cleaver, Robert, 183, 184, 186, 187, 189n.21, 189–90n.22, 212, 215, 219, 228
Cleopatra (*Antony and Cleopatra*): death of, 263–64, 279; as destabilizing principle, 246; language and, 241–43, 251–52, 262; in male role, 278; as other, 243, 245; as Romanized, 263–64; as schemer, 278–80; sociopolitical concerns of, 276–77; as subversive, 241; textual operation and, 15, 253–58
Colie, Rosalie, 265n.3
Colonialist discourse, 11, 22n.11
Coriolanus (Shakespeare), 105, 123n.2, 138, 157
Coryat, Thomas, 195, 196
Crane, Mary Thomas, 55, 68n.2, 70n.13
Cressy, David, 16, 69n.7, 70n.10
Cross-dressing, 22n.11, 253, 261
Cultural materialism, 11, 20, 21n.10, 272
Cymbeline (Shakespeare), 106, 109, 287

D'Amico, Jack, 205
Danby, John, 154, 265n.2
Demetrius (*Titus Andronicus*), 57, 58, 60, 63
De Quincy, Thomas, 128n.32
Desdemona (*Othello*), 14, 171–90; activity of, 177–78; autonomy of, 217–18, 219; choice of, 199–201; death of, 221–22; as defiant, 226; as heroic, 217, 219; as inanimate cargo, 178; lies of, 217, 220–21; marriage and, 14–15; military imagery and, 234n.14; as other, 295; as pattern, 181; sexual ideology of, 216–17; transformations in, 182–83; as victim, 223; willfulness, 180–81
Discoverie of Witchcraft (Scot), 79, 86

Dismemberment: body politic and, 66; torture and, 71n.21; witchcraft and, 114

Docherty, Thomas, 68n.3, 69n.6

Dod, John, 183, 184, 186, 187, 189n.21, 189–90n.22, 212, 215, 219, 228

Dollimore, Jonathan, 21n.10, 80

Doran, Madeline, 292–93

Duchess of Malfi, The (Webster), 15, 36, 211; class conflict in, 224, 225, 226–28; marriage scene in, 226–27; public vs. private sphere in, 224; sexual conflict in, 224

Duncan (Macbeth), 114; gender transformation of, 109–10, 125n.10; as ideal father, 108–109, 138; weakness of, 109–10, 115, 116, 125n.11

Eagleton, Terry, 21–22n.10, 24n.14

Eaton, Sarah, 12–13

Eisenstein, Elizabeth, 55

Elizabeth (Richard III), 37, 289

Elizabeth I, patronage and, 142, 143, 161–62n.18

Emilia (Othello), 8–9, 179–80, 182, 189n.18, 222–23, 229

Empson, William, 161n.15

Enobarbus (Antony and Cleopatra), 251–52, 255, 256, 260

Fawcett, Mary Laughlin, 68–69n.3, 70–71n.18

Female Malady, The (Showalter), 76

Feminist criticism, 15, 21n.9, 135; language and, 241; love and, 272; representation and, 244–45

Fly, Richard, 152, 159–60n.4

Fortune, 14, 136–38, 152–53, 160n.6; misogyny and, 298–99

Foucault, Michel, 76, 80, 93, 95, 97n.3, 280; language as madness and, 98n.10

Fulton, Robert, 154–55

Garner, Shirley Nelson, 12, 15, 16–17, 206n.11

Gender: as analytic category, 8; genre and, 12; hero and, 302–303; madness and, 80, 81, 82–83, 88–89, 94; testing of roles, 261; tragedy and, 300; violence and, 109–10. See also Women

Genre: conventions of, 10; gender and, 12; love as, 269–73; romance as, 269–71; universalism and, 10

Goldberg, Jonathan, 58–60, 70n.11, 130n.44, 143–44

Goneril (King Lear), 1, 5, 19n.1, 92

Gosson, Stephen, 33

Gouge, William, 213, 214

Green, Douglas E., 69n.6

Greenblatt, Stephen, 8, 80, 91, 189n.16

Greene, Gayle, 8, 16

Hall, Edward, 32, 38, 40

Hall, John, 75, 76, 99n.20

Halpern, Richard, 44

Hamlet (Hamlet), 13; feigned madness of, 82–83; as proleptic, 21n.10; as subversive, 93

Hamlet (Shakespeare), 108, 109; as document in madness, 81; language in, 58, 59; misogyny in, 287; platea and, 32

Harsnett, Samuel, 79, 90, 91

Hendricks, Margo, 14

Henry IV (Shakespeare), 36

Henry V (Shakespeare), 6, 46

Henry VI plays, 31, 36, 37, 39

Hero, 301; action and, 223–24, 233; as actor, 43; character and, 3; displacement of, 9, 11; Elizabethan concept of, 210; as exceptional, 3–4; gender identity of, 302–303; lost past and, 230, 231–33; marriage and, 211, 213; misogyny and, 288, 303; political/ideological fields and, 22n.10; psychological growth of, 63; selfhood and, 11; suffering and, 228. See also Heroine

Heroine, 223; psychological growth and, 63; suffering of, 228–30; wife as, 211, 213–15, 216–17, 219–20, 225. See also Hero; Women

Heywood, Thomas, 32, 34

Hicks, Jane, 69n.3

History: audience conception of, 42–43; fictional narrative and, 272; self-representation and, 274; vs. tragedy, 32–33, 36

"History into Tragedy: The Case of Richard III" (Rackin), 12

History play: chronicle form of, 12; goal of, 37; idealizing of past in, 35, 36; identity and, 43–44; masculinity of, 33; as short-lived, 43; women as adversaries in, 37

Hodgdon, Barbara, 38, 47

Horatio (Hamlet), 17, 300–301

Humanism: challenges to, 21n.10, 68n.2; literacy and, 54–55; public vs. private spheres, 67n.1, 70n.13; silencing of women and, 67; women's education and, 62–63. See also Liberal humanist criticism

Iago (Othello), 179, 180, 201, 206–207n.12

Identity: autonomy and, 105–106; language as constructing, 312; Roman, 246–50; writing and, 59. See also Masculine identity

Irigaray, Luce, 15, 80, 244; on feminine style, 254, 256–57; on language of death, 263; on mimeticism, 252–53; representation and, 246, 251; on women's sexuality, 261–62

James I, 106, 123n.3, 130n.44, 157–58; compulsive giving of, 13–14, 142–47; on crown as property, 4, 44

Jardine, Lisa, 62

Jed, Stephanie, 56

Joan (I Henry VI), 37–38, 47

Johnson, Samuel, 241
Jones, Ann Rosalind, 196
Jorden, Edward, 77

Kahn, Coppélia, 8, 13–14, 100n.29, 123n.2, 128n.32
Kerrigan, William, 273
King Lear (Shakespeare), 5, 138, 157; contemporary analysis of, 80; emotional representation in, 151; historical anecdote and, 7; madness and, 80; maternal power in, 110; misogyny in, 287; representation of humanity in, 5, 6–7; retelling of, 1–3; storm in, 91, 100–101n.29, 110, 113; versions of, 18n.1
King Lear in Our Time (Mack), 4–7
Klein, Joan, 98n.14
Kozikowski, Stanley J., 123n.3, 123–24n.4

La Belle, Jenijoy, 126n.17
Lacan, Jacques, 200–201, 243, 244
Language: appropriation of, 47; blank verse and, 37; curses, 39; of death, 263; as feminine, 241, 242–43; feminine style, 254, 256–57; foreign nationality and, 36–37; humanism and, 54–55; identity and, 312; lying and, 61, 222, 311–12; of madness, 79, 80–87, 98n.11; mimesis and, 252–53; as order, 310, 311; paradox and, 251–52, 266n.4; patriarchy and, 18; as power, 55; production of, 58–60; public vs. private, 54, 59–60, 65–66; quibbles, 241, 242, 263; representation and, 262–63; rhetorical art and, 61; sexuality and, 222; signification and, 16; silencing and, 65–66, 243–44; structure of, 80–81; as subversive, 15; as transformative, 257–58; transition to modern, 312; violence and, 54, 55, 56, 61–62, 63, 65–67, 70n.15; witchcraft and, 38; women and, 65–66, 243–44, 251; writing and, 58–59. *See also* Literacy
Laslett, Peter, 176
Lavinia (*Titus Andronicus*), 12–13, 54–61, 61–62; as changing piece, 64, 65; humanist pedagogy and, 57–58; Ovid and, 69n.6; sexualization of, 63; as symbol of disorder, 68n.1; as text, 66
Lear (*King Lear*), 13; discourse of, 92; madness of, 91; as subversive, 92–93
Leggatt, Alexander, 40–41
Lessing, Doris, 313–14
Levin, Richard, 4, 17, 18, 19–20n.5, 20n.7; attack on feminist criticism, 9–10; on Timon, 159n.4; on women in the theater, 34
Lewkenor, Lewes, 195, 197, 199, 200
Liberal humanist criticism, 268–84; American politics and, 280–82, 283–84n.13, 284n.14; great individual concept, 270, 272; reconstruction of love, 279–80; transcendence and, 277, 281–82, 282n.6
Lindenberger, Herbert, 50n.10

Literacy, 12; in Shakespeare's time, 16, 70n.10; violence and, 54–55; as weapon, 55; writing and, 70n.11. *See also* Language
Locus, 31, 41, 101n.30
Love: eighteenth-century views of, 269–71, 282n.5; empire and, 275–76; as essentialized, 273; history and, 273; mythic consciousness and, 272, 273; as narrative, 268–69, 273; as natural, 272–73; politics and, 274; reconstruction of, 279–80; rhetoric of, 274–75; sociopolitical realm of, 272, 276–77; transcendence and, 272, 274, 277; as universalized, 273
Luborsky, Ruth Samson, 172

McAlindon, T., 190n.24
Macbeth (*Macbeth*), 13, 290; control of by women, 108, 111, 117, 124n.9; rejection of, 138
Macbeth (Shakespeare), 105–31, 157, 163n.27; Birnam Wood imagery, 121, 122, 130n.41; Bloody Child image in, 117; cosmology in, 114, 127–28n.26, 131n.45; diminishment of women in, 121–22; ending of, 116; family tree in, 121–22, 130n.43; fantasies of manhood in, 119–20; feminizing of men in, 118–19; Freudian readings of, 125–26n.15; Gowrie conspiracy and, 106, 123n.3; male and female realms in, 118–19, 128n.32; natural order in, 121–22, 129–30n.40; Oedipal issues in, 126n.16; platea and, 32; suicide in, 84–85; witches in, 85–87, 112–13
Macbeth, Lady (*Macbeth*), 13, 126n.16, 154; control of Macbeth, 124–25n.9; diminishment of, 121; as frightening, 112, 114; madness of, 84–87; as male, 115–16; rejection of son in, 138; witches and, 85, 86. *See also* Maternal power
MacCaffrey, Wallace, 142
MacDonald, Michael, 21, 87, 97n.5, 99n.20
Macdonwald (*Macbeth*), 118–19, 119–20
Macduff (*Macbeth*), 110, 116, 117; contradictions in, 119–20, 129n.39; family relations of, 120, 121, 122, 129n.38
Macduff, Lady (*Macbeth*), 120, 121
Macfarlane, Alan, 86, 127n.25
Machiavelli, Niccolò, 298–99
Mack, Maynard, 4–7, 8, 17, 18, 288; lack of gender analysis, 300, 301
McLeod, Randall, 19n.1
McNaron, Toni A. H., 294
McPherson, David C., 194
Madness, 12, 13, 75–101; alienated discourse of, 81–85, 91, 92; bewitchment and, 77–78; bodily boundaries and, 93–94; categorization of, 87–89; class issues and, 92; construction of humanity and, 95; discrediting of, 78–79, 82, 83, 88, 97n.2; dramatic function of, 79–87; early studies on, 76–79; fascination with, 75; feigned vs. actual, 82–83, 89–90, 91; as gendered, 80, 81,

82–83, 87, 88–89, 94; hallucinations and, 92; hysteria, 78; impostors and, 78–79; justice and, 92; language of, 79, 95–96; maternal power and, 90; melancholy, 76–77; misogyny and, 90, 91, 92, 100n.28; normalizing discourse of, 94–95; prose and, 98n.12; quotation and, 80, 98n.11; religion and, 91; remedies for, 78, 93–95; rhetorical structure of, 79–87; seventeenth century and, 87–89, 97–98n.7; sexuality and, 78, 82, 83; as social critique, 96; social formulas and, 80–83, 85, 92; stage introductions and, 81, 85, 98n.13; suicide and, 83, 84–85, 94, 99n.16; supernaturality and, 76–77, 79, 80, 81, 85–87; theater and, 95–96; witchcraft and, 19, 79, 85–87, 99n.18
Madness and Civilization (Foucault), 76
Margaret of Anjou (*Richard III*), 39, 47
Marriage, 14–15, 35–36, 210–35; contradictions in, 215–16, 218–19; feudalism and, 44–46; as heroic, 211, 213–14, 216, 217, 218, 220, 221, 225; as means of salvation, 212; military imagery and, 213, 217; Protestant discourse of, 14–15, 45; state imagery and, 211, 212; submission of wife in, 214–15, 216, 219; suffering and, 213–14; transformations in, 44–45
Martin, Emily, 71n.21
Masculine identity: as bloodthirsty, 37, 107–10, 116–17, 118, 129n.36; Italian, 205; male fears and, 105; paterfamilias and, 46–48; performance and, 43, 44; as rigid, 123n.2; status and, 45. *See also* Identity
Maternal power, 12, 105–31, 135–63; Amazonian mythology and, 155; androgynous parent and, 108–109; betrayal and, 136, 151–52, 160n.8; bounty and, 136, 141–42; Caesarean section and, 119–22, 124n.8, 129n.35; as castrating, 125n.13; destructive rage and, 110, 111, 115; dual role of, 138; elimination of, 122–23; fantasy of escape from, 105–107, 108, 115, 116; fantasy of omnipotence and, 105, 106; Fortune and, 152–53; infant dependency and, 137, 150, 152, 158–59, 160–61n.11; infanticide and, 29, 110–11, 114–15, 128n.27, 138, 154; James I and, 14; madness and, 90; male potency and, 114–15; male subjection to, 111; mother as male and, 115–16; nursing and, 110–12, 114–15, 126–27n.19, 154; rejection of son and, 136; as seductive, 157; in *Titus Andronicus*, 61, 65, 67; unnatural birth and, 106–107, 111–12; usurping role and, 13–14; witches and, 110–14; womb and, 106–107. *See also* Macbeth, Lady
Merchant of Venice, The (Shakespeare), 197–98
Merry Wives of Windsor, The (Shakespeare), 205
Middleton, Thomas, 159n.2
Midsummer Night's Dream, A (Shakespeare), 155, 174
Miller, Nancy K., 80

Modleski, Tania, 269, 279, 283n.7
Montrose, Louis Adrian, 21n.10, 142, 155
More, Thomas, 40
Mullaney, Steven, 95

Napier, Richard, 87–89, 94, 97n.5
Nashe, Thomas, 33, 35, 42–43
Neely, Carol Thomas, 8–9, 13, 19n.4
Neiditz, Minerva, 139, 161n.13
Neill, Michael, 193, 204
New Criticism, 4, 6, 11; close reading and, 291; textual analysis of, 8
New historicism, 11, 21n.9, 135
Newman, Karen, 38, 45
Niccholes, Alexander, 212, 213, 219
Novy, Marianne, 19n.2

Octavia (*Antony and Cleopatra*), 249
Oliver, H. J., 159n.4, 161n.15
Ophelia (*Hamlet*), 17; feminist analysis of, 80; gendered madness of, 82–83; language structure of, 81–82; mourning and, 98n.15; representations of, 98n.8; as subversive, 93
Orgel, Stephen, 130n.44
Orlin, Lena Cowen, 14, 68n.1
Othello (*Othello*), 14; fear of sexual activity of, 194; as insider, 199–200; narcissism of, 234n.14; as royal, 234n.16; as unfit for marriage, 183–85
Othello (Shakespeare), 22n.11, 171–90, 193–207, 211; anxiety in, 193–94, 201, 204; Centaur imagery in, 172–75, 176, 188n.9; citadel imagery in, 181–82; class issues in, 19n.4; cultural assumptions in, 194; decentered reading of, 8–9; desire in, 295; dislocation in, 9; domestic prescription in, 183; dual sexual discourse in, 216; homoeroticism in, 295; justice in, 197, 202, 204, 206n.8; language in, 217, 222; location in, 171–72, 194; public vs. private life in, 221; race issues in, 19n.4, 193, 199–200, 202–203, 204–205, 295; Saggitar/y in, 172–74, 177, 184, 188n.5; senses in, 202; student response to, 301; Venice as racial persona in, 194; zodiacal man in, 173, 174. *See also* Venice
Ovid, 69n.4

Parker, Patricia, 61, 65–66, 70n.14, 195; on *Othello*, 193, 207n.15
Paster, Gail, 33
Patriarchal ideology, 15; as destabilizing, 68n.1; fear of marriage and, 184–85; jealousy and, 185–86; language and, 18; otherness and, 69n.9; possession and, 185; procreation and, 143–44; women's location within, 175, 181
Patronage, 135–63; contradictions of, 147; fantasy

and, 158–59; humiliation and, 161n.14; lending at interest and, 145–46; prestation, 142–43; ritualized, 162n.20

Platea, 12, 31, 32, 41, 48, 101n.30; exclusion of women from, 49n.2; tragic hero and, 43

Pocock, J. G. A., 194, 199

Pompey (*Antony and Cleopatra*), 249, 258

Poor Tom (*King Lear*), 26, 90, 91, 92, 100n.25

Poststructuralism, 10, 11

Prince, The (Machiavelli), 298–99

Protestant discourse: double standard and, 214–16; equality of sexes and, 214, 215, 216; of family, 233n.2; of marriage, 210–16, 219–20; public vs. private sphere in, 211–12, 221, 232–33

Psychoanalysis, Lacanian, 10–11, 20n.8

Puttenham, George, 61

Rackin, Phyllis, 12

Radical Tragedy (Dollimore), 80

Radway, Janice, 271

Rape of Lucrece, The (Shakespeare), 56, 125n.12

Reading: adolescence and, 313; consequences of, 57; practice of, 8, 54

Regan (*King Lear*), 5, 92

Reid, Stephen A., 156

Reinventing Shakespeare (Taylor), 18

Reiss, Timothy J., 232

Renaissance Self-Fashioning (Greenblatt), 8

Representation, 246; challenges to, 15; conventions of, 262–63; history and, 273–74; in history plays, 40, 43, 339; repressions in, 243–45; women and, 251

Representing Shakespeare: New Psychoanalytic Essays (Schwartz, Kahn), 8

Richard II (Shakespeare), 288

Richard III (*Richard III*), 124n.7; accounts of as tragic, 32; appropriation of women's part by, 39–40; maternal power and, 106–108, 116; as tragic hero, 49n.3

Richard III (Shakespeare), 31–51; folio vs. quarto, 32; marriage in, 46–47; masculine identity and, 44–48; misogyny in, 288–89; nation as feminine in, 47–48; opening soliloquy, 41; royal authority and, 44; transformation of women's roles in, 36; women's language in, 36–37

Ridley, M. R., 199

Roderigo (*Othello*), 175–76

Rose, Mary Beth, 14–15, 36, 45

Rosenberg, Marvin, 126n.16

Ross, Lawrence, 3, 187n.2

Scarry, Elizabeth, 71n.21

Scot, Reginald, 79, 86

Scott, William O., 161n.15

Seneca, 149–50, 162–63n.24, 214

Shakespeare, William: ambiguity in, 301; ambivalence toward women, 305; as conservative, 230–31; idealization of, 296–98; Italian city-states and, 194; misogyny of, 16; parable and archetype in, 5; racism and, 301–302; as relationship, 312, 313; teaching of, 287, 296; women's roles and, 49n.2

Shakespearean Meanings (Burckhardt), 242

Shakespearean Tragedy (Bradley), 3–4, 80

Showalter, Elaine, 76, 97n.3

Sidney, Philip, 33

Sinfield, Alan, 189n.20

Smiley, Jane, 1–3, 17

Smith, Henry, 179

Snitow, Ann Barr, 283n.7

Sprengnether, Madelon (Gohlke), 126n.6, 128n.32, 265n.1

Stallybrass, Peter, 64, 66, 85, 127n.21, 130n.44, 131n.45; on *Othello*, 189n.18

Steppat, Michael, 270

Stone, Lawrence, 146, 147, 215

Stranger in Shakespeare, The (Fiedler), 301

Taming of the Shrew, The (Shakespeare), 95, 298

Tamora (*Titus Andronicus*), 55, 58, 60–61, 64, 65

Tawney, R. H., 145–46, 147

Theater: construction of humanity and, 95; demonic associations with, 40; madness and, 79, 89–90, 95–96; trials and, 38; women's absence from, 245

Thousand Acres, A (Smiley), 1–3, 17

Tilney, Edmund, 189n.21

Timon (*Timon of Athens*): changing character of, 136, 159–60n.4; distancing of, 140; as Fortuna, 139–40; James I compared with, 142, 146, 147, 157–58; magical thinking of, 152, 153–54; misanthropy of, 156, 161n.16; as narcissistic, 156, 163n.26

Timon of Athens (Shakespeare), 135–63; Amazonian mythology in, 155; cannibalism in, 141; fortune's role in, 136–38; fraternal betrayal in, 141–42; friendship in, 147–50; gift-giving in, 138–39; grave imagery in, 156–57; homoeroticism in, 150–51; Jacobean patronage in, 142–47; lack of family in, 136; maternal power and, 13–14; Middleton's co-authorship of, 159n.2; missing father in, 138–39; rejection of son in, 136, 138; as topical, 158; usury in, 148–50, 151; women as whores in, 153–55

Titus Andronicus (Shakespeare), 12–13, 54–71, 174; class issues in, 64–65; dismemberment in, 54–57, 59, 61, 66, 69n.9; politics of "kind" in, 56, 58, 60, 61, 64, 69n.7; rape in, 55, 56; rhetorical rules in, 61; sexualization of women in, 56; teaching imagery in, 58; texts in, 56–57

Tragedy, 1–51; as aristocratic form, 231; audience conception of, 16, 42–43; beneficial effects of, 33–35; challenges to, 8; conventions of, 10; critical traditions and, 3; cultural change and, 36, 211; desire in, 3; as domestic subgenre, 34; as effeminate, 6, 33, 49n.5; elegiac function of, 15; of existence, 6–7; gender and, 3, 35–36, 287, 300, 302–303; as genre, 1, 8; history and, 32–33, 233n.1; humanist evaluation of, 18; Jacobean, 230, 231; masculine identity and, 43; misogyny and, 287–88, 303, 305; modernity and, 43; public vs. private sphere in, 211, 232, 274; radicalism in, 230, 231; science and, 232; social change and, 232; social codes and, 11; structure of, 12; subjectivity and, 1–2, 12; as universalizing, 17, 18, 270; vulnerability and, 7; women's roles in, 8, 37, 50n.11, 50n.14, 211
Traub, Valerie, 194
Treatise of Melancholy (Bright), 76–77
Troilus and Cressida (Shakespeare), 19n.2, 174, 260, 261, 274, 279

Venice, 206n.4; early modern discourse of, 14; as female body, 194–95, 196, 202; irrationality and, 197, 200, 203; myth of, 194, 197; race issues and, 194, 196, 205; as whore, 195–96, 203
Vives, Juan Luis, 65
Volumnia (*Coriolanus*), 138, 154

Walker, Lewis, 160n.6
Wallace, John, 162–63n.24
Warning for Fair Women, A, 35
Watson, Robert N., 124n.8, 129n.35
Wayne, Valerie, 21n.9
Webster, John, 224, 226

Weimann, Robert, 31, 49n.3, 93, 101n.30
Weldon, Anthony, 143
Whately, William, 177, 212, 213, 215, 218
Wheeler, Richard, 13, 125n.10, 130n.44
Whigham, Frank, 225
White, Hayden, 272
Wilbern, David, 126n.16, 129n.35
Winter's Tale, The (Shakespeare), 287
Witchcraft, 288; cannibalism and, 113–14; diminishment of, 112–14, 127n.22; English vs. Continental, 24, 113–14, 127nn.20,25; in *Othello*, 197, 200; weakening of, 112–13
Woman's Part: Feminist Criticism of Shakespeare, The (Lenz, Greene, Neely), 7
Women: boys in the role of, 245, 251, 262, 263, 277; changes in portrayal of, 12, 31; comic roles of, 35–36; dependence on men, 289–90; disempowerment of, 36, 39, 42; dualizing of, 210, 211, 216, 224–25, 226, 230; education of, 62–63; effect of tragedy on, 33–35; ennobling of, 36, 39, 42; eros and, 210, 211, 216, 223–24, 232; as form of exchange, 63–64; home as proper place for, 47, 178–80; humanist view of, 62–63; as interpreters of tragedy, 16; lack of insight into, 1; language and, 36–37, 251; learned, 12–13, 54–71; as other, 243, 244–45, 265n.1, 295, 314; patriarchal location of, 171–76; Protestant discourse of, 210–16; as race, 204; rape and, 54, 56, 58, 64, 65; role in tragedy, 8, 14, 37, 50n.11, 211; scholars, 293–94; sexualization of, 56, 62–63; silencing of, 65–66, 80, 222–23; as students, 298, 302; as unruly, 62–63, 65–66, 71n.20; victimization of, 15; as victims, 37; as whores, 153–55. *See also* Gender; Heroine
Wrightson, Keith, 145

Lightning Source UK Ltd.
Milton Keynes UK
UKOW05f0612170217
294640UK00005B/71/P